N

QUICK

REFERENCE™

BIBLE
PEOPLE &
PLACES

Publishers since 1798

Thomas Nelson Publishers

Nashville

© 1993 by Thomas Nelson, Inc.

Published in Nashville, Tennessee, by Thomas Nelson, Inc.

Library of Congress Cataloging-in-Publication Data

Nelson's quick reference Bible people and places.
    Rev. ed. of: All the people and places of the Bible.
    ISBN 0-8407-6912-1
    1. Bible—Dictionaries.   I. Thomas Nelson Publishers.   II. All the people and places of the Bible.   III. Title: Bible people and places.
BS440.A46   1993
220.3—dc20   93–4592
                                                   CIP

Printed in the United States of America
1 2 3 4 5 6 7 8 — 00 99 98 97 96 95 94 93

INTRODUCTION

This volume identifies all of the people and places of the Bible, excluding the Apocrypha. Names are arranged alphabetically by their spellings in the New King James Version. When a person and a place share the same name, separate entries are made for each with the person listed first.

A typical entry lists the name, followed by any variant spellings enclosed with brackets. Parentheses surround the phonetic spelling of the word and the meaning of the name, the latter set in italics. A short description of the person or place follows, plus selected biblical references where it may be found. Dates have been provided for persons, where these are known.

The meanings of biblical names are far from certain. Many have such obscure origins that they can present only interesting possibilities at best. The fact that reference books vary in defining these meanings attests to this uncertainty.

Biblical names also present other challenges. Because countless generations continuously inhabited a certain area, throughout its history it might be known by different names. Thus, Acco and Ptolemais refer to the same city, but each in a different period of history. Because these changes often confuse Bible students, in this volume names are grouped under the most familiar biblical word and are cross-referenced to others.

Names of people are challenging for other reasons. Frequently, more than one person bears the same name. For instance, no fewer than eleven men are called Joseph. When this is the case, each person is listed in the entry in correct biblical order. A bracketed number designates each individual.

Some biblical characters are called by more than one

name. Often this is due to nothing more than foreign speakers referring to someone in their own languages. Thus, Saul (Hebrew) of Tarsus is also called Paul (Greek). However, many differences are not explained as easily. For example, why is the same person called both Reuel and Deuel? Or why is Jemuel also called Nemuel? In some cases, scribes could have made errors in transcribing Scripture and their errors were passed from generation to generation without correction. Whatever the reason, this volume harmonizes many of these differences. Note that the Deuel entry includes a reference to Reuel.

Many of these difficulties arise because biblical names originated in ancient and foreign settings. The variant spellings of people and places could be contractions that posed little difficulty for readers in ancient times. Also, some names were altered or omitted from genealogies for reasons that were clear then but are unclear to us. Therefore, even genealogies do not always help us to distinguish one person from an ancestor with the same name. The user of this volume will be spared some frustration if the differences between the ancient and modern situations are kept in mind.

Besides standard abbreviations of Bible book names, other abbreviations used include:

q.v.	"which see"
KJV	King James (Authorized) Version
NASB	New American Standard Bible
NEB	New English Bible
NIV	New International Version
RSV	Revised Standard Version

Six maps of the biblical world (beginning with page 374) locate many of the Bible places identified herein.

Aaron (ār′un; *enlightened, rich, mountaineer*). 1450 B.C. The older brother and companion of Moses during the Exodus. He became the first high priest of the Hebrew nation (Exod. 4:14, 30; 7:2, 19; 17:9–12; 29; Num. 12; 17).

Abaddon (a-bad′don; *destroyer, destruction*). The Hebrew name for the king of the bottomless pit referred to in Revelation 9:11. The Greek term for this figure is Apollyon, meaning *destroyer*.

Abagtha (a-bag′tha; *happy, prosperous*). 475 B.C. One of the seven chamberlains of King Ahasuerus (Esther 1:10).

Abanah (a-ba′na; *stony*). The chief river that runs through Damascus, purported to have healing qualities (2 Kings 5:12). A more accurate rendering of the name would be Amana.

Abarim (ab′a-rim; *mountain beyond*). A large mountain range in Moab near Heshbon. Includes Mount Nebo from which Moses surveyed the Promised Land before he died (Num. 27:12; 33:47–48; Deut. 32:49).

Abda (ab′da; *servant; worshiper*). [1] 975 B.C. Father of Solomon's tribute officer, Adoniram (1 Kings 4:6). [2] 450 B.C. A chief Levite after the Exile (Neh. 11:17). He is called Obadiah in First Chronicles 9:16.

Abdeel (ab′dē-el; *servant of God*). 625 B.C. The father of Shelemiah, who was commanded by Jehoiakim, king of Judah to arrest Baruch the scribe and Jeremiah the prophet (Jer. 36:26).

Abdi (ab′di; *servant of Jehovah*). [1] 1075 B.C. Grandfather of Ethan, whom David set over the song service (1 Chron. 6:44). [2] 750 B.C. Father of Kish, a Levite contemporary with Hezekiah (2 Chron. 29:12). **[3]** 450 B.C. A Jew who took a foreign wife during the Exile (Ezra 10:26).

Abdiel (ab'di-el; *servant of God*). Ancestral head of the tribe of Gad (1 Chron. 5:15).

Abdon (ab'don; *service, servile*). **[1]** 1075 B.C. A judge who led Israel for eight years (Judg. 12:13–15). **[2]** A descendant of Benjamin who dwelt in Jerusalem (1 Chron. 8:23). **[3]** 1075 B.C. Firstborn son of Jeiel and an ancestor of King Saul, mentioned in Chronicles (1 Chron. 8:30; 9:36). **[4]** 625 B.C. An official sent by King Josiah to Huldah to inquire of the meaning of the Law (2 Chron. 34:20). He is called Achbor in Second Kings 22:12. Possibly he is identical with **[2]**.

Abdon (ab'don; *servile*) KJV, Ebron. A city belonging to the tribe of Asher, located at the present site of Khirbet Abdeh (Josh. 19:28, 21:30; 1 Chron. 6:71). See Hebron **[2]**.

Abed-nego (a-bed'ne-gō; *servant of Nego* [a Babylonian God]). The Chaldean name given to Azariah, one of the three friends of Daniel who were carried captive to Babylon. The three were thrown into a fiery furnace and were miraculously protected by God. (Dan. 1:7; 2:49; 3:12–30).

Abel (ā'bel; *breath, vapor*). Second son of Adam and Eve, slain by his brother Cain (Gen. 4:1–10; Heb. 11:4; 12:24).

Abel (ā'bel; *meadow, brook*). A prefix attached to several towns. **[1]** In Second Samuel 20:14–18, a city specifically related to Abel Beth Maacah is mentioned. Some suppose that Abel and Beth Maacah were towns so close together that they were thought of as being one. However, others believe only one town is referred to in this passage. **[2]** The KJV reading in First Samuel 6:18, "the great stone of Abel," is not very likely. It is a combination of the Hebrew, *the great meadow* [*abel*], and the Septuagint, *the great stone*. A city is not referred to here. *See* Abel Beth Maacah.

Abel Acacia Grove (ā'bel a-kā'sha grōv). A site northeast of the Dead Sea in the plains of Moab. The Israelites camped here just before they crossed the Jordan River to enter the Promised Land (Num. 25:1; Josh. 2:1, 3:1; Mic. 6:5). *See* Abel Shittim.

Abel Beth Maacah (ā'bel-beth-mā'a-ka; *meadow of the house of Maacah*). A fortified town near Dan in the area of the tribe of Naphtali, located in northern Palestine. Attacked by Joab (2 Sam. 20:14), Ben-Hadad (1 Kings 15:20), and Tiglath-Pileser (2 Kings 5:29). *See also* Abel **[1]**, Abel Maim.

Abel Cheramim (ā'bel ker'a-mim). A form of Abel Keramim.

Abel Keramim (ābel ker'a-mim; *meadow of vineyards*). A city located east of the Jordon River and southwest of Rabbah. The farthest point reached by Jephthah in his military campaign against the Ammonites (Judg. 11:33).

Abel Maim (ā'bel-mā'im; *meadow of waters*). Probably another name for Abel Beth Maacah (2 Chron. 16:4).

Abel Mayim (ā'bel ma-im). A form of Abel Maim.

Abel Meholah (ā'bel-me-ho'lah; *meadow of dancing*). The home (and possibly the birthplace) of Elisha. Located on the western side of the Jordan Valley (Judg. 7:22; 1 Kings 4:12).

Abel Mizraim (ā'bel-miz'rā-im; *meadow of Egypt*). *See* Atad.

Abel Shittim (ā'bel-shit'im; *meadow of Acacias*). A form of Abel Acacia Grove.

Abez [Ebez] (ā'bez [e'bez]). A town in northern Palestine apportioned to the tribe of Issachar (Josh. 19:20).

Abi (a'bi; *my father*). 750 B.C. A daughter of Zechariah and the wife of Ahaz. Also the mother of King Hezekiah of Judah (2 Kings 18:2). *Abi* is a contraction of *Abijah (Jehovah is father)*, which she is called in Second Chronicles 29:1. *See* Abi-albon; Abiezer.

Abia [Abiah, Abijah] (a-bī'a [a-bī'ja, a-bī'ja]; *Jehovah is father*). A form of Abijam.

Abi Albon (a'bī-al'bon; *father of strength*). A form of Abiel.

Abiasaph [Ebiasaph] (a-bī'a-saf (e-bī'a-saf]; *my father has gathered*). A Levite whose descendants were doorkeepers of the Tabernacle (Exod. 6:24; 1 Chron. 6:23; 9:19).

Abiathar (a-bī'a-thar; *father of abundance*). 1000 B.C. The only priest to escape Saul's massacre at Nob. When David became king, Abiathar was appointed joint high priest, along with Zadok, in the royal court (2 Sam. 8:17; 1 Chron. 18:16). When David's son Absalom tried to overthrow him, Abiathar and Zadok carried the Ark of the Covenant out of Jerusalem, later returning it at David's command (2 Sam. 15:29). When Solomon became the new ruler, Abiathar was banished to Anathoth, where his role and privileges as a Jerusalem priest were taken away. (1 Kings 1:7–25, 2:22–35). Some scholars believe that Abiathar wrote portions of 1 and 2 Samuel that describe life in the royal court of King David. No strong evidence supports this theory.

Abida [Abidah] (a-bī'da [a-bī'da]; *father of knowledge*). 2000 B.C. The fourth son of Midian, the fourth son of Abraham and Keturah (Gen. 25:4; 1 Chron. 1:33).

Abidan (a-bī′dan; *my father is judge*). 1450 B.C. Son of Gideoni and leader of the Benjamites. Represented his tribe when a census was taken during their trek in the wilderness. (Num. 1:11; 2:22; 7:60, 65; 10:24).

Abiel (ā′bi-el; *my God is father*). The name of two men in the Old Testament: **[1]** 1100 B.C. Ancestor of Saul (1 Sam 9:1; 19:51). **[2]** 1000 B.C. An Arbathite who served as one of David's thirty mighty men (1 Chron. 11:32). Also called Abi Albon (2 Sam. 23:31).

Abiezer (a′bi-ē′zer [a′bi-ē′zer]: *father of help*). **[1]** A descendant of Manasseh (Josh. 17:2; Judg. 8:2; 1 Chron. 7:18). *See* Jeezer. **[2]** 1000 B.C. One of David's mighty men (2 Sam. 23:27; 1 Chron. 11:28; 27:12).

Abigail (ab′i-gāl; *father of delight*). **[1]** 1000 B.C. A wife of Nabal the Carmelite. After his death, became the wife of David (1 Sam. 25:3, 14–44). **[2]** 1000 B.C. A sister or half-sister of David and the mother of Amasa, whom Absalom made captain of the army instead of Joab (2 Sam. 17:25; 1 Chron. 2:16–17).

Abigal (ab′i-gāl). A form of Abigail.

Abihail (ab′i-hāl; *father of strength*). **[1]** 1475 B.C. A Levite who was the Father of Zuriel (Num. 3:35). **[2]** The wife of Abishur (1 Chron. 2:29). **[3]** Head of a family of Gad (1 Chron. 5:14). **[4]** 975 B.C. A wife of Rehoboam (2 Chron. 11:18). **[5]** 500 B.C. Father of Esther (Esther 2:15; 9:29).

Abihu (a-bī′hū; *he is my father*). 1450 B.C. A son of Aaron, destroyed with his brother Nadab for offering "profane fire" to God (Exod. 6:23; Lev. 10:1).

Abihud (a-bī′hud; *father of honor*). 1825 B.C. A son of Bela, the oldest son of Benjamin, listed in Chronicles (1 Chron. 8:3).

Abijah (a-bī′ja; *the Lord is my father*). The name of nine persons in the Old Testament: **[1]** 1825 B.C. Seventh of the nine sons of Becher; son of Benjamin (1 Chron. 7:8). **[2]** Wife of Hezron, who was a descendant of Judah (1 Chron. 2:24). **[3]** 1050 B.C. A son of Samuel who was a corrupt judge of Israel (1 Sam. 8:1–5). **[4]** 1000 B.C. A descendant of Aaron who was a priest in the time of David (1 Chron. 24:10). **[5]** 925 B.C. Son of Jeroboam I, King of Israel. He died as a child (1 Kings 14:1–8). **[6]** Ruled 913–910 B.C. A son of Rehoboam and Macaah the daughter of Absalom (2 Chron. 11:20, 22). Also see Abijam. **[7]** 750 B.C. Mother of Hezekiah; King of Judah (2 Chron. 29:1). Also called Abi (2 Kings 18:2). **[8]** 525 B.C. A priest who returned to Jerusalem with Zerubbabel after the Exile (Neh. 12:1–4; 12–17). **[9]** 450 B.C. A priest who signed the covenant renewal with God in Nehemiah's time (Neh. 10:7).

Abijam (a-bī′jam; *father of the sea [or west]*). Ruled 913–910 B.C. Son of Rehoboam and Macaah, daughter of Absalom. Succeeded Rehoboam to the throne of Judah. Also called Abijah (2 Chron. 11:20, 22).

Abilene (ab-i-lē′ne; *meadow, brook*). A Syrian tetrarchy deriving its name from its capital, Abila, located 29 to 32 km. (18 to 20 mi.) northwest of Damascus (Luke 3:1).

Abimael (a′bim′a-el; *my father is God*). A son of Joktan listed in Genesis and Chronicles (Gen. 10:26–28; 1 Chron. 1:20–22). The name may denote an Arabian tribe. Some scholars suggest a locality in Arabia is intended.

Abimelech (a-bim′e-lek; *my father is king*). The name of five men in the Old Testament: **[1]** 2050 B.C. A Philistine king of Gerar who made a covenant with Abraham (Gen. 20:1–18; 21:22–34). Some scholars believe that the name Abimelech is not a proper name but rather a royal title of Philistine kings, as the term Pharaoh was a title of Egyptian kings. **[2]** 1950 B.C. A king of Gerar in the time of Isaac (Gen. 26:1–31). **[3]** Ruled 1129–1126 B.C. Ruler of the city of Shechem during the period of the judges (Judg. 8:30–10:1; 2 Sam. 11:21) and king of Israel for three years (Judg. 9:22). Son of Gideon who killed all of Gideon's other sons in order to eliminate any who might challenge his authority (Judg. 9:5). Killed in a battle at Thebez (Judg. 9:50–54; 2 Sam. 11:21). **[4]** 1025 B.C. A Philistine king whom David met while fleeing from King Saul (Psalm 34, title). This king of Gath's actual name was Achish (1 Sam. 21:10–15). **[5]** 975 B.C. A priest in the time of David (1 Chr. 18:16).

Abinadab (a-bin´a-dab; *father of liberality*). **[1]** 1025 B.C. A man of Judah in whose house the ark was placed (1 Sam. 7:1; 2 Sam. 6:3–4; 1 Chron. 13:7). **[2]** 1025 B.C. The second son of Jesse and a brother of David (1 Sam. 16:8; 17:13; 1 Chron. 2:13). **[3]** 1025 B.C. Son of Saul slain at Mount Gilboa by the Philistines (1 Sam. 31:2; 1 Chron. 8:33; 9:39; 10:2). **[4]** 950 B.C. Father of one of Solomon's officers (1 Kings 4:11).

Abiner (ab´i-ner). A form of Abner.

Abinoam (a-bin´ō-am; *father of pleasantness*). 1250 B.C. Father of Barak the general who served under Deborah the judge (Judg. 4:6, 12; 5:1, 12).

Abiram (a-bī´ram; *my father is exalted*). **[1]** 1450 B.C. A Reubenite who conspired against Moses and was destroyed (Num. 16:1–33; Psa. 106:17). **[2]** 850 B.C.

Firstborn son of Hiel who died when his father began to rebuild Jericho (1 Kings 16:34; cf. Josh. 6:26).

Abishag (ab′i-shag; *my father was a wanderer*). 975 B.C. A beautiful young woman chosen to nurse the aged David (1 Kings 1:3, 15; 2:17, 21–22).

Abishai (a-bish′a-ī; *source of wealth*). 1000 B.C. A son of David's half-sister, Zeruiah, and brother of Joab and Asahel. He was one of David's mighty men (1 Sam. 26:6–9; 2 Sam. 2:18; 10:10; 23:18).

Abishalom [Absalom] (a-bish′a-lom [ab′sa-lom]; *father of peace*). 975 B.C. Grandfather of Maachah, the wife of Rehoboam (1 Kings 15:2, 10). He is called Absalom, another form of the name, in Second Chronicles 11:20–21, and Uriel in Second Chronicles 13:2. May be the same as Absalom, son of David. *See* Absalom.

Abishua (a-bish′ū-a; *father of deliverance*). [1] A son of Phinehas; descendant of Aaron and fourth high priest of Israel (1 Chron. 6:4–5, 50; Ezra 7:5). [2] 1825 B.C. A descendant of Benjamin listed in Chronicles (1 Chron. 8:4).

Abishur (ab′i-shur; *my father is a wall*). The second son of Shammai, of the tribe of Judah (1 Chron. 2:28–29).

Abital (ab′i-tal; *father of dew*). 1000 B.C. A wife of David and mother of Shephatiah (2 Sam. 3:4; 1 Chron. 3:3).

Abitub (ab′i-tub; *my father is good*). A descendant of Benjamin listed in Chronicles (1 Chron. 8:11).

Abiud (a-bī′ud; *my father is majesty*). A son of Zerubbabel and ancestor of Jesus (Matt. 1:13).

Abner [Abiner] (ab′ner [ab′i-ner]; *my father is a lamp*). 1025 B.C. A shortened form of *Abiner;* the captain of the army under Saul (1 Sam. 14:50–51; 26:5, 7; 2 Sam. 2; 3).

Abraham [Abram] (ā′bra-ham [ā′bram]). The founder

of the Jewish nation and an ancestor of Jesus. His name was changed from Abram *(the father is exalted)* to Abraham *(father of a multitude)* (Gen. 11–26; Matt. 1:1–2).

Absalom (ab'sa-lom; *father of peace*). 975 B.C. A son of David and Macaah who tried to usurp the throne from his father (2 Sam. 3:3; 13–19). *See* Abishalom.

Accad [Akkad] (ak'ad [ak'ad]; *fortress*). A city built by Nimrod of the Plain of Shinar (Sumer), north of Babylonia (Gen. 10:10). Later the name came to describe the land of Accad, the northern division of Babylonia.

Accho (ac'kō). A form of Acco.

Acco [Accho] (ac'kō [ac'ko]; *hot sand*). A town of Palestine on the Mediterranean coast about 40 km. (25 mi.) south of Tyre, apportioned to the tribe of Asher (Judg. 1:31); also called Ptolemais in Acts 21:7.

Achaia (a-kā'ya). In Roman times, the region including all of Greece except Thessaly (Acts 18:12; Rom. 15:26).

Achaicus (a-kā'i-kus; *belonging to Achaia*). A.D. 55. A Corinthian Christian who visited Paul at Philippi (1 Cor. 16:17).

Achan [Achar] (ā'kan [ā'kar]; *trouble*). 1400 B.C. One who stole part of the spoil of Jericho and brought "trouble" on his people. He was killed for this (Josh. 7:1–24). In First Chronicles 2:7, he is called *Achar. Also see* Achor.

Achaz (a'kaz). A form of Ahaz.

Achbor (ak'bor; *a mouse*). **[1]** Father of the Edomite king Baal-hanan (Gen. 36:31, 38–39; 1 Chron. 1:49). **[2]** The father of Elnathan, who was sent by Jehoiakim to bring Urijah from Egypt (Jer. 26:22; 36:12). **[3]** *See* Abdon **[4]**.

Achim (ā'kim; *woes*). Ancestor of Jesus (Matt. 1:14).

Achish (ā'kish). [1] 1025 B.C. A king of Gath to whom David fled for safety (1 Sam. 21; 27–29). [2] 975 B.C. Another king of Gath who bore the same name but reigned during Solomon's time (1 Kings 2:39–40). However, many believe the kings to be identical.

Achmetha [Ecbatana] (ak'me-tha [ek-ba-ta'na]; *fortress*). Capital of the Median Empire. Later became capital of the Persian and Parthian Empires. Captured by Cyrus the Great of Persia in 550 B.C. It became the summer residence of Persian kings (Ezra 6:2). Conquered by Alexander the Great in 330 B.C. The city stood near present-day Hamadan.

Achor (ā'kōr; *trouble*). A valley south of Jericho, in which Achan was stoned (Josh. 7:24); and which formed the northern boundary of Judah (Josh. 15:7).

Achsah [Achsa; Acsah] (ak'sah; [ak'sah; ak'sah] *ankle ornament*). The only daughter of Caleb, who married her cousin Othniel (Josh. 15: 16–17; Judg. 1:12–13; 1 Chron. 2:49).

Achshaph (ak'shaf; *sorcery*). A city of Canaan captured by Joshua (Josh. 12:20); and a landmark on the boundary of the land apportioned to the tribe of Asher (Josh. 19:25).

Achzib [Chezib] (ak'zib [ke'zib]; *falsehood*). [1] A Canaanite city in the lowlands of Judah, captured by Joshua (Josh. 15:44). Probably the same town as Chezib (Gen. 38:5) and Chozeba (1 Chron. 4:22). [2] A town in western Galilee on the Mediterranean Sea; near the border of ancient Phoenicia (Josh. 19:29; Judg. 1:31).

Acre (a-krē'). A form of Acco.

Acsah (ak-sah'). A form of Achsah.

A

Adadah [Arahah] (ad′a-dah [ar′a-hah]). A town in the southern district of Judah (Josh. 15:22).

Adah (ā′da; *adornment*). [1] One of the two wives of Lamech and the mother of Jabal and Jubal. (Gen. 4:19–20, 23). [2] 1950 B.C. One of the wives of Esau and the daughter of Elon the Hittite (Gen. 36:2, 4, 10, 12, 16). She was the mother of Eliphaz, Esau's firstborn son. *See* Esau's Wives.

Adaiah (ad-ā′ya; *Jehovah has adorned*). [1] A son of Shimhi found in First Chronicles 8:12–21. [2] A Levite ancestor of Asaph (1 Chron. 6:41). Also called Iddo (1 Chron. 6:21). [3] 1675 B.C. Father of Jedidah, the mother of King Josiah (2 Kings 22:1). [4] 850 B.C. Father of a captain who aided Jehoiada (2 Chron. 23:1). [5] 525 B.C. One whose descendants resided in Jerusalem and a member of the royal line of David (Neh. 11:5). [6] 450 B.C. One who married a foreign wife (Ezra 10:29). [7] 450 B.C. Another who did the same (Ezra 10:39). [8] 450 B.C. A Levite descendant from Aaron who settled in Jerusalem after the Exile (1 Chron. 9:12; Neh. 11:12).

Adalia (a-dā′li-a). 475 B.C. One of the ten sons of Haman slain by the Jews (Esther 9:8–10).

Adam (ad′am; *of the ground*). The first man. His sin caused a curse to fall upon all the human race (Gen. 2—3; 1 Cor. 15:22, 45). He is listed in the genealogy of Christ (Luke 3:38).

Adam (ad′am; *red; of the earth*). A city near Zarethan on the east bank of the Jordan River that was given to the tribe of Reuben (Josh. 3:16).

Adamah (ad′a-ma; *earth*). A fortified city in northern Palestine apportioned to the tribe of Naphtali (Josh. 19:36); its exact location is not known.

Adami Nekeb [Adami] (ad'a-mī nē'keb [ad'a-mi]; *Adam of the pass*). A town assigned to the tribe of Naphtali at the border of Zebulun (Josh. 19:33).

Adar [Addar] (ā'dar [ā'dar]; *height*). A fortress town located on the southwestern border of Judah between Kadesh Barnea and Karka (Josh. 15:3). This place is called Hazar Addar in Numbers 34:4.

Adbeel (ad'bi-el; *God has disciplined*). 2025 B.C. The third of twelve sons of Ishmael, listed in Genesis and Chronicles (Gen. 25:13; 1 Chron. 1:29).

Addan (ad'dan; *strong*). A man who was unable to prove his Jewish ancestry when he returned from the Exile (Neh. 7:61; Ezra 2:59).

Addan (ad'dan). A place in Babylon that served as a staging area for exiles returning to Israel (Ezra 2:59; Neh. 7:61).

Addar (ad'dar; *height*). 1850 B.C. A son of Bela and grandson of Benjamin listed in Chronicles (1 Chron. 8:3). Also called Ard (Num. 26:40).

Addi (ad'dī; *my witness*). An ancestor of Joseph listed in the geneology of Jesus (Luke 3:28).

Addon (ad'don). A form of Addan.

Ader (ā'der). A form of Eder.

Adiel (ā'di-el; *ornament of God*). [1] 1025 B.C. Father of David's treasurer, Asmaveth (1 Chron. 27:25). [2] 700 B.C. A descendant of Simeon in the time of Hezekiah (1 Chron. 4:36). [3] 450 B.C. A Levite priest whose son Maasai helped rebuild the Temple after the Captivity (1 Chron. 9:12).

Adin (ā'din; *ornament*). [1] Ancestor of returned captives (Ezra 2:15; Neh. 7:20). [2] One whose descendant returned with Ezra (Ezra 8:6). [3] 450 B.C. A Jewish leader who sealed the covenant in Nehemiah's time (Neh. 10:14–16).

Adina (ad'i-na; *ornament*). 1000 B.C. Son of Shiza the Reubenite. One of David's thirty mighty men (1 Chron. 11:42).

Adino (ad'i-nō; *he wielded his spear*). 1000 B.C. The name given Jashobeam when he killed 800 men at one time (2 Sam. 23:8). *See also* Josheb-Basshebeth.

Adithaim (ad-i-tha'im; *two ways*). A town in the lowlands of Judah (Josh. 15:36). Exact location not known.

Adlai (ad'lā-i; *Jehovah is just*). 1025 B.C. Father of Shaphat, an overseer of David's herds (1 Chron. 27:29).

Admah (ad'mah; *redness*). One of the Cities of the Plain that God destroyed with Sodom and Gomorrah (Gen. 19:25–29); its location may now be submerged by the southern end of the Dead Sea.

Admatha (ad'ma-tha; *God-given*). 475 B.C. One of the seven princes of Persia (Esther 1:14).

Adna (ad'na; *pleasure*). [1] 525 B.C. A priest listed in Nehemiah who returned with Zerubbabel from the Captivity. (Neh. 12:12–15). [2] 450 B.C. A Jew who took a foreign wife (Ezra 10:30).

Adnah (ad'nah; *pleasure*). [1] 1000 B.C. A captain who joined David at Ziklag (1 Chron. 12:20). [2] 875 B.C. A chief captain of Jehoshaphat (2 Chron. 17:14).

Adoni-bezek (a-dō'ni-bē'zek; *lord of lightning* [*Bezek*]). A king of Bezek who was captured by Israel (Judg. 1:5–7).

Adonijah (a-dō-nī'jah; *Jehovah is my lord*). [1] 975 B.C. A son of David, executed by Solomon for trying to usurp the throne (2 Sam. 3:4; 1 Kings 1:2). [2] 875 B.C. One sent by Jehoshaphat to teach the law (2 Chron. 17:8). [3] 450 B.C. One who sealed the new covenant with

God after the Exile (Neh. 10:14–16). Also called Adonikam (Ezra 2:13). [4] *See* Tob-adonijah.

Adonikam (a-don-ī'kam; *my lord is risen*). Ancestral head of a family that returned to Palestine after the Exile (Ezra 2:13). Apparently also the Adonijah of Nehemiah 10:16.

Adoniram [Adoram; Hadoram] (a-do-nī'ram, [a-dōr'am; ha-dōr'am]; *lord of height*). 975 B.C. The son of Abda and an officer in the armies of David, Solomon, and Rehoboam. (2 Sam. 20:24; 1 Kings 4:6; 5:14; 12:18; 2 Chron. 10:18).

Adoni-zedek (a-do'ni-ze'dek; *lord of justice or righteousness*). 1400 B.C. A king of Jerusalem defeated by Joshua (Josh. 10:1–27).

Adoraim (ad-ō-rā'im). A city in Judah fortified by Rehoboam. (2 Chron. 11:9).

Adoram (a-dō'ram). A form of Adoniram and Hadoram.

Adrammelech (a-dram'mel-ek; *Adar is king*). [1] 725 B.C. A pagan god to whom a group of colonists of Samaria sacrificed their children (2 Kings 17:31). [2] 625 B.C. A son of the Assyrian king Sennacherib who, with his brother, killed his father (2 Kings 19:37; Isa. 37:38).

Adramyttium (a-dra-mit'ti-um; *from Adramys, brother of Craesus*). A port city of Mysia in the northwestern part of the Roman province of Asia (Acts 27:2; cf. 16:7).

Adria (ā'dri-a; *from [the city] Adria of Italy*). Originally a name referring to the sea east of Italy. In later times, the term included the Mediterranean between Greece and Sicily (Acts 27:27).

Adriel (ā'dri-el; *my help is God*). 1025 B.C. Son of Barzillai the Meholathite, of the tribe of Issachar. The man whom Merab married although she had been promised to David (1 Sam. 18:19; 2 Sam. 21:8).

Adullam (a-dul'lam; *refuge*). A town of Judah near Succoth. David made the headquarters of his rebellion against Saul in a cave near this town (Josh. 12:7–15; 1 Sam. 22; 2 Sam 23:13).

Adummim (a-dum'im; *bloody*). A pass from the Jordan Valley to the hill country of Judah. It is the shortest route from Jericho to Jerusalem, and may have been the setting for Jesus' parable of the good Samaritan (Josh. 15:7; cf. Luke 10:30–37).

Aeneas (e nē'as; *praise*). A.D. 35. The paralyzed man of Lydda who was healed by Peter (Acts 9:33–34).

Aenon (ē'non; *springs*). A place in Palestine near Salim noted for its abundant supply of water, where John baptized his converts. Most likely this site was at the head of the Valley of Shechem (John 3:23).

Agabus (ag'a-bus; *locust*). A.D. 45. A Christian prophet of Jerusalem who foretold suffering for Paul if he went to Jerusalem (Acts 11:28; 21:10).

Agag (ā'gag; *high; warlike*). A name or title of the kings of Amalek; it is probably not a proper name. However, if it is a proper name, it is used to refer to two persons: **[1]** A king mentioned by Balaam (Num. 24:7). **[2]** 1025 B.C. A king that Saul spared, but who was later executed by Samuel (1 Sam. 15).

Agar (ā'gar; *wandering*). The Greek form of Hagar (q.v.).

Agee (ag'ē; *fugitive*). 1025 B.C. A Hararite, father of one of David's mighty men (2 Sam. 23:11).

Agrippa (a-grip'a). *See* Herod.

Agur (ā'gur; *he who gathers*). A son of Jakeh and sage who wrote Proverbs 30.

Ahab (ā'hab; *father is brother*). **[1]** The seventh king of Israel. He was wicked and idolatrous and married a woman of the same character—Jezebel (1 Kings 16:28—22:40). [2] 600 B.C. A false prophet killed by Nebuchadnezzar (Jer. 29:21–22).

Aharah (a-har´ah; *brother's follower*). 1860 B.C. Third son of Benjamin (1 Chron. 8:1). Also called Ehi (Gen 46:21) and Ahiram (Num. 26:38).

Aharhel (a-har´hel; *brother of Rachel*). A descendant of Judah (1 Chron. 4:8).

Ahasai (a-hā´sī; *my holder; protector*). *See* Jahzerah.

Ahasbai (a-has´bī; *blooming; shining*). 1025 B.C. Father of one of David's mighty men (2 Sam. 23:34).

Ahasuerus (a-haz-u-ē´rus; *mighty man*). [1] 575 B.C. The father of Darius of Mede (Dan. 9:1). [2] The king of Persia who ruled from 486–465 B.C. and married Esther. He is known as Xerxes to historians (Esther 1:1; 2:16; 10:3). [3] Another name for Cambyses, king of Persia (Ezra 4:6).

Ahava (a-hā´va; *water*). A site about 14 km. (9 mi.) north of Babylon; a staging area for Jews preparing to return to Palestine (Ezra 8:15, 31).

Ahaz [Achaz] (ā´haz [a´kaz]; *he has grasped*). [1] 950 B.C. Son of Micah and father of Jehoaddah. A Benjamite who was a descendant of King Saul (1 Chron. 8:35–36; 9:41–42). [2] 742–725 B.C. The eleventh king of Judah and an ancestor of Christ (1 Kings 15:38—16:20; Matt. 1:9). He was an ungodly ruler who burned a son as a human sacrifice in the worship of Molech (2 Chron. 28:1–4; Isa. 7).

Ahaziah [Azariah] (ā-ha-zi´a [a-za-rī´a]; *Jehovah sustains*). [1] The ninth king of Israel. He was weak and idolatrous (1 Kings 22:49, 50, 51—2 Kings 1:18). [2] The sixth king of Judah; he reigned only one year

(2 Kings 8:24–29; 9:16ff.). He was also known as Jehoahaz (2 Chron. 21:17; 25:23). His being called Azariah in Second Chronicles 22:6 is an error; over fifteen Hebrew manuscripts and all recent versions read Ahaziah. *See* Jehoahaz.

Ahban (a′ban; *brother of intelligence*). The son of Abishur of Judah (1 Chron. 2:29).

Aher (ā′her; *one that is behind*). A descendant of Benjamin (1 Chron. 7:12). His name may be a shortened form of Ahiram (Num. 26:38) or Aharah (1 Chron. 8:1).

Ahi (ā′hī; *my brother*). [1] Head of a family of Gad (1 Chron. 5:15). [2] A man of the tribe of Asher (1 Chron. 7:34).

Ahiam (a-hī′am; *a mother's brother*). 1000 B.C. A son of Sharar the Hararite and one of David's mighty men (2 Sam. 23:33; 1 Chron. 11:35).

Ahian (a-hī′an; *brotherly*). A descendant of Manasseh (1 Chron. 7:19).

Ahiezer (a-hī-ē′zer; *helping brother*). [1] 1450 B.C. A prince of Dan who helped Moses take a census (Num. 1:12; 2:25; 7:66). [2] 1000 B.C. One who joined David at Ziklag (1 Chron. 12:3).

Ahihud (a-hī′hūd; *brother of honor*). [1] 1400 B.C. A prince of Asher who helped to divide the land upon entering Canaan. (Num. 34:27). [2] A member of the family of Ehud, descended from Benjamin (1 Chron. 8:7).

Ahijah [Ahiah] (a-hī′jāh, [a-hī′-ah]; *my brother is Jehovah*). [1] A son of Jerahmeel, a descendant of Judah (1 Chron. 2:25). [2] 1025 B.C. A son of Ahitub who was priest during Saul's reign. Many scholars identify him as Ahimelech (1 Sam. 14:3; 22:9). [3] 1000 B.C.

One of David's mighty men (1 Chron. 1:36). **[4]** 1000 B.C. A Levite set over the temple treasures (1 Chron. 26:20). *See also* Ahimelech. **[5]** 950 B.C. A scribe in Solomon's time, son of Shisha (1 Kings 4:3). **[6]** 925 B.C. A prophet from Shiloh who prophesied the splitting away of the ten tribes (1 Kings 11:29–30; 14:2, 4–5). **[7]** 925 B.C. Father of Baasha who conspired against Nadab (1 Kings 15:27, 33; 21:22). **[8]** A descendant of Benjamin who forced the inhabitants of Geba to move to Manahath (1 Chron. 8:7).

Ahikam (a-hī′kam; *my brother has risen*). 625 B.C. An officer in King Josiah's court and a delegate sent to consult Huldah the prophetess (2 Kings 22:12; 14; 25:22; Jer. 26:24; 39:14).

Ahilud (a-hī′lud; *a brother is born*). 1025 B.C. Father of Jehosaphat, who was appointed by David as recorder (2 Sam. 8:16; 20:24; 1 Kings 4:3, 12).

Ahimaaz (a-him′a-az; *powerful brother*). **[1]** 1050 B.C. Father of Ahinoam, wife of Saul (1 Sam. 14:50). **[2]** 950 B.C. One of Solomon's officers (1 Kings 4:15). **[3]** 925 B.C. Son of Zadok who remained loyal to David (2 Sam. 15:27, 36; 17:17, 20; 18:19–29).

Ahiman (a-hī′man; *brother of man of fortune*). **[1]** 1400 B.C. A son of Anak who dwelt in Hebron (Num. 13:22; Josh. 15:14; Judg. 1:10). **[2]** 450 B.C. A Levite gatekeeper in the Temple (1 Chron. 9:17).

Ahimelech (a-him′e-lek; *my brother is king*). **[1]** 1025 B.C. A Hittite friend of David (1 Sam. 26:6). **[2]** 1025 B.C. One of the priests of Nob slain for helping David (1 Sam. 21:1–8; 22:9–20). *See also* Abimelech. **[3]** 975 B.C. A priest, son of Abiathar and grandson of [2] (2 Sam. 8:17; 1 Chron. 24:6). Some think the readings in these passages have been transposed (i.e.; they speak of Ahimelech the son of Abiathar instead of Abiathar the son of Ahimelech). But this seems unlikely, especially in First Chronicles 24. He is called Abimelech in First Chronicles 18:16. The Septuagint has Ahimelech here also.

Ahimoth (a-hī'moth; *brother of death*). A son of Elkanah the Levite (1 Chron. 6:25).

Ahinadab (a-hin'a-dab; *brother of liberality*). 950 B.C. Son of Iddo and one of Solomon's royal merchants (1 Kings 4:14).

Ahinoam (a-hin'ō-am; *my brother is joy*). [1] 1025 B.C. Wife of King Saul (1 Sam. 14:50). [2] 1000 B.C. Mother of Amnon, David's firstborn son (1 Sam. 25:43; 27:3; 1 Chron. 3:1).

Ahio (a-hi'ō; *his brother*). [1] A descendant of Benjamin (1 Chron. 8:14). [2] 1075 B.C. A descendant of Saul (1 Chron. 8:31; 9:37). [3] 1000 B.C. Son of Abinadab, in whose house the ark stayed for 20 years (2 Sam. 6:3–4; 1 Chron. 13:7).

Ahira (a-hī'ra; *brother of evil*). 1450 B.C. A chief of the tribe of Naphtali (Num. 1:15; 2:29; 7:78).

Ahiram (a-hī'ram; *my brother is exalted*). 1850 B.C. A descendant of Benjamin (Num. 26:38). He is called Ehi, possibly a contraction of Ahiram, in Genesis 46:21 and Aharah in First Chronicles 8:1. He is possibly the same as Aher (q.v.).

Ahisamach (a-his'a-mach; *supporting brother*). 1475 B.C. A craftsman of the tribe of Dan who helped build the tabernacle in the wilderness (Exod. 31:6; 35:34; 38:23).

Ahishahar (a-hish'a-har; *brother of the dawn*). One of the sons of Bilhan (1 Chron. 7:10).

Ahishar (a-hī'shar; *brother of song*). 950 B.C. An officer of Solomon (1 Kings 4:6).

Ahithophel (a-hith'o-fel; *brother of foolishness*). 975 B.C. The real leader of Absalom's rebellion against David. When he saw that victory was impossible, he committed suicide (2 Sam. 15–17).

Ahitub (a-hī'tub; *my brother is goodness*). **[1]** 1050 B.C. A son of Phinehas (1 Sam. 14:3; 22:9, 11–12, 20). **[2]** 1050 B.C. Father of Zadok the high priest (2 Sam. 8:17; 15:27; 1 Chron. 6:7–8). **[3]** The father of Meraioth and a high priest of the same family who served during Nehemiah's time (1 Chron. 6:11; 9:11; Neh. 11:11).

Ahlab (ah'lab; *fertile*). A town assigned to Asher, but never captured from the Canaanites (Judg. 1:31); its probable location is about 6 km. (4 mi.) northeast of Tyre.

Ahlai (a'li). **[1]** A daughter of Sheshan and descendant of Perez (1 Chron. 2:31) Matt. 1:3;. **[2]** 1025 B.C. Father of one of David's mighty men (1 Chron. 11:41).

Ahoah (a-hō'ah; *Jehovah is brother*). 1825 B.C. A son of Bela (1 Chron. 8:4). Called Ahijah in 1 Chron. 8:7.

Aholiab [Oholiab] (a-hō'li-ab [ō-hō'li-ab]; *a father's tent*). One of the workers who erected the tabernacle (Exod. 31:6; 35:34; 36:1–2).

Aholibamah [Oholibamah] (a-hōl-i-bā'mah [ō-hō-li-ba'ma]; *tent of the high place*). **[1]** 1950 B.C. A wife of Esau (Gen. 36:2, 5, 14, 18). In Genesis she is called Judith. **[2]** A duke of Edom (Gen. 36:41). *See also* Esau's Wives.

Ahumai (a-hū'mī). A son of Jahath descendant of Judah (1 Chron. 4:2).

Ahuzam [Ahuzzam] (a-hū'zam, [a-hū'zam]; *possessing*).

A son of Ashur, a descendant of Judah through Caleb (1 Chron. 4:16).

Ahuzzath (a-huz′zath). 2025 B.C. A friend of Abimelech, king of Philistia (Gen. 26:26).

Ahzai [Ahasai] (a′zīh [a′hah-zīh]; *Jehovah has seized*). A priest in Nehemiah's time (Neh. 11:13).

Ai [Aiath; Aija] (ā′ī [ā-ī′ath; ā-ī′ja]; *heap of ruins*). [1] One of the strongest Canaanite cities, located east of Bethel (Josh. 7:2; Neh. 11:31). In Isaiah 10:28 the Hebrew feminine form of the name (Aiath) occurs. [2] A city of the Ammonites, probably located near Heshbon (Jer. 49:3).

Aiah (ā-ī′ah; *a falcon*). 1075 B.C. Father of Saul's concubine. Rizpah (2 Sam. 3:7; 21:8, 10–11).

Aijalon [Ajalon] (ā′ja-lon [aj′a-lon]; *place of deer*). [1] A town located 22.5 km. (14 mi.) northwest of Jerusalem, designated as a Levitical city (Josh. 19:42; 21:24; 2 Chron. 28:18). [2] A site belonging to the tribe of Zebulun west of the Sea of Galilee, where the judge Elon was buried (Judg. 12:12). Its exact location is unknown.

Ain (a′ēn; *fountain*). [1] A town of Judah near Rimmon, assigned to the Levites serving the tribe of Simeon (Josh. 15:32; 19:7; 21:16; 1 Chron. 4:32). [2] A site on the boundary line of the Promised Land, west of Riblah (Num. 34:11). Its exact location is unknown.

Ajah (ā′ya; *hawk*). 1975 B.C. A son of Zibeon (Gen. 36:24; 1 Chron. 1:40).

Ajalon (aj′a-lon). *See* Aijalon.

Akan (ā′ken; *twisted*). 1925 B.C. Son of Ezar and grandson of Seir (Gen. 36:27).

Akel Dama [Aceldama] (a-kel da′ma [a-kel da′ma]; *field of blood*). A field located outside the walls of Jerusalem, also called the *potter's field*, purchased by the priests of Jerusalem with the 30 pieces of silver which they had paid to Judas for his betrayal of Jesus (Matt. 27:5–10). According to Luke, the field was purchased by Judas himself (Acts 1:18–19).

Akkub (ak'kub). **[1]** Ancestor of a family of porters (Ezra 2:42; Neh. 7:45). **[2]** Ancestor of Nethinim who returned from the Exile (Ezra 2:45). **[3]** 450 B.C. A porter in the Temple after the Exile (1 Chron. 9:17; Neh. 11:19; 12:25). **[4]** 450 B.C. A priest who helped the people understand the Law (Neh. 8:7). **[5]** One descendant from David mentioned in Chronicles (1 Chron. 3:24).

Akrabbim, Ascent of (a'krab'bim). A mountain pass that marks the southeast border of Judah near the Dead Sea and the wilderness of Zin (Josh. 15:3; Num. 34:4).

Alammelech (a-lam'me-lek; *king's oak*). A village assigned to the tribe of Asher (Josh. 19:26).

Alemeth Alameth (al'e-meth [al'a-meth]; *hiding place*). **[1]** A son of Becher and grandson of Benjamin (1 Chron. 7:8). **[2]** A descendant of Jonathan, son of Saul (1 Chron. 8:36; 9:42).

Alemeth [Almon] (al'e-meth [al'mōn]; *hidden*). A city given to the priests of the tribe of Benjamin (1 Chron. 6:60; Josh. 21:18).

Alexander (al-ex-an'der; *defender of men*). **[1]** A.D. 30. A kinsman of Annas and a leading man in Jerusalem (Acts 4:6). **[2]** A.D. 50. A son of the Simon who bore Christ's cross (Mark 15:21). **[3]** A.D. 55. A Jew who was with Paul when the Ephesians had a riot (Acts 19:33). Perhaps the same as **[1]**. **[4]** A.D. 65. A convert who apostatized (1 Tim. 1:20). **[5]** A.D. 65. A person who did much harm to Paul (2 Tim. 4:14). Perhaps the same as [4].

Alexandria (al-ex-an′dri-a; *city of Alexander the Great*). A city on the Mediterranean coast of Egypt, which served as Egypt's capital city for many years (Acts 27:6; 28:11–13).

Aliah [Alvah] (a-lī′ah [al′va]; *sublimity*). A duke of Edom (1 Chron. 1:51). He is called Alvah in Genesis (Gen. 36:40).

Alian [Alvan] (a-lī′an [al′van]; *sublime*). 1950 B.C. The oldest son of Shobal and a descendant of Seir (1 Chron. 1:40). He is called Alvan in Genesis 36:23.

Allon (al′lun; *an oak*). A son of Jedediah and father of Shiphi, of the tribe of Simeon (1 Chron. 4:37).

Allon Bachuth (a′lun bak′uth; *oak of weeping*). Burial place of Deborah, nurse of Rebekah, near Bethel.

Almodad (al-mō′dad; *God is a friend*). A son of Joktan (Gen. 10:26; 1 Chron. 1:20).

Almon (al′mōn, *hiding place*). A priestly town near the territory of Benjamin (Josh. 21:18), also called Alemeth. Probably the same place as Khirbet Almit, a mound northeast of Jerusalem.

Almon Diblathaim (al′mon dib-la-tha′im). A site between Dibon Gad and the mountains of Abarim where the Israelites camped during their wandering in the wilderness (Num. 33:46).

Aloth (ā′loth; *ascents*). A district in northern Palestine from which King Solomon drew provisions (1 Kings 4:16). Possibly the same place as Bealoth.

Alphaeus (al-fē′us; *leader; chief*) [1] A.D. 1. The father of Levi (Matthew) the apostle (Mark 2:14). [2] A.D. 1. The father of the apostle James the Less (Matt. 10:3; Mark 3:18; Acts 1:13).

Alush (ā'lush; *wild place*). A site where the Israelites camped on their journey from Egypt to Mount Sinai (Num. 33:14).

Alvah (al'va). *See* Aliah.

Alvan (al'van). *See* Alian.

Amad (a'mad; *station*). A frontier town of the tribe of Asher (Josh. 19:26).

Amal (a'mal; *sorrow*). A son of Helem in the line of Asher (1 Chron. 7:35).

Amalek (am'a-lek; *warlike*). A grandson of Esau and son of Eliphaz and progenitor of the Amalekites (Gen. 36:12, 16; 1 Chron. 1:36; cf. Exod. 17:8–9).

Amam (a'mam; *gathering place*). A village in southern Judah, exact location unknown. (Josh. 15:26).

Amana (a-ma'na; *constant*). A range of mountains in Lebanon, probably south of the Amana [Abana] River (Song of Sol. 4:8).

Amariah (am-a-rī'a; *Jehovah has said*). [1] 1100 B.C. Son of the priest Meraioth, a descendant of Phineas, and grandson of Aaron (1 Chron. 6:7, 52; Ezra 7:3). [2] Son of Azariah, a high priest in Solomon's time (1 Chron. 6:11). [3] A Levite who was a descendant of Kohath (1 Chron. 23:19; 24:23). [4] 875 B.C. A chief priest in the reign of Jehoshaphat (2 Chron. 19:11). [5] Ancestor of Zephaniah the prophet (Zeph. 1:1). [6] 725 B.C. A Levite appointed by King Hezekiah to distribute the tithes (2 Chron. 31:15). [7] 525 B.C. One who sealed the new covenant with God after the Exile (Neh. 10:3; 12:2, 13). [8] 450 B.C. One who took a foreign wife during the Exile (Ezra 10:42). [9] One whose descendants dwelled in Jerusalem after the Exile (Neh. 11:4).

Amasa (am'a-sa; *burden-bearer*). [1] 975 B.C. A nephew

of David who became the commander of Absalom's army (2 Sam. 17:25; 19:13; 20:4–12). **[2]** 750 B.C. A leader of the Ephraimites and son of Hadlai who opposed making slaves of captured Jews (2 Chron. 28:12).

Amasai (a-mas'ā-ī; *Jehovah has borne*). **[1]** A son of Elkanah in the genealogy of Kohath (1 Chron. 6:25, 35; 2 Chron. 29:12). **[2]** 1000 B.C. A captain who joined David at Ziklag (1 Chron. 12:18). **[3]** 1000 B.C. A priest who assisted in bringing up the ark of the covenant to Jerusalem (1 Chron. 15:24).

Amashai [Amashsai] (a-mash'ā-ī [a-mash'sā-ī]; *carrying spoil*). 450 B.C. A priest of the family of Immer (Neh. 11:13).

Amasiah (am-a-sī'a; *burden of Jehovah*). 875 B.C. A son of Zichri and chief captain of Jehoshaphat (2 Chron. 17:16).

Amau [Amaw] (a'mōe [a'mōe]). The land from which Balak summoned Balaam the soothsayer (Num. 22:5).

Amaziah (am-a-zī'a; *Jehovah is mighty*). **[1]** A Levite descendant from Merari (1 Chron. 6:45). **[2]** Ruled 796–767 B.C. Son and successor of Joash to the throne of Judah. He was murdered at Lachish (2 Kings 12:21–14:20). **[3]** 775 B.C. An idolatrous priest of Bethel who tried to silence the prophet Amos (Amos 7:10, 12, 14). **[4]** 725 B.C. Father of Joshah (1 Chron. 4:34).

Ami [Amon] (ā'mī [ā'mon]; *faithful*). 950 B.C. A servant of Solomon whose descendants returned from captivity (Ezra 2:57). In Nehemiah 7:59, he is called Amon.

Aminadab (a-min'a-dab; *my people is noble*). Greek form of Amminadab (q.v.).

Amittai (a-mit′ī; *faithful*). 775 B.C. Father of the prophet Jonah (2 Kings 14:25; Jon. 1:1).

Ammah (am′ma; *mother* or *beginning*). A hill in the country of Benjamin; Joab and Abishai stopped here after their victory over Abner in the battle of Gibeon. (2 Sam. 2:24).

Ammiel (am′i-el; *kinsman of God*). [1] 1450 B.C. One of those sent by Moses to spy out the Promised Land (Num. 13:12). [2] 1025 B.C. Father of Machir, David's friend (2 Sam. 9:4–5; 17:27). [3] 1025 B.C. Father of Bathsheba (1 Chron 3:5). *See* Eliam (2 Sam. 11:3). [4] 1000 B.C. A son of Obed-edom who served as a gate-keeper of the tabernacle in the time of David (1 Chron. 26:5).

Ammihud (am-mi′hud; *man of praiseworthiness*). [1] 1450 B.C. Father of Elishama, the chief of Ephraim (Num. 1:10; 2:18; 7:48). [2] 1400 B.C. A Simeonite whose son helped to divide the Promised Land (Num. 34:20). [3] 1400 B.C. A Naphthalite whose son helped divide the Promised Land (Num. 34:28). [4] 1025 B.C. Father of Talmai, king of Geshur (2 Sam. 13:37). [5] 450 B.C. A descendant of Judah through Perez and a son of Omri (1 Chron. 9:4).

Amminadab [Aminadab] (am-min′a-dab [a-min′a-dab]; *my people is noble*). [1] A son of Kohath (1 Chron. 6:22). Also called Izhar (1 Chron. 6:37–38). [2] 1500 B.C. Aaron's father-in-law (Exod. 6:23). [3] 1000 B.C. One of the Levites who helped to bring the ark of the covenant from the house of Obed-edom (1 Chron. 15:10–11). [4] A prince of Judah and ancestor of Christ (Num. 1:7; 2:3; Ruth 4:19–20; Matt. 1:4).

Ammishaddai (am-mi-shad′dā-ī; *the Almighty is my kins-*

man). 1500 B.C. Father of Ahiezer, a captain of Dan during the wilderness journey (Num. 1:12; 2:25).

Ammizabad (am-miz′a-bad; *the kinsman has endowed*). 975 B.C. One of David's captains (1 Chron. 27:6).

Ammon (am′mon; *kinsman* or *people*). [1] 2025 B.C. The son of Lot and the person referred to as Ben-ammi in Gen. 19:38. [2] The land settled by the Ammonites located north and east of Moab. *See* Ben-ammi.

Amnon (am′non; *faithful*). [1] A son of Shimon of the family of Caleb (1 Chron. 4:20). [2] 1000 B.C. Eldest son of David, by Ahinoam, slain by Absalom (2 Sam. 3:2; 13:1–39).

Amok (a′mok; *unsearchable*). 525 B.C. A priest who returned to Jerusalem with Zerubbabel (Neh. 12:7, 20).

Amon (ā′mon; *trustworthy*). [1] 875 B.C. Governor of Samaria in Ahab's time (1 Kings 22:26; 2 Chron. 18:25). [2] Ruled 642–640 B.C. Son and successor of Manasseh to the throne of Judah; an ancestor of Christ (2 Kings 21:19–25; Jer. 1:2; Zeph. 1:1; Matt. 1:10). [3] *See* Ami.

Amos (ā′mos; *burden-bearer*). [1] 775 B.C. A prophet during the reigns of Uzziah and Jeroboam (Amos 1:1; 7:10–12; 14). [2] An ancestor of Christ (Luke 3:25).

Amoz (ā′moz; *strong*). 775 B.C. Father of the prophet Isaiah (2 Kings 19:2, 20; Isa. 1:1; 2:1; 13:1).

Amphipolis (am-fip′o-lis; *surrounded city*). The chief city of Macedonia, located in the region of Thrace (Acts 17:1).

Amplias [Ampliatus] (am′pli-as [am-plih-a′tus]; *large*). A.D. 55. A Roman Christian to whom Paul sent greetings (Rom. 16:8).

Amram [Hamram; Hemdan] (am′ram [ham′ran; hem-

'dan]; *people exalted*). **[1]** 1525 B.C. A descendant of Levi and father or ancestor of Aaron, Moses, and Miriam (Exod. 6:18, 20; Num. 3:19; 26:58–59). **[2]** 450 B.C. One who had taken a foreign wife (Ezra 10:34). **[3]** *See* Hemdan.

Amraphel (am′ra-fel). 2100 B.C. A king of Shinar who warred against Sodom (Gen. 14:1, 9).

Amzi (am′zi; *my strength*). **[1]** A Levite of the family of Merari (1 Chron. 6:46). **[2]** An ancestor of returned exiles (Neh. 11:12).

Anab (ā′nab; *grape*). A town in the mountains of Judah (Josh. 11:21; 15:50).

Anah (ā′nah; *answering* or *speech*). **[1]** Zibeon's daughter and one of Esau's wives (Gen. 36:2, 14, 18, 25). If the father, he is the same as Beeri the Hittite (Gen. 26:34). *See* Esau's Wives. **[2]** 1950 B.C. A son of Seir and a chief of Edom (Gen. 36:20, 29; 1 Chron. 1:38). **[3]** A son of Zibeon (Gen. 36:24; 1 Chron. 1:40–41).

Anaharath (a-ña′ha-rath; *gorge*). A frontier town of the tribe of Issachar (Josh. 19:19).

Anaiah (a-nī′a; *Jehovah answers*). **[1]** 450 B.C. One who stood with Ezra at the reading of the Law (Neh. 8:4). **[2]** 450 B.C. One who sealed the new covenant with God after the Exile (Neh. 10:22).

Anak (ā′nak; *giant*). Ancestor of the giant Anakim (Num. 13:22, 28, 33; Josh. 15:14).

Anamim (an′a-mim; *rockmen*). Descendants of Mizraim (Gen. 10:13; 1 Chron. 1:11). Possibly an unknown Egyptian tribe.

Anan (ā′nan; *cloud*). 450 B.C. One who sealed the new covenant with God after the Exile (Neh. 10:26).

Anani (a-nā′nī; *God has appeared*). A descendant of David who lived after the Babylonian Captivity (1 Chron. 3:24).

Ananiah (an-a-nī′a; *Jehovah is a protector*). **[1]** 500 B.C. Grandfather of Azariah (Neh. 3:23).

Ananiah (an-a-nī′a; *Jehovah is a protector*). A town inhabited by the tribe of Benjamin after the Exile (Neh. 11:32).

Ananias (an-a-nī′as; *Jehovah is gracious*). **[1]** A.D. 30. A disciple struck dead for trying to deceive the apostles (Acts 5:1, 3, 5). **[2]** A.D. 35. A disciple of Damascus who helped Paul after receiving a vision (Acts 9:10–17; 22:12). **[3]** A.D. 60. A high priest in Jerusalem who opposed Paul (Acts 23:2; 24:1).

Anath (ā′nath). 1225 B.C. Father of the judge Shamgar (Judg. 3:31; 5:6).

Anathoth (an′a-thoth; *answered prayers*). **[1]** 1800 B.C. A son of Becher (1 Chron. 7:8). **[2]** 450 B.C. One who sealed the new covenant with God after the Exile (Neh. 10:19).

Anathoth (an′a-thoth; *answered prayers*). A town of the tribe of Benjamin, located about 4 km. (2.5 mi.) northeast of Jerusalem (Josh. 21:18; Ezra 2:23); the birthplace of the prophet Jeremiah (Jer. 1:1; 11:21).

Andrew (an′drew; *manly; conqueror*). A.D. 25. The brother of Peter and one of the twelve apostles (Matt. 4:18; 10:2; John 1:40, 44; 6:8).

Andronicus (an-dro-nī′kus; *conqueror*). A.D. 55. A kinsman of Paul at Rome, to whom Paul sent greetings (Rom. 16:7).

Anem (ā′nem; *two fountains*). A city of the tribe of Issachar, assigned to the Levites (1 Chron. 6:73). It is identical with En Gannim **[2]**.

Aner (ā'ner; *sprout; waterfall*). 2100 B.C. An Amorite chief (Gen. 14:13, 24).

Aner (ā'ner; *sprout; waterfall*). A city of the tribe of Manasseh located west of the Jordan; it was assigned to the Levites (1 Chron. 6:70).

Aniam (a-nī'am; *lamentation*). A descendant of Manasseh (1 Chron. 7:19).

Anim (a'nim; *fountains*). A town in the hills of Judah (Josh. 15:50).

Anna (an'a; *favor*). 5 B.C. A prophetess of the tribe of Asher in Christ's time (Luke 2:36).

Annas (an'as; *grace of Jehovah*). High priest of the Jews from A.D. 6 to A.D. 15, who first tried Christ (Luke 3:2; John 18:13, 24; Acts 4:6).

Antioch (an'ti-ok). **[1]** A Syrian city on the south side of the Orontes River, where the followers of Jesus were first called Christians (Acts 11:19–26). **[2]** A city of Phrygia near the border of Pisidia, visited by Paul and Barnabas on their missionary journey (Acts 13:14).

Antipas (an'ti-pas; *against all*). A.D. 80. A Christian martyr of Pergamos (Rev. 2:13).

Antipatris (an-tip'a-tris; *for his father*). A city built on the Plain of Sharon by Herod the Great (Acts 23:31).

Antothijah [**Anthothijah**] (an-to-thī'jah [an-thō-thī'jah]; *belonging to Anathoth*). A son of Shashak (1 Chron. 8:24).

Anub (ā'nub). A descendant of Judah through Caleb (1 Chron. 4:8).

Apelles (a-pel'ēz). A.D. 55. A Roman Christian to whom Paul sent greetings (Rom. 16:10).

Aphek [**Aphik**] (ā'fek [ā'fik]; *fortress*). **[1]** A city north of Sidon (Josh. 13:4). **[2]** A town assigned to the tribe of Asher but never captured from the Canaanites; located just southeast of Accho (Josh. 19:30; Judg. 1:31). **[3]** A town on the Plain of Sharon northeast of Joppa, whose king was killed by Joshua (Josh. 12:18). **[4]** A town between Shunem and Jezreel, whose soldiers fought in the war between Saul and the Philistines (1 Sam. 28:4; 29:1, 11; 31:1). This may have been the town where Benhadad fought Ahab (1 Kings 20:26–30), and where "Jehoash" of Israel would defeat the Syrians (2 Kings 13:14–19). However, these two passages may refer to Aphek in Golan, about 5 km. (3 mi.) east of the Sea of Galilee.

Aphekah (a-fē′kah; *fortress*). A city of Judah (Josh. 15:53).

Aphiah (a-fī′a). A Benjamite; ancestor of Saul (1 Sam. 9:1).

Aphrah (aph′rah). A form of Beth Aphrah.

Aphses (aph′ses). A form of Happizzez.

Apollonia (ap-o-lō′ni-a; *city of Apollo*). A Macedonian town visited by Paul on his way to Thessalonica (Acts 17:1).

Apollos (a-pol′los; *destroyer*). A.D. 50. A Jewish Christian, mighty in the scripture, who came to Ephesus and was instructed by Aquila and Priscilla (Acts 18:24; 19:1; 1 Cor. 1:12; 3:4–6; Titus 3:13).

Appaim (ap′pa-yim; *nostrils*). A son of Nadab and the father of Nishi (1 Chron. 2:30).

Apphia (af′i-a; *endearment*). A.D. 60. A female Christian Paul mentioned when writing Philemon (Philem. 2).

Appii Forum (ap-i-ī fō′rum; *marketplace of Appius*). A town in Italy about 64 km. (40 mi.) from Rome. Roman Christians met Paul here when he was brought to plead his case before Caesar (Acts 28:15).

Aqabah, Gulf of. *See* Red Sea.

Aquila (ak'wi-la; *eagle*). A.D. 50. A pious Jewish Christian, husband of Priscilla and friend of Paul (Acts 18:2, 18, 26; Rom. 16:3; 1 Cor. 16:19).

Ar (ar; *city*). The chief city of Moab, located on the northern boundary of Moabite territory (Num. 21:15; Isa. 15:1).

Ara (a'ra; *strong*). A son of Jether of the tribe of Asher (1 Chron. 7:38).

Arab (a'rab; *ambush*). A town in the hills of Judah east of Dumah (Josh. 15:52).

Arabah (ar'a-bah; *desert, plain*). The depression of land holding the Sea of Galilee and the Dead Sea (Josh. 18:18). The "valley" of Joshua 11:2 probably refers to the Arabah.

Arabia (a-rā'bia; *desert*). A large peninsula bounded on the east by the Persian Gulf and the Gulf of Oman, on the west by the Red Sea, and on the south by the Indian Ocean. It was the home of many nomadic tribes, and was sometimes called the "East Country" (2 Chron. 21:16; Isa. 13:20).

Arad (a'rad; *fugitive*). One of the chief men of Aijalon (1 Chron. 8:15).

Arad (a'rad; *wild ass*). A Canaanite city in the wilderness of Judea (Josh. 12:14).

Arah (a'rah; *wayfarer*). [1] A son of Ulla; member of the tribe of Asher (1 Chron. 7:39). [2] Ancestor of a family returned from the Exile (Ezra 2:5; Neh. 7:10). Grandfather of the wife of Tobiah, who opposed Nehemiah in rebuilding the temple (Neh. 6:18).

Aram (a'ram; *high; exalted*). [1] A son of Shem (Gen. 10:22–23; 1 Chron. 1:17). The Aramean people possibly are referred to. [2] 2000 B.C. A son of Abraham's nephew, Kemuel (Gen. 22:21). [3] A descendant from

Asher (1 Chron. 7:34). **[4]** The Greek form of Ram, the father of Amminadab (q.v.).

Aram (a'ram; *high*). The plain extending eastward from the Lebanon Mountains beyond the Euphrates River, occupied by the Aramaeans, mistakenly termed "Syrians" by the KJV (Num. 23:7; 1 Kings 20:1).

Aram Dammesek (ar'am dam'e-sek). An ancient name for Syria of Damascus, conquered by David (2 Sam. 8:5–6).

Aram-naharaim (a'ram-nuh-ha-rā'im; *Aram of the two rivers*). The northern section of the land located between the Tigris and Euphrates Rivers (Psa. 60, title).

Aran (ar'an). 1950 B.C. A son of Dishan and a descendant of Seir the Horite (Gen. 36:28; 1 Chron. 1:42).

Ararat (ar'a-rat). A mountainous, hilly land in western Asia (Jer. 51:27) later known as Armenia (Isa. 37:38; 2 Kings 19:37). Noah's ark rested on mountains in this area (Gen. 8:4).

Araunah [Ornan] (a-ra'na [ōr'nan]). A Jebusite who owned a threshing floor, a site of which David purchased to build an altar to the Lord (2 Sam. 26:16–24).

Arba (ar'ba; *four*). An ancestor of the Anak and founder of Kirjath Arba (Josh. 14:15; 15:13; 21:11).

Archelaus (ar-ke-lā'us; *people's chief*). 4 B.C. to A.D. 6. The son of Herod the Great who succeeded his father as the ruler of Idumea, Judea, and Samaria (Matt. 2:22).

Archippus (ar-kip'us; *chief groom*). A.D. 60. A "fellow-soldier" whom Paul addresses (Col. 4:17; Philem. 2).

Ard (ard; *descent*). **[1]** 1825 B.C. A son of Benjamin (Gen. 46:21). **[2]** A son of Bela listed in Numbers 26:40. Possibly identical with the Addar of First Chronicles 18:3.

Ardon (ar'don; *descendant*). A son of Caleb of Judah mentioned in Chronicles (1 Chron. 2:18).

Areli (a-rē′li; *valiant; heroic*). One of the sons of Gad (Gen. 46:16; Num. 26:17).

Areopagus (ar-e-op′a-gus; *hill of Ares [Mars]*). A hill west of the acropolis in Athens, where Paul addressed several Greek philosophers; also known as Mars Hill (Acts 17:19–34).

Aretas (ar′e-tas; *pleasing; virtuous*). A.D. 35. Aretas IV; Philopatris, King of the Nabataeans whose deputy tried to seize Paul (2 Cor. 11:32).

Argob (ar′gob; *stony*). 750 B.C. An officer of Pekahiah slain by Pekah (2 Kings 15:25).

Argob (ar′gob; *region of clods*). A district of Bashan that was taken by King Solomon (Deut. 3:4; Josh. 13:30; 1 Kings 4:13).

Aridai (a-rid′ā-ī; *delight of Hari*). 475 B.C. A son of Haman slain by the Jews (Esther 9:9).

Aridatha (a-rīd′a-tha; *given by Hari*). 475 B.C. A son of Haman, hanged with his father (Esther 9:8).

Arieh (ar-yā; *lion of Jehovah*). 750 B.C. A man of Israel killed by Pekah (2 Kings 15:25).

Ariel (ar′i-el; *lion of God*). [1] 450 B.C. One sent by Ezra to secure the temple ministers (Ezra 8:16). [2] Symbolic name of Jerusalem (Isa. 29:1–2).

Arimathea (a-ri-ma-the′a; *height*). The home of a businessman named Joseph, who gained permission to bury the body of Jesus (Matt. 27:57; Luke 23:51). Its exact location is not known, but is generally believed to have been about 16 km. (10 mi.) northeast of Lydda on the western edge of the hill country of Ephraim. *See also* Ramah.

Arioch (ar′i-ok). [1] 2100 B.C. A king of Ellasar in Assyria who took part in the expedition against Sodom and Gomorrah (Gen. 14:1, 9). [2] 600 B.C. A captain of

Nebuchadnezzar's guard commanded to slay the "wise men" (Dan. 2:14–15, 24–25).

Arisai (a-ris'ī). 475 B.C. A son of Haman slain by the Jews (Esther 9:9).

Aristarchus (a-ris-tar'kus; *the best ruler*). A.D. 55. A faithful companion who accompanied Paul on his third missionary journey (Acts 19:29; 20:4; Col. 4:10).

Aristobulus (a-ris-to-bū'lus; *best counselor*). A.D. 55. A person in Rome whose household Paul saluted (Rom.16:10).

Armageddon (ar-ma-ged'on; Hebrew, *Har Megiddo—hill of Megiddo*). The site of the final battle between Christ and Satan (Rev. 16:16). *See also* Megiddo.

Armoni (ar-mō'ni; *of the palace*). 1000 B.C. A son of Saul by Rizpah (2 Sam. 21:8).

Arnan (ar'nan; *quick; strong*). A descendant of David and founder of a family (1 Chron. 3:21).

Arnon (ar'non; *rushing water*). A river that pours into the Dead Sea (Num. 21:13; Josh. 13:16).

Arod [Arodi] (ā'rod [ā'rō-dī]; *hunchbacked*). 1900 B.C. A son of Gad, progenitor of the tribe of Arodi (Num. 26:17; cf. Gen. 46:16).

Aroer (ar'ō-er; *ruins*). [1] A town on the northern bank of the Arnon River (Deut. 2:36; Josh. 12:2). [2] A city of Gilead east of Rabbath-Ammon (Josh. 13:25). [3] A village of Judah about 19 km. (12 mi.) southeast of Beersheba (1 Sam. 30:28).

Arpad [Arphad] (ar'pad [ar'fad] *resting place*). A Syrian city 20 km. (13 mi.) north of Aleppo (Isa. 36:19; Jer. 42:23).

Arphaxad (ar-fax'ad; *one who heals*). A son of Shem and an ancestor of Christ (Gen. 10:22, 24; 1 Chron. 1:17–18; Luke 3:36). Possibly the reference is to a tribe or

people. Formerly identified with the mountainous land
north of Nineveh.

Artaxerxes (ar-ta-zerk´sēz; *possessor of an exalted kingdom*).
[1] A king of Persia, Artaxerxes I Longimanus, at whose
court Ezra and Nehemiah were officials (Ezra 7:1, 7, 11–
12; Neh. 2:1; 5:14). [2] Some suppose that Ezra 4:7
uses "Artaxerxes" to refer to the pseudo-Smerdis king of
Persia, but the reference is probably to [1].

Artemas (ar´te-mas; *whole; sound*). A.D. 65. A friend of
Paul at Nicopolis (Titus 3:12).

Arubboth (ar´u-bōth; *lattices*). A district belonging to
King Solomon (1 Kings 4:10).

Arumah (a-rū´ma; *lofty*). A town near Shechem once
occupied by Abimelech (Judg. 9:41).

Arvad (ar´vad; *refuge*). The northernmost Phoenician
city, noted for its mariners (Ezek. 27:8). The modern
city of Ruwad is located on this site.

Arza (ar´za; *delight*). 900 B.C. A steward of King Elah of
Israel (1 Kings 16:9).

Asa (ā´sa; *physician; healer*). [1] 910–869 B.C. The third
king of Judah and an ancestor of Christ (1 Kings 15:8–
16:29; Matt. 1:7–8). [2] Head of a Levite family
(1 Chron. 9:16).

Asahel (ās´a-hel; *God is doer*). [1] 1025 B.C. A son of
David's sister, Zeruiah. He was slain by Abner (2 Sam.
2:18–32; 3:27, 30). [2] 875 B.C. A Levite sent to teach
the Law (2 Chron. 17:8). [3] 725 B.C. A Levite employed as an officer of the offerings and tithes (2 Chron.
31:13). [4] 450 B.C. Father of Jonathan, appointed to
take a census of foreign wives (Ezra 10:15).

Asahiah [Asaiah] (ā-sa-hī´a [ā-sa-ī´a]; *Jehovah is doer; Jehovah has made*). 625 B.C. One sent to inquire of the Lord

concerning the Book of the Law (2 Kings 22:12, 14;
2 Chron. 34:20).

Asaiah (ā-sa-ī′a; *Jehovah is doer; Jehovah has made*). **[1]**
1000 B.C. A descendant of Merari who helped bring
up the ark (1 Chron. 6:30; 15:6, 11). **[2]** 725 B.C. A
prince of Simeon who helped defeat the people of
Gedor (1 Chron. 4:36). **[3]** 450 B.C. A resident of
Jerusalem after the Exile (1 Chron. 9:5). **[4]** *See also*
Asahiah.

Asaph (ā′saf; *Jehovah has gathered*). **[1]** One whose
descendants were porters in David's time (1 Chron.
26:1). The text should possibly read Abiasaph (q.v.). **[2]**
1000 B.C. One of David's three chief musicians
(1 Chron. 6:39; 15:17, 19). Author of Psalms 50, 73—
83. **[3]** A levite whose descendants lived in Jerusalem
(1 Chron. 9:15). **[4]** 725 B.C. Father of Joah the recorder to Hezekiah (2 Kings 18:18, 37; 2 Chron.
29:13). **[5]** 450 B.C. A keeper of the royal forests in Judah (Neh. 2:8).

Asareel [Asarel] (a-sar′e-el [a-sā′rel]; *God is joined*). A
descendant of Judah through Caleb (1 Chron. 4:16).

Asarelah (as-a-re′la). A form of Asharelah.

Asenath (as′e-nath). 1875 B.C. The Egyptian wife of
Joseph (Gen. 41:45, 50; 46:20).

Aser (ā′ser). Greek form of Asher (q.v.).

Ashan (ā′shan; *smoke*). A lowland town assigned to the
tribe of Judah, then to Simeon (Josh. 15:42; 19:7;
1 Chron. 4:32); probably located just northwest of
Beer-sheba. It is possibly identical with Chor-ashan
(q.v.).

Asharelah [Asarelah; Jesarela; Jesharelah] (ash-a-re′la
[as-a-re′la; jes-a-re′la; jesh-a-re′la]; *God has fulfilled with
joy*). 1000 B.C. A son of Asaph, appointed by King

David to be musician in the Temple (1 Chron. 25:2, 14).

Ashbea (ash'be-a). A place where linen workers lived (1 Chron. 4:21); its exact location is unknown.

Ashbel (ash'bel; *man of Baal*). 1850 B.C. Son of Benjamin (Gen. 46:21; Num. 26:38; 1 Chron. 8:1).

Ashchenaz [Ashkenaz] (ash'ken-az [ash'ken-az]; *a fire that spreads*). A son of Gomer (Gen. 10:3; 1 Chron. 1:6). Possibly a race or tribe who dwelt near Ararat and Minni in eastern Armenia.

Ashdod (ash'dod; *stronghold*). One of the five chief Canaanite cities; the seat of the worship of the fish god Dagon; located halfway between present-day Jaffa and Gaza (Josh. 11:22; 1 Sam. 5:1). In the N.T. the city is called Azotus (Acts 8:40).

Asher [Aser] (ash'er [ā'ser]; *happy*). 1900 B.C. The eighth son of Jacob and an ancestor of one of the twelve tribes of Israel (Gen. 30:13; 35:26; 46:17; 49:20; 1 Chron. 2:2).

Asher (ash'er; *happy*). A town on the southern border of Manasseh (Josh. 17:7).

Ashhur [Ashur] (ash'ur [ash'ur]). A son of Hezron and Abiah; father of Tekoa (1 Chron. 2:24; 4:5).

Ashkelon [Askelon] (ash'ke-lon [as'ke-lon]; *wandering*). One of the five chief Canaanite cities, the seat of the worship of the goddess Derceto; located about 19 km. (12 mi.) north of the present-day city of Gaza (Josh. 13:3; Jer. 47:5).

Ashkenaz (ash'ke-naz). *See* Ashchenaz.

Ashnah (ash'na; *hard; firm*). **[1]** A village in the lowlands of Judah near Zorah (Josh. 15:33). **[2]** Another village of Judah, farther south (Josh. 15:43).

Ashpenaz (ash'pe-naz). 600 B.C. Prince of Nebuchadnezzar's eunuchs who had charge of the captives from Judah (Dan. 1:3).

Ashriel (ash'ri-el). *See* Asriel.

Ashtaroth [Astaroth] (ash'ta-roth [as'ta-roth]). **[1]** The plural form of Ashtoreth, a pagan goddess (1 Sam. 31:10; 1 Kings 11:5). Often connected with Baal as his female partner. **[2]** A city in the northern Transjordan region of Israel. Served as one of the Cities of Refuge. In time of Joshua, Ashtaroth was the home of Og, King of Bashan.

Ashteroth karnaim (ash'te-roth-kar-na'im; [*the goddess*] *Ashtaroth of the two horns*). A town of Bashan, the seat of the worship of the goddess Ashtaroth (Gen. 14:5). The city is possibly to be identified with Astaroth (Ashtaroth) (Deut. 1:4; Josh. 9:10), though this is not certain.

Ashtoreth (ash'tō-reth; *wife, goddess*). A form of Ashtaroth.

Ashurbanipal (ash-ur-ban'i-pal; *Ashur is creating an heir*). 669–626 B.C. The last of the great Assyrian kings. Identified by most scholars as Osnapper (Ezra 4:10). Son and successor of Esarhaddon.

Ashurnasirpal (ash-ur-nas'ir-pal). A king of Assyria who reigned while Assyria was at its peak in power (c.884–860 B.C.).

Ashvath (ash'vath; *wrought*). A son of Japhlet; a descendant of Asher (1 Chron. 7:33).

Asia (ā'sha; *eastern*). The term used by the Bible to refer to Asia Minor (1 Cor. 16:19; Acts 2:9).

Asiel (ā'si-el; *God is doer or maker*). A descendant of Simeon and grandfather of Jehu (1 Chron. 4:35).

Askelon (as'ke-lon). *See* Ashkelon.

Asnah (as'na; *thornbush*). One whose descendants returned from Exile (Ezra 2:50).

Asnapper (as'nap-er). Alternative form of Osnapper.

Aspatha (as-pā'tha; *horse-given*). 475 B.C. Son of Haman, slain by the Jews (Esther 9:7).

Asriel [Ashriel] (as'ri-el [ash'ri-el]; *God has filled with joy*). A son of Manasseh listed in the second census taken in the wilderness (Num. 26:31; 1 Chron. 7:14).

Asshur [Assur] (ash'ur [as'ur]; *level plain*). [1] A son of Shem (Gen. 10:22; 1 Chron. 1:17). Possibly the people of Assyria are intended. [2] Genesis 10:11, if denoting a person, refers to a son of Ham or to [1]. However, many scholars translate: "From that land he (Nimrod) went into Assyria (Asshur)."

Asshur [Assur] (ash'ur [as'ur]; *level plain*). A city in Assyria which was sometimes the capital, or the nation itself may be referred to (Num. 24:22, 24).

Assir (as'sir; *prisoner*). [1] A son of Korah (Exod. 6:24; 1 Chron. 6:22). [2] A son of Ebiasaph (1 Chron. 6:23, 37). [3] A son of Jehoiachin, king of Judah (1 Chron. 3:17).

Assos (as'os; *approaching*). A seaport of Mysia, near Troas (Acts 20:13).

Assur (as'ur). *See* Asshur.

Assyria (a-sir'i-a; *country of Assur*). A Semitic nation on the Tigris River, whose capital was Nineveh (Gen. 2:14; 2 Kings 15:10, 20).

Asuppim (a-sup'im). A word which should be translated "storehouse" as in Nehemiah 12:25. First Chronicles 26:15 should read: "The lot for the South Gate (southward) fell to Obed-edom, and the lot for the storehouse fell to his sons."

Asyncritus (a-sing'kri-tus; *incomparable*). A.D. 55. One at Rome whom Paul salutes (Rom. 16:14).

Atad (ā'tad; *thornbush*). The campsite near Hebron used by Joseph and his brothers as they prepared to take Jacob's body back to Canaan (Gen. 50:11). The new name given the site was a pun: The Canaanites saw the mourning [Hebrew *ēbhel*] of the Egyptians and called the place *Abel* [Hebrew, *ābhel*]—"meadow"; *mizraim*—"of the Egyptians."

Atarah (at'a-ra; *crowning; ornament*). A wife of Jerahmeel and mother of Onam (1 Chron. 2:26).

Ataroth (at'a-roth; *crowns*). **[1]** A town east of the Jordan River rebuilt by the tribe of Gad (Num. 32:3, 34). **[2]** A town on the edge of the Jordan Valley at the border of Ephraim (Josh. 16:7). **[3]** The house of Joab mentioned in the genealogy of Judah (1 Chron. 2:54). The site is unknown. Some take the "House of Joab" to be part of the town's title; in Hebrew this would be Atroth-bethjoab. **[4]** *See also* Ataroth Addar.

Ataroth Addar [Ataroth Adar] (at'a-roth ad'dar [at-a-roth a'dar]; *crown of Addar*). A village on the southern frontier of Ephraim (Josh. 16:5; 18:13). The town is probably to be identified with Ataroth (Josh. 16:2).

Ater (ā'ter; *bound; lame*). **[1]** 450 B.C. One who sealed the new covenant with God after the Exile (Neh. 10:17). **[2]** Ancestor of a family of gatekeepers (Ezra 2:42; Neh. 7:45). **[3]** Ancestor of a family that returned from the Exile (Ezra 2:16; Neh. 7:21).

Athach (ā'thak; *stopping place*). A town in southern Judah, to which David sent some of the spoil of Ziklag (1 Sam. 30:30).

Athaiah (ath-a'ya; *Jehovah is helper*). 450 B.C. A son of Uzziah and descendant of Judah dwelling in Jerusalem (Neh. 11:4).

Athaliah (a-tha-lī'ah; *Jehovah is strong*). **[1]** Ruled 841–835 B.C. The daughter of Jezebel, wife of King Jehoram, and afterwards ruler of Israel for six years (2 Kings 8:26; 11:1–20; 2 Chron. 22:2—23:21). [2] A son of Jeroham (1 Chron. 8:26). [3] 475 B.C. Father of a returned exile (Ezra 8:7).

Athens (ath'enz; *city of Athena*). The greatest city of classical Greece, capital of the Greek city-state of Attica, where Paul founded a Christian church (Acts 17:15–18).

Athlai (ath'lī; *Jehovah is strong*). 450 B.C. A son of Bebai who divorced his pagan wife (Ezra 10:28).

Atroth Beth Joab (at'roth beth jō'ab; *the crowns of the house of Joab*). A town of Judah, apparently near to Bethlehem, the inhabitants of which were descendants of Caleb (1 Chron. 2:54).

Attai (ā'tā-ī; *seasonable; timely*). [1] 1000 B.C. One who joined David at Ziklag (1 Chron. 12:11). [2] 900 B.C. A son of king Rehoboam (2 Chron. 11:20). [3] Grandson of Sheshan the Jerahmeelite, son of Ahlai and Jarha (1 Chron. 2:35–36).

Attalia (at-a-li'a). A seaport of Pamphylia near Perga through which Paul and Barnabas passed after their first missionary journey (Acts 14:25).

Augustus (a-gus'tus; *consecrated* or *holy*). Acts 25:21, 25; 27:1 use the Greek rendering of the title "reverend" in this fashion, since Augustus had been dead many years.

Augustus Caesar (a-gus'tus sē'zer). 63 B.C.—A.D. 14. The imperial name of Octavian, a nephew of Julius Caesar who became emperor of Rome. During his reign, Christ was born (Luke 2:1).

Ava [Avva] (āv'a [āv'va]; *region*). An Assyrian city that sent settlers to colonize Samaria (2 Kings 17:24).

Aven (ā′ven; *wickedness*). [1] Another name for the Egyptian city of On, called Heliopolis by the Greeks (Ezek. 30:17). [2] A valley town in the kingdom of Damascus; probably Awaniyek (Amos 1:5). [3] A shortened form of Beth Aven (Hos. 10:8).

Avim [Avvim] (av′im [av′vim]; *villagers* A city of the tribe of Benjamin, probably near Bethel (Josh. 18:23). Some translate "Bethel and (the village of) the Avvim," thus indicating a group of people (Deut. 2:23; Josh. 13:3).

Avith (ā′vith; *ruins*). A city of Edom, home of King Hadad (Gen. 36:35; 1 Chron. 1:46).

Ayyah (eye′yah; *heap, ruin*). A town settled by the Ephraimites (1 Chron. 7:28). May be the same as Aija (Neh. 11:31).

Azal (ā′zal; *slope*). A place near Jerusalem; location unknown (Zech. 14:5).

Azaliah (az-a-lī′a; *Jehovah is noble*). 650 B.C. Father of Shaphan the scribe (2 Kings 22:3; 2 Chron. 34:8).

Azaniah (az-a-nī′a; *Jehovah is hearer*). 475 B.C. Father of Jeshua, a Levite who signed the new covenant with God after the Exile (Neh. 10:9).

Azarael [Azareel; Azarel] (a-zā′rē′el [a-zā′rē′el; a-zā′rel]; *God is helper*). [1] 1000 B.C. A Korahite who joined David at Ziklag (1 Chron. 12:6). [2] 1000 B.C. One who ministered in the song service of the temple (1 Chron. 25:18). [3] 1000 B.C. A prince of Dan (1 Chron. 27:22). [4] 450 B.C. One who took a foreign wife (Ezra 10:41). [5] A priest of the family of Immer (Neh. 11:13). [6] 450 B.C. One who played the trumpet at the dedication of the new temple (Neh. 12:36).

Azariah (az-a-rī'a; *Jehovah has helped*). **[1]** 975 B.C. A son of Ahimaaz (1 Chron. 6:9). **[2]** An ancestor of Samuel the prophet (1 Chron. 6:36). **[3]** A descendant of Jerahmeel (1 Chron. 2:38–39). **[4]** Ancestor of Zadok and Ezra (Ezra 7:3). **[5]** 950 B.C. A high priest and grandson of [2]. (1 Chron. 6:10–11). **[6]** 950 B.C. A descendant of David's high priest (1 Kings 4:2). **[7]** 950 B.C. A ruler of Solomon's officers (1 Kings 4:5). **[8]** 900 B.C. A prophet who went to Asa (2 Chron. 15:1). **[9]** 850 B.C. A son of King Jehoshaphat (2 Chron. 21:2). **[10]** 850 B.C. A captain who helped to place Joash on the throne (2 Chron. 23:1). **[11]** 850 B.C. Another man who helped Joash (2 Chron. 23:1). **[12]** 792–740 B.C. Tenth king of Judah; also called Uzziah (2 Kings 14:21; 1 Chron. 3:12). **[13]** 775 B.C. A high priest who opposed Uzziah (2 Chron. 26:17, 20). **[14]** 750 B.C. A chief of Ephraim (2 Chron. 28:12). **[15]** 750 B.C. A descendant of Kohath and father of Joel (2 Chron. 29:12). **[16]** 725 B.C. One who helped cleanse the temple (2 Chron. 29:12). **[17]** 725 B.C. A chief of the family of Zadok, priest in Hezekiah's time (2 Chron. 31:10, 13). **[18]** 600 B.C. A son of Hilkiah the high priest under Josiah (1 Chron. 6:13–14; 9:11; Ezra 7:1). **[19]** 600 B.C. A captive carried to Babylon with Daniel (Dan. 1:6–7, 11, 19; 2:17). *See* Abed-nego. **[20]** 575 B.C. One who charged Jeremiah with false prophecy (Jer. 43:2). **[21]** 525 B.C. One who came up to Jerusalem with Zerubbabel (Neh. 7:7). Perhaps this is another name of Seraiah (Ezra 2:2); if not, his name is omitted in this passage. **[22]** 450 B.C. One who repaired the wall of Jerusalem (Neh. 3:23–24). **[23]** 450 B.C. A priest who explained the Law (Neh. 8:7). **[24]** A prince of Judah

(Neh. 12:33). **[25]** A descendant of Judah (1 Chron. 2:8).

Azaz (ā'zaz; *Jehovah is strong*). A descendant of Reuben (1 Chron. 5:8).

Azaziah (ā-za-zī'a; *Jehovah is strong*). **[1]** 1025 B.C. Father of a prince of Ephraim in David's time (1 Chron. 27:20). **[2]** 1000 B.C. A Levite who took part in the musical service when the ark was brought to the temple (1 Chron. 15:21). **[3]** 725 B.C. A Levite who had the oversight of the dedicated things of the temple under Hezekiah (2 Chron. 31:13).

Azbuk (az'buk; *pardon*). The father of a man named Nehemiah (Neh. 3:16).

Azekah (a-zē'ka; *a place tilled*). A city in the lowlands of Socoh, less than 32 km. (20 mi.) southwest of Jerusalem; the kings besieging Gibeon were driven here (Josh. 10:10; 1 Sam. 17:1).

Azel (ā'zel; *noble*). Son of Eleasah and a descendant of King Saul (1 Chron. 8:37–38; 9:43–44).

Azem (ā'zem). *See* Ezem.

Azgad (az'gad; *Gad is strong*). **[1]** One whose descendants returned from the Exile with Zerubbabel (Ezra 2:12; Neh. 7:17). **[2]** One who came back to Jerusalem with Ezra (Ezra 8:12). **[3]** 450 B.C. One who sealed the new covenant with God after the Exile (Neh. 10:15).

Aziel (ā'zi-el; *God has nourished*). 1000 B.C. A Levite musician who participated in the return of the Ark of the Covenant to Jerusalem (1 Chron. 15:20). *See* Jaaziel.

Aziza (a-zī'za; *strong*). 450 B.C. Son of Zattu. Divorced his pagan wife after the Exile (Ezra 10:27).

Azmaveth (az-ma'veth; *strong as death*). **[1]** 1000 B.C. One of David's mighty men (2 Sam. 23:31; 1 Chron.

11:33). **[2]** A descendant of Saul (1 Chron. 8:36; 9:42). **[3]** 1000 B.C. Father of two men who joined David at Ziklag (1 Chron. 12:3). **[4]** 1000 B.C. A treasury officer during David's reign (1 Chron. 27:25).

Azmaveth (az-ma′veth). *See* Beth Azmaveth.

Azmon (az′mon; *fortress*). A place on the western boundary of Canaan (Num. 34:4).

Aznoth Tabor (az′noth tā′bor; *peaks [ears] of Tabor*). An incline near Mount Tabor, west of Kadesh Barnea (Josh. 19:34).

Azor (ā′zōr; *helper*). An ancestor of Jesus (Matt. 1:13–14).

Azotus (a-zō′tus). The Greek name for Ashdod.

Azriel (az′ri-el; *God is helper*). **[1]** 1000 B.C. Father of Jerimoth, a ruler of Naphtali in David's time (1 Chron. 27:19). **[2]** 750 B.C. A chief of the tribe of Manasseh (1 Chron. 5:24). **[3]** 625 B.C. Father of Seraiah, an officer sent to capture Baruch (Jer. 36:26).

Azrikam (az′ri-kam; *my help has risen*). **[1]** A son of Azel of the family of Saul (1 Chron. 8:38; 9:44). **[2]** 750 B.C. The governor of Ahaz's house (2 Chron. 28:7). **[3]** A descendant of Merari (1 Chron. 9:14; Neh. 11:15). **[4]** One of the family of David (1 Chron 3:23).

Azubah (a-zu′bah; *forsaken*). **[1]** Wife of Caleb, the son of Hezron (1 Chron. 2:18–19). **[2]** 900 B.C. The mother of King Jehoshaphat (1 Kings 22:42; 2 Chron. 20:31).

Azur [Azzur] (ā′zur [ā′zur]; *helper*). **[1]** 625 B.C. Father of the false prophet Hananiah (Jer. 28:1). **[2]** 575 B.C. Father of a prince that Ezekiel saw in a vision (Ezek.

11:1). **[3]** 450 B.C. A leader who signed the covenant renewal with God (Neh. 10:17).

Azzan (az´zan; *sharp*). 1450 B.C. Father of a chief of Issachar (Num. 34:26).

B

Baal (bā´al; *master; lord*). **[1]** A descendant of Reuben (1 Chron. 5:5). **[2]** The fourth of ten sons of Jehiel (1 Chron. 8:29–30; 9:36).

Baal (bā´al; *master; lord*). A city of Simeon, identical with Baalath Beer (1 Chron. 4:33).

Baal Gad (bā´al gad; *the lord of Gad*). A town at the foot of Mount Hermon that marked the northern limit of Joshua's conquest (Josh. 11:17; 12:7).

Baal Hamon (bā´al hā´mon; *lord of a multitude*). A place where King Solomon had a vineyard (Song of Sol. 8:11); its exact location is unknown.

Baal-hanan (bā´al-hā´nan; *Baal is gracious*). **[1]** The seventh of the kings of Edom (Gen. 36:38–39; 1 Chron. 1:49–50). **[2]** 1000 B.C. A tender of olive and sycamore trees in David's time (1 Chron. 27:28).

Baal Hazor (bā´al hā´zōr; *lord of Hazor*). The place near Ephraim where Absalom's servants killed Ammon (2 Sam. 13:23); the probable site is about 7 km. (4.5 mi.) northeast of Bethel.

Baal Hermon (bā´al her´mon; *lord of Hermon*). **[1]** A mountain located east of Lebanon (Judg. 3:3). **[2]** A city near Mount Hermon where Canaanite worship took place (1 Chron. 5:23).

Baal Meon (bā´al mē´on; *lord of meon*). An Amorite city on the north border of Moab (Num. 32:38; Ezek. 25:9). The city is called Beon in Numbers 32:3, Beth Baal Meon in Joshua 13:17 and Beth Meon in Jeremiah 48:23.

Baal Perazim (bā′al pe-rā′zim; *lord of breaches*). A place near the Valley of Rephaim, where King David won a battle with the Philistines (2 Sam. 5:20). It is called simply Perazim in Isaiah 28:21.

Baal Shalisha (bā′al shal′i-sha; *lord of Shalisha*). A village of Ephraim that presented food to the prophet Elisha; probably located about 22 km. (13.5 mi.) northwest of Gilgal (2 Kings 4:42).

Baal Tamar (bā′al Tā′mar; *lord of palms*). A place in Benjamin near Gibeah and Bethel in the territory of Benjamin, where the Israelites prepared for battle with the army of Gibeah (Judg. 20:33).

Baal Zephon (bā′al se′fon; *lord of winter*). The site that the Israelites faced when they encamped between Migdol and the Red Sea on their Exodus from Egypt (Exod. 14:2; Num. 33:7).

Baalah [Balah] (bā′a-la [bā′lah]; *mistress*). **[1]** A Simeonite town in southern Judah (Josh. 15:29). The city is also called Bilhah (1 Chron. 4:29) and Balah in Joshua 19:3. **[2]** A hill in Judah between Ekron and Jabneel (Josh. 15:11). **[3]** *See* Kirjath Jearim.

Baalath (bā′a-lath; *mistress*). A town of the tribe of Dan, located near Gezer (Josh. 19:44; 1 Kings 9:18; 2 Chron. 8:6).

Baalath Beer (bā′a-lath-bē′er; *mistress of a well*). A border town of the tribe of Simeon, sometimes called "Ramah of the South" (1 Sam. 30:27; Josh. 19:8). It is identical with the city of Baal (q.v.) *Also see* Bealoth.

Baale Judah (bā′a-lē-jū′da). *See* Kirjath Jearim.

Baalis (bā′a-lis; *lord of joy*). 575 B.C. The king of the Ammonites after Jerusalem was taken (Jer. 40:14).

Baanah [Baana] (bā′a-na [bā′a-na]; "*son of grief*"). **[1]** 1050 B.C. Father Heled, of one of David's mighty men (2 Sam. 23:29; 1 Chron. 11:30). **[2]** 1000 B.C. A captain in Ishbosheth's army (2 Sam. 4:2, 5–6, 9). **[3]** 950 B.C. One of Solomon's royal merchants (1 Kings 4:16). **[4]** 950 B.C. Another merchant of Solomon, responsible for Asher (1 Kings 4:12). **[5]** 525 B.C. One who returned from the Exile with Zerubbabel (Ezra 2:2; Neh. 7:7; 10:27). **[6]** 475 B.C. Father of Zadok, the builder of the temple (Neh. 3:4).

Baara (bā′a-ra; *the burning one*). A Moabite wife of Shaharaim, a Benjamite (1 Chron. 8:8).

Baaseiah (bā′a-sē′ya; *Jehovah is bold*). An ancestor of Asaph (1 Chron. 6:40) and descendant of Gershon (1 Chron. 6:43).

Baasha (bā′a-sha; *Baal hears*). 908–886 B.C. The son of Ahijah of the tribe of Isaachar, and third king of Israel; war and wickedness characterized his reign (1 Kings 15:16–16:13).

Babylon (bab′i-lon). **[1]** The capital city of the Babylonian Empire, famous for its hanging gardens; a focal point of the Jewish captivity beginning in 586 B.C. (2 Kings 17:24–25; Isa. 39:3, 6–7). **[2]** Most scholars believe the references in First Peter 5:13 and Revelation 14:8; 18:2, 10–21 are to Rome. However, some believe Peter refers to **[1]**.

Babylonia (bab-i-lō′ni-a). The eastern portion of the Fertile Crescent having Babylon (2 Kings 17:24–25) for its capital. It is also called Shinar (Gen. 10:10) and the land of the Chaldeans (Jer. 24:5; Ezek. 12:13) in the Old Testament.

Baca, Valley of (bā'ka). A valley of Palestine; possibly the Valley of Rephaim, where many balsam trees are found (Psa. 84:6).

Bahurim [Bahurum] (ba-hū'rim [ba-hū'rum]; *young men*). A village near the Mount of Olives on the road from Jerusalem to the Jordan River (2 Sam. 3:16; 16:5; 17:18; 19:16).

Bajith (bā'jith; *house*). A Moabite city or temple (Isa. 15:2).

Bakbakkar (bak-bak'er; *diligent; searcher*). 450 B.C. A Levite who returned from the Babylonian Captivity (1 Chron. 9:15). *See* Bakbukiah **[3].**

Bakbuk (bak'būk; *flask*). One whose descendant returned from the Exile (Ezra 2:51; Neh. 7:53).

Bakbukiah (bak-bū-kī'a; *Jehovah's pitcher*). **[1]** 525 B.C. A Levite who returned with Zerubbabel (Neh. 12:9). **[2]** 475 B.C. A Levite and guard of the temple storehouse (Neh. 12:25). **[3]** A Levite who lived in Jerusalem (Neh. 11:17). Perhaps identical with Bakbakkar (q.v.).

Balaam (bā'lam; *lord [Baal] of the people*). 1400 B.C. A prophet that the king of Moab induced to curse Israel. God put words of blessing in his mouth (Num. 22—24; 31:8).

Balac (bā'lak). Greek form of Balak (q.v.).

Baladan (bal'a-dan). 750 B.C. Father of Merodach-Baladan, the king of Babylon in Hezekiah's time (2 Kings 20:12; Isa. 39:1).

Balah (bā'la). *See* Baalah [1].

Balak [Balac] (bā'lak [ba'lak]; *destroyer*). 1400 B.C. The king of Moab that hired Balaam to curse Israel (Num. 22—24; Josh. 24:9).

Bamah (bā'ma; *high place*). The reference in Ezekiel

20:29 is possibly to a prominent high place of idolatrous worship like the one at Gibeon (1 Kings 3:4).

Bamoth (bā′moth; *high places*). An Israelite encampment north of the Arnon River (Num. 21:19). The city is probably the Bamoth Baal of Numbers 22:41.

Bamoth Baal (bā′moth bā′al; *high places of Baal*). *See* Bamoth.

Bani (bā′nī; *built*). [1] A descendant of Merari (1 Chron. 6:46). [2] 1000 B.C. One of David's mighty men (2 Sam. 23:36). [3] A descendant of Judah through Peres (1 Chron. 9:4). [4] Father of a family that returned from the Babylonian Captivity (Ezra 2:10; 10:29). In Nehemiah 7:15, he is called Binnui. [5] One whose descendants had taken foreign wives during the Exile (Ezra 10:34). [6] A descendant of [5] who took a foreign wife during the Exile (Ezra 10:38). [7] 475 B.C. A Levite who helped to repair the wall of Jerusalem (Neh. 3:17; 8:7). [8] 450 B.C. A Levite who assisted in the devotions of the people (Neh. 9:4; 10:13). [9] 450 B.C. One who sealed the new covenant with God after the Exile (Neh. 10:14). [10] A Levite whose son was an overseer of the Levites after the Exile. Perhaps the same as [7] or [8] (Neh. 11:22). [11], [12], [13] 450 B.C. Three Levites who participated in the temple worship (Neh. 9:4–5).

Bar (bar; Aramaic for the Hebrew *ben, son*). "Bar" and "ben" are frequently prefixed to names to indicate direct relationship. Thus Peter is called Bar-jonah *(son of Jonah)* because his father was named Jonah (Matt. 16:17) and perhaps Nathanael was called Bartholomew *(son of Tolmai)* because his father was named Tolmai. It can also designate characteristics or conditions. For example,

Joses was called Barnabas *(son of consolation)* because of the aid he rendered the apostles (Acts 4:36).

Barabbas (bar-ab′as; *son of Abbas*). A.D. 30. A murderer whom the people demanded that Pontius Pilate should release instead of Christ (Matt. 27:17, 20–21, 26; Mark 15:7), *See* Bar.

Barachel [Barakel] (bar′a-kel [bar′a-kel]; *blessed of God*). Father of Elihu, a figure in Job (Job 32:2, 6).

Barachiah [Barachias] (bar-a-kī′ah;) [bar-a-kīe′as]. Forms of Berechiah.

Barak (bar′ak; *lightning*). 1225 B.C. The general of the judge Deborah; he helped to defeat Sisera (Judg. 4:6–5:15).

Bariah (ba-rī′ah; *fugitive*). A son of Shemiah, of the tribe of Judah (1 Chron. 3:22).

Bar-jesus (bar-jē′sus; *son of Jesus*). A.D. 45. A false prophet struck blind because he opposed the gospel (Acts 13:4–12). Also called Elymas.

Bar-jonah (bar-jō′nah). *See* Peter; Bar.

Barkos (bar-kos). An ancestor of captives returning from the Exile (Ezra 2:53; Neh. 7:55).

Barnabas (bar′na-bas; *son of encouragement*). A.D. 35. A Jewish Christian who traveled widely with Paul (Acts 4:36; 9:27; 11:22–30; Gal. 2:1). His original name was Joses, but he was named Barnabas by the apostles (Acts 4:36); obviously they considered him to be *their* consoler. *See* Bar.

Barsabas [Barsabbas] (bar′sa-bas [bar′sab-bas]; *son of the Sabbath*). **[1]** A.D. 30. The nickname of Joseph, surnamed Justus, who was one of the two disciples proposed to replace Judas Iscariot as an apostle. **[2]** A.D. 50. The nickname of Judas, a disciple who was sent with Silas to accompany Paul and Barnabas to Antioch of Syria (Acts 15:22, 27). *See* Bar; Joseph [11]; Juda [12].

Bartholomew (bar-thol′ō-mū; *son of Tolmai*). A.D. 25. One of Jesus' twelve apostles (Matt. 10:3; Mark 3:18; Acts 1:13). He is probably the same as Nathanael (q.v.) *See* Bar.

Bartimaeus [Bartimeus] (bar-ti-mē′us [bar-ti-mē′us]; Aramaic "bar" *son* and Greek "timaios," *honorable*). A.D. 25 A blind beggar healed by Christ (Mark 10:46–52). *See* Bar.

Baruch (ba′ruk; *blessed*). **[1]** 600 B.C. Jeremiah's friend and scribe (Jer. 32:12–13, 16; 36). **[2]** 475 B.C. A descendant of Perez who returned from the Exile (Neh. 11:5). **[3]** 450 B.C. One who helped to rebuild the wall of Jerusalem (Neh. 3:20; 10:6). **[4]** 450 B.C. A man who sealed the covenant with Nehemiah (Neh. 10:6). May be the same as [3].

Barzillai (bar-zil′ā-i; *made of iron*). **[1]** 1050 B.C. Husband of Merab, Saul's eldest daughter, and father of Adriel (2 Sam. 21:8). **[2]** 1000 B.C. One who befriended David when he fled from Absalom (2 Sam. 17:27; 19:31–39). **[3]** 975 B.C. A priest whose genealogy was lost during the Exile (Ezra 2:61; Neh. 7:63).

Basemath [Bashmath; Basmath] (bas′e-math [bash′-math; bas′math]; *sweet-smelling perfume*). **[1]** 1950 B.C. Wife of Esau and daughter of Elon the Hittite (Gen. 26:34). Also called Adah. **[2]** 1925 B.C. Another of Esau's wives; daughter of Ishmael. Also called Mahaloth (Gen. 28:9) and may be the same person as [1]. **[3]** 925 B.C. A daughter of Solomon and wife of Ahimaaz (1 Kings 4:15). *See* Esau's Wives.

Bashan (ba'shan; *fertile plain*). A district stretching from the Upper Jordan Valley to the Arabian Desert, containing "the whole region of Arzob" (Deut. 3:4–5, 10, 13; 1 Kings 4:13; Psa. 22:12; Ezek. 27:6; 39:18).

Bashan, Mountain of (ba'shan). Probably a name for Mount Hermon (Psa. 68:15).

Bath Rabbim (bath-rab'im; *daughter of multitudes*). A gate of Heshbon (Song of Sol. 7:4).

Bathsheba (bath-shē'ba). 1000 B.C. The beautiful wife of Uriah the Hittite, and afterward the wife of David (2 Sam. 11:3; 12:24; 1 Kings 1:11–2:19). She was the mother of Solomon and an ancestor of Christ (Matt. 1:6). She is called Bathshua in First Chronicles 3:5.

Bathshua (bath-shū'a; *daughter of Shua*). [1] 1875 B.C. The wife of Judah. In Genesis 38:2 and First Chronicles 2:3, the KJV incorrectly renders her name as "daughter of Shua"; Bathshua is really a proper name. [2] Another name of Bathsheba (q.v.)

Bavai [Bavvai] (bav'a-i [bav'va-i]; *wisher*). One who helped to rebuild the wall of Jerusalem (Neh. 3:18).

Bazlith [Bazluth] (baz'lith [baz'luth]; *asking*). One whose descendants returned from the Exile (Ezra 2:52; Neh. 7:54).

Bealiah (be-a-li'a; *Jehovah is lord*). 1000 B.C. A man who joined David at Ziklag (1 Chron. 12:5).

Bealoth (bē'a-loth; *possessors*). A village in southern Judah (Josh. 15:24). May be the same as Baalath Beer (Josh. 19:8).

Beautiful Gate. *See* Gates, Through the.

Bebai (bē'bā-ī; *fatherly*). [1] An ancestor of captives returning from the Exile (Ezra 2:11; Neh. 7:16). [2] 450 B.C. An ancestor of some returning from the Exile with

Ezra (Ezra 8:11; 10:28); perhaps the same as [1]. **[3]** 450 B.C. One who sealed the new covenant with God after the Exile (Neh. 10:15).

Becher (bē'ker; *youth*). **[1]** 1850 B.C. A son of Benjamin (Gen. 46:21). **[2]** A son of Ephraim (Num. 26:35); perhaps the same as Bered in First Chronicles 7:20. He may be the same person as [1].

Bechorath [Becorath] (be-kō'rath [be-kō'rath] *first born*). An ancestor of Saul (1 Sam. 9:1).

Bedad (bē'dad; *separation*). Father of Hadad, fourth king of Edom (Gen. 36:35; 1 Chron. 1:46).

Bedan (bē'dan; *son of judgment*). **[1]** A leader of Israel mentioned as a deliverer of the nation (1 Sam. 12:11). The Septuagint, Syriac, and Arabic read *Barak* instead; however, many think this is a reference to Abdon. **[2]** A descendant of Manasseh (1 Chron. 7:17).

Bedeiah (be-dē'ya; *servant of Jehovah*). 450 B.C. One who divorced his pagan wife after the Exile (Ezra 10:35).

Beeliada (bē'e-li'a-da; *Baal knows*). 1000 B.C. A son of David (1 Chron. 14:7) also known as Eliada (2 Sam. 5:16; 1 Chron. 3:8).

Beer (bē'er; *a well*). **[1]** A temporary encampment of the Israelites in the wilderness (Num. 21:16–18); possibly the same as Beerelim. **[2]** A place where Jotham sought refuge from his brother Abimelech (Judg. 9:21); possibly the same as Beeroth.

Beer Elim (bē'er-ē'lim; *well of Elim*). A village in southern Moab (Isa. 15:8).

Beer Lahai Roi [Lahai Roi] (bē'er la-hī'roi [la-hī'roi]; *well of the Living One*). The well of Hagar, located between Kadesh and Bered on the road to Shur, about 80 km. (50 mi.) southwest of Beersheba (Gen. 16:14).

Beera (be-ē'ra [be-ē'ra]; *expounder*). A descendant of Asher (1 Chron. 7:37).

Beerah (be-ē'ra; *expounder*). 750 B.C. A prince of the Reubenites who was taken into captivity by Tiglath-pilesar, king of Assyria.

Beeri (be-ē'ri; *man of a fountain*). [1] 1975 B.C. Father of Judith, a wife of Esau (Gen. 26:34). *See also* Esau's Wives. [2] 1725 B.C. Father of the prophet Hosea (Hos. 1:1).

Beeroth (bē-ē'roth; *wells*). [1] A place on the border of Edom where the wandering Israelites camped; also called Beeroth, Bene-Jaakan or Bene Jaakan (Deut. 10:6; Num. 33:31). [2] A city of Gibeon assigned to the tribe of Benjamin (Josh. 9:17; 18:25).

Beeroth Bene Jaakan (bē-e-roth' ben'e jāy'uh-kan). A form of Beeroth.

Beersheba (bē'er-shē'ba; *well of the seven*). A city in southern Judah, site of Abraham's covenant with Abimelech; it is located about 45 km. (28 mi.) southwest of Hebron (Gen. 21:14, 22–31; Josh. 15:28).

Bela [Belah] (bē'la [be'la]; *consuming* or *devouring*). [1] 1850 B.C. A son of Benjamin and one of the left-handed heroes (Gen. 46:21; 1 Chron. 7:6–7). [2] A king of Edom, the first mentioned in Scripture (Gen. 36:32–33; 1 Chron. 1:43–44). [3] Descendant of Reuben (1 Chron. 5:8).

Bela [Belah] (bē'la [be'la]; *consuming* or *devouring*). One of the Cities of the Plain, probably Zoar (Gen. 14:2).

Belshazzar (bel-shaz'er; Hebrew form of the Babylonian name Bel-shar-usur—[*the god*] *Bel has protected the king* [*ship*]. The son of Nabonidus and co-regent in Babylon from 550–539 B.C. He witnessed strange handwriting on the wall of his palace before his kingdom was overthrown by Persia (Dan. 5; 7:1; 8:1).

Belteshazzar (bel-te-shaz´er; Hebrew form of the Babylonian name, Balat-usu-usur—*protect his life!*). 600 B.C. The name given to Daniel in Babylon (Dan. 1:7). *See* Daniel.

Ben (ben; *son*). An assistant in the temple musical service at the time of David (1 Chron. 15:18).

Ben-abinadab (ben-a-bin´a-dab; *son of Abindab*). 950 B.C. One of Solomon's twelve officers, married to Solomon's daughter Taphath (1 Kings 4:11).

Ben-ammi (ben-am´i; *son of my people*). 2025 B.C. The ancestor of the Ammonites (Gen. 19:38), born to Lot and his daughter.

Ben-dekar [Ben Deker] (ben-di-kar´ [ben-dek´ur]; *son of Deker*). 950 B.C. One of Solomon's twelve officers who provided food for the royal household (1 Kings 4:9).

Ben-geber (ben-ge´bur; *son of a strong man*). 950 B.C. One of Solomon's officers who provided food for the king and his household (1 Kings 4:13).

Ben-hadad (ben-hā´dad; *son of [the god] Hadad*). [1] 875 B.C. Ben-hadad I, the king of Syria who made a league with Asa of Judah and invaded Israel (1 Kings 15:18, 20; 2 Chron. 10:2, 4). [2] 850 B.C. Ben-hadad II, another king of Syria defeated by Ahab; he eventually laid siege to Samaria itself (1 Kings 20; 2 Kings 6:24; 8:7, 9. [3] 800 B.C. The son and successor of Hazael who reigned over Syria as the empire disintegrated (2 Kings 13:3, 24–25; Amos 1:4). [4] Possibly a general title of the Syrian kings (Jer. 49:27).

Ben-hail [Ben-hayil] (ben-hā´il [ben-hā´il]; *strong; son of strength*). 875 B.C. A prince of Judah under Jehoshaphat (2 Chron. 17:7). *Ben-hanan* (ben-hā´nen; *son of* *grace*). A son of Shimon of the tribe of Judah (1 Chron. 4:20).

Ben-hesed (ben-hē′sid; *faithfulness*). 950 B.C. One of Solomon's twelve supply officers (1 Kings 4:10).

Ben-hur (ben-hur′; *son of Hur*). 950 B.C. One of Solomon's twelve supply officers, in charge of supplying food to Solomon's household (1 Kings 4:8).

Ben-jahaziel (ben-jāzē-el; *son of Jahaziel*). A chief of the people who returned from the Captivity (Ezra 8:5).

Ben Josiphiah (ben jōsi-fi′-ah; *son of Josiphiah*). One of the sons of Bani who returned from the Captivity (Ezra 8:10).

Ben-oni (ben-ō′ni; *son of my pain*). 1875 B.C. Name given to Rachel's child as she died bearing him; Jacob changed his name to Benjamin (q.v.).

Ben-zoheth (ben-zō′heth; *son of Zoheth*). A son of Ishi and descendant of Judah through Caleb (1 Chron. 4:20).

Benaiah (be-nā′ya; *Jehovah has built*). **[1]** 1025 B.C. Father of one of David's counselors (1 Chron. 27:34). **[2]** 1000 B.C. The third leader of David's army, counselor to the kings, and loyal friend of both David and Solomon (2 Sam. 8:18; 20:23; 1 Kings 1:8—2:46). **[3]** 1000 B.C. Benaiah the Pirathonite, one of David's mighty men (2 Sam. 23:30; 1 Chron. 11:31). **[4]** 1000 B.C. One of David's priests and a Temple musician (1 Chron. 15:18, 20, 24; 16:5–6). **[5]** 925 B.C. The grandfather of Jahaziel (2 Chron. 20:14). **[6]** 725 B.C. Head of a family of the tribe of Simeon (1 Chron. 4:36). **[7]** 725 B.C. An overseer of the temple during Hezekiah's reign (2 Chron. 31:13). **[8], [9], [10], [11], [12],** 625 B.C. Father of Pelatiah, a prince of Judah (Ezek. 11:1, 13). 450

B.C. Four men who married foreign wives during the Exile (Ezra 10:25, 30, 35, 43).

Bene Berak (ben´e bē´rak; *sons of lightning*). A town of the tribe of Dan about 6 km. (4 mi.) east of modern Jaffa (Josh. 19:45).

Bene Jaakan (ben-jāv´-kan; *sons of Jaakan*). *See* Beeroth [1].

Beninu (be-ni´nū; *our son*). 450 B.C. A Levite who sealed the new covenant with God after the Exile (Neh. 10:13).

Benjamin (ben´ja-min; *son of the right hand*). [1] 1875 B.C. The youngest son of Jacob; his descendants became one of the twelve tribes of Israel (Gen. 35:18, 24; 42:4, 36; 43—45. [2] A descendant of Benjamin (1 Chron. 7:10). [3] 450 B.C. A descendant of Harim (Ezra 10:32). [4] 450 B.C. One who helped to repair the wall of Jerusalem (Neh. 3:23). [5] 450 B.C. One who helped to dedicate the wall of Jerusalem (Neh. 12:34).

Beno (bēnō´; *his son*). A Levite descendant of Merari (1 Chron. 24:26–27).

Beon (be-ōn´; *house of On*). An ancient Amorite city located east of the Jordan River and north of Moab (Num. 32:3). Also called Baal Meon (Num. 32:38) and Beth Baal Meon (Josh. 13:17). *See* Baal meon.

Beor [Bosor] (be´sor [bō´or]; *a torch*). [1] Father of Bela, the king of Edom (Gen. 36:32; 1 Chron. 1:43). [2] 1425 B.C. Father of the prophet Balaam (Num. 22:5; 24:3, 15; 31:8). Also called Bosor (2 Pet. 2:15).

Bera (bē´ra). 2100 B.C. A king of Sodom in the time of Abram (Gen. 14:2).

Beracah [Berachah] (ber´a-ka [ber´a-ka]; *blessing*). 1000 B.C. One who joined David at Ziklag (1 Chron. 12:3).

Berachah (ber'a-ka; *blessing*). A valley in Judah near Tekoa, named by Jehoshaphat (2 Chron. 20:26).

Beraiah (ber-a-ī'a; *Jehovah has created*). A chief of the tribe of Benjamin (1 Chron. 8:21).

Berea [Beroea] (be-rē'a [be-rē-a]). A city in Macedonia about 80 km. (50 mi.) west of Thessalonica (Acts 17:10); now called Verria, or Salonica.

Berechiah [Barachiah; Barachias; Berachiah] (ber-a-kī'a *[bar-a-kī'ah; bar-a-kī'as; ber-a-kī'a]*; *Jehovah is blessing*). **[1]** 1025 B.C. Father of Asaph, the chief singer (1 Chron. 6:39; 15:17). **[2]** 1000 B.C. One of the tabernacle doorkeepers (1 Chron. 15:23). **[3]** 750 B.C. A descendant of Ephraim in the time of Pekah (2 Chron. 28:12). **[4]** 550 B.C. The father of the prophet Zechariah (Zech. 1:1, 7).**[5]** 500 B.C. A descendant of Jehoiakim (1 Chron. 3:20). **[6]** 475 B.C. Father of one who repaired the wall of Jerusalem (Neh. 3:4, 30; 6:18). **[7]** 450 B.C. A Levite who lived near Jerusalem (1 Chron. 9:16).

Bered (bē'red; *hail*). A descendant of Ephraim (1 Chron. 7:20); perhaps the same as Becher (Num. 26:35).

Bered (bē'red; *hail*). A place in the wilderness of Shur in southern Palestine, not far from Kadesh (Gen. 16:14).

Beri (bē'ri; *expounder*). A descendant of Asher (1 Chron. 7:36).

Beriah (be-rī'a; *tragedy, misfortune*). **[1]** 1850 B.C. A descendant of Asher (Gen. 46:17; Num. 26:44–45; 1 Chron. 7:30–31). **[2]** 1825 B.C. A descendant of Ephraim (1 Chron. 7:23). **[3]** A descendant of Benjamin (1 Chron. 8:13, 16). **[4]** A descendant of Levi (1 Chron. 23:10–11).

Bernice (ber-nī'sē; *victorious*). A.D. 50. The immoral daughter of Herod Agrippa I. She and her brother

Agrippa (with whom she was living in incest) sat in judgment on Paul (Acts 25:13, 23; 26:30).

Berodach-baladan (be-rō′dak-bal′a-dan). A copyist's mistake or another form of Merodach-baladan (q.v.).

Berothah [Berothai; Berutha; Cun] (be-rō′tha [be-rō′thi; be-rū′tha; kun]; *wells*). A town in northern Palestine between Hamath and Damascus, captured by David; also called Cun (2 Sam. 8:8; 1 Chron. 18:8; Ezek. 47:16).

Besai (bē′sī′. One who returned to Jerusalem with Zerubbabel (Ezra 2:49; Neh. 7:52).

Besodeiah (bes-o-dē′ya; *given to trust in Jehovah*). 475 B.C. One of the repairers of the old gate of Jerusalem (Neh. 3:6).

Besor (bē′sōr; *cold*). A brook south of Ziklag (1 Sam. 30:9–10, 21).

Betah (bē′ta; *confidence*). A city of Amam-Zobah (2 Sam. 8:8). It is identical with Tibhath (q.v.).

Beten (bē′ten; *abdomen*). A village of the tribe of Asher (Josh. 19:25); Eusebius noted that it was about 12 km. (7.5 mi.) east of Accho.

Beth Acacia (beth a-kā′sha; *house of acacia*). A town located in the Jordan Valley between Zerarah and Jezreel (Judg. 7:22). Also known as Beth-shittah.

Beth Anath [Beth Anoth] (beth ā′nath [beth ā′noth] **[1]** A fortress town of the tribe of Naphtali (Josh. 19:38; Judg. 1:33). **[2]** A town in the mountains of Judah, about 6 km. (4 mi.) from Hebron (Josh. 15:59).

Beth Aphrah (beth ′af′ra; *house of dust*). A Philistine city (Mic. 1:10). *See* Aphrah.

Beth Arabah (beth ar′a-ba; *house of the desert*). A village in the Judean wilderness on the boundary between the territories of Judah and Benjamin (Josh. 15:6, 61; 18:22).

Beth Aram [Beth Haram; Beth Haran] (beth a'ram [beth ha'ram; beth a'ran]; *house of the heights*). A town of the tribe of Gad, located in the Jordan Valley and noted for its hot springs (Num. 32:36; Josh. 13:27).

Beth Arbel (beth ar'bel; *house of ambush*). A town destroyed by Shalman (Hos. 10:14). Now known as Irbid, it is located about 6 km. (4 mi.) west-northwest of Tiberias.

Beth Aven (beth ā'ven; *house of idols*). A town of the tribe of Benjamin, located in the wilderness near Ai (Josh. 7:2; 18:12; 1 Sam. 13:5).

Beth Azmaveth (beth az-mā'veth; *house of Azmaveth*). A town near Jerusalem, halfway between Geba and Anathoth; perhaps the same as Hizmeh (Neh. 7:28). It is also called simply Azmaveth (Ezra 2:24; Neh. 12:29).

Beth Baal Meon (beth bā'al mē'on; *Baal's dwelling place*). *See also* Baal Meon, Beth Meon, Beon.

Beth Barah (beth ba'ra; *house of crossing*). A place in the vicinity of the Jordan Valley, possibly a ford or crossing near the confluence of the Jordan and the Wadi Farah (Judg. 7:24). Not to be confused with Bethabara (John 1:28), a place east of the Jordan River.

Beth Birei [Beth Biri] (beth bir'e-ī bir'[beth]; *house of my creation*). A town of southern Judah of the tribe of Simeon (1 Chron. 4:31); perhaps the same as Beth Lebaoth (q.v.).

Beth Car (beth kar'; *house of a lamb*). A Philistine stronghold in Judah, site of a battle between the Israelites and the Philistines (1 Sam. 7:11).

Beth Dagon (beth dā'gon; *house of Dagon*). **[1]** A town located on the border between Asher and Zebulun

(Josh. 19:27); probably modern Jelamet el-Atika at the foot of Mount Carmel. **[2]** A town in the Judean lowlands (Josh. 15:33, 41); possibly modern Khirbet Dajun.

Beth Diblathaim (beth dib-la-thā'im; *house of two fig cakes*). A town in Moab (Jer. 48:21–22); possibly the same as Almon diblathaim (q.v.)

Beth Eden (beth ē'den; *house of delight*). A city-state in Mesopotamia (Amos 1:5). Called Bit-adini in Assyrian records. Located on both sides of the Euphrates River.

Beth Eked of the Shepherds (beth ē'ked; *house of shearing*). A town on the road from Jezreel to Samaria where Jehu killed 42 relatives of King Ahaziah of Judah (2 Kings 10:12–14).

Beth Emek (beth ē'mek; *house of the valley*). A town near the border of Asher; it is bounded on the north side by the ravine of Jipthah El (Josh. 19:27). The modern name of this site is Amkah.

Beth-Ezel (beth-ē'zel; *adjoining house*). A town of Judah (Micah 1:11); present-day Deil el-'Asal.

Beth-gader (beth-gā'der; *house of walls*). A town of Judah founded by Hareph (1 Chron. 2:51); possibly the same place as Geder (Josh. 12:13).

Beth Gamul (beth gā'mul; *place of recompense*). A city of Moab about 10 km. (6 mi.) east of Dibon (Jer. 48:23).

Beth Haccerem [Beth Haccherem] (beth hak-sē'rem [beth-hak-ker'um]; *house of the vineyard*). A town of Judah that maintained a beacon station (Neh. 3:14; Jer. 6:1); probably present-day Ain Karim, 7 km. (4 mi.) west of Jerusalem.

Beth Haram [Beth Haran]. *See* Beth Aram.

Beth Hogla [Beth Hoglah] (beth-hog'la [beth hog'-

lah]; *partridge house*). A Benjamite village about 6 km. (4 mi.) southeast of Jericho (Josh. 15:6; 18:19).

Beth Horon (beth-hō′ron; *cave house*). Twin towns located on the boundary between the territories of Ephraim and Benjamin. Upper Beth Horon was situated on a mountain pass between Jerusalem and the plain to the west. Lower Beth Horon was about 2 km. (1.5 mi.) farther northwest (Josh. 16:3; 18:13; 2 Chron. 8:5; 1 Kings 9:17). The modern names for these towns are Beit 'Ur et Tahta (Lower) and Beit 'Ur el Foka (Upper).

Beth Jeshimoth [Beth Jesimoth] (beth jesh′i-moth [beth jes′i-moth]; *house of the wastes*). A town in Moab near the Dead Sea (Num. 33:49; Josh 12:3).

Beth-le-aphrah (beth-le-af-′rah). A form of Beth Aphrah.

Beth Lebaoth (beth le-bā′oth; *house of lionesses*). A town of southern Judah assigned to the tribe of Simeon (Josh. 19:6). The city is also known as Lebaoth (Josh. 15:32). It is perhaps identical with Beth-birei (q.v.).

Beth Marcaboth (beth mar′ka-both; *house of chariots*). A city of the Simeonites in the Negeb near Ziklag (Josh. 19:5).

Beth Meon (beth mē′on; *dwelling place*). *See also* Baal Meon.

Beth Millo (beth mil′-lō; *place of a mound*). An ancient fortification in or near Shechem (Judg. 9:6).

Beth Nimrah (beth nim′ra; *house of the leopard*). A fortified city built by the tribe of Gad east of the Jordan River (Num. 32:36); also called Nimrah (Num. 32:3).

Beth Pazzez (beth paz′ez; *house of destruction*). A town of the tribe of Issachar (Josh. 19:21); its modern name is Kerm el-Had-datheh.

Beth-Palet [Beth-phelet] (beth-pā'let [beth-fē'let]; *house of escape*). A town in the southernmost part of Judah (Josh. 15:27; Neh. 11:26); probably modern el-Meshash.

Beth Peor (beth pē'or; *house of the openings*). A town of Moab near Pisgah where the Israelites placed their main camp while warring against Og (Deut. 3:29; 4:46).

Beth Rapha (beth ra'fa; *house of healing*). A descendant of Judah and son of Eshton (1 Chron. 4:12).

Beth Rehob (beth rē'hob; *place of a street*). A town of the Upper Jordan Valley (Judg. 18:28; 2 Sam. 10:6). The city is called Rehob (Num. 13:21).

Beth-shan [Beth-shean] (beth-shan [beth-shē'an]; *place of security*). The southern border town of the region of Galilee; largest of the ten cities of the Decapolis (Josh. 17:11; 1 Chron. 7:29).

Beth Shemesh (beth shē'mesh; *house of the sun*). **[1]** A town on the road from Ashkelon and Ashdod to Jerusalem; it is located about 38 km. (24 mi.) west of Jerusalem (Josh. 15:10). **[2]** A Canaanite city in the territory of Naphtali (Josh. 19:38; Judg. 1:33). **[3]** A city of the tribe of Issachar, probably on the Jordan River near the Sea of Galilee (Josh. 19:22). **[4]** Another name for the Egyptian city of Heliopolis (Jer. 43:13).

Beth-shittah (beth-shit'a; *house of acacia*). A town of the Jordan Valley between Jezreel and Zererah, noted for its acacia trees (Judg. 7:22). A form of Beth Acacia.

Beth Tappuah (beth tap'u-a; *house of apricots*). A settlement in the hills of Judah about 8 km. (5 mi.) west of Hebron (Josh. 15:53).

Beth Zur (beth zur'; *house of rock*). A city in the hill country of Judah, fortified during the era of Rehoboam

(Josh. 15:58; 2 Chron. 11:7). **[2]** A son of Maon (1 Chron. 2:45).

Bethabara (beth-ab'a-ra; *house at the ford*). A place on the eastern side of the Jordan River where John the Baptist baptized his converts (John 1:28). The majority of Greek manuscripts read Bethany here instead; however, this city was not identical with Bethany proper.

Bethany (beth'a-ni; *house of unripe figs*). **[1]** A settlement on the hill leading to the Mount of Olives, about 2.6 km. (1.6 mi.) from Jerusalem (Mark 11:1; Luke 19:29). **[2]** A village in Transjordan where John the Baptist baptized. The exact location is not known.

Bethel (beth'-el; *house of God*). **[1]** A town located about 18 km. (11 mi.) north of Jerusalem; an important site throughout the history of Israel (cf. Gen. 13:3; 28:18–19; Josh. 16:2; Judg. 21:19). It was formerly called Luz. The modern town of Bertin is located near the ruins. **[2]** *See also* Bethuel.

Bether (bē'ther; *division, split*). A small range of hills located between Bethlehem and Jerusalem (Song. 2:17).

Bethesda (be-thez'da; *house of grace*). A pool near the Sheep Gate of Jerusalem reputed to have healing qualities (John 5:2–3).

Bethlehem (beth'-le-hem; *house of bread*). **[1]** A town about 10 km. (6 mi.) south of Jerusalem; birthplace of Jesus Christ (Matt. 2:5) and Ephrath (Gen. 35:16, 19; Ruth 4:11; cf. Mic. 5:2). Only in later times was it known as Bethlehem. It was originally called Ephrath (Ephrath) (Gen. 35:16; Ruth 4:11). **[2]** A city of the tribe of Zebulun located about 11 km. (7 mi.) northwest of Nazareth (Josh. 19:15). **[3]** A son of Salma, a descendant of Caleb (1 Chron. 2:51).

Bethphage (beth'fa-jē; *house of unripe figs*). A settlement near Bethany on the road from Jerusalem to Jericho, probably at the descent from the Mount of Olives (Matt. 21:1; Mark 11:1).

Bethsaida (beth-sā´i-da; *fish house*). A fishing town on the Sea of Galilee; birthplace of Philip, Andrew, and Simon (Matt. 11:21; Luke 9:10; Mark 6:45).

Bethuel (be-thū´el; *abode of God*). 2050 B.C. A son of Nahor, Abraham's brother (Gen. 22:22–23; 28:5).

Bethuel [Bethul] (be-thū´el [bē´thul]; *abode of God*). A town apportioned to the tribe of Simeon (Josh. 19:4; 1 Chron. 4:30). The town was also called Bethel (1 Sam. 30:27).

Betonim (bet´o-nim; *pistachio nuts*). A town east of the Jordan River assigned to the tribe of Gad (Josh. 13:26).

Beulah (bū´la; *married*). Isaiah's name for the Promised Land after the Babylonian Captivity (Isa. 62:4).

Bezai (bā´za-ī). [1] An ancestor of 323 captives returning from the Exile (Ezra 2:17; Neh. 7:23). [2] 450 B.C. One who sealed the new covenant with God after the Exile (Neh. 10:18).

Bezaleel [Bezalel] (be-zal´e-el [be-zal´el]; *in the shadow of God*). [1] 1450 B.C. A chief worker and designer of the tabernacle (Exod. 31:2; 35:30; 36:1–2). [2] 450 B.C. One who had married a foreign wife (Ezra 10:30).

Bezek (bē´zek; *lightning*). [1] A town near Jerusalem (Judg. 1:4–5). [2] The place where Saul assembled his army (1 Sam. 11:8).

Bezer (bē´zer; *strong*). One of the heads of Asher (1 Chron. 7:37).

Bezer (bē´zer; *fortress*). A fortified city within the territory of Reuben (Deut. 4:43; Josh. 20:8); probably present-day Unim el-Ammad, about 9 km. (5.5 mi.) east of Heshbon.

Bichri [Bicri] (bik'ri [bik'ri]; *firstborn*). An ancestor of Sheba, who rebelled against David (2 Sam. 20:1).

Bidkar (bid'kar). 850 B.C. 850 B.C. A captain in the service of Jehu who executed the sentence on Ahab's son (2 Kings 9:25).

Bigtha (big'tha; *gift of God*). 475 B.C. A chamberlain of Ahasuerus (Esther 1:10).

Bigthan [Bigthana] (big'than [big-thā'na]; *gift of God*). 475 B.C. A chamberlain who conspired against Ahasuerus (Esther 2:21; 6:2).

Bigvai (big'va-ī; *fortunate*). [1] Head of one of the families who returned with Zerubbabel (Ezra 2:2, 14; 8:14; Neh. 7:7, 19). [2] 450 B.C. One who sealed the covenant with Nehemiah (Neh. 10:16).

Bildad (bil'dad). One of Job's three "friends" (Job 2:11; 8:1; 18:1; 25:1; 42:9).

Bileam (bil'e-am; *place of conquest*). A settlement on the western side of the Jordan River assigned to the tribe of Manasseh (1 Chron. 6:70).

Bilgah (bil'ga; *brightness*). [1] 1000 B.C. A priest in the tabernacle service (1 Chron. 24:14). [2] 525 B.C. A priest who came up to Jerusalem with Zerubbabel (Neh. 12:5, 18).

Bilgai (bil'ga-i; *cheerfulness*). 450 B.C. One who sealed the new covenant with God after the Exile (Neh. 10:8); perhaps the same as Bilgah [2].

Bilhah (bil'ha; *unconcerned*). 1925 B.C. The handmaid of Rachel and mother of Dan and Naphtali (Gen. 29:29; 30:3–5, 7).

Bilhah (bil'ha). *See* Baalah [1].

Bilhan (bil'han; *foolish*). [1] 1925 B.C. A descendant of Seir (Gen. 36:27; 1 Chron. 1:42). [2] A descendant of Benjamin (1 Chron. 7:10).

Bilshan (bil'shan; *their lord*). 525 B.C. A prince who returned from the Exile (Ezra 2:2; Neh. 7:7).

Bimhal (bim'hal; *circumcised*). A descendant of Asher (1 Chron. 7:33).

Binea (bin'e-a; *wanderer*). A descendant of Jonathan, son of Saul (1 Chron. 8:37; 9:43).

Binnui (bin'nū-i; *a building up*). [1] 450 B.C. A Levite appointed by Ezra to weigh gold and silver (Ezra 8:33). [2], [3] 450 B.C. Two men who married foreign wives during the Exile (Ezra 10:30, 38). [4] 450 B.C. One who repaired the wall of Jerusalem (Neh. 3:24; 10:9). [5] A Levite who came up with Zerubbabel (Neh. 12:8). [6] *See* Bani [4].

Birsha (bir'sha; *thick; strong*). 2100 B.C. A king of Gomorrah in the days of Abraham (Gen. 14:2).

Birzaith [Birzavith] (bir'zā'ith, bir'z̄-vith] *well of the olive tree*). Descendant of Asher (1 Chron. 7:31).

Bishlam (bish'lam; *peaceful*). 475 B.C. A foreign colonist who wrote a letter of complaint against the Jews (Ezra 4:7).

Bithiah (bi-thī'a; *daughter of Jehovah*). A daughter of Pharaoh and wife of Mered (1 Chron. 4:18); her name implies her conversion.

Bithron (bith'ron). A gorge in the Aravah east of the Jordan River (2 Sam. 2:29).

Bithynia (bi-thin'i-a). A country of northwestern Asia Minor, bounded on the north by the Black Sea (Acts 16:7; 1 Pet. 1:1).

Biziothiah [Bizjothjah] (biz-ē-ah-thē-a, [biz-joth'ja]). A town in the southernmost portion of Judah (Josh. 15:28).

Biztha (biz'tha; *bound*). 475 B.C. One of Ahasuerus' eunuchs (Esther 1:10).

Blastus (blas'tus; *a bud*). A.D. 50. The chamberlain of Herod Agrippa I (Acts 12:20).

Boanerges (bo-a-nur'jez; *sons of thunder*). 25 B.C. The surname bestowed upon James and John, the sons of Zebedee (Mark 3:17).

Boaz [Booz] (bō'az [bō'oz]; *strength*). 1100 B.C. A Bethlehemite of Judah who became the husband of Ruth and an ancestor of Christ (Ruth 2–4; Matt. 1:5; Luke 3:32).

Bocheru (bō'ke-roo; *youth*). One of the six sons of Azel, a Benjamite descendant of King Saul (1 Chron. 8:38; 9:44).

Bochim [Bokim] (bō'kim [bō'kim]; *weepers*). A site near Gilgal where the Israelites repented of their sins (Judg. 2:1–5).

Bohan (bō'han; *thumb*). A descendant of Reuben for whom a boundary stone between Judah and Benjamin was named (Josh. 15:6; 18:17).

Bohan (bō'han; *thumb*). The "stone of Bohan" was a boundary mark separating the northeast frontier of Judah from Benjamin. The site is uncertain (Josh. 18:17).

Booz (bō'oz). Greek form of Boaz (q.v.).

Boscath (bos'kath). *See* Bozkath.

Bosor (bō'sor). Greek form of Beor. (q.v.). **Bozez** (bō'z'es; *shining*). The name of two crags near Geba; the northernmost crag faces Michmash (1 Sam. 14:4).

Bozkath [Boscath] (boz'kath [bos'kath]; *height*). A town near Lachish in southern Judah (Josh. 15:39; 2 Kings 22:1).

Bozrah (boz'ra; *shepherd*). [1] The capital of Edom (Gen. 36:33; 1 Chron. 1:44). [2] A city of Moab; probably Bezer (Jer. 48:24).

Brook of the Willows. *See* Willows, Brook of the.

Bukki (buk´ī; *proved of Jehovah*). **[1]** 1400 B.C. A prince of the tribe of Dan (Num. 34:22). **[2]** A son of Abishua who was an ancestor of Ezra and descendant of Aaron (1 Chron. 6:5, 51; Ezra 7:4).

C

Bukkiah (bu-kī´a; *proved of Jehovah*). 1000 B.C. A son of Heman and musician in the temple (1 Chron. 25:4, 13).

Bunah (boo´na; *understanding*). A son of Jerahmeel (1 Chron. 2:25).

Bunni (bun´ī; *my understanding*). **[1]** An ancestor of She-maiah the Levite (Neh. 11:15). **[2]** 450 B.C. A Levite who helped Ezra in teaching the Law (Neh. 9:4). **[3]** 450 B.C. One who sealed the new covenant with God after the Exile (Neh. 10:15).

Buz (booz; *contempt*). **[1]** 2050 B.C. The second son of Nahor, the brother of Abraham (Gen. 22:21). **[2]** A descendant of Gad (1 Chron. 5:14).

Buz (booz; *contempt*). A place probably located in northern Arabia from which Elihu's father came (Jer. 25:23; Job 32:2).

Buzi (booz´i). 1625 B.C. A descendant of Aaron and father of Ezekiel (Ezek. 1:3).

C

Cabbon (kab´on; *surround*). A town of lowland Judah (Josh. 15:40).

Cabul (kā´bul; *sterile, unproductive*). **[1]** A town of the tribe of Asher noted for its dry climate (Josh. 19:27). **[2]** A district of Galilee; the northern part of the territory of Naphtali (1 Kings 19:13).

Caesar (sē'zer). The name of a branch of the artistocratic family of the Julii, which gained control of the Roman government; afterward it became a formal title of the Roman emperors. *See* Augustus Caesar; Tiberius Caesar; Claudius Caesar.

Caesarea [Caesarea Maritima] (ses-a-rē'a [ses-a-rē'a ma-ri-tē'ma]; *pertaining to Caesar*). Coastal city of Palestine that served as capital of the Roman province (Acts 8:40). Built by Herod the Great, it is located 37 km. (23 mi.) from the foot of Mount Carmel; also called Caesarea Maritima.

Caesarea Philippi (ses-a-rē'a fi-lip'ī; *Caesar's city of Philippi*). A town located at the foot of Mount Hermon; the northernmost extent of Jesus' ministry (Matt. 16:13–20).

Caiaphas (kā'ya-fas; *a searcher*). A.D. 30. The high priest who took a leading role in the trial of Jesus (Matt. 26:3, 57–68; John 11:49).

Cain (kān; *possessed*). The eldest son of Adam who killed his brother Abel (Gen. 4:1–25). *See also* Tubal-cain.

Cain [Kain] (kān [kān]; *possessed*). A town in the hill country of Judah (Josh. 15:57).

Cainan [Kenan] (ka-ī'nan [kē'nan]). **[1]** A son of Enosh and ancestor of Christ (Gen. 5:9; Luke 3:37). The KJV inconsistently spells the same name *Kenan* in First Chronicles 1:2. **[2]** A son of Arphaxad and an ancestor of Christ (Luke 3:36). It should be noted that this name occurs in the Septuagint text and not in the Hebrew of Genesis 10:24; 11:12. The presence of this name shows that the early lists in Genesis were not meant to be complete.

Calah (kā'la; *holy gate*). A city built by Nimrod that later became the capital of the Assyrian Empire; located about 29 km. (18 mi.) south of Nineveh (Gen. 10:11).

Calcol [Chalcol] (kal'kol [kal'kol]; *sustaining* or *nourishment*). A descendant of Judah (1 Chron. 2:6; 1 Kings 4:31).

Caleb [Chelubai] (kā'leb [ke-lū'bī]; *dog*). **[1]** A son of Hezron and grandfather of [1] (1 Chron. 2:18–19, 42). **[2]** 1400 B.C. One of the spies sent out by Moses to see the Promised Land (Num. 13:6; Josh. 14–15). **[3]** A son of Hur (1 Chron. 2:24). Some translations have this as a place. *See* Caleb Ephrathah.

Caleb Ephrathah (kā'leb ef'ra-tha). The place where Hezron died (1 Chron. 2:24). Many scholars translate the verse: ''after the death of Hezron, Caleb went into Ephrathah, the wife of Hezron his father, and she bore him Ashhur, the father of Tekoa'' (RSV) following the LXX. *See also* Ephratah.

Calneh (kal'ne; *fortress*). **[1]** A city in Mesopotamia belonging to Nimrod (Gen. 10:10). **[2]** A city located about 10 km. (6 mi.) from Arpad (Amos 6:2); probably the present-day Kullani.

Calno (kal'nō; *futility*). A city conquered by the Assyrians (Isa. 10:9); probably the same as Calneh [2].

Calvary (kal'var-ē'. The name used in the KJV and NKJV for the place where Jesus was crucified (Luke 23:33). Located outside Jerusalem. *See* Golgotha.

Camon [Kamon] (kā'mon [kā'mon]; *standing place*). The place where Jair the Gileadite was buried (Judg. 10:5).

Cana (kā'na; *place of reeds*). A village of Galilee where Jesus performed the miracle of changing water into wine. It is located 16 km. (10 mi.) northeast of Nazareth (John 2:1, 11; 4:46).

Canaan (kā'nan; *merchant* or *trader*). A son of Ham and grandsom of Noah (Gen.10:6–19; 1 Chron. 1:8, 13). Possibly a reference to the inhabitants of Canaa.

Canaan (kā'nan; *merchant* or *trader*). The native name of Palestine, the land given to Abraham and his descendants (Gen. 11:31; Exod. 6:4).

Candace (kan'da-sē; *queen* or *ruler of children*). A dynastic title of Ethiopian queens. The eunuch of the Candace was converted to Christianity by Philip (Acts 8:27).

Canneh (kā'neh; *distinguished*). A town on the southern coast of Arabia (Ezek. 27:23); present-day Canne.

Capernaum (ka-per'na-um; *village of Nahum*). A town on the northwest shore of the Sea of Galilee; an important center of Jesus' ministry (Matt. 4:13; Luke 4:31).

Caphtor (kaf'tor). The island or seacoast region from which the Philistines originally came (Jer. 47:4; Amos 9:7); probably Crete and other nearby islands.

Caphtorim [Caphthorim] (kaf-tor-im' [kaf-thor-im]. A reference to the people from Caphtor (Gen. 10:14; 1 Chron. 1:12).

Cappadocia (kap-a-dō'shi-a). A Roman district in eastern Asia Minor (Acts 2:9; 1 Pet. 1:1).

Carcas [Carkas] (kar'kas [kar'kas] *vulture*). 475 B.C. A chamberlain of Ahasuerus (Esther 1:10).

Carchemish [Charchemish] (kar'ke-mish [kar'kem-ish]; *city* [*fortress*] *of Chemosh*). A city west of the Euphrates River; the eastern capital of the Hittites (2 Chron. 35:20; Isa. 10:9; Jer. 46:2).

Careah (ka-rē'a). *See* Kareah.

Carmel (kar'mel; *orchard*). [1] A string of mountains that run about 24 km. (15 mi.) through central Palestine and jut into the Mediterranean Sea (Jer. 46:18). [2] A town in the mountains of Judah about 14 km. (9 mi). south-southeast of Hebron (Josh. 15:55; 1 Sam. 25:5); modern Kermel.

Carmi (kar'mī; *vinedresser*). **[1]** 1850 B.C. A son of Reuben who went to Egypt with him (Gen. 46:9; Exod. 6:14; 1 Chron. 5:3). **[2]** 1425 B.C. A descendant of Judah (Josh. 7:1; 1 Chron. 2:7). **[3]** 1425 B.C. Another son of Judah (1 Chron. 4:1); some identify him with [2].

Carpus (kar'pus; *fruit*). A.D. 65. A friend with whom Paul left his cloak (2 Tim. 4:13).

Carshena (kar-shē'na; *plowman*). 475 B.C. One of the seven princes of Persia and Media during Ahasuerus; reign (Esther 1:14).

Casiphia (ka-sif'i-a). An unidentified place in Babylon to which Ezra sent for ministers of the house of God (Ezra 8:17).

Casluhim (kas'lū'him; *people of Kasluh*). A son of Mizraim (Gen. 10:14; 1 Chron. 1:12). Possibly a people related to the Egyptians. They were the ancestors of the Philistines.

Cenchrea [Cenchreae] (sen'kre-a [sen'krē-a]). A harbor about 11 km. (7 mi.) east of Corinth, visited by Paul (Acts 18:18).

Cephas (sē'fas; *rock*). The Aramaic name given to Simon, son of Jonah, by Jesus (John 1:42).

Chalcol (kal'kol; *sustaining*). A form of Calcol.

Chaldea (kal-dē'a). The southern region of the Babylonian Empire (Jer. 50:10; Ezek. 11:24).

Charran (kar'an). Greek form of Haran (q.v.).

Chebar (kē'bar; *joining*). A "river" of Chaldea; the Jewish exiles, including Ezekiel, lived along its banks (Ezek. 1:3). Probably not actually a river, but the Royal Canal of Nebuchadnezzar that connected the Tigris and Euphrates Rivers.

Chedorlaomer (ked-or-la-ō'mer; Elamite, Kutir-Lakamar—*servant of [the Canaanite god] Lakamar*). 2100 B.C. A king of Elam who came up against Sodom and Gomorrah (Gen. 14:1–24).

Chelal (ke'lal; *completeness*). 450 B.C. A man who married a foreign wife during the Exile (Ezra 10:30).

Chelluh [Cheluh; Cheluhi] (kel'a [kel'uh; ke-lū'hī] *perfect*). 450 B.C. A man who married a foreign wife during the Exile (Ezra 10:35).

Chelub (ke'lub; *bird's cage*). [1] A descendant of Judah (1 Chron. 4:11). [2] 1025 B.C. Father of Ezri (1 Chron. 27:26).

Chelubai (ke-lū'bī *bold*). A son of Hezron and the grandfather of Caleb (1 Chron. 2:9, 18, 42).

Chenaanah (ke-nā'a-na). [1] A son of Bilhan (1 Chron. 7:10). [2] 875 B.C. Father of the false prophet Zedekiah (1 Kings 22:11, 24).

Chenani (ken'a-nī; *Jehovah has established*). 450 B.C. A Levite in the time of Ezra (Neh. 9:4).

Chenaniah (ken-a-ni'a; *established by Jehovah*). [1] 1000 B.C. A head Levite when David brought the ark of the covenant to the temple (1 Chron. 15:22, 27). [2] 975 B.C. An officer of David (1 Chron. 26:29).

Chephar Haammonai (kē'far ha-am'o-ni; *village of the Ammonites*). A town assigned to the tribe of Benjamin (Josh. 18:24); probably modern Khirbet Kafr 'Ana, east of Jifna.

Chephirah (ke-fī'ra; *town*). A city of Gibeon given to the tribe of Benjamin (Josh. 9:17); modern Kefireh, located 13 km. (8 mi.) west-northwest of Jerusalem.

Cheran (kē'ran; *lyre*). 1925 B.C. A son of Dishon (Gen. 36:26; 1 Chron. 1:41).

Cherith (ke'rith; *gorge*). A wadi (dry riverbed) of Gilead, east of the Jordan River, where birds fed the prophet Elijah (1 Kings 17:3–5).

Cherub (kē'rub; *held fast*). A place in Babylonia where some Jewish citizens lived during the Captivity. (Ezra 2:59; Neh. 7:61).

Chesalon (kes'a-lon; *slope*). A town near Mount Jearim of Judah, about 16 km. (10 mi.) west of Jerusalem (Josh. 15:10).

Chesed (ke'sed; *gain*). 2050 B.C. Son of Nahor and Milcah and nephew of Abraham (Gen. 22:22).

Chesil (ke'sil; *fool*). A village in the southernmost portion of Judah (Josh. 15:3); perhaps the same as Bethuel (q.v.).

Chesulloth (ke-sul'oth; *loins*). A town 6 km. (4 mi.) southeast of Nazareth in the territory of Issachar (Josh. 19:18).

Chezib (ke'zib; *deceitful*). A form of Achzib.

Chidon [Nachon] (kī'don [nā'kon]; *javelin*). The place where Uzzah was struck dead for touching the ark of the covenant (1 Chron. 13:9); in Second Samuel 6:6 the place is called Nachon. Its exact location is unknown.

Chileab (kil'e-ab; *restraint of father*). 975 B.C. A son of David (2 Sam. 3:3); also called Daniel (1 Chron. 3:1).

Chilion (kil'i-un; *pining*). Son of Naomi and husband Orpah (Ruth 1:2, 5).

Chilmad (kil'mad; *closed*). A nation on the Euphrates River that traded with Tyre (Ezek. 27:23). The exact location is unknown.

Chimham (kim'ham; *of a pallid face*). 1000 B.C. A friend and political supporter of David (2 Sam. 19:37–38, 40; Jer. 41:17).

Chinnereth [Chinneroth; Cinneroth] (kin′e-reth [kin′e-roth; sin′e-reth]; *harps*). **[1]** An early name for the Sea of Galilee (Num. 34:11; Josh. 12:3). **[2]** A fortified city of Naphtali on the north shore of the Sea of Galilee (Deut. 3:17. **[3]** The region of Naphtali surrounding the city of Chinnereth (1 Kings 15:20).

Chios (kī′os; *open*). An island of the Greek chain at the entrance to the Gulf of Smyrna (Acts 20:15).

Chislon (ki′lon; *strength*). 1400 B.C. A prince of the tribe of Benjamin; father of Elidad. (Num. 34:21).

Chisloth Tabor (kis′loth ta′bor; *loins of tabor*). A city of Zebulun at the foot of Mount Tabor (Josh. 19:12).

Chittim (kit′im). A form of kittim.

Chloe (klō′e; *tender sprout*). A.D. 55. A Corinthian woman or an Ephesian woman who knew of the problems at Corinth (1 Cor. 1:11).

Chorashan (kōr′a-shan; *smoking furnace*). A town in Judah given to Simeon (1 Sam. 30:30). It is possibly identical with Ashan (q.v.).

Chorazin (ko-rā′zin; *secret*). A coastal city north of the Sea of Galilee where Jesus Christ performed many miracles (Matt. 11:21; Luke 10:13).

Chozeba (ko-zē′ba; *untruthful*). A village of Judah inhabited by the descendants of Shelah (1 Chron. 4:22); probably the same as Achzib (Josh. 15:44; Mic. 1:14) and Chezib (Gen. 38:5).

Christ (krīst). *See* Jesus.

Chub (kub). A people who joined with Egypt to fight against the Babylonians during the time of Nebuchadnezzar (Ezek. 30:5). Many scholars believe this is a textual error and should be read as in the LXX, "Lub," i.e., Libya (q.v.) (Ezek. 30:5).

Chun (kun). A town in Syria (1 Chron. 18:8).

Chuza (koo'za; *little jug*). A.D. 25. Steward of Herod Antipas whose wife ministered to Christ and the apostles (Luke 8:3).

Cilicia (si-lish'i-a). A district of southeast Asia Minor. Paul was born in Tarsus, the principal city of this district (Acts 21:39).

Cis (sis). Greek form of Kish (q.v.).

City of David. [1] Jebusite city of Zion captured by David's men. David made it his royal city and renamed it Jerusalem (2 Sam. 5:6–9; 1 Chron. 11:5, 7). [2] *See* Bethlehem.

Cities of the Plain. Five cities located on the Plain of Jordan: Sodom, Gomorrah, Admah, Zeboim, and Zoar (Gen. 10:19; 13:10).

Cities of Refuge. Six Levitical cities set aside as sanctuaries for certain criminals: Bezer, Ramoth Gilead, Golan, Kedesh, Shechem, and Kirjath-arba (Deut. 4:41–43: Josh. 20:7–9).

City, Holy. Another name for Jerusalem, the religious center of the Jewish people (Neh. 11:1; Dan. 9:24).

City of Salt. A city in the wilderness of Judah near Engedi (Josh. 15:62).

City of Waters. An expression which refers to the lower part of the Ammonite city Rabbah, distinguishing it from Citadel (the upper city) (2 Sam. 12:27).

Clauda [Cauda] (klo'da [ko'da]). An island southwest of Crete passed by Paul during his journey to Rome (Acts 27:16).

Claudia (klo'di-a; *lame*). A.D. 65. A Roman Christian who sent greetings to Timothy (2 Tim. 4:21).

Claudius (klo′di-us sē′zer; *lame*). A.D. 41–54. Fourth emperor of the Roman Empire, Tiberius Claudius Nero Germanicus who banished the Jews from Rome (Acts 18:2).

Claudius Lysias (klo′di-us lis′i-as; *lame dissolution*). *See* Lysias.

Clement (klem′ent; *merciful*). A.D. 60. A co-worker with Paul at Philippi (Phil. 4:3).

Cleopas (klē′o-pas; *renowned father*). A.D. 30. One of the two disciples whom Jesus met on the way to Emmaus (Luke 24:18).

Cleophas [Clopas] (klē′uh-fus] [klō′puhs]). A.D. 30. The husband of Mary, one of the women present at the crucifixion, of Jesus (John 19:25). Believed to be the same person as Alphaeus, father of James the Less and Joses (Matt. 10:3; Mark 15:40).

Cnidus (nī′dus; *age*). A city of the province of Caria on the southwestern coast of Asia Minor near the Isle of Cos passed by Paul on his journey to Rome (Acts 27:7).

Col-hozeh (kol-hō′zeh; *wholly a seer*). **[1]** Father of Baruch of the tribe of Judah (Neh. 11:5); possibly the same as [2]. **[2]**. 475 B.C. Father of Shallum, who helped to rebuild the wall of Jerusalem (Neh. 3:15).

Colosse [Colossae] (ko-los′e [ko-los′e]). A city in the Roman province of Asia (Col. 1:2).

Conaniah (kon-a-nī′a; *Jehovah establishes*). 625 B.C. A chief of the Levites who assisted in the Passover celebration during King Josiah's reign (2 Chron. 35:9).

Coniah (cōnī′a). *See* Jehoiachin.

Cononiah (kon-on-ī′a; *Jehovah establishes*). 725 B.C. A Levite in charge of overseeing tithes and offerings at the

Temple during the reign of King Hezekiah (2 Chron. 31:12–13).

Coos (kō′os). A form of Cos.

Core (kōre). Greek form of Korah (q.v.).

Corinth (kor′inth). A Greek city located on the Isthmus of Corinth between the Peloponnesus and mainland Greece, about 64 km. (40 mi.) west of Athens (Acts 18:1; 1 Cor. 1:2).

CORINTH AT THE CROSSROADS

Corinth rose from ashes to occupy a position of prominence at the trading crossroads of the ancient world. The original city was destroyed in 146 B.C. in a Greek revolt against the Roman Empire. Rebuilt in the time of Julius Caesar (*ca.* 46 B.C.) Corinth soon regained its former position as a center of commerce. Within twenty-one years, this rapidly growing metropolis became the capital of the province of Achaia in Greece.

Corinth was one of the wealthiest and most influential cities of its time. Located on a narrow strip of land between mainland Greece and the Peloponnesus (the peninsula of southern Greece), Corinth had two main harbors, which gave the city access to the Aegean and Ionian seas. This strategic location allowed Corinth to control the traffic of the eastern and western seas, along a principal trade route of the Roman Empire. Corinth was the fourth largest city of the empire (after Rome, Alexandria, and Antioch), and had a population of nearly half a million.

Corinth was also situated at a cultural crossroads. Residents migrated to this rapidly developing area from every corner of the Mediterranean world. Egyptians, Syrians, Orientals, and Jews who settled there brought a wide variety of cultural influences.

One might well call ancient Corinth a "sin city." While rather low moral values were held by the general Roman public, Corinth had a reputation for embracing the lowest of the low. Even prior to the time of the apostle Paul, "to live like a Corinthian" was a slang phrase denoting loose, immoral conduct.

Oddly, religion contributed to this atmosphere of moral corruption. Many of the fertility cults that existed in the city included acts of magic and sexual perversion as part of their "worship." Corinth's temple of Aphrodite, the goddess of love, at one time had one thousand priestess-prostitutes within its confines.

To this complex city came the apostle Paul. Arriving around A.D. 52, Paul remained there for about a year and a half, ministering to one of the greatest churches of Jesus Christ. A city at the crossroads, both physically and spiritually, Corinth heard the gospel of Christ through Paul's ministry.

Corinth was rebuilt after earthquakes in 1858 and 1928. The Doric columns of one old temple of Apollo are one of the few reminders of Corinth's early days left. Corinth today has a population of about 20,000. It is still an important sea town, with exports of olive oil, silk, and currants, which take their name from the city.

Cornelius (kor-nē′li-us). A.D. 40. A Roman centurion who was converted to Christianity (Acts 10:1–31).

Corner Gate. A gate near the northwest corner of the wall of Jerusalem (2 Kings 14:13).

Cos [Coos] (kahz [kooz]). A small island between Miletus and Rhodes off the coast of Asia Minor (Acts 21:1).

Cosam (kō′sam; *diviner*). An ancestor of Christ (Luke 3:28).

Coz (koz). A form of Koz.

Cozbi (koz′bi; *deceitful*). 1400 B.C. A Midianite woman slain by Phinehas at Shittim (Num. 25:6–18).

Crescens (kres′enz; *increasing*). A.D. 65 An assistant with Paul at Rome (2 Tim. 4:10).

Crete (krē). A large island in the Mediterranean Sea southeast of Greece (Titus 1:5).

Crispus (kris′pus; *curled*). A.D. 58. A ruler of the Jewish synagogue at Corinth who was converted to Christ (Acts 18:7–8; 1 Cor. 1:14).

Cush (kūsh; *black*). **[1]** Eldest son of Ham (Gen. 10:6–8; 1 Chron. 1:8–10). **[2]** 1000 B.C. A descendant of Benjamin and enemy of David (Psa. 7, title).

Cush (kūsh; *black*). **[1]** A land that bordered the Gihon River, which was one of the four rivers of the Garden of Eden (Gen. 2:10–14). Is thought to have been in or near Mesopotamia. **[2]** An area South of Egypt which includes part of the countries Sudan and Ethiopia; also called Nubia. The Persian Empire of Ahasuerus (Xerxes 486–465 B.C.) extended to this point (Esth. 1:1, 8:9; Job 28:19; Isa. 11:11, 18:1–7).

Cushan (kū'shan; *belonging to Cush*). The name of a place or people, possibly Midian (Hab. 3:7). Possibly the same person as Cushan-rishathaim, king of Mesopotamia (Judg. 3:8, 10).

Cushan-rishathaim (kū'shan-rish-a-thā'im; *double wickedness*). 1382–1374 B.C. A king of Mesopotamia that God chose to punish Israel (Judg. 3:8, 10).

Cushi (kū'shi; *black*). **[1]** Great-grandfather of Jehudi (Jer. 36:14). **[2]** 675 B.C. Father of Zephaniah (Zeph. 1:1).

Cuth Cuthah (kuth [kū'thuh]; *burning*). A Babylonian city (2 Kings 17:30); present-day Tell Ibrahim, northeast of Babylon.

Cyprus (sī'prus). An island in the northeastern Mediterranean Sea about 96 km. (60 mi). east of Syria (Acts 13:4; 15:39). The name Cyprus does not appear in the Old Testament, many scholars believe Elishah (Gen. 10:4; 1 Chron. 1:7; Ezek. 27:7) and Kittim (Gen. 10:4; 1 Chron. 1:7) refer to Cyprus.

Cyrene (sīrē'nē). A city of Libya in Northern Africa (Matt. 27:32); probably modern Shahhat.

Cyrenius [Quirinius] (sī-rēni-us [kwī-rin′i-us]; *of Cyrene*). The governor of Syria (Luke 2:2).

Cyrus (sī′rus). Ruler of the Persian Empire (559–530 B.C.); he returned the Jews to their land (Ezra 1:1–4, 7; 3:7; Isa. 44:28; 45:1–4; Dan. 6:28).

D

Dabbasheth [Dabbesheth] (dab′e-sheth [dab′be-sheth]; *camel hump*). A border town of the tribe of Zebulun (Josh. 19:11).

Daberath [Dabareh] (dab′e-rath [dab′a-reh]; *pasture*). A city of the tribe of Issachar, assigned to the Levites (Josh. 19:12; 1 Chron. 6:72); probably modern Daburiyeh at the western base of Mount Tabor. The KJV renders the same Hebrew word as Dabareh in Joshua 21:28.

Dalaiah (da-lī′a). A form of Delaiah.

Dalmanutha (dal-ma-nū′tha). A fishing village on the western coast of the Sea of Galilee (Mark 8:10). The parallel passage in Matthew 15:39 calls this place Maydala (KJV, NKJV) and Magaden (RSV).

Dalmatia (dal-mā′shē-a). A province of Illyricum on the eastern shore of the Adriatic Sea; noted for its wild inhabitants (Rom. 15:19; 2 Tim. 4:10). Dalmatia later became the official name of the province.

Dalphon (dal′fon). A son of Haman who was an advisor to King Ahasuerus. He was slain by his father (Esther 9:6–7, 10).

Damaris (dam′a-ris). An Athenian woman converted by Paul (Acts 17:34).

Damascus (da-mas'kus). An important Syrian trade center; Paul was converted on the road from Jerusalem to this city (Gen. 14:15; Acts 9:2). The capital of Syria.

Dan (dan; *judge*). 1900 B.C. The fifth son of Jacob and ancestor of one of the twelve tribes of Israel (Gen. 30:6; 49:16–17).

Dan (dan; *judge*). A town of the tribe of Dan in the northwest portion of Palestine (Josh. 19:47; Judg. 20:1).

Daniel (dan'yel; *God is my judge*). [1] 975 B.C. One of the sons of David (1 Chron. 3:1). *See* Chileab. [2] 600 B.C. A prophet at the time of Nebuchadnezzar and Cyrus. His wisdom and faith earned him a position of esteem under Nebuchadnezzar and Darius (Dan. 1:1–6; 2; 6:1–2. [3] 450 B.C. A Levite of the line of Ithamar (Ezra 8:2; Neh. 10:6).

Dan Jaan (dan jā'an). A place or city in northern Palestine between Gilead and Sidon: possibly Dan (2 Sam. 24:6).

Dannah (dan'na; *stronghold*). A small village in the hill country of Judah (Josh. 15:49); modern Deir esh-Shemish or Simya.

Dara (da'ra; *bearer [pearl] of wisdom*). A son of Zerah of the tribe of Judah (1 Chron. 2:6). Possibly the same as Darda (q.v.).

Darda (dar'da; *bearer [pearl] of wisdom*). A wise man with whom Solomon was compared (1 Kings 4:31). *See also* Dara.

Darius (da-rī'us). [1] 539–538 B.C. The sub-king of Cyrus who received the kingdom of Belshazzar (Dan. 5:30–6:28); also known as Darius the Mede. [2] 522–486 B.C. The fourth king of Persia (Ezra 4:5; Hag. 1:1; Zech. 1:1); also called Hystaspis. [3] 424–405 B.C.

Darius II (Nothus) who ruled Persia and Babylon (Neh. 12:22).

Darkon (dar'kon, *bearer* or *carrier*). 950 B.C. A servant of Solomon whose descendants returned to Palestine after the Exile (Ezra 2:56; Neh. 7:58).

Dathan (dā'than; *strong*). 1450 B.C. A chief of the tribe of Reuben who tried to overthrow Moses and Aaron (Num. 16; 26:9; Deut. 11:6).

David (dā'vid; *beloved*). Reigned 1010–970 B.C. The great statesman, general, and king of Israel. He united the divided tribes of Israel and made many preparations for the temple, which his son Solomon would complete (1 Sam. 16—1 Kings 2:11). He was an ancestor of Christ (Matt. 1:6).

David, City of. [1] The name given to Jebus or Zion, the city of the Jebusites, after it was captured by David (2 Sam. 5:6–9; 1 Chron. 11:4–7). David moved his royal capital here (1 Kings 3:1; 2 Kings 8:24, 2 Chron. 5:2). [2] The town of Bethlehem in Judea, birthplace of Jesus, called the City of David because it was also the birthplace of David (1 Sam. 17:12). *See also* Zion.

Dead Sea. A salt sea in southern Palestine and the lowest point on the earth. Referred to as the Salt Sea (Gen. 14:3; Josh. 3:16) and the East Sea (Ezek. 47:18; Joel 2:20) in the Old Testament. Also called the Sea, or Plain, of Arabah (Deut. 3:17).

Debir (dē'bir; *speaker*). 1400 B. C. A king of Eglon defeated by Joshua (Josh. 10:3).

Debir (dē'bir; *speaker*). [1] A town in the hill country of Judah assigned to the Levites (Josh. 15:15). The city is called Kirjath Sannah (Josh. 15:49) and Kirjath Sepher (Judg. 1:11–13). [2] A town near the Valley of Achor, probably on the road between Jerusalem and Jericho

(Josh. 15:7). **[3]** A border town of the tribe of Gad, located east of the Jordan River near Mahanaim (Josh. 13:26).

Deborah (deb'ō'ra;; *wasp*). **[1]** 2025 B.C. The nurse of Rebekah and wife of Isaac (Gen. 24:59; 35:8). **[2]** 1225 B.C. Prophetess and fifth judge of Israel who helped to deliver her people from Jabin and Sisera (Judg. 4:4–14; 5).

Decapolis (de-kap'ō-lis; *ten cities*). A league of ten cities forming a Roman district on the Plain of Esdraelon and the Upper Jordan Valley (Matt. 4:25).

Dedan (dē'dan; *low*). **[1]** A descendant of Cush (Gen. 10:7). Possibly a people of Arabia in the neighborhood of Edom. **[2]** 2000 B.C. A son of Jokshan and grandson of Abraham (Gen. 25:3).

Dedan (dē'dan; *low*). A district near Edom between Sela and the Dead Sea (Jer. 25:23; Ezek. 25:13). Isaiah 21:13 mentions the "caravans of the Dedanim" in the wilds of Arabia.

Delaiah [Dalaiah] (de-lī'a [da-lī'a]; *Jehovah is deliverer*). **[1]** 1000 B.C. One of David's priests (1 Chron. 24:18). **[2]** 600 B.C. A prince who urged Jehoiakim not to destroy the roll containing Jeremiah's prophecies (Jer. 36:12, 25). **[3]** Ancestor of a postexilic family that had lost its genealogy (Ezra 2:60; Neh. 7:62). **[4]** 475 B.C. The father of Shemaiah (Neh. 6:10).

Delilah (de-lī'la; *dainty one*). 1075 B.C. A Philistine woman whom the Philistines paid to find Samson's source of strength (Judg. 16).

Demas (dē'mas). A.D. 60. A friend of Paul at Rome who later forsook him (Col. 4:14; 2 Tim. 4:10; Philem. 24).

Demetrius (de-mē'tri-us; *belonging to Demeter*). **[1]** A.D.

90. A silversmith who led the opposition against Paul at Ephesus (Acts 19:24–41). **[2]** A.D. 55. A Christian praised by John (3 John 12).

Derbe (der´bē). A city of southeastern Asia Minor, where Paul sought refuge after being stoned at Lystra (Acts 14:6–20).

Deuel (dū´el; *knowledge of God*). 1475 B.C. Father of Eliasaph (Num. 1:14). He is called Reuel in Numbers 2:14; we do not know which name is original.

Diblah [Diblath] (dib´lah, [dib´lath]). A place or city in Palestine (Ezek. 6:14); its exact location is unknown, but it was probably the same place as Riblah.

Diblaim (dib´lāim; *two cakes of figs*). 775 B.C. Father-in-law of Hosea (Hos. 1:3).

Dibon [Dimon; Dimonah] (dī´bon [dī´mon; di-mō´na]; *wasting*). **[1]** A city of the tribe of Gad located north of the Arnon River. Also called Dimon (Num. 21:30; 32:3; Isa. 15:9); the famous Moabite Stone was found here in 1868. **[2]** A village of southern Judah near the boundary of Edom; also known as Dimonah (Neh. 11:25; Josh. 15:22).

Dibon Gad (dī´bon gad; *wasting of Gad*). A halting place of the Israelites leaving Egypt (Num. 33:45–46). It is probably the same as Dibon [1].

Dibri (dib´ri; *talkative*). 1475 B.C. A descendant of Dan whose daughter married an Egyptian; her son was stoned for blasphemy (Lev. 24:11).

Didymus (did´i-mus; *twin*). A.D. 25. The Greek name of Thomas (John 11:16; 20:24; 21:2).

Diklah (dik´la; *place of palms*). A son of Joktan (Gen. 10:27; 1 Chron. 1:21). Possibly an oasis in southern Arabia is intended.

Dilean (dil'e-an; *cucumber*). A city in the lowlands of Judah (Josh. 15:38). Possibly the same place as Tell en-Najileh.

Dimnah (dim'na; *dung*). A border town in Zebulun assigned to Levites of the Merari family (Josh. 21:35).

Dimon (dī'mon). *See* Dibon.

Dimonah (dī'mō'na). *See* Dibon [2]. **Dinah** (dī'na; *one who judges*). 1900 B.C. The daughter of Jacob and Leah who was violated by Hamor; this resulted in a tribal war (Gen. 34).

Dinhabah (din'ha-ba; *give judgment*). A city belonging to Bela, the king of Edom (Gen. 36:32; 1 Chron. 1:43); its exact location is unknown.

Dionysius the Areopagite (di-o-nish'i-us). A.D. 50. A member of the supreme court at Athens, converted by Paul (Acts 17:34).

Diotrophes (dī-ot'ruh-fēz; *nourished by Jupiter*). A.D. 90. A person who opposed John's authority (3 John 9—10).

Diphath (dif'ath) The second son of Gomer (Gen. 10:3; 1 Chron. 1:6). Probably the same person as Riphath.

Dishan (dī'shan; *antelope*). 1950 B.C. A son of Seir (Gen. 36:21, 28, 30; 1 Chron. 1:38). [2] 1950 B.C. A grandson of Seir (Gen. 36:25; 1 Chron. 1:41). *See also* Dishon.

Dishon (dī'shon; *antelope*). [1] 1950 B.C. A son of Seir (Gen. 36:21, 30; 1 Chron. 1:38, 42). *See also* Dishan.

Dizahab (dī'z'a-hab; *abounding in gold*). A place in the Arabian desert near where Moses gave his farewell speech to the nation of Israel (Deut. 1:1); its exact location is unknown, but it may be Edh-Dheilbeh, east of Heshbon.

Dodai (dō''dī). *See* Dodo.

Dodanim [Rodanim] (dōd'a-nim [rod'a-nim]). The son of Javan (Gen. 10:4). First Chronicles 1:7 states his name as Rodanim; many scholars consider Rodanim to be original. Possibly a reference to the inhabitants of Rhodes and the neighboring islands.

Dodavah [Dodavahu] (dōd'a-va [dōd'a-va'hū']; *beloved of Jehovah*). 875 B.C. Father of Eliezer of Mareshah (2 Chron. 20:37).

Dodo [Dodai] (dō'do [dō'dī]; *beloved*). [1] 1175 B.C. The grandfather of Tola, a judge (Judg. 10:1). [2] 1025 B.C. A commander of one of the divisions of David's army and father of Eleazar [3] (2 Sam. 23:9; 1 Chron. 11:12; 27:4). [3] 1025 B.C. Father of Elhanan [2] (2 Sam. 23:24; 1 Chron. 11:26).

Doeg (dō'eg; *timid*). 1000 B.C. A servant of King Saul who executed the priests of Nob on Saul's orders (1 Sam. 21:7; 22:9–19).

Dophkah (dof'ka; *drover*). A place in the wilderness of Sinai between the Red Sea and Rephidim (Num. 33:12–13).

Dor (dōr; *habitation*). A Canaanite town on the Mediterranean coast about 13 km. (8 mi.) north of Caesarea (Josh. 11:2; 12:23).

Dorcas (dor'kas). A.D. 35. A Christian woman from Joppa who was known for helping the poor (Acts 9:36–43); also called Tabitha. She was raised from the dead by the apostle Peter. *See* Tabitha.

Dothan (do'than; *two wells*). A city of the tribe of Manasseh west of the Jordan River and northeast of Samaria, near Mount Gilboa; here Joseph was sold into slavery (Gen. 37:17; 2 Kings 6:13).

Dragon Well. *See* Serpent Well.

Drusilla (drūsil´a; *watered by dew*). A.D. 60. The youngest daughter of Herod Agrippa I and wife of Felix; she and Felix heard a powerful message of Paul's (Acts 24:24–25).

Dumah (dū´ma; *silence*). 2025 B.C. A descendant of Ishmael (Gen. 25:14; 1 Chron. 1:30).

Dumah (dū´ma; *silence*). [1] A town in Judah (Josh. 15:52). [2] A symbolic name of Edom or a place in Arabia (Isa. 21:11).

Dung Gate. A gate in the southwest wall of Jerusalem (Neh. 2:13; 12:31).

Dura (dū´ra; *circle* or *circuit*). The Babylonian plain where King Nebuchadnezzar set up a golden idol (Dan. 3:1).

E

Eastern Sea. *See* Dead Sea.

Ebal [Obal] (ē´bal [ō´bal]; *bare*). [1] 1950 B.C. A son of Shobal the Horite (Gen. 36:23; 1 Chron. 1:40). [2] A son of Joktan, descendant of Shem (1 Chron 1:22). He is called Obal in Genesis 10:28. Possibly an Arabian people is meant.

Ebal (ē´bal; *bare*). A mountain north of Shechem and beside Mount Gerizim (Deut. 27:12–13); modern Jebel Eslamiyeh.

Ebed (ē´bed; *servant*). [1] 1150 B.C. Father of Gaal who rebelled against Abimelech (Judg. 9:26–35). [2] 450 B.C. A companion of Ezra on his return to Jerusalem (Ezra 8:6).

Ebed-Melech (ē´bed-mē´lek; *the king's servant*). 600 B.C.

An Ethiopian eunuch who served Zedekiah and rescued Jeremiah (Jer. 38:7–12; 39:16).

Ebenezer (eb'en-ē'zer; *stone of help*). **[1]** c. 1080 B.C. The site of the defeat of Israel by the Philistines (1 Sam. 4:1–22). It was in the north of Sharon near Aphek. **[2]** Name of a stone Samuel erected to commemorate his victory over the Philistines (1 Sam. 7:12). The stone was possible named after [1] to give the idea that Israel's defeat there had been reversed.

Eber (ē'ber; *the other side; across*). **[1]** A descendant of Shem and an ancestor of Christ (Gen. 10:21, 24–25; 11:14–17; Luke 3:35). His name occurs as Heber in Luke 3:35. Possibly the Hebrews and certain Aramean people are intended. **[2]** Descendants of Eber or possibly those who lived "across" the Euphrates (Num. 24:24). **[3]** A family of the tribe of Gad (1 Chron 5:13). **[4]** A descendant of Benjamin (1 Chron. 8:12). **[5]** 500 B.C. Head of a priestly family (Neh. 12:20). *See* Heber.

Ebez (ē'bez). *See* Abez.

Ebiasaph (e-bī'a-saf; *the father has gathered*). A Levite whose descendants were doorkeepers of the tabernacle (1 Chron. 6:23; 9:19). Also spelled Abiasaph (Exod. 6:24).

Ebron [Hebron] (ēē'bron [hē'brun]). A town in the territory alloted to the tribe of Asher (Josh. 19:28). May be the same place as Abdon (Josh. 21:30; 1 Chron. 6:74).

Ebronah (eb-rō'na). A form of Abronah.

Ecbatana (ek'bat-uh-nuh). A form of Achmetha.

Eden (ē'den; *delight*). **[1]** 725 B.C. A descendant of Gershom (2 Chron. 29:12). **[2]** 700 B.C. A Levite in the time of Hezekiah (2 Chron. 31:15).

Eden (ē´den; *pleasure*). **[1]** The garden that God created as the first residence of man (Gen. 2:15); its exact location is unknown. It may have been between the Tigris and Euphrates Rivers near the head of the Persian Gulf. **[2]** A region in Mesopotamia (2 Kings 19:12; Isa. 37:12).

Eder [Ader] (ē´der [ā´der] *flock*). A grandson of Merari, son of Levi (1 Chron. 23:23; 24:30).

Eder [Edar] (ē´der [ē´dar]; *flock*). **[1]** A tower or possibly a town between Bethlehem and Hebon; Jacob once camped near here (Gen. 35:21). **[2]** A town of southern Judah about 7 km. (4.5mi.) south of Gaza (Josh. 15:21); modern el-Adar.

Edom (ē´dom; *red*). Name given to Esau, the elder son of Isaac, because of his red skin (Gen. 25:30). *See* Esau.

Edom (ē´dom; *red*). A mountainous region south of Moab, which stretches from the Dead Sea to the Gulf of Aqabah. It was settled by the descendants of Esau, the Edomites (Gen. 32:3; Exod. 15:15).

Edrei (ed´re-ī). **[1]** The capital of Bashan; site of Israel's battle with Og (Deut. 3:10; Josh. 12:4). **[2]** A city of Naphtali between Kedesh and En-hazor (Josh. 19:37).

Eglah (eg´la; *calf*). 1000 B.C. One of David's wives and mother of Ithream (2 Sam. 3:5; 1 Chron. 3:3).

Eglath-shelishiya (egg´luth-shel-ih-shē´-a). An unknown city, the name of which is mentioned in prophetic oracles declared against Moab (Isa. 15:5; Jer. 48:34).

Eglaim (eg´la-im; *twin springs*). A town of Moab (Isa. 15:8).

Eglon (eg´lon; *young bull*). 1334–1316 B.C. A king of Moab who oppressed Israel in the days of the judges (Judg. 3:12–17).

Eglon (eg′lon; *young bull*). An Amorite city in the low-lands of Judah (Josh. 15:39); its exact location is un-known.

Egypt (ē′jipt). Northeast corner of Africa where the Isra-elites were held in bondage until Moses led them to the Promised Land (Gen. 45:9; 47:6).

Ehi (ē′hi; *unity*). A son of Benjamin (Gen. 46:21). Also called Ahiram (Num. 26:38).

Ehud (ē′hud; *strong*). [1] 1316–1235 B.C. A judge who delivered Israel from the oppression of Eglon of Moab (Judg. 3:15–30). [2] Great-grandson of Benjamin (1 Chron. 7:10; 8:6); perhaps the same as [1].

Eker (ē′ker; *offspring*). A son of Ram and descendant of Judah (1 Chron. 2:27).

Ekron (ek′ron; *barren place*). The northernmost of the five chief cities of Palestine, apportioned to the tribe of Judah (Josh. 13:3); present-day 'Akir, located 10 km. (6 mi.) west of Gezer.

El Paran (el par′an; *god of Paran*). A place in the Wilder-ness of Paran in southern Palestine during the time of Abraham (Gen. 14:6).

Eladah Eleada (el′a-da [el-ē′a-da]; *God has adorned*). A descendant of Ephraim (1 Chron. 7:20).

Elah (ē′la; *oak*). [1] A chieftain of Edom (Gen. 36:41; 1 Chron. 1:52). [2] Father of a commissary officer un-der Solomon (1 Kings 4:18). [3] 1375 B.C. A son of Caleb, son of Jephunneh (1 Chron. 4:15). [4] 886–885 B.C. The son and successor of Baasha, king of Israel. He was murdered by Zimri (1 Kings 16:6–14). [5] 775 B.C. The father of Hoshea, last king of Israel (2 Kings 15:30; 17:1). [6] A descendant of Benjamin (1 Chron. 9:8).

Elah (ē′la; *oak*). A valley mentioned in First Samuel 17:2. Quite possibly the Wadi Es-Sant ("valley of the terebinth") or part of it is intended. Es-Sant is 11 mi. south-west of Jerusalem.

Elam (ē'lam; *high land*). **[1]** A son of Shem (Gen. 10:22; 1 Chron. 1:17). Many scholars consider the people of Elam, a region beyond the Tigris east of the Babylonia, to be intended. It was bounded on the north by Assyria and Media, on the south by the Persian Gulf, and on the east and southeast by Persia. **[2]** A descendant of Benjamin (1 Chron. 8:24). **[3]** 1000 B.C. A descendant of Korah (1 Chron. 26:3). **[4]** 450 B.C. A leader of the people who sealed the new covenant with God after the Exile (Neh. 10:14). **[5]** 450 B.C. A priest of Nehemiah's time who helped to cleanse Jerusalem (Neh. 12:42). **[6]** One whose descendants returned from the Exile (Ezra 2:7). **[7]** Another whose descendants returned from the Exile (Ezra 2:31). **[8]** Yet another whose descendants returned from the Exile (Ezra 8:7). **[9]** Ancestor of some who married foreign wives during the Exile (Ezra 10:2).

Elasah (el'a-sa; *God has made*). **[1]** 600 B.C. Ambassador of Zedekiah (Jer. 29:3). **[2]** 450 B.C. One who married a foreign wife (Ezra 10:22). **[3]** *See* Eleasah.

Elath [Eloth] (e'lath [ē'loth]; *palm grove*). A major port city of the Gulf of Elath or Aqabah on the Red Sea (Deut. 2:8).

Eldaah (el'da; *whom God calls*). 1975 B.C. A son of Midian (Gen. 25:4; 1 Chron. 1:33).

Eldad (el'dad; *God has loved*). 1450 B.C. One of two elders who received the prophetic powers of Moses (Num. 11:26–27).

Elead (el'e-ad; *God is witness*). 1800 B.C. A descendant of Ephraim slain by invaders (1 Chron. 7:21).

Eleadah (el-ī-ah´duh). A form of Eladah.

Elealeh (e-le-a´le; *God id exalted*). A town of the tribe of Reuben about 3 km. (2 mi.) north-northeast of Heshbon (Num. 32:3); modern el-Al.

Eleasah (el-ē´a-sa; *God has made*). [1] A son of Helez, of the tribe of Judah (1 Chron. 2:39–40). [2] A son of Raphah and descendant of King Saul (1 Chron. 8:37; 9:43). *See* Elasah.

Eleazar (el-e-ā´zer; *God is helper*). [1] 1400 B.C. Third son of Aaron and successor to the high priest's office (Exod. 6:23; Num. 3:32; 20:28). [2] 1000 B.C. One sanctified to keep the ark of the covenant (1 Sam. 7:1). [3] 1000 B.C. One of David's mighty men (2 Sam. 23:9; 1 Chron. 11:12). [4] A descendant of Merari who had no sons (1 Chron. 23:21–22; 24:28). [5] 450 B.C. A priest who accompanied Ezra when he returned to Jerusalem (Ezra 8:33). [6] 450 B.C. A priest who assisted at the dedication of the walls of Jerusalem (Neh. 12:42); possibly the same as [5]. [7] An ancestor of Jesus (Matt 1:15).

Eleph [Ha-Eleph] (e´lef [ha´el´ef]). A city of the tribe of Benjamin, near Jerusalem (Josh. 18:28).

Elhanan (el-hā´nan; *God is gracious*). [1] 1000 B.C. The warrior who killed Lahmi, the brother of Goliath (1 Chron. 20:5; 2 Sam. 21:19). [2] 1000 B.C. One of David's mighty men (2 Sam. 23:24; 1 Chron. 11:26).

Eli (ē´lī; *Jehovah is high*). 1180–1120 B.C. High priest at Shiloh and judge of Israel. He is remembered for his lack of firmness (1 Sam 1–4).

Eliab (e-lī´ab; *God is father*). [1] 1475 B.C. Father of the wicked pair, Dathan and Abiram (Num. 16:1, 12; 26:8). [2] 1450 B.C. A prince of Zebulun (Num. 1:9; 2:7; 7:24, 29; 10:16). [3] Son of Jesse and brother of

David (1 Sam. 16:6); he is called Elihu in First Chronicles 27:18. **[4]** Ancestor of Samuel (1 Chron. 6:27); he is called Eliel in First Chronicles 6:34 and Elihu in First Samuel 1:1. **[5]** 1000 B.C. A warrior of David (1 Chron. 12:8–9, 14). **[6]** 1000 B.C. A Levite musician in the time of David (1 Chron. 15:18, 20; 16:5). **[7]** *See* Eleil.

Eliada [Eliadah] (e-lī′a-da [e-lī′a-da]; *God knows*). **[1]** 1000 B.C. A son of David (2 Sam. 5:16); also called Beeliada (1 Chron. 14:7). *See* Beeliada. **[2]** 950 B.C. Father of Rezon (1 Kings 11:23). **[3]** 875 B.C. A mighty man of Jehoshaphat (2 Chron. 17:17).

Eliah (e-lī′a). *See* Elijah.

Eliahba (e-lī′a-ba; *God hides*). 1000 B.C. One of David's mighty men (2 Sam. 23:32; 1 Chron. 11:33).

Eliakim (e-lī′a-kim; *God is setting up*). **[1]** 700 B.C. Successor of Shebna as master of Hezekiah's household (2 Kings 18:18, 26; Isa. 22:20). **[2]** 609–598 B.C. Original name of King Jehoiakim (q.v.). **[3]** 450 B.C. A priest in Nehemiah's time (Neh. 12:41). **[4]** An ancestor of Christ descended from Zerubbabel (Matt. 1:13). **[5]** An ancestor of Christ of the line of David who lived before the Captivity (Luke 3:30).

Eliam (ē-lī-am; *people's God*). **[1]** Father of Bathsheba (2 Sam. 11:3). By transposition of the two parts of the name he is called Ammiel (1 Chron. 3:5). **[2]** One of David's mighty men (2 Sam. 23:34).

Elias (e-lī′as). Greek form of Elijah (q.v.).

Eliasaph (e-lī′a-saf; *God has added*). **[1]** 1450 B.C. Head of the tribe of Gad (Num. 1:14; 2:14; 7:42, 47). **[2]** 1450 B.C. A prince of Gershon (Num. 3:24).

Eliashib (e-lī′a-shib; *God restores*). **[1]** 1000 B.C. A priest in the time of David (1 Chron. 24:12). **[2]** A descendant of David (1 Chron. 3:24). **[3]** 475 B.C. The high priest in Nehemiah's time (Neh. 3:1, 20–21). **[4]** 475 B.C. One who assisted Ezra in resolving the matter of the foreign wives (Ezra 10:6; Neh. 12:10); possibly the same as **[3]**. **[5]**, **[6]**, **[7]** 450 B.C. Three men who married foreign wives during the Exile (Ezra 10:24, 27, 36).

Eliathah (e-li'a-tha; *God is come*). 1000 B.C. One appointed for the song service in the Temple during David's reign (1 Chron. 25:4, 27).

Elidad (e-lī'dad; *God is a friend*). 1400 B.C. A chief of the tribe of Benjamin (Num. 34:21).

Eliehoenai (el-i-hō-ē'nī). A form of Elioenai **[3]** and Elihoenai.

Eliel (ē'li-el; *God is God*). **[1]** Head of a family of the tribe of Manasseh (1 Chron. 5:24). **[2]** A descendant of Benjamin (1 Chron. 8:20). **[3]** Another descendant of Benjamin in Chronicles (1 Chron. 8:22). **[4]** 1000 B.C. A captain of David's army (1 Chron. 11:46). **[5]** 1000 B.C. One of David's mighty men (1 Chron. 11:47). **[6]** 1000 B.C. One who joined David at Ziklag (1 Chron. 12:11); perhaps the same as **[4]** or **[5]**. **[7]** 1000 B.C. A chief of Judah (1 Chron. 15:9); perhaps **[4]**. **[8]** 1000 B.C. A chief Levite whom David commissioned to bring the ark of the convenant to the temple (1 Chron. 15:11). **[9]** 725 B.C. The Levite overseer of the dedicated things of the temple under Hezekiah (2 Chron. 31:13). **[10]** *See* Eliab **[4]**.

Elienai (el-i-ē'nī; *unto God are my eyes*). A son of Shimei of the tribe of Benjamin (1 Chron. 8:20).

Eliezer (el-i-ē'zer; *God is helper*). **[1]** 2100 B.C. Abraham's chief servant (Gen. 15:2). **[2]** 1825 B.C. A descendant of Benjamin (1 Chron. 7:8). **[3]** 1450 B.C. The second son of Moses and Zipporah (Exod. 18:4; 1 Chron.

23:15, 17). **[4]** 1000 B.C. A priest who assisted with bringing the ark of the covenant to the temple (1 Chron. 15:24). **[5]** 1000 B.C. A prince of Reuben in the time of David (1 Chron. 27:16). **[6]** 850 B.C. A prophet who rebuked Jehoshaphat (2 Chron. 20:37). **[7]** 450 B.C. A leader who induced others to return to Jerusalem (Ezra 8:16). **[8]**, **[9]**, **[10]** 450 B.C. Three men who took foreign wives during the Exile (Ezra 10:18, 23, 31). **[11]** An ancestor of Christ (Luke 3:29). *Also see* Eleazar.

Elihoenai (el-i-ho-ē´nī; *to Jehovah are my eyes*). Ancestor of some returned exiles (Ezra 8:4).

Elihoreph (el-i-hō´ref; *God of harvest grain*). 950 B.C. A son of Shisha and scribe of Solomon (1 Kings 4:3).

Elihu (e-lī´hū; *He is my God*). **[1]** The youngest "friend" of Job (Job 32:2, 4–6). **[2]** *See* Eliab [3]. **[3]** *See* Eliab [4]. **[4]** 1000 B.C. One who joined David at Ziklag (1 Chron. 12:20). **[5]** 1000 B.C. A porter at the tabernacle at the time of David (1 Chron. 26:7).

Elijah [Eliah; Elias] (e-li´ja [e-lī´a; e-lī´as]; *Jehovah is my God*). **[1]** 875 B.C. A great prophet of God; he strenuously opposed idolatry and was caught up in a chariot of fire at death (1 Kings 17:1—2 Kings 2:11; Matt. 17:3). **[2]** A chief of the tribe of Benjamin (1 Chron. 8:27). **[3]** 450 B.C. One who married a foreign wife during the Exile (Ezra 10:26). **[4]** 450 B.C. Another who took a foreign wife during the Exile (Ezra 10:21).

Elika (e-lī´ka; *God has rejected*). 1000 B.C. One of David's warriors (2 Sam. 23:25).

Elim (ē´lim; *large trees*). The second resting place of the Israelites after they crossed the Red Sea (Exod. 15:27; 16:1); probably the modern oasis of Wadi Gharandel, located 101 km. (63 mi.) from Suez.

Elimelech (e-lim'e-lek; *my God is King*). 1100 B.C. The husband of Naomi and father-in-law of Ruth. He died in Moab (Ruth 1:2–3; 2:1, 3; 4:3, 9).

Elioenai (e-li-o-ē'nī; *to Jehovah are my eyes*). [1] 1825 B.C. A chief of Benjamin (1 Chron. 7:8). [2] A chief of the tribe of Simeon (1 Chron. 4:36). [3], [4] 450 B.C. Two men who had married foreign wives during the Exile (Ezra 10:22, 27). [5] 450 B.C. A priest in the days of Nehemiah (Neh. 12:41); possibly the same as [3]. [6] A descendant of David (1 Chron. 3:23–24). [7] A doorkeeper of the temple (1 Chron. 26:3). [8] *See* Elihoenai.

Eliphal (e-lī'fal; *God is judge*). 1000 B.C. One of David's mighty men (1 Chron. 11:35).

Eliphalet [Eliphelet; Elpalet] (e-lif'a-let [e-lif'e-let; el-pā'let]; *God is deliverance*). [1] 1000 B.C. One of David's mighty men (2 Sam. 23:34). [2] 975 B.C. The last of David's thirteen sons (2 Sam. 5:16; 1 Chron. 3:8; 14:7). [3] 975 B.C. Another of David's sons (1 Chron. 3:6); called Elpalet in First Chronicles 14:5. [4] A descendant of Benjamin and Saul (1 Chron. 8:39). [5] 450 B.C. One who came back to Jerusalem with Ezra (Ezra 8:13). [6] 450 B.C. One who took a foreign wife during the Exile (Ezra 10:33).

Eliphaz (el'i-faz; *God is victorious*). [1] The leader of Job's three "friends" who confronted him (Job 2:11; 4:1; 15:1). [2] 1925 B.C. A son of Esau (Gen. 36:4, 10–12; 1 Chron. 1:35–36).

Elipheleh (e-lif'e-le; *whom God makes distinguished*). 1000 B.C. A Levite set over the choral service of the temple when the ark of the covenant was returned (1 Chron. 15:18, 21).

Eliphelehu. A form of Elipheleh.

Eliphelet (e-lif′e-let). *See* Eliphalet.

Eliseus (el-i-sē′us). Greek form of Elisha (q.v.).

Elisha [Eliseus] (e-lī′sha [el-i-sē′us]; *God is Savior*). **[1]** 850 B.C. The disciple and successor of Elijah; he held the prophetic office for 55 years (1 Kings 19:16–17s, 19; 2 King 2–6; Luke 4:27).

Elishah (e-lī′sha; *God is Savior*). Eldest son of Javan and grandson of Noah (Gen. 10:4). Possibly the people of Cyprus or the inhabitants of Alasiya, a country near Cilicia. Others suggest it includes the Italians and Peloponnesians.

Elishama (e-lish′a-ma; *God is hearer*). **[1]** 1450 B.C. Grandfather of Joshua (Num. 1:10; 2:18; 1 Chron. 7:26). **[2]** A descendant of Judah (1 Chron. 2:41). **[3]** 975 B.C. A son of King David (2 Sam. 5:16; 1 Chron. 3:8). **[4]** 975 B.C. Another son of David (1 Chron. 3:6); also called Elishua in Second Samuel 5:15 and First Chronicles 14:5. **[5]** 875 B.C. A priest sent by Jehoshaphat to teach the Law (2 Chron. 17:8). **[6]** 600 B.C. One of the "royal seed" and grandfather of Gedaliah (2 Kings 25:25; Jer. 41:1). **[7]** 600 B.C. A scribe or secretary of Jehoiakim (Jer. 36:12, 20–21).

Elishaphat (e-lish′a-fat; *God is judge*). 850 B.C. One of the captains of hundreds commissioned by Jehoiada to overthrow Athaliah in favor of Joash. (2 Chron. 23:1).

Elisheba (e-lish′e-ba; *my God is fullness*). 1450 B.C. The wife of Aaron and mother of Nadab, Abihu, Eleazar, and Ithamar (Exod. 6:23).

Elishua (e-līsh-u-a; *God is salvation*). 975 B.C. A son of David born at Jerusalem (2 Sam. 5:15; 1 Chron. 14:5). *See* Elishama [4].

Eliud (e-lī′ud; *God is majestic*). A son of Achim and the father of Eleazer; an ancestor of Jesus (Matt. 1:14–15).

Elizabeth (e-liz′a-beth; *God is my oath*). 5 B.C. The wife of Zacharias and mother of John the Baptist (Luke 1:5–57).

Elizaphan [Elzaphan] (e-liz′a-fan [el′za-fan]; *God has concealed*). [1] 1450 B.C. A chief of the family of Kohath (Num. 3:30; 1 Chron. 15:8); he is also called Elizaphan (Exod. 6:22; Lev. 10:4). [2] 1400 B.C. A prince of the tribe of Zebulun and son of Parnach (Num. 34:25).

Elizur (e-lī′zur; *God is a rock*). 1450 B.C. A chief of the tribe of Reuben who assisted Moses in taking the census (Num. 1:5; 2:10; 7:30, 35).

Elkanah [Elkonah] (el-kā′na [el-kō′na]; *God has possessed*). [1] Grandson of Korah (Exod. 6:24; 1 Chron. 6:23). [2] 1100 B.C. Father of the prophet Samuel and a descendant of [1] (1 Sam. 1:1–23; 2:11, 20). [3] A descendant of Levi (1 Chron. 6:25, 36). [4] A descendant of Levi (1 Chron. 6:26, 35); perhaps the same as [3]. [5] A Levite ancestor of Berechiah (1 Chron. 9:16). [6] 1000 B.C. One who joined David at Ziklag (1 Chron. 12:6). [7] 1000 B.C. A doorkeeper of the ark of the covenant (1 Chron. 15:23); perhaps the same as [6]. [8] 750 B.C. An officer of King Ahaz (2 Chron. 28:7).

Elkosh (el′kosh). The birthplace of Nathan the prophet (Nah. 1:1).

Ellasar (el-lā′sar). A country of Mesopotamia, possibly the same as Larsa (Gen. 14:1, 9); present-day Senkereh.

Elmodam [Elmadam] (el-mō′dam [el-mā′-dam]). The son of Er and an ancestor of Christ (Luke 3:28).

Elnaam (el-nā′am; *God is pleasant*). 1025 B.C. The father of two of David's warriors (1 Chron. 11:46).

Elnathan (el-nā′than; *God has given*). [1] 600 B.C. Leader of the delegation sent to bring Uriah out of Egypt (Jer. 26:22). (2 Kings 24:8; Jer. 26:22). [2], [3], [4] 450 B.C. Three Levites in the time of Ezra (Ezra 8:16).

Elon (ē′lon; *oak*). [1] 1950 B.C. Father of a wife of Esau (Gen. 26:34; 36:2). [2] 1850 B.C. A son of Zebulun (Gen. 46:14; Num. 26:26). [3] 1100 B.C. A judge of Israel for ten years (Judg. 12:11–12).

Elon (ē′lon; *oak*). A city assigned to the tribe of Dan (Josh. 19:43); its exact location is unknown.

Elon Beth Hanan (ē′lon beth hā′nan; *oak of Hanon*). One of three towns of the tribe of Dan that formed a district of King Solomon (1 Kings 4:9).

Eloth (ē′loth). *See* Elath.

Elpaal (el-pā′al; *God is working*). A descendant of Benjamin (1 Chron. 8:11–12).

Elpelet [Elpalet; Eliphalet] (el-pē′let [el-pā′let; e-lif′a-let]; *God is deliverance*). One of David's sons (1 Chron. 14:5). *See* Eliphalet [3].

Eltekeh (el′te-keh; *meeting place*). A town of the tribe of Dan assigned to the Levites (Josh. 19:40, 44; 21:20, 23); probably modern Khirbet elMukanna, located about 10 km. (6 mi.) south-southeast of Akir (Ekron).

Eltekon (el′te-kon; *founded by God*). A village in the hill country of Judah (Josh. 15:59); probably modern Khirbet el-Deir, located about 6 km. (4 mi.) west of Beersheba.

Eltolad (el-tō′lad). A town about 21 km. (13 mi.) southeast of Beersheba in southern Judah; appointed to the tribe of Simeon (Josh. 19:4) in First Chronicles 4:29 the city is simply called Tolad.

Eluzai (e-lū´zā-ī; *God is my strength*). 1000 B.C. One who joined David at Ziklag (1 Chron. 12:5).

Elymas (el´i-mas). A.D. 50. A false prophet who opposed Saul and Barnabas at Paphos (Acts 13:8); he was also called Bar-Jesus (v. 6).

Elzabad (el´za-bad; *God is endowing*). [1] 1000 B.C. One who joined David at Ziklag (1 Chron. 12:12). [2] 975 B.C. A descendant of Levi (1 Chron. 26:7).

Elzaphan (el´za-fan). *See* Elizaphan.

Emek Keziz (eh´meck keh´zēz; *valley cut off*). A city of the tribe of Benjamin near Jericho and Beth Hoglah (Josh. 18:21; Valley of Keziz, KJV).

Emmaus (e-mā´us; *warm wells*). A settlement about 16 km. (10 mi.) west of Jerusalem (Luke 24:13); its exact location is unknown.

Emmor (em´mor). Greek form of Hamor (q.v.).

En Dor (en´dor; *fountain of habitation*). A town of the tribe of Manasseh where Saul consulted a witch about his future (Josh. 17:11); probably modern Indur on the northeastern shoulder of the Little Hermon Mountain, 10 km. (6 mi.) southeast of Nazareth.

En Eglaim (eneg´la-im *fountain of two calves*). A place on the northwestern coast of the Dead Sea. (Ezek. 47:10).

En Gannim (en gan´im; *fountain of gardens*). [1] A town of lowland Judah (Josh. 15:20, 34). [2] A border town of the tribe of Issachar, about 11 km. (7 mi.) southwest of Mount Gilboa (Josh. 19:21); sometimes called Anem (1 Chron. 6:73). Its modern name is Jenin.

En Gedi (en gē´dī; *fountain of a kid*). A town on the western shore of the Dead Sea assigned to the tribe of Judah; originally called Hazazon Tamar (Josh. 15:62; 2 Chron. 20:2).

En Haddah (en had´a; *flowing strongly*). A village of the tribe of Issachar, located about 10 km. (6 mi.) east of Mount Tabor (Josh. 19:21).

En Hakkore (en hak'o-re; *well of the one who called*). A spring at Lehi, which God brought forth as an answer to Samson's prayer (Judg. 15:18–19).

En hazor (en hā'zor; *fountain of an enclosure*). A fortified city of the tribe of Naphtali (Josh. 19:37). It has been identified with modern Khirbet Hasireh, near the ruins of Hazyter.

En Mishpat (en mish'pat; *fountain of judgment*). *See also* Kadesh Barnea.

En Rimmon (en'rim'on; *spring of the pomegranate*). A city of Judah, south of Jerusalem, where the tribe of Judah settled on their return from the Babylonian Captivity (Neh. 11:29). Usually identified with Khirbet Umm er-Ramamin, northeast of Beersheba.

En Rogel (en rō'gel; *fuller's fountain*). A spring outside the city of Jerusalem near the Hinnom Valley (2 Sam. 17:17).

En Shemesh (en she'mesh; *spring of the sun*). A well and town east of Bethany on the road between Jerusalem and Jericho (Josh. 15:1, 7).

En Tappuah (en tap'u-a; *apple spring*). A town on the border of Ephraim (Josh. 17:7–8).

Enam (ē'nam; *double fountains*). A village of lowland Judah near Jarmuth (Josh. 15:20, 34).

Enan (ē'nan; *fountains*). 1475 B.C.Father of a prince of Naphtali (Num. 1:15; 2:29).

Enoch [Henoch] (ē'nuk [hē'nuk]; *initiated* or *dedicated*). **[1]** The eldest son of Cain (Gen. 4:17–18). **[2]** A son of Jared and an ancestor of Christ (Gen. 5:18–19, 21; 1 Chron. 1:3; Luke 3:37; Heb. 11:5).

Enoch (ē'nuk; *initiated*). A city built by Cain (Gen. 4:17).

Enos [Enosh] (ē'nos [ē'nosh] *man, mankind*). Son of Seth and ancestor of Christ (Gen. 4:26; 5:6–11; 1 Chron. 1:1; Luke 3:38).

Enosh (ē'nosh). *See* Enos.

Epaenetus (e-pē'ne-tus; *praiseworthy*). A.D. 55. A Christian at Rome to whom Paul sent greetings (Rom. 16:5).

Epaphras (ep'a-fras; shortened form of *Epaphroditus—charming*). A.D. 60. A Christian worker with Paul who served as missionary to Colossae (Col. 1:7; 4:12; Philem. 23).

Epaphroditus (e-paf-ro-dī'tus; *charming*). A.D. 60. A Philippian Christian who worked so strenuously that he lost his health (Phil. 2:25; 4:18).

Ephah (ē'fa; *obscurity*). [1] A concubine of Caleb (1 Chron. 2:46). [2] A descendant of Judah (1 Chron. 2:47). [3] A grandson of Abraham (Gen. 25:4; 1 Chron. 1:33).

Ephai (ē'fa; *birdlike*). 625 B.C. One whose children were left in Judah after the Exile (Jer. 40:8).

Epher (ē'fer; *gazelle*). [1] 1975 B.C. A grandson of Abraham and son of Midian (Gen. 25:4; 1 Chron. 1:33). [2] One of the descendants of Judah (1 Chron. 4:17). [3] 750 B.C. A chief of the tribe of Manasseh east of the Jordan River (1 Chron. 5:24).

Ephes Dammim [Pasdammim] (ē'fes dam'im [pas'-dam'im]; *boundary of blood*). A Philistine settlement near Socoh, apportioned to the tribe of Judah (1 Sam. 17:1). It is called Pas-dammim ("portion of blood") in First Chronicles 11:13.

Ephesus (ef'e-sus). A town on the western coast of Asia

Minor between Miletus and Smyrna; an important trading center (Acts 19:1).

Ephlal (ef'lal; *judging*). A descendant of Perez through Jerahmeel (1 Chron. 2:37).

Ephod (ē-fod; *oracular*). Father of Hanniel of the tribe of Manasseh (Num. 34:23).

Ephraim (e'fra-im; *doubly fruitful*). 1850 B.C. The second son of Joseph by Asenath. Although Ephraim was the younger of the two sons of Joseph, he received the firstborn's blessing. He was an ancestor of one of the twelve tribes of Israel (Gen. 41:52; 46:20; 48; 50:23).

Ephraim (e'fra-im; *double grainland*). [1] The territory allotted to the tribe of Ephraim in the Promised Land (Num. 1:33). [2] A city near Baal-hazor, probably the same as "Ephraim near the Wilderness" (2 Sam. 13:23; John 11:54). It is identified with modern et-Taiyibeh, about 6 km. (4 mi.) northeast of Bethel. [3] A gate on the north wall of old Jerusalem (2 Kings 14:13; 2 Chron. 25:23). [4] A rough area (not forest) where Absalom was slain (2 Sam. 18:6). [5] Mountains west of the Jordan River, extending as far south as Ramah and Bethel (1 Sam. 1:1; 2 Chron. 13:4), allotted to the tribe of Ephraim.

Ephrain e'fra-in). A city that Abijah took from Jeroboam (2 Chron. 13:19); probably another name for Ephraim [2].

Ephratah [Ephrath] (ef'ra-ta [ef'rath]; *fertility*). The second wife of Caleb (1 Chron. 2:19, 50; 4:4).

Ephratah (ef'ra-ta). *See* Bethlehem [1].

Ephrath (ef'rath). *See* Bethlehem [1].

Ephron (ē'fron; *dust*). 2025 B.C. A Hittite from whom Abraham bought a field with a cave, which became Sarah's burial place (Gen. 23:8, 10, 13–14; 49:30).

Ephron (ē'fron; *dust*). A ridge of mountains between Nephtoah and Kirjath-jearim on the boundary between Judah and Benjamin (Josh. 15:1, 9).

Er (ur; *watcher*). [1] 1875 B.C. Eldest son of Judah, slain by God (Gen. 38:3, 6–7; 1 Chron. 2:3). [2] A son of Shelah (1 Chron. 4:21). [3] An ancestor of Jesus (Luke 3:28).

Eran (ē'ran; *watcher; watchful*). The son of Ephraim's oldest son (Num. 26:36).

Erastus (e-ras'tus; *beloved*). [1] A.D. 55. Christian sent with Timothy into Macedonia while Paul stayed in Asia (Acts 19:22). [2] A.D. 55. An important person in Corinth sending greetings to Rome (Rom. 16:23). [3] A.D. 65. One who remained at Corinth (2 Tim. 4:20). Perhaps some or all of the above are identical.

Erech (ē'rek). A city built by Nimrod on the Plain of Shinar, south of Babylon (Gen. 10:10).

Eri (ē'ri; *watcher*). 1875 B.C. A son of Gad (Gen. 46:16: Num. 26:16).

Esaias (e-zā'yas). Greek form of Isaiah (q.v.).

Esarhaddon (e-sar-had'on). 680–669 B.C. The son of Sennacherib and a powerful king of Assyria (2 Kings 19:37; Ezra 4:2; Isa. 37:38).

Esau (ē'so). 1950 B.C. Eldest son of Isaac and twin brother of Jacob. He is the progenitor of the tribe of Edom (Gen. 25:25). He sold his birthright to Jacob (Gen. 25:26–34; 27; 36).

Esau's Wives: There are two lists of Esau's wives—Genesis 26:34; 28:9 list them in this fashion: [1] Judith, the daughter of Beeri the Hittite. [2] Basemath, daughter of Elon the Hittite and [3] Mahalath, the daughter of Ishmael, Abraham's son. The other list in Genesis 36:2–3 runs thus: [1] Aholibamah, the daughter of Anah the daughter of Zibbeon. **[2]** Adah, the daughter of Elon the Hittite and **[3]** Basemath, the daughter of Ishmael. Some scholars suppose we are dealing with six women, but this seems unlikely. In the ancient world, many women received new names at marriage and this fact would account for the different names. Thus, [1] Judith is Aholibamah, [2] Basemath is Adah, and [3] Mahalath is Basemath. As far as Judith is concerned, Beeri might be her father and Anah her mother; or perhaps Anah is another name of Beeri. Some even think Beeri ("man of the springs") is a nickname rather than a proper name.

Esek (ē'sek; *strife*). A well dug by Isaac in the Valley of Gerar; claimed by the Philistines (Gen. 26:20).

Esh Baal (esh'ba-al; *man of Baal*). Altered to a curse. *See* Ishbosheth.

Eshban (esh'ban). 1925 B.C. Son of Dishon (Gen. 36:26; 1 Chron. 1:41).

Eshcol (esh'kol; *a cluster of grapes*). 2100 B.C. The brother of Mamre and Aner who helped Abraham defeat Chedorlaomer (Gen. 14:13–24).

Eshcol (esh'kol; *cluster of grapes*). A valley north of Hebron, famous for its grapes (Num. 13:24).

Eshean (esh'e-an [ē'shan]; *support*). A mountain village near Dumah, about 16 km. (10 mi.) from Hebron; apportioned to the tribe of Judah (Josh. 15:52).

Eshek (ē'shek; *oppressor*). A descendant of King Saul (1 Chron. 8:39).

Eshtaol (esh'ta-ol). A settlement in the hills of Judah about 21 km. (13 mi.) west of Jerusalem; burial place of Samson (Josh. 15:33; Judg. 13:25).

Eshtemoa (esh-te-mō'a; *listening post*). A Maacathite, a son of Ishbah (1 Chron. 4:17). **[2]** A descendant of Caleb who was of the tribe of Judah (1 Chron. 4:17).

Eshtemoa [Eshtemoh] (esh-te-mō′a [esh-te-mō]; *listening post*). A village in the hill country of Judah about 14 km. (9 mi.) south of Hebron, famed for its prophetic oracle (Josh. 15:20, 50).

Eshton (esh′ton). A descendant of Judah through Caleb (1 Chron. 4:11–12).

Esli (es′lī). An ancestor of Christ (Luke 3:25).

Esrom (ez′rom). Greek form of Hezron (q.v.).

Esther (es′ter; *star*). 475 B.C. The Persian name of Hadassah, who was chosen by Ahasuerus to be his queen. The Book of Esther tells her story.

Etam (ē′tam; *place of birds of prey*). A name occurring in Judah's genealogy list (1 Chron. 4:3). It may be a place name.

Etam ē′tam; *place of birds of prey*). **[1]** A town of the tribe of Simeon (1 Chron. 4:32); identified with modern 'Aitun, about 18 km. (11 mi.) west-southwest of Hebron. **[2]** A cleft of rock near Zorah (Judg. 15:8, 11). **[3]** A resort town near Jerusalem, used by King Solomon (2 Chron. 11:6); Josephus wrote that it was located about 11 km. (7 mi.) from Jerusalem.

Etham (ē′tham; *fortress*). A place where the Israelites camped before they entered the wilderness of Sinai (Exod. 13:20; Num. 33:6); apparently it was located north of Timsah Lake.

Ethan (ē′than; *long-lived*). **[1]** A wise man in the days of Solomon (1 Kings 4:31; Psa. 89 title). **[2]** A descendant of Judah (1 Chron. 2:6, 8). He is possibly identical with **[1]**. **[3]** *See* Jeduthun. **[4]** 1000 B.C. A descendant of Levi (1 Chron. 6:42).

Ethbaal (eth'ba-al; *with him is Baal*). 875 B.C. King of-Sidon and father of Ahab's wife Jezebel (1 Kings 16:31).

Ether (ē'ther; *plenty*). **[1]** A village of the tribe of Judah located within 3 km. (2 mi.) of modern Beit-Jibrin (Josh. 15:42). **[2]** A village of the tribe of Simeon (Josh. 19:7), sometimes called Tochen (1 Chron. 4:32). This is probably modern Khirbet 'Attic, 25 km. (15.5 mi.) northeast of Beersheba.

Ethiopia (e-thi-ō'pi-a; *burnt face*). A nation located in the upper region of the Nile River (Psa. 68:31; Isa. 18:1). It is not the same as modern Ethiopia. *See also* Cush.

Eth Kazin [Ittah Kazin] (eth kā'zin [it'a kā'zin]). A town on the eastern border of Zebulun (Josh. 19:13).

Ethnan (eth'nan; *gift*). Grandson of Ashur through Caleb, son of Hur (1 Chron. 4:7).

Ethni (eth'ni; *gift*). One whom David set over the song service of the temple (1 Chron. 6:41).

Eubulus (u-bū'lus; *of good counsel*). A.D. 65. One of the Roman Christians that remained loyal to Paul (2 Tim. 4:21).

Eunice (u-nī'se; *good victory*). A.D. 30. The pious mother of Timothy (2 Tim. 1:5; cf. Acts 16:1).

Euodia [Euodias] (u-ō'di-a [u-ō'di-a]; *good journey*). A.D. 60. A Christian woman at Philippi (Phil. 4:2).

Euphrates (u-frā'tēz). A major river of western Asia, which begins in Armenia and joins the Tigris River before flowing into the Persian Gulf. It formed the western boundary of Mesopotamia (Gen. 2:14; 15:18).

Eutychus (u'ti-kus; *fortunate*). A.D. 55. A young man at Troas whom Paul restored to life (Acts 20:6–12).

Eve (ēv) *life-giving*). The first woman, Adam's wife (Gen. 3:20; 4:1; 2 Chron. 11:3).

Evi (ē′vī; *desire*). 1400 B.C. One of the five kings of Midian slain by Israel (Num. 31:8; Josh. 13:21).

Evil-merodach (ē′vil-me-rō′dak; Babylonian, Arvil-Marduk—*the man of* [the god] *Marduk*). 562–560 B.C. The king of Babylon who released Jehoiachin from imprisonment. He succeeded his father, Nebuchadnezzar (2 Kings 25: 27–30; Jer. 52:31).

Ezar (ē′zar). *See* Ezer [6].

Ezbai (ez′bā-ī; *shining*). 1000 B.C. The father of one of David's mighty men (1 Chron. 11:37).

Ezbon (ez′bon). [1] 1875 B.C. A son of Gad (Gen. 46:16), called Ozni (*Jehovah hears*) in Numbers 26:16. [2] 1825 B.C. A descendant of Benjamin (1 Chron. 7:7).

Ezekias (ez-e-kī′as). Greek form of Hezekiah (q.v.).

Ezekiel (e-zēk′yel; *God strengthens*). 575 B.C. A prophet of a priestly family carried captive to Babylon. He prophesied to the exiles in Mesopotamia by the river Chevar, and is the author of the book bearing his name (Ezek. 1:3; 24:24).

Ezel (ē′zel; *division*). A craggy hiding place of David during his rebellion against Saul (1 Sam. 20:19).

Ezem [Azem] (ē′zem [ā′zem]; *mighty*). A village about 5 km. (3 mi.) south of Beersheba, near the border of Edom (Josh. 15:29).

Ezer (ē′zer; [God is a] *help*). [1] 1975 B.C. a son of Seir (Gen. 36:21, 27, 30; 1 Chron. 1:42); he is also called Ezar (1 Chron. 1:38). *See* Abiezer; Romamti-ezer. [2] 1800 B.C. A son of Ephraim slain by the inhabitants of Gath (1 Chron. 7:21). [3] A descendant of Judah through Caleb (1 Chron. 4:4); perhaps the same as Ezra [2]. [4] 1000 B.C. A valiant man who joined David at Ziklag (1 Chron. 12:9). [5] 450 B.C. A Levite who

assisted in repairing the wall of Jerusalem (Neh. 3:19).
[6] 450 B.C. A priest in Nehemiah's time (Neh.
12:42).

Ezion Geber [Ezion Gaber] (ē′zi-on gē′ber [ē′zi-on
gā′ber]; *backbone of a man*). A village west of the port of
Elath on the Gulf of Aqaba (Num. 33:35).

Eznite (ez′nite). A nickname given to Josheb-Basshebeth
the Tachmonite, a chief of David's mighty men (2 Sam.
23:8).

Ezra (ez′ra; *God is a help*). **[1]** Head of one of the courses
of priests that returned from the Exile (Neh. 12:1).
The full form of his name, *Azariah,* occurs in Nehemiah 10:2. **[2]** A descendant of Judah through Caleb (1 Chron. 4:17). *See* Ezer [3]. **[3]** 450 B.C. A
prominent scribe and priest descended for Hilkiah
the high priest (Ezra 7:1–12; 10:1; Neh. 8:1–13). *See*
Azariah.

Ezri (ez′rī; *God is my help*). 1975 B.C. One of David's su-
perintendents of farm workers (1 Chron. 27:26).

F

Fair Havens. An anchorage on the southern coast of the
island of Crete, near Lasea (Acts 27:8).

Felix (fē′lix; *happy*). A.D. 60. Roman governor of Judea
that presided over the trial of Paul at Caesarea (Acts
23:23–27; 24:22–27).

Festus Porcius (fes′tus-pōr′shē-us). A.D. 60. Successor
of Felix to the governorship of Judea. He continued the
trial of Paul begun under Felix (Acts 25:26).

Field of Sharp Swords. The site of a bloody battle between Israel and Judah, located near the pool of Gibeon (2 Sam. 2:16).

Fortunatus (for-tu-na′tus *fortunate*). A.D. 55. A Corinthian Christian who cheered and comforted Paul at Ephesus (1 Cor. 16:17–18).

Fuller's Field. A place outside the walls of Jerusalem where launderers washed and dried clothes (2 Kings 18:17; Isa. 36:2).

G

Gaal (gā′al; *rejection*). 1125 B.C. A Son of Ebed. He tried to lead a rebellion against Abimelech (Judg. 9:26–41).

Gaash (gā′ash; *trembling*). A hill in the territory of Ephraim, just south of Timnath Serah; the burial place of Joshua (Josh. 24:30).

Gaba (gā′ba). *See* Geba.

Gabbai (gab′a-ī; *taxgatherer*). 450 B.C. A chief of the tribe of Benjamin after the return from the Exile (Neh. 11:8).

Gabbatha (gab′a-tha; *elevated place*). An open space at the front of Herod's temple in Jerusalem, where Pontius Pilate sat to judge Jesus Christ (John 19:13).

Gabriel (gā′brē-el; *God is great*). The archangel who brings messages from God to Daniel (Dan. 8:16), Zacharias (Luke 1:19), and the Virgin Mary (Luke 1:26–38).

Gad (gad; *fortune*). [1] 1875 B.C. The seventh son of Jacob and an ancestor of one of the twelve tribes (Gen. 30:11; 49:19). [2] 1000 B.C. David's seer who frequently advised him (1 Sam. 22:5; 1 Chron. 21:9–19). [3] A pagan god (Isa. 65:11).

Gad (gad; *lot; fortune*). The territory settled by the tribe of Gad, east of the Jordan River (1 Sam. 13:7; Josh. 13:24).

Gadara (gad'a-ra; *walls*). A town located east of the Jordan River, 11 km. (7 mi.) south of the Sea of Galilee (Mark 5:1; Luke 8:26). It was one of the Decapolis cities (q.v.).

Gaddi (gad'ī; *my fortune*). 1450 B.C. One of those sent to spy out Canaan (Num. 13:11).

Gaddiel (gad'i-el; *God is my fortune*). 1450 B.C. One of the spies (Num. 13:10).

Gadi (gā'dī; *my fortune*). 775 B.C. Father of King Menahem of Israel (2 Kings 15:14, 17).

Gaham (gā'ham; *burning brightly*). 2050 B.C. A son of Nahor (Gen. 22:24).

Gahar (gā'har; *concealment*). One whose family returned from captivity (Ezra 2:47; Neh. 7:49).

Gaius (gā'yus). [1] A.D. 50. A convert whom Paul baptized at Corinth (1 Cor. 1:14); some think he is identical with [2]. [2] A.D. 55. The host to Paul when he wrote to the Romans (Rom. 16:23). [3] A.D. 55. A man of Derbe who accompanied Paul as far as Asia (Acts 20:4). [4] A.D. 55. A native of Macedonia and a companion of Paul (Acts 19:29). [5] A.D. 90. One to whom John's third epistle is addressed (3 John 1).

Galal (ga'lal; *rolling*). [1] 450 B.C. A returned exile (1 Chron. 9:15). [2] A Levite who returned from the Exile (1 Chron. 9:16; Neh. 11:17).

Galatia (ga-lā'shi-a). A district of central Asia Minor (Acts 16:6).

Galeed (gal′e-ed; *heap of witness*). A pile of stones erected by Jacob and Laban as a sign of their covenant of peace and to mark the boundary between their lands.

Galilee (gal′i-lē; *circle*). One of the largest Roman districts of Palestine; the primary region of Jesus' ministry (Luke 3:1; 23:6).

Galilee, Sea of. A large lake in northern Palestine, fed by the Jordan River; several of Jesus' disciples worked as fishermen on this lake (John 6:1). The lake was also known as the Sea of Chinnereth (q.v.), the Sea of Tiberias, and the Sea of Gennesaret (q.v.). *See also* Chinnereth [1] and Gennesaret [2].

Gallim (gal′im; *heaps*). A village near Gibeah of Saul (Isa. 10:29–30; 1 Sam. 25:44); probably modern Kirbet Kakul.

Gallio (gal′i-ō). A.D. 50. Roman proconsul of Achaia before whom Paul was tried in Corinth (Acts 18:12–17).

Gamaliel (ga-mā′li-el; *God is my recompense*). [1] 1450 B.C. A prince of the tribe of Manasseh (Num. 1:10; 2:20). [2] A.D. 35. A great Jewish teacher of the Law. He persuaded his fellow Jews to let the apostles go free (Acts 5:33–40; 22:3).

Gammad (gam′mad). A city mentioned in the Book of Ezekiel, where warriors who manned the towers of Tyre are referred to as the "men of Gammad" (Ezek. 27:11). May be the same as Kumidi in northern Syria.

Gamul (gā′mul; *weaned*). 1000 B.C. A chief priest (1 Chron. 24:17).

Gareb (ga′reb; *reviler; despiser*). 1000 B.C. One of David's mighty men (2 Sam. 23:38 1 Chron. 11:40).

Gareb (ga′reb; *reviler, despiser*). A hill in the vicinity of Jerusalem (Jer. 31:39).

Gashmu (gash'mu). *See* Geshem.

Gatam (gā'tam; *burnt valley*). 1875 B.C. An Edomite chief, grandosn of Esau (Gen. 36:11; 16: 1 Chron. 1:36).

Gath (gath; *wine press*). One of the five chief Philistine cities; home of the giant Goliath (1 Sam. 17:4; 2 Kings 12:17; 2 Chron. 26:6). Its exact location is not known.

Gath Hepher [Gittah-hepher] (gath hē'fer [git-a-hē'fer]; *wine press of the well*). A city of the tribe of Zebulun, located about 5 km. (3 mi.) northeast of Nazareth; home of the prophet Jonah (Josh. 19:13; 2 Kings 14:25).

Gath Rimmon (gath rim'on; *pomegranate press*). [1] A city of the tribe of Dan assigned to the Levites; it probably was located on the Plain of Joppa (Josh. 19:45; 1 Chron. 6:69). [2] A town of the tribe of Manasseh, assigned to the Levites (Josh. 21:25); probably the same as Bileam.

Gaza (gā'za; *stronghold*). [1] The southernmost of the five chief Philistine cities, located 72 km. (44.5 mi.) south of modern Jaffa and 4 km. (2.4 mi.) from the Mediterranean Sea. It was the scene of Samson's exploits (Josh. 11:22; Judg. 16:1–3; 2 Kings 18:8; Jer. 25:20).

Gazez (gā'zez; *sheep shearer*). [1] A son of Caleb (1 Chron. 2:46). [2] A grandson of Caleb (1 Chron. 2:46).

Gazzam (gāz'am; *bird of prey*). One whose descendants returned (Ezra 2:48; Neh. 7:51).

Geba (gē'ba; *mountain*). A Benjamite city in the extreme northern portion of Judah, about 10 km. (6 mi.) north-northeast of Jerusalem (Josh. 18:24); modern Jeba'.

G

THROUGH THE GATES

Cities in biblical times were bounded by protective walls. Set in these were any number of gates, massive wooden doors through which traffic passed. Often reinforced with brass or iron for greater security, these gates were opened during the day to allow the city's citizens to come and go. But they were generally closed at night as a safety measure. In the event of attack, the gates were closed and barred to keep out the enemy.

Goods were often bought and sold and important legal matters were discussed just inside the city gate (Ruth 4:11). Because of their central location, gates were often spoken of in the Bible as symbols of power and authority. God promised Abraham that his descendants would possess the gates of their enemies (Gen. 22:17).

Gates of Jerusalem and the Temple: The Bible mentions numerous gates by specific names. But keeping these names straight is complicated by the fact that as the walls of Jerusalem expanded to incorporate new areas, or were destroyed and rebuilt, different names were used for the same gate (or gate site). Unless the Bible gives a clear indication, as in the case of "the Beautiful Gate of the Temple" (Acts 3:10), it is difficult to distinguish between gates of the Temple and gates of the city wall.

Exactly how many gates the city of Jerusalem had is unknown. The number of gates probably varied from century to century. In John's vision of the New Jerusalem, the holy city had 12 gates—three gates on each of its four sides (east, north, south, and west). Each of these gates was inscribed with the name of one of the 12 tribes of Israel (Rev. 21:12–13). John's portrayal of the New Jerusalem seems to be based on the prophecy of Ezekiel (Ezekiel 48). The gates described in the Book of Revelation may not correspond to the number of gates of the Old Jerusalem.

As various modern versions of the Bible are compared, more than a dozen of the gates of Jerusalem are given different names by the different translations. A list of the gates of Jerusalem and the Temple follows:

Beautiful Gate (Acts 3:10)
Benjamin's Gate (Jer. 38:7; Zech. 14:10)

Corner Gate (2 Kin. 14:13; 2 Chr. 25:23; 26:9; Jer. 31:38;
   Zech. 14:10)
East Gate (1 Chr. 26:14; 2 Chr. 31:14)
Ephraim, Gate of (2 Kin. 14:13; 2 Chr. 25:23; Neh. 8:16;
   12:39)
First Gate (Zech. 14:10; Former Gate, RSV, NEB)
Fish Gate (2 Chr. 33:14; Neh. 3:3; 12:39; Zeph. 1:10)
Foundation, Gate of the (2 Chr. 23:5)
Fountain Gate (Neh. 3:15; 12:37)
Horse Gate (2 Chr. 23:15; Neh. 3:28; Jer. 31:40)
Joshua, Gate of (2 Kin. 23:8)
King's Gate (1 Chr. 9:18)
Middle Gate (Jer. 39:3)
Miphkad Gate (Neh. 3:31; Inspection Gate, NIV, NASB;
   Muster(ing) Gate, RSV, NEB)
New Gate (Jer. 36:10)
North Gate (1 Chr. 26:14)
Old Gate (Neh. 3:6; 12:39; Jeshanah Gate, NIV, NEB)
Potsherd Gate (Jer. 19:2)
Prison, Gate of the (Neh. 12:39; Gate of the Guard (house)
   RSV, NIV, NASB)
Refuse Gate (Neh. 2:13; 3:13–14; 12:31; Dung Gate, RSV,
   NIV, NEB, KJV)
Shallecheth Gate (1 Chr. 26:16; Shalleketh Gate, NIV)
Sheep Gate (Neh. 3:1, 32; 12:39; John 5:2; Sheep Market,
   KJV; Sheep-Pool, NEB)
South Gate (1 Chr. 26:15)
Upper Gate (2 Kin. 15:35; 2 Chr. 23:20; 27:3; High(er)
   Gate, KJV)
Valley Gate (2 Chr. 26:9; Neh. 2:13, 15; 3:13)
Water Gate (Neh. 3:26; 8:1, 3, 16; 12:37)
West Gate (1 Chr. 26:16).

G

Gebal (gē′bal; *mountain*). **[1]** A Phoenician seaport 68
km. (42 mi.) north of Sidon; also called Byblos (Ezek.
27:9). **[2]** The northern portion of the mountains of
Edom (Psa. 83:7).
Geber (gē′ber; *strong one*). **[1]** The father of one of Sol-

omon's officers (1 Kings 4:13). **[2]** 950 B.C. One of Solomon's commissaries (1 Kings 4:19).

Gebim (gē′bim; *ditches*). A settlement just north of Jerusalem near Michmash (Isa. 10:31).

Gedaliah (ged-a-lī′a; *Jehovah is great*). **[1]** 1000 B.C. A Levite musician (1 Chron. 25:3, 9). **[2]** Grandfather of the prophet Zephaniah (Zeph. 1:1). **[3]** 600 B.C. A chief of Jerusalem that imprisoned Jeremiah (Jer. 20:1–6). **[4]** Reigned 587 B.C. Governor of Jerusalem after the Exile (2 Kings 25:22; Jer. 40:5–6). **[5]** 450 B.C. A priest who had married a foreign wife during the Exile (Ezra 10:18).

Gedeon (ged′e-on). Greek form of Gideon (q.v.).

Geder (gē′der; *fence*). A town in the extreme southern portion of Judah, captured by Joshua (Josh. 12:13); perhaps the same as modern Beth Gador or Gedor.

Gederah (ge-de′ra; *sheepfold*). A town in the lowlands of Judah, 6 km. (4 mi.) northwest of Zorah (Josh. 15:36); modern Jedireh.

Gederoth (ged′e-roth; *sheepfolds*). A town in the lowlands of Judah, about 6 km. (4 mi.) southwest of Ekron (Josh. 15:41); modern Katrah.

Gederothaim (ged′e-ro-thā′im; *two sheepfolds*). A town of Judah (Josh. 15:36), perhaps the same as Gederoth.

Gedor (gē′dor; *wall*) **[1]** A descendant of Judah (1 Chron. 4:18). **[2]** A descendant of Judah (1 Chron. 4:4). **[3]** 1075 B.C. An ancestor of Saul (1 Chron. 8:31).

Gedor (gē′dor; *wall*). **[1]** A town in the hills of Judah about 11 km. (7 mi.) northwest of Hebron (Josh. 15:58). **[2]** A town of the tribe of Simeon, near the southwestern limits of Palestine (1 Chron. 4:39). **[3]** A village in the territory of Benjamin (1 Chron. 12:7); modern Khirbet el-Judeira.

Ge-harashim (gi-har′a-shim; *valley of craftsmen*). A valley in Judah (1 Chron. 4:14) in which Benjamites settled following the Babylonian Captivity (Neh. 11:35).

Gehazi (ge-hā′zī; *valley of vision*). 850 B.C. The dishonest servant of Elisha (2 Kings 4:12–37; 5:20–27; 8:4).

Geliloth (gel′i-lōth; *circles*). A landmark on the southern boundary of Benjamin (Josh. 18:17).

Gemalli (ge-mal′i; *camel owner*). 1475 B.C. Father of Ammiel (Num. 13:12).

Gemariah (gem-a-rī′a; *Jehovah has accomplished*). [1] 600 B.C. One who sought to stop Jehoiakim from burning Jeremiah's prophecies (Jer. 36:10–12, 25). [2] 600 B.C. One of Zedekiah's ambassadors to Babylon (Jer. 29:3).

Gennesaret (ge-nes′a-ret; *garden of riches*). [1] The region on the northwest shore of the Sea of Galilee (Matt. 14:34). [2] Another name for the Sea of Galilee (Luke 5:1). [3] A town on the west shore of the Lake of Gennesaret (Josh. 19:35). Commonly called Chinnereth.

Genubath (ge-nū′bath). 925 B.C. A son of Hadad the Edomite (1 Kings 11:20).

Gera (gē′ra; *sojourner, pilgrim*). [1] 1850 B.C. A son of Benjamin (Gen. 46:21). [2] 1825 B.C. A son of Bela (1 Chron. 8:3, 5, 7). [3] 1350 B.C. Father of Ehud (Judg. 3:15). [4] 1000 B.C. Father or ancestor of Shimei (2 Sam. 16:5; 19:16, 18; 1 Kings 2:8). [Note: All of these may be identical.]

Gerar (gē′rar; *halting place*). A Philistine city on the southern edge of Palestine, near Gaza (Gen. 26:1; 2 Chron. 14:13); its exact location is unknown.

Gerasa [Gadarenes; Gerasenes] (gur′ge-sa). A town or district which would have been located on the eastern side of the Lake of Galilee. Its location is not certain, but some have suggested modern-day Kersa (Matt. 8:28).

Some scholars have questioned the reliability of the Gospel accounts of the healing of the demoniac, for Matthew says that it occurred in Gerasa while Mark 5:1 and Luke 8:26 says that it occurred in Gadara. However, this really is no problem for Gadara was a strong city and probably had economic and political influence over the entire area.

Gerizim (ger'i-zīm). A steep mountain in central Palestine facing Mount Ebal (Deut. 11:29); its peak is 872 m. (2,840 ft.) above sea level.

Gershom (gur-shom; *sojourner*). [1] 1450 B.C. Firstborn son of Moses and Zipporah (Exod. 2:22; 18:3). [2] *See* Gershon. [3] Father of Jonathan, a Levite during the time of the judges (Judg. 18:30). [4] 450 B.C. A descendant of Phinehas (Ezra 8:2).

Gershon [Gershom] (gur'shun [gur'shom]; *exile*). 1875 B.C. An important priest, the eldest son of Levi (Gen. 46:11; Exod. 6:16; 1 Chron. 6:1). He is also called Gershom (1 Chron. 6:16–17, 20; 15:7).

Geshan (gē'shan). A descendant of Caleb (1 Chron. 2:47).

Geshem [Gashmu] (gē'shem [gash'mu]; *rain*). 450 B.C. An Arabian opponent of Nehemiah (Neh. 2:19; 6:1–2).

Geshur (gē'shur; *bridge*). An Aramean kingdom just east of Maacah, between Mount Hermon and the district of Bashan. Absalom sought refuge here after he killed his half-brother Amnon (2 Sam. 3:3; 13:37).

Gether (gē'ther; *fear*). [1] A descendant of Shem (1 Chron. 1:17). Possibly an unknown family of Arameans is meant. [2] The third of Aram's sons (Gen. 10:23).

Gethsemane (geth-sem'a-nē; *olive press*). A garden east of

Jerusalem, beyond the brook Kidron at the foot of Mount Olivet; the site of Christ's betrayal (Matt. 26:36–56).

Geuel (ge-ū′el; *majesty of God*). 1450 B.C. The spy sent out from Gad to bring back word about Canaan (Num. 13:15).

Gezer [Gazer] (gez′er [gā′zer]; *portion, division*). A Canaanite town beside the Mediterranean Sea near Lachish and Lower Beth Horon; a battleground in King David's wars (2 Sam. 5:25; 1 Chron. 14:16).

Giah (gī′ah; *bubbling spring*). A settlement between Gibeon and a ford across the Jordan River (2 Sam. 2:24).

Gibbar (gib′ar; *mighty man*). One who returned to Jerusalem with Zerubbabel (Ezra 2:20).

Gibbethon (gib′e-thon; *height*). A village of the tribe of Dan where Nadab was assassinated (Josh. 19:44; 1 Kings 15:27); probably modern Tell el-Milat, directly east of Ekron.

Gibea (gib′e-a; *hill*). A descendant of Caleb (1 Chron. 2:49).

Gibeah Gibeath (gib′e-a [gib′e-ath]; *hill*). **[1]** A Judean town about 16 km. (10 mi.) northwest of Hebron (Josh. 15:57). **[2]** A town midway between Jerusalem and Ramah; home and capital of King Saul (1 Sam. 10:26; 15:34). The town is called Gibeath in Joshua 18:28. **[3]** A town or hill in the territory of Ephraim (Josh. 24:33); probably near Timnah [1]. **[4]** A hill in Kiriath Jearim on which was located the house of Abinadad (2 Sam. 6:3–4).

Gibeon (gib′e-on; *pertaining to a hill*). The chief city of the Hivites, assigned to the tribe of Benjamin; located 9 km. (5.5 mi.) north-northwest of Jerusalem (Josh. 11:19; 2 Sam. 20:1–9). Its modern name is El-Jib.

Giddalti (gi-dal′tī; *I have magnified God*). 1000 B.C. A son of Heman in charge of one of the courses at the temple (1 Chron. 25:4).

Giddel (gid′el; *magnified*). [1] 950 B.C. Head of a family of Solomon's servants (Ezra 2:56; Neh. 7:58). [2] One whose descendants returned to Jerusalem with Zerubbabel (Ezra 2:47; Neh. 7:49).

Gideon [Gedeon] (gid′e-on [ged′e-on]; *warrior*). Ruled 1169–1129 B.C. The great judge of Israel who delivered his people from Midian (Judg. 6—8); he was given the name Jerubbaal (q.v.).

Gideoni (gid-e-ō′ni; *feller*). 1450 B.C. A descendant of Benjamin (Num. 1:11; 2:22).

Gidom (gī′dom; *desolation*). A village of the tribe of Benjamin, located between Gibeah [1] and Rimmon [2] (Judg. 20:45).

Gihon (gī′hon; *stream*). [1] One of the four rivers of Eden [1] (Gen. 2:13). [2] An intermittent spring outside the walls of Jerusalem, south of the temple area (1 Kings 1:38–45; 2 Chron. 32:30).

Gilalai (gil′a-lī; *weighty*). 450 B.C. One of a party of priests who played on David's instruments at the consecration of the Jerusalem walls under Ezra (Neh. 12:36).

Gilboa (gil-bō′a; perhaps *bubbling fountain*). A mountain overlooking the Plain of Jezreel; site of King Saul's death (1 Sam. 28:4; 31:1); modern Jebel Fuku'a.

Gilead (gil′e-ad; *mound of stones*). [1] 1825 B.C. A son of Machir (Num. 26:29–30). [2] 1125 B.C. Father of Jephthah the judge (Judg. 11:1–2). [3] A descendant of Gad (1 Chron. 5:14).

Gilead (gil′e-ad; *mound of stones*). A region east of the Jordan River, stretching from Moab to the Yarmuk River (Deut. 3:16–17). [2] A mountain jutting onto the Plain of Jezreel (Judg. 7:3). **[3]** A city in the region of Gilead (Hos. 6:8).

Gilgal (gil´gal; *circle of stones*). **[1]** The first campsite of the Israelites after they crossed the Jordan River into Canaan, probably near Jericho (Josh. 4:19–24). **[2]** A village 11 km. (7 mi.) northeast of Bethel, from which Elijah and Elisha began their journey (2 Kings 2:1–4; 4:38); present-day Jiljilia. **[3]** A town on the edge of the Plain of Sharon, about 8 km. (5 mi.) north-northeast of Antipatris (Josh. 10:6–9, 15).

Giloh (gī´lo; *circle*). A town in the hill country of Judah, 8 km. (5 mi.) north-northwest of Hebron (Josh. 15:51).

Gimzo (gim´zo; *sycamores*). A town of northern Judah, about 5 km. (3 mi.) southeast of Lydda (2 Chron. 28:18); modern Jimzu.

Ginath (gī´nath). 900 B.C. Father of Tibni (1 Kings 16:21–22).

Ginnetho [Ginnethon] (gin´e-tho [gin´e-thon]; *gardener*). 450 B.C. A prince or priest who sealed the new covenant with God after the Exile (Neh. 10:6; 12:4, 16).

Ginnethon (gin´e-thon). *See* Ginnetho.

Gishpa (gis´pa; *attentive*). 450 B.C. An overseer of the Nethinim (Temple servants) (Neh. 11:21).

Gittah Hepher (git´a hē´fer) *See* Gath Hepher.

Gittaim (git´a-im; *two winepresses*). A Benjamite town of refuge near Beeroth (Neh. 11:33); probably the site of modern el-Ramleh.

Goath [Goah] (gō´ath; [gō´ah]). A site near Jerusalem (Jer. 31:39); its exact location is unknown.

Gob (gob; *cistern*). A site of several battles during Israel's wars with the Philistines (2 Sam. 21:18); its exact location is unknown, but may be the same as Gezer or Gath.

Gog (gog; *golden ornament*). **[1]** A descendant of Joel, of the tribe of Reuben (1 Chron. 5:4). **[2]** A prince of Rosh, Meshech, and Tubal (Ezek. 38:2; 39:1, 11). In Revelation 20:7 Gog appears to have become a nation as is Magog, thus indicating the name is to be understood symbolically. *See also* Magog.

Golan (gō'lan; *circle*). A city of Bashan east of the Jordan River, assigned to the Levites as a city of refuge (Deut. 4:43; Josh. 21:27). It is probably the site of modern Sam el-Jaulan, 27 km. (17 mi.) east of the Sea of Galilee.

Golgotha [Calvary] (gol'go-tha; *place of a skull*). A hill just outside the walls of ancient Jerusalem; the site of Jesus' crucifixion (Matt. 27:33; John 19:17). Its exact location is unknown, but it was probably inside the walls of what is now called the "old city."

Goliath (go-lī'ath; *soothsayer*). **[1]** 1025 B.C. The Philistine giant who was slain by David (1 Sam. 17:4–54). **[2]** 1000 B.C. Another giant, possibly the son of [1] (2 Sam. 21:19).

Gomer (gō'mer; *complete*). **[1]** Eldest son of Japheth (Gen. 10:2–3; 1 Chron. 1:5–6). Possibly a people inhabiting the north, probably including or identical with the Cimmerians of classical history. **[2]** 750 B.C. The immoral wife of Hosea (Hos. 1:3; 3:1–4).

Gomorrah (go-mor'ra; *submersion*). One of the five Cities of the Plain destroyed along with Sodom (Gen. 18:20; 19:24, 28). Many scholars believe it was submerged by the southeastern tip of the Dead Sea.

Goshen (gō'shen; *mound of earth*). **[1]** A cattle-raising district of the Nile delta assigned to the Israelites before they were placed in bondage (Gen. 46:28). **[2]** A town in the hill country of Judah (Josh. 15:51); probably modern Dahariyeh, about 21 km. (13 mi.) southwest of Hebron. **[3]** A region of Judah that probably derived its name from the town of Goshen (Josh. 10:41; 11:16).

Gozan (gō′zan; *quarry*). A district and town of Mesopotamia, located on the Habor River (2 Kings 17:6; 18:11). The KJV and NKJV refer to it as a river, but the river is actually the Habor, and Gozan is the area through which it flows.

Greece [Grecia] (grēs [grē′shi-a]). A country of Southern Europe between Italy and Asia Minor; one of the most powerful nations of the ancient world (Dan. 8:21; Zech. 9:13; Acts 16:1).

Gudgodah (gud-gō′da; *incision*). A place where the Israelites camped in the wilderness, near Ezion Geber (Deut. 10:7); also called Hor Hagidgad (q.v.).

Guni (gū′nī; *protected*). **[1]** 1850 B.C. Son of Naphtali found in three lists (Gen. 46:24; Num. 26:48; 1 Chron. 7:13). **[2]** Father of Abdiel (1 Chron. 5:15).

Gur, Ascent to (gur; *lion's cub*). A hill near Ibleam where Jehu killed Ahaziah (2 Kings 9:27).

Gur Baal (gur bā′al; *dwelling place of Baal*). A desert district south of Beersheba between Canaan and the Arabian peninsula (2 Chron. 26:7).

H

Haahashtari (hā-a-hash′ta-ri; *courier*). A son of Ashur listed in the descendants of Judah (1 Chron. 4:6).

Habaiah (ha-ba′ya; *Jehovah has hidden*). Ancestor of a priestly family (Ezra 2:61; Neh. 7:63).

Habakkuk (ha-bak´uk; *embraced by God*). 600 B.C. A prophet during the reigns of Jehoiakim and Josiah (Hab. 1:1; 3:1).

Habazziniah [Habaziniah] (hab-az-zin-ī´a [hab-a-zi-nī´a]). 650 B.C. The grandfather of Jaazaniah, the founder of a Jewish sect (Jer. 35:3).

Habor (hā´bor). A tributary of the Euphrates River (2 Kings 17:6; 18:11); probably the Khabur River.

Hacaliah [Hachaliah] (hak-a-lī´a [hak-a-lī´a]; *Jehovah is hidden*). 475 B.C. The father of Nehemiah, the governor of Israel (Neh. 1:1).

Hachilah (ha-kī´la; *gloomy*). A hill in the wilderness southeast of Hebron, near Maon (1 Sam. 26:1–3).

Hachmoni [Hacmoni] (hak´mo-nī [hak´mo-nī] *wise*). Father of Jehiel, the royal tutor (1 Chron. 27:32).

Hadad [Hadar] (hā´dad [hā´dar]; *thunderer*). **[1]** One of the twelve sons of Ishmael and grandson of Abraham (1 Chron. 1:30). He is called Hadar, due to a copyist's mistake or a dialectal variant in Genesis 25:15. **[2]** A king of Edom who fought Midian (Gen. 36:35–36; 1 Chron. 1:46). **[3]** The last of Edom's early kings (1 Chron. 1:50–51). Due to a copyist's mistake or dialectal variant he is called Hadar in Genesis 36:39. **[4]** 950 B.C. A member of the royal family of Edom who opposed Israel's rule of Edom (1 Kings 11:14–22, 25). **[5]** An ancient god of storms.

Hadadezer [Hadarezer] (ha-dad-ē´zer [ha-da-rē´zer]; [the god] *Hadad is my help*). The king of Zobah in Syria that warred against David and Joab (2 Sam. 8:3–12). His name is also written Hadarezer; perhaps this is a dialectal variant (2 Sam. 10:16; 1 Chron. 18:3–10).

Hadad Rimmon (ha-dad rim´on; compound of two divine names: Hadad and Rimmon). The KJV takes this as a reference to a place in the Valley of Jezreel, near Megiddo (Zech. 12:11). Many believe, however, the reference is to the lamentation for a divinity analogous to the weeping for Tammuz (Ezek. 8:14).

Hadar (hā'dar). *See* Hadad [1], [3].

Hadarezer (ha-da-rē'zer). *See* Hadadezer.

Hadashah (had'-a-sha; *new*). A village in the lowlands of Judah about 5 km. (3 mi.) from Beth Horon (Josh. 15:37); perhaps modern Khirbet el-Judeideh.

Hadassah (ha-das'sa; *myrtle*). The Hebrew name of Esther (q.v.).

Hadattah [Hazor-hadattah] (ha-dat'a [ha'zor-ha-dah'ta]; *new Hazor*). A town in southern Judah (Josh. 15:25).

Hades (hād'ēz). *See* Hell.

Hadid (hā-did; *sharp*). A Benjamite town located 5 km. (3 mi.) east-northeast of Lydda (Ezra 2:33; Neh. 11:34).

Hadlai (had'lī; *fat*). 775 B.C. The father of Amasa, a chief man of the tribe of Ephraim (2 Chron. 28:12).

Hadoram (ha-dō'ram; *Hadad is exalted*). [1] The son of Joktan, a descendant of Noah (Gen. 10:27; 1 Chron. 1:21). Possibly the name denotes an Arabian tribe. [2] 975 B.C. The son of Tou, the king of Hamath; he bore presents to David (1 Chron. 18:10). He is called Joram, in Second Samuel 8:9–10, perhaps as a token to honor David's God (i.e., Joram means *Jehovah is high*). [3] The superintendent of forced labor under David, Solomon, and Rehoboam. He is variously called Adoniram (*my lord is exalted*), and Adoram, a contraction of the former (2 Sam. 20:24; 1 Kings 4:6; 12:18; 2 Chron. 10:18). *See also* Jehoram.

Hadrach (hā-drak). A Syrian country associated with Hamath and Damascus, encompassing an area along the Orontes River south of Hamath (Zech. 9:1).

Hagab (hā'gab; *locust*). An ancestor of captives returning with Zerubbabel (Ezra 2:46). *See* Hagaba.

Hagaba [Hagabah] (hag'a-ba [hag'a-ba]; *locust*). An ancestor of some of the captives returning with Zerubbabel (Ezra 2:45; Neh. 7:48). *See* Hagab.

Hagabah (hag'a-ba). *See* Hagaba.

Hagar [Agar] (hā'gar [ā'gar]; *flight*). 2075 B.C. An Egyptian servant of Sarah; she became the mother of Ishmael by Abraham (Gen. 16:1–16; 21:14–17).

Haggai (hag'gā-ī; *festive*). 525 B.C. The first of the prophets who prophesied after the Babylonian Captivity (Ezra 5:1; Hag. 1:1, 3, 12).

Haggeri (hag'ge-ri). A form of Hagri.

Haggi (hag'i; *born on a feast day*). 1875 B.C. The second son of Gad (Gen. 46:16; Num. 26:15).

Haggiah (hag-gī'a; *festival*). A descendant of Levi (1 Chron. 6:30).

Haggith (hag'gith; *festival*). 1000 B.C. The fifth wife of David and mother of Adonijah (2 Sam. 3:4; 1 Kings 1:5, 11).

Hakkatan (hak'a-tan; *the little one*). 475 B.C. The father of Johanan, who returned with Ezra (Ezra 8:12).

Hakkoz (hak'oz; perhaps *the thorn*). 1000 B.C. A priest and chief of the seventh course of service in the sanctuary (1 Chron. 24:10). *See* Koz [1].

Hakupha (ha-kū'fa; *crooked*). Ancestor of a family returning from captivity (Ezra 2:51; Neh. 7:53).

Halah (hā'la). A portion of the Assyrian kingdom, encompassing the basin of the Habor and Saorkas Rivers (2 Kings 17:6; 1 Chron. 5:26).

Halak (hā'lak; *bald mountain*). A mountain in southern

Palestine (Josh. 11:17; 12:7); possibly present-day Jebel Halaq, just north-northeast of Abdeh.

Halhul (hal′hul). A Judean village located about 6 km. (4 mi. north of Hebron (Josh. 15:58); said to be the burial place of Jonah.

Hali (hā′lī; *ornament*). A town of Judah, located near the border of Asher (Josh. 19:25).

Hallohesh [Halohesh] (ha-lō′hesh [ha-lō′hesh]; *the whisperer*). **[1]** 475 B.C. The father of one who repaired the wall (Neh. 3:12). **[2]** A man or family that sealed the new covenant with God after the Exile (Neh. 10:24); some identify him with **[1]**.

Halohesh (ha-lō′hesh). *See* Hallohesh.

Ham (ham; *hot*). The youngest son of Noah. Because of his wickedness, his son Canaan was cursed (Gen. 5:32; 9:22–27).

Ham (ham; *hot*). **[1]** A name for Egypt used only in poetry (Psa. 78:51). **[2]** A place between Ashteroth Karnaim in Bashan and the Moabite country (Gen. 14:5). Possibly modern Ham about 5 mi. south of Irbid in the 'Ajlūn district.

Haman (hā′man). 475 B.C. The prime minister of Ahasuerus who plotted against the Jews (Esther 3—9).

Hamath (hā′math; *fortress*). **[1]** A Hittite city on the Orontes River about 200 km. (125 mi.) north of Damascus; a supply base for Solomon's armies (2 Chron. 8:4). **[2]** The ideal northern boundary of Israel (Num. 13:21; 34:8).

Hamath Zobah (hā′moth zō′ba). A city captured by Solomon (2 Chron. 8:3).

Hammath [Hamath] (ham′eth [ham′eth]; *hot spring*). Father of the house of Rechab (1 Chron. 2:55).

Hammath (hām′ath; *hot spring*). A city on Naphtali alaloted to the Levites (Josh. 19:35). It is probably identical with Hammon (1 Chron. 6:76) and Hammoth dor (Josh. 21:32).

Hammedatha (ham-e-dā'tha; *given by the moon*). 500 B.C. The father of Haman the Agagite (Esther 3:1).

Hammelech (ham'e-lek). The father of Jerahmeel and Malchiah. This is probably not a proper name. It is a general title that means "the king" (Jer. 36:26; 38:6).

Hammolecheth (ha-mol'e-keth). A form of Hammoleketh.

Hammoleketh (ha-mol'e-keth; *she who reigns*). An ancestor of Gideon. It may be a proper name or title (1 Chron. 7:18).

Hammon (ham'on; *hot spring*). [1] A frontier village of the tribe of Asher, assigned to the Levites, located about 16 km. (10 mi.) south of Tyre (Josh. 19:28). [2] *See* Hammath.

Hammoth Dor (ham'moth dōr; *warm springs of Dor*). *See* Hammath.

Hamonah (ham'o-na; *multitude*). Symbolic name of the city where Gog is to be defeated (Ezek. 39:16).

Hamon Gog (hā'mon gog; *multitude of Gog*). The valley where Gog and his armies will be defeated in their final struggle against God's people (Ezek. 39:11–15).

Hamor [Emmor] (hā'mor [em'mor]; *donkey*). 1925 B.C. The prince of Shechem whose son Shechem brought destruction on himself and his family (Gen. 33:19; 34:2–26).

Hamran (ham'ran). *See* Hemdan.

Hamuel [Hammuel] (ha-mū'el [ham-mū'el]; *God protects*). A descendant of Simeon (1 Chron. 4:26).

Hamul (hā-mul; *spared by God*). 1850 B.C. The younger son of Perez (Gen. 46:12; 1 Chron. 2:5).

Hamutal (ha-mū′tal; *father-in-law is protection*). 650 B.C. One of King Josiah's wives (2 Kings 23:31; 24:18; Jer. 52:1).

Hanameel [Hanamel] (ha-nam′e-el [ha-nam′el]; *God is gracious*). A cousin of Jeremiah's who sold him a field (Jer. 32:6–9).

Hanan (hā′nan; *merciful*). **[1]** A descendant of Benjamin (1 Chron. 8:23). **[2]** 1000 B.C. One of David's heroes (1 Chron. 11:43). **[3]** A descendant of Benjamin through Saul (1 Chron. 8:38; 9:44). **[4]** A returned captive (Ezra 2:46; Neh. 7:49). **[5]** 625 B.C. A temple officer whose sons had a chamber in the temple (Jer. 35:4). [Note: This name should not be confused with Baal Hanan.] **[6]** 450 B.C. A Levite who assisted Ezra when reading the Law (Neh. 8:7). **[7]** 450 B.C. A Levite who sealed the covenant with Nehemiah (Neh. 10:10; 13:13). Perhaps identify with [6]. **[8]** 450 B.C. A chief or family who also sealed the covenant (Neh. 10:26). **[9]** A chief or family who sealed the covenant with Nehemiah (Neh. 10:22).

Hananel [Hanamel] (ha-nan′e-el [ha-na′nel]; *God is merciful*). A tower of Jerusalem, located near the Sheep's Gate (Jer. 31:38; Zech. 14:10).

Hanani (ha-nā′nī; *gracious gift of the Lord*). **[1]** 975 B.C. A musician and head of one of the courses of the temple services (1 Chron. 25:4, 25). **[2]** 900 B.C. The father of the prophet Jehu; cast into prison by Asa (1 Kings 16:1, 7; 2 Chron. 16:7–10). **[3]** 450 B.C. A priest who married a foreign wife (Ezra 10:20). **[4]** 450 B.C. A brother of Nehemiah and a governor of Jerusalem under him (Neh. 1:2; 7:2). **[5]** 450 B.C. A priest and musician who helpled to purify the walls of Jerusalem (Neh. 12:36).

Hananiah (han-a-nī'a; *Jehovah is gracious*). **[1]** A descendant of Benjamin (1 Chron. 8:24). **[2]** 975 B.C. The leader of the sixteenth division of David's musicians (1 Chron 25:4, 23). **[3]** 775 B.C. An officer of Uzziah (2 Chron. 26:11). **[4]** 650 B.C. The grandfather of Irijah (Jer. 37:13). **[5]** 600 B.C. The father of a prince under Jehoiakim (Jer. 36:12). **[6]** 600 B.C. A false prophet who opposed Jeremiah (Jer. 28). **[7]** 600 B.C. One of Daniel's friends at Babylon (Dan. 1:7, 11, 19). *See also* Shadrach. **[8]** 500 B.C. A son of Zerubbabel (1 Chron. 3:19, 21). **[9]** 500 B.C. A priest present at the dedication of the walls of Jerusalem (Neh. 12:12, 41). **[10]** 450 B.C. A Levite who married a foreign wife during the Exile (Ezra 10:28). **[11]** 450 B.C. A druggist and priest who helped to rebuild the wall of Jerusalem (Neh. 3:8). **[12]** 450 B.C. One who helped to rebuild the gate of Jerusalem (Neh. 3:30); perhaps the same as [11]. **[13]** 450 B.C. A faithful Israelite placed in charge of Jerusalem (Neh. 7:2). **[14]** 450 B.C. One who sealed the new covenant with God after the Exile (Neh. 10:23).

Hanes (ha'nez). An unidentified place in Egypt (Isa. 30:4).

Haniel [Hanniel] (han'i-el; *grace of God*). **[1]** 1400 B.C. A prince of the tribe of Manasseh (Num. 34:23). **[2]** A hero of Asher (1 Chron. 7:39).

Hannah (han'a; *gracious*). 1125 B.C. A prophetess, the mother of Samuel (1 Sam. 1).

Hannathon (han'a-thon; *dedicated to grace*). A town of the tribe of Zebulun located on a road between Megiddo and Accho (Josh. 19:14).

Hanniel (han'i-el). *See* Haniel.

Hanoch [Enoch, Henoch] (hā'nok [ē'nok, hē'nuk]; *dedicated*). **[1]** 1950 B.C. A grandson of Abraham (Gen.

25:4), called Henoch in First Chronicles 1:33. **[2]** 1900 B.C. The eldest son of Reuben, and founder of the Hanochite clan (Gen. 46:9; 1 Chron. 5:3).

Hanun (hā′nun; *gracious*). **[1]** 1000 B.C. A king of Ammon who involved the Amonites in a disastrous war with David (2 Sam. 10:1–6). **[2]** 450 B.C. One who repaired the wall (Neh. 3:30). **[3]** 450 B.C. One who repaired the valley gate of Jerusalem (Neh. 3:13).

Haphraim (haf-ra′yim; *two pits*). A frontier town assigned to the tribe of Issachar (Josh. 19:19). It may be modern Khirbet el-Farriyeh, about 10 km. (6 mi.) northwest of Megiddo; or it may be modern et Faryibeh, northwest of Bethshean.

Happizzez (hap′i-zēz; *scattering*). 1000 B.C. A descendant of Aaron. His family became the 18th of David's 24 divisions of priests.

Hara (ha′ra; *mountains*). A place in Assyria to which the Israelite captives were taken (1 Chron. 5:26); it may be the proper name of a settlement or the Hebrew term for *mountains of the Medes*.

Haradah (har′a-da; *fear*). A place where the Israelites camped during their wilderness wanderings (Num. 33:24); its exact location is unknown.

Haran (ha′ran). **[1]** 2100 B.C. A brother of Abraham who died before his father (Gen. 11:26–31). **[2]** A descendant of Levi (1 Chron. 23:9). **[3]** A son of Caleb (1 Chron. 2:46).

Haran [Charran] (ha′ran [kā ran]). A Mesopotamian city located 386 km. (240 mi.) northwest of Nineveh and 450 km. (280 mi.) north-northeast of Damascus (Gen. 11:31; 12:4–5).

Harbona [Harbonah] (har-bō′na; *donkey-driver*). 475 B.C. A chamberlain under Ahasuerus (Esther 1:10; 7:9).

Hareph (ha'ref; *autumn*). A son of Caleb (1 Chron. 2:51), not to be confused with Hariph (q.v.).

Hareth (ha'reth). A form of Hereth.

Harhaiah (har-hā'ya). 475 B.C. Father of Uzziel, a builder of the wall of Jerusalem (Neh. 3:8).

Harhas [Hasrah] (har'has [has'ra]; *splendor*). 657 B.C. Grandfather of Shallum, the husband of the prophetess Huldah (2 Kings 22:14). Another form of the name is Hasrah (2 Chron. 34:22).

Harhur (har'hur). Ancestor of returned captives (Neh. 7:53; Ezra 2:51).

Harim (hā'rim; *dedicated to God*). [1] 1000 B.C. A priest in charge of the third division of temple duties (1 Chron. 24:8; Ezra 2:39; 10:21; Neh. 3:11). [2] An ancestor of some returning from captivity (Ezra 2:32; Neh. 7:35). Harim's descendants took foreign wives during the Exile (Ezra 10:31). [3] One who sealed the new covenant with God after the Exile (Neh. 10:5). [4] 450 B.C. A family that sealed the new covenant with God after the Exile (Neh. 10:27).

Hariph (hā'rif; *autumn*). [1] An ancestor of returning captives (Neh. 7:24). [2] 450 B.C. Head of a family who sealed the new covenant with God after the Exile (Neh. 10:19). He is called Jorah in Ezra 2:18.

Harmon (har'mon). A place to which the people of Samaria were exiled, perhaps in the area of Rimmon (Amos 4:3).

Harnepher (har-nē'fer; *Horus is merciful*). A descendant of Asheer (1 Chron. 7:36).

Harod (hā'rod; *terror*). A spring (Judg. 7:1); commonly thought to be modern 'Ain Jalud on the northwest side of Mount Gilboa, about 1.5 km. (1 mi.) southeast of Jezreel.

Haroeh (har′o′e; *the seer*). A descendant of Judah (1 Chron. 2:52); perhaps Reaiah (1 Chron. 4:2).

Harosheth Hagoyim (ha-rō′sheth ha-goy′ēm; *forest of the Gentiles*). A small village on the northern bank of the Kishon River 26 km. (16 mi.) north-northwest of Megiddo (Judg. 4:2, 13).

Harsha (har′sha; *silent*). An ancestor of returning captives (Ezra 2:52; Neh. 7:54).

Harum (hā′rum; *exalted*). A descendant of Judah (1 Chron. 4:8).

Harumaph (ha-rū′maf; *mutilated nose*). 475 B.C. Father of Jedaiah the wall-builder (Neh. 3:10).

Haruz (hā′ruz; *gold*). 700 B.C. A man of Jotbah in Judah (2 Kings 21:19).

Hasadiah (has-a-dī′a; *Jehovah is faithful*). 425 B.C. A descendant of Jehoiakim (1 Chron. 3:20).

Hasenuah (has-e-nū′a). A form of Hassenuah.

Hashabiah (hash-a-bī′a; *Jehovah has taken account*). **[1]** A descendant of Levi (1 Chron. 6:45). **[2]** 975 B.C. A son of Jeduthun (1 Chron. 25:3). **[3]** 975 B.C. A descendant of Kohath (1 Chron. 26:30). **[4]** 975 B.C. A son of Kemuel who was a prince of the Levites (1 Chron. 27:17). **[5]** 625 B.C. A chief of a Levite clan (2 Chron. 35:9). **[6]** Another descendant of Levi (1 Chron. 9:14). **[7]** An attendant of the temple (Neh. 11:22). **[8]** 500 B.C. A priest in the days of Jeshua (Neh. 12:21). **[9]** 450 B.C. One who repaired the wall of Jerusalem (Neh. 3:17). **[10]** 450 B.C. One who sealed the covenant with Nehemiah (Neh. 10:11). **[11]** A Levite in charge of certain temple functions (Neh. 11:15). **[12]** 450 B.C. A Levite who returned with Ezra from Babylon (Ezra 8:19). **[13]** 450 B.C. A chief of the family of Kohath (Ezra 8:24). **[14]** 450 B.C. A chief Levite (Neh. 12:24). [Note: It is quite possible that [7], [9], [14] refer to the same person.]

Hashabnah (ha-shab'na; *Jehovah has considered*). 450 B.C. One who sealed the new covenant with God after the Exile (Neh. 10:15).

Hashabniah (ha-shab-nī'a; *Jehovah has considered*). [1] 475 B.C. Father of Hattush who helped to rebuild the wall of Jerusalem (Neh. 3:10). [2] 450 B.C. A Levite who officiated at the fast under Ezra and Nehemiah when the covenant was sealed (Neh. 9:5).

Hashbadana [Hashbaddana (hash-bad'a-na [hash-bad'-da-na]; *judge*). 450 B.C. An assistant to Ezra at the reading of the Law (Neh. 8:4).

Hashem (hā-shem; *shining*). 1000 B.C. Father of several of David's guards (1 Chron. 11:34).

Hashmonah (hash-mō'na; *fruitfulness*). A place where the Israelites camped in the wilderness (Num. 33:29–30); possibly modern Wadi el-Hashim.

Hashub [Hasshub (hā'shub [has'shub]; *considerate*). [1] 475 B.C. A Levite chief (1 Chron. 9:14; Neh. 11:15). [2] 450 B.C. A builder of the wall of Jerusalem (Neh. 3:11). [3] 450 B.C. One of the signers of the new covenant with God after the Exile (Neh. 10:23). [4] 450 B.C. One who repaired the wall of Jerusalem (Neh. 3:23).

Hashubah (ha-shū'ba; *Jehovah has considered*). 425 B.C. A descendant of Jehoiakim (1 Chron. 3:20).

Hashum (hā'shum; *broad-nosed*). [1] One whose descendants returned from the Babylonian Captivity (Ezra 2:19; 10:33; Neh. 7:22). [2] 450 B.C. One who sealed the covenant [3] A priest who helped Ezra at the reading of the Law (Neh. 8:4).

Hashupha (ha-shoo'fa). A form of Hasupha.

Hasrah (has'ra, *splendor*). 675 B.C. The grandfather of Shallum (2 Chron. 34:22). *See* Harhas.

Hassenaah (has-en-'āa; *thorny*). An ancestor of those who rebuilt the Fish Gate at Jerusalem (Neh. 3:3). The name is probably identical with the Senaah of Ezra 2:35 and Nehemiah 7:38, which most English translators have understood to have the Hebrew definite article (Ha-) prefixed.

Hassenuah (has-se-nū'a; *hated*). Father of Hodaviah (1 Chron. 9:7).

Hasshub (has'shub; *considerate*). [1] 475 B.C. The father of Shemaiah (1 Chron. 9:14). [2] 450 B.C. An Israelite who helped rebuild the wall of Jerusalem (Neh. 3:23). [3] 450 B.C. A head of a family who sealed the covenant after the Captivity (Neh. 10:23). *See* Hashub.

Hassophereth (hass'sō-fear'eth). A form of Sophereth.

Hasupha (ha-soo'fa; *swift*). 950 B.C. An ancestor of a family of Nethinim (Temple servants) who returned from the Captivity with Zerubbabel (Ezra 2:43).

Hatach [Hathach] (ha'tach [ha'thach]; *good*). 475 B.C. A chamberlain of Ahasuerus (Esther 4:5–10).

Hathath (hā'thath; *terror*). 350 B.C. Son of Othniel (1 Chron. 4:13).

Hatipha (ha-tī'fa; *taken; captive*). An ancestor of returning captives (Ezra 2:54; Neh. 7:56).

Hatita (hat'i-ta). A temple gatekeeper or porter whose descendants returned from the Babylonian Captivity (Ezra 2:42; Neh. 7:45).

Hattil (hat'il; *talkative*). 950 B.C. An ancestor of some who returned from the Babylonian Captivity (Ezra 2:57; Neh. 7:59).

Hattush (hat'ush; *contender*). [1] 525 B.C. A priest who returned frm the Exile with Zerubbabel (Neh. 12:2). [2]

450 B.C. Descendant of the kings of Judah, perhaps of Shechaniah (1 Chron. 3:22). [3] 450 B.C. A descendant of David who returned from the Exile with Ezra (Ezra 8:2). [4] 450 B.C. One who helped to rebuild the wall of Jerusalem (Neh. 3:10). [5] 450 B.C. A priest who signed the covenant (Neh. 10:1, 4). [Note: entries [1], [2], [3], and [5] may refer to the same person.]

Hauran (ha-oo-ran'; *black land*). A district bordering the region of Gilead south of Damascus, noted for the fertility of its soil (Ezek. 47:16, 18).

Havilah (hav'i-la; *district*). [1] Son of Cush (Gen. 10:7; 1 Chron. 1:9). Possibly an unknown tribe is intended. [2] A descendant of Shem in two genealogies (Gen. 10:29; 1 Chron. 1:23). Possibly a tribe of Arabians who inhabited central or south Arabia is meant.

Havilah (hav'i-la; *district*). A region of central Arabia populated by the descendants of Cush (Gen. 10:7; 1 Sam. 15:7; cf. Gen. 25:18). This term may have referred to the territory of the Arabian Desert for several hundred miles north of modern Al-Yamanah.

Havoth Jair (hā'voth jā'ir). An area in the northwest part of Bashan, containing several unwalled cities (Num. 32:41). The area is called Havoth jair in Deuteronomy 3:14.

Hazael (haz'a-el; *God has seen*). 850 B.C. The murderer of Ben-hadad II who usurped the throne of Syria (1 Kings 19:15, 17; 2 Kings 8:8–29).

Hazaiah (ha-zā'ya *Jehovah sees*). A descendant of Judah (Neh. 11:5).

Hazar Addar (hā'zar ad'ar). *See* Adar.

Hazar Enan (hā'zar ē'nan; *village of fountains*). A small village on the northern border of Palestine (Num. 34:9; Ezek. 48:1); probably modern Kiryatein.

Hazar Gaddah (hā′zar gad′a; *village of Gad*). A village on the southern border of Judah southwest of Ras Zuiveira (Josh. 15:27); possibly modern Khirbet Ghazza.

Hazar Hatticon [Hazer-hatticon] (hā′zar hat′i-kon; *middle village*). A village on the border of Havran (Ezek. 47:16).

Hazarmaveth (hā′zar-mā′veth). The third son of Joktan (Gen. 10:26; 1 Chron. 1:20). Possibly the name refers to a people who dwelt in the peninsula of Arabia.

Hazarmaveth (hā′zar-mā′veth). A very small district of Arabia in the southern portion of the Arabian Peninsula (Gen. 10:26).

Hazar Shual (hā′zar shū′al; *village of the jackal*). A town in southern Judah apportioned to the tribe of Simeon (Josh. 15:28; 19:3). Perhaps it is modern el-Watan, located between Beersheba and Tell es-Saba.

Hazar Susah [Hazar Susim] (hā′zar soo′za [hā′zar soo′-zim]; *village of horses*). A small village in the extreme south of the territory of Simeon (Josh. 19:5; 1 Chron. 4:31); it may be modern Susiyeh, located 3 km. (2 mi.) east of Eshtemoa.

Hazazon Tamar [Hazezon Tamar] (haz′a-zon tā′mar [haz′e-zon tā′mar]; *the palm tree*). Said to be another name for En-gedi (Gen. 14:7; 2 Chron. 20:2); this name may in fact refer to modern Tamar, about 32 km. (20 mi.) south-southeast of the Dead Sea on the road to Elath.

Hazelelponi [Hazzelelponi] (haz-e-lel-pō′nī [haz-e-lel-pō′nī]; *give shade*). A daughter of Etam in the genealogy of Judah (1 Chron. 4:3).

Hazeroth (ha-zē′roth; *villages*). A place where the Israelites camped in the wilderness (Num. 11:35); possibly modern Ain Hudra, about 58 km. (36 mi.) north-northeast of Mount Sinai.

Haziel (hā'zi-el; *God is seeing*). A descendant of Levi in the time of David (1 Chron. 23:9).

Hazo (hā'zō; *visionary*). 2075 B.C. A son of Nahor and nephew of Abraham (Gen. 22:22).

Hazor (hā' zor; *enclosure*). [1] The capital of the Canaanite kingdom, later included in the territory of Naphtali in northern Palestine (Josh. 11:1, 10, 13); site of a major archaeological excavation. [2] A place in extreme southern Judah (Josh. 15:23); possibly modern el-Jebariyeh. [3] Another city in southern Judah (Josh. 15:25). Hezron was a district or region of the city or another name for the city itself (v. 25). [4] A village of the tribe of Benjamin, to which the Jewish exiles returned (Neh. 11:33); modern Khirbet Hazzur, 6 km. (4 mi.) north-northwest of Jerusalem. [5] A region of the Arabian Desert east of Palestine (Jer. 49:28, 30, 33).

Heber [Eber] (hē'ber [e'ber]; *associate*). [1] 1850 B.C. A descendant of Asher (Gen. 46:17; 1 Chron. 7:31–32). [2] 1225 B.C. The husband of Jael, who killed Sisera (Judg. 4:11, 17, 21; 5:24). [3] Head of a clan of Judah (1 Chron. 4:18). [4] A descendant of Benjamin (1 Chron. 8:17). [5] Head of a family of Gad (1 Chron. 5:13). [6] A descendant of Benjamin (1 Chron. 8:22).

Hebrews (hē'brews). An ethnic term referring to the lineage of the Jewish people. Abraham (q.v.) was the first person in the Bible to be called a Hebrew (Gen. 14:13). His descendants through Isaac and Jacob were known as Hebrews (Gen. 40:15; 43:32). The term's origin is mysterious. Some believe the term came from a prominent man of the region known as Eber (q.v.), a descendant of Noah and an ancestor of Abraham. The literal meaning of Eber, *on the other side of,* may allude to Abraham's departure from Ur, east of the Euphrates. Others believe the Hebrews sprang from the Habiru, a people mentioned in clay tablets as early as the 19th century B.C. and in the Nuzian-Hittite and Amarna documents of the 14th and 15th centuries B.C. Some evidence suggests that the Hebrews saw themselves as a composite race (Deut. 26:5), especially in their wandering tribal days and in their early years in Canaan, when they intermarried with surrounding peoples (Gen. 24:10; 25:10; 28–29).

Hebron (hē′brun; *alliance*). **[1]** 1850 B.C. A son of Kohath (Exod. 6:18; Num. 3:19; 1 Chron. 6:2, 18). **[2]** A descendant of Caleb (1 Chron. 2:42–43).

Hebron [Ebron] (hē′brun [ē′brun]; *alliance*). **[1]** A city in the hills of Judah, 32 km. (20 mi.) south of Jerusalem (Gen. 13:18; Num. 13:22). **[2]** A town of the tribe of Asher, more frequently called Abdon (Josh. 19:28).

Hegai [Hege] (heg′a-ī [hē′ge]). 475 B.C. A chamberlain of Ahasuerus (Esther 2:3, 8, 15).

Helah (hē′lah; *necklace*). A wife of Asher (1 Chron. 4:5, 7).

Helam (hē′lam; *fortress*). A place east of the Jordan, where David defeated the king of Syria (2 Sam. 10:16–19). Possibly 'Almā or 'Ilmā, 10 mi. southwest of Busr el-Harīrī.

Helbah (hel′ba; *fertile*). A town of the tribe of Asher on the Phoenician plain northeast of Tyre (Judg. 1:31); probably the same as Ahlah.

Helbon (hel′bon; *fruitful*). A village of Syria near Damascus, known for its wines (Ezek. 27:18); probably modern Khalbun, 21 km. (13 mi.) north-northwest of Damascus.

Heldai [Heleb; Heled] (hel´dī [hel´eb; hel´ed]; *worldly*).
[1] 975 B.C. A captain of the temple service (1 Chron. 27:15). **[2]** 525 B.C. An Israelite who returned from the Babylonian Captivity and was given special honors (Zech. 6:10); he is called Helem in verse 14.

HEBRON AND HISTORY

The city of Hebron is first mentioned in the Bible when Abram separated his camp from Lot's and settled at Hebron (Gen. 13:18). Years later, Abraham bought the cave at Machpelah in Hebron to bury Sarah. The burial place later served for Abraham, Isaac and Rebecca, and Jacob and Leah (Gen. 49:29–33).

When the Hebrews returned from Egyptian bondage to inhabit the Promised Land, they feared the size of the inhabitants; so they only gradually captured Canaan from the clans of Anak, or made alliances with them (Num. 13:14). After Hebron's king joined with other kings to attack a Hebrew ally, Gibeon, the Hebrews attacked and captured Hebron and other cities (Josh. 10). The Bible gives credit for the capture of Hebron to three people or groups of people; Caleb (Josh. 15:13–15), the tribes of Judah (Judg. 1:8–10), and Joshua (Josh. 10:36–37). After the capture, Hebron was turned over to Caleb, as God had promised earlier (Num. 14).

Generations later, the inhabitants of Hebron assisted David and his army as he pursued the Philistines. Victorious, David shared "the spoil of the enemies of the Lord (1 Sam. 30–31) with the people of Hebron and other cities. As David grew in power, the men of Judah gathered at Hebron and anointed him their king. David ruled the southern kingdom from Hebron.

After David united the two kingdoms (with the seat of government at Jerusalem), Hebron is mentioned only briefly in the Bible. David's son Absalom launched an unsuccessful revolt against him from Hebron (2 Sam. 15:7–10). Later Rehoboam strengthened the city's fortifications so that Hebron could protect Jerusalem, which lay about nineteen miles to the north (2 Chron. 11:5, 10).

Hebron was designated a city of the Levites. The descendants of Levi (i.e., the priests) were given these cities and surrounding pastures as places to live (cf. Josh. 21:1–12). Hebron was also named a city of refuge. If a person unintentionally killed someone, he could flee to one of the six cities of refuge, where he would be protected until he stood trial (Num. 35:9–15).

Modern Hebron has a population of about 40,000 and is located on an important road junction in the highland area of western Jordan. The stone-built town has small, winding streets, and active marketplaces, which sell the wares of local craftsmen, such as glassblowers. Dr. Philip C. Hammond of the University of Utah, who has excavated many artifacts at Hebron, considers the city the oldest continuously occupied unwalled city in the world.

H

Heleb [Heled] (hē′leb [hē′led]). A form of Heldai **[1]**.

Heled (hē′led). A form of Heldai.

Helek (hē′lek; *portion*). A descendant of Manasseh (Num. 26:30; Josh 17:2).

Helem (hē′lem; *strength*). **[1]** A descendant of Asher (1 Chron. 7:35). **[2]** A man of whom the prophet Zechariah speaks (Zech. 6:14). May be another name for Heldai **[2]** (q.v.)

Heleph (hē′lef). A town marking the boundary of the tribe of Naphtali, just northeast of Mount Tabor (Josh. 19:33).

Helez (hē′lez; *God has saved*). **[1]** 1000 B.C. One of David's mighty men (2 Sam. 23:26; 1 Chron. 11:27; 27:10). **[2]** A descendant of Judah (1 Chron. 2:39).

Heli (hē′lī; *God is high*). Heli is the Greek form of Eli.). 25 B.C. The father of Joseph in Luke's genealogy (Luke 3:23).

Helkai (hel′ka-ī; *Jehovah is my portion*). 500 B.C. The head of a priestly family (Neh. 12:15).

Helkath (hel′kath; *part*). A town marking the boundary

of the tribe of Asher (Josh. 19:25); probably modern Tell el-Harboj. Also called Hukok (1 Chron. 6:75).

Helkath-hazzurim (hel'kath-haz'u-rim; *field of sharp swords*). An area of smooth ground near the pool of Gibeon (2 Sam. 2:16).

Hell (hel). The place of woe for the departed. "Hades" is the New Testament name for "Sheol," which was conceived as a place where the souls of all dead rised (Psa. 16:10; Matt. 11:23; Acts 2:27). The KJV also has *hell* as its translation of *Gehenna,* a valley outside Jerusalem that Jesus used as a symbol of woe for lost souls. For believers, He said that Hades would be a paradise (Luke 23:43); for the godless, it would be "Gehenna" (cf. Luke 16:22–23).

Helon (hē'lon; *strength*). 1475 B.C. The father of Eliab, the prince of Zebulun (Num. 1:9; 2:7; 7:24; 10:16).

Hemam [Homam] (hē'mam [hō'mam]). 1950 B.C. A son of Lotan and the grandson of Seir (Gen. 36:22).

Heman (hē'man; *faithful*). **[1]** A wise man with whom Solomon was compared (1 Kings 4:31; 1 Chron. 2:6). He composed a meditative Psalm (Psa. 88, title). **[2]** 1000 B.C. A musician and seer appointed by David as a leader in the temple's vocal and instrumental music (1 Chron. 6:33; 15:17; 2 Chron. 5:12; 35:15).

Hemdan (hem'dan; *pleasant*). 1925 B.C. A descendant of Seir (Gen. 36:26). The KJV wrongly rendered his name *Amram* in First Chronicles 1:41—the reading there is Hamran, possibly a copyist's mistake.

Hen (hen; *grace*). 525 B.C. A son of Zephaniah (Zech. 6:14); he is probably the same as *Josiah* in verse 10.

Hena (hē'na). A city about 32 km. (20 mi.) from Babylon (2 Kings 19:13; Isa. 37:13); probably the same as modern Anah on the Euphrates River.

Henadad (hen'a-dad; *Hadad is gracious*). A head of a Levite family that helped to rebuild the temple (Ezra 3:9; Neh. 3:18, 24; 10:9).

Henoch (hē'nuk). *See* Hanoch [1] and Enoch [2].

Hepher (hē'fer; *a well*). [1] The youngest son of Gilead and founder of the Hepherites (Num. 26:32; Josh. 17:2). [2] A man of Judah (1 Chron. 4:6). [3] 1000 B.C. One of David's heroes (1 Chron. 11:36).

Hepher (hē'fer; *a well*). A town west of the Jordan River (Josh. 12:17); probably modern Tell Ibshar on the Plain of Sharon.

Hephzibah (hef'zi-ba; *my delight is in her*). 725 B.C. The mother of King Manasseh (2 Kings 21:1).

Heresh (he'resh; *silent*). 450 B.C. Head of a Levite family (1 Chron. 9:15).

Hereth [Hareth] (hēr'eth [har'eth]; *thicket*). A forest in the hill country of Judah. David hid from Saul in a cave near this place (1 Sam. 22:5).

Hermas (hur'mas; *Mercury*). A.D. 55. A Christian to whom Paul sent greetings (Rom. 16:14).

Hermes (hur'mēz). A.D. 55. A Greek Christian in Rome to whom Paul sent greetings (Rom. 16:14).

Hermogenes (hur-moj'e-nēz; *born of Hermes*). A.D. 65. A Christian who deserted Paul at Rome or Ephesus (2 Tim. 1:15).

Hermon (hur'mun; *sacred mountain*). The highest mountain of the Anti-Lebanon range, marking the northeast boundary of Palestine (Deut. 3:8; Josh. 11:17; 1 Chron. 5:23).

Herod (her'ud). [1] 37–4 B.C. Herod the Great, the sly king of Judea when Christ was born. In order to maintain power, he murdered the children of Bethlehem, thinking that he would be killing the Messiah (Matt.

2:1–22; Luke 1:5). **[2]** 4 B.C.–A.D. 39. Herod Antipas, son of the former, was tetrarch of Galilee and Perea. He was the murderer of John the Baptist (Matt. 14:1–10; Luke 13:31–32; Luke 23:7–12). **[3]** 4 B.C.–A.D.31. Herod Philip, son of Herod the Great, was tetrarch of Iturea and Trachonitis (Luke 3:1). **[4]** A.D. 25. Herod Philip, another son of Herod the Great, is the Philip whose wife Herod Antipas lured away (Matt. 14:3). **[5]** A.D. 37–44. Herod Agrippa I, tetrarch of Galilee and eventual ruler of his grandfather's (i.e., Herod the Great's) old realm. He bitterly persecuted Christians (Acts 12:1–23). **[6]** A.D. 50–100. Herod Agrippa II, son of Agrippa I and king of various domains, witnessed the preaching of Paul (Acts 25:13–26; 26:1–32).

Herodias (he-rō′di-as). A.D. 25. Granddaughter of Herod the Great, wife of Antipas, and ultimate cause of John the Baptist's death (Matt. 14:3–9; Luke 3:19).

Herodion (he-rō′di-on; *heroic*). A.D. 55. A Jewish Christian to whom Paul sent greetings (Rom. 16:11).

Heshbon (hesh′bon; *stronghold*). The Amorite capital on the boundary between Reuben and Gad, standing between the Arnon and Jabbok Rivers (Num. 21:26; Josh. 13:17).

Heshmon (hesh′mon; *fruitfulness*). A place in the far southern region of Judah (Josh. 15:27); possibly same as Azmon.

Heth (heth; *terrible*). A son of Canaan (Gen. 10:15; 1 Chron. 1:13). Possibly a reference to the Hittite people.

Hethlon (heth′lon). A mountain pass at the northern border of Palestine, connecting the Mediterranean coast with the Plain of Hamath (Ezek. 47:15; 48:1).

Hezeki (hez′e-kī). A form of Hizki.

Hezekiah [Ezekias; Hizkiah] Hizkijah; (hez-e-kī′a [ez-e-kī′as; hiz-kī′a; hiz-kī′a]; *Jehovah is strength*). **[1]** 728–697 B.C. The thirteenth king of Judah; an ancestor of Christ. He instituted religious reform and improved the overall safety and prosperity of the nation (2 Kings 18—20; 2 Chron. 29—32; Matt. 1:9–10). **[2]** 525 B.C. One who returned from Babylon (Ezra 2:16; Neh. 7:21). He, or his representative, is called Hizkijah (a form of Hezekiah) in Nehemiah 10:17. **[3]** A son of Neariah, a descendant of the royal family of Judah (1 Chron. 3:23). **[4]** The great-great grandfather of the prophet Zephaniah (Zeph. 1:1).

Hezion (hē′zi-on). 950 B.C. The grandfather of Ben-Hadad I, king of Syria (1 Kings 15:18). Many scholars identify him with Rezon (q.v.).

Hezir (hē′zir; *swine*). **[1]** 1000 B.C. A Levite in the time of David (1 Chron. 24:15). **[2]** 450 B.C. A chief of the people that sealed the new covenant with God after the Exile (Neh. 10:20).

Hezrai [Hezro] (hez′rī [hez′rō]). 1000 B.C. One of David's warriors (2 Sam. 23:35). He is also called Hezro (1 Chron. 11:37).

Hezro (hez′rō). *See* Hezrai.

Hezron [Esrom] (hez′ron [ez′rom]; *enclosure*). **[1]** 1875 B.C. A son of Reuben (Gen. 46:9; Exod. 6:14). **[2]** 1825 B.C. A son of Perez and an ancestor of Christ (Gen. 46:12; 1 Chron. 2:5, 9, 18, 21, 24–25; Matt. 1:3; Luke 3:33).

Hezron (hez′ron; *enclosure*). **[1]** A place on the southern border of Judah, not far from Kadesh Barnea (Josh. 15:3).

Hiddai [Hurai] (hid′a-ī [hū′rai-ī]). 1000 B.C. One of

David's mighty men (2 Sam. 23:30). He is called Hurai (*free; noble*) in First Chronicles 11:32.

Hiddekel (hid'e-kel). An archaic name for the Tigris River (Gen. 2:14; Dan. 10:4). It is narrower than the Euphrates, but carries more water. It joins the Euphrates 100 miles from the Persian Gulf at Al Qurna.

Hiel (hī'el; *God is living*). 875 B.C. A man who rebuilt Jericho (1 Kings 16:34) and sacrificed his sons, in fulfillment of Joshua's curse (Josh. 6:26).

Hierapolis (he-er-ap'o-lis; *priestly*). A city of the province of Phrygia in Asia Minor, at the confluence of the Lycas and Meander Rivers (Col. 4:13).

Hilen [Holon] (hī'len [hō'lon]; *strong place*). A city of the tribe of Judah, allotted to the Levites (Josh. 15:51; 1 Chron. 6:58).

Hilkiah (hil-kī'a; *Jehovah is my portion*). [1] A Levite who kept the children of the temple officials (1 Chron. 6:45). [2] 975 B.C. A gatekeeper of the tabernacle (1 Chron. 26:11). [3] 725 B.C. Master of the household of King Hezekiah (2 Kings 18:18, 26; Isa. 22:20; 36:3). [4] 625 B.C. High priest and the discoverer of the Book of the Law in the days of Josiah (2 Kings 22:4, 8; 23:4). [5] 625 B.C. A priest of Anathoth and father of Jeremiah (Jer. 1:1). [6] 600 B.C. The father of Gemariah (Jer. 29:3). [7] 525 B.C. A chief of priests who returned from captivity (Neh. 12:7) and his later descendants (Neh. 12:12, 21). [8] 450 B.C. One who stood with Ezra at the reading of the Law (Neh. 8:4).

Hillel (hil'lel; *he has praised*). 1100 B.C. The father of Abdon, one of the judges (Judg. 12:13, 15).

Hinnom (hin'om; *gratis*). An unknown person who had a son(s) after whom a valley near Jerusalem was named. Human sacrifices took place there in Jeremiah's day, and garbage was later incinerated in this defiled place (Josh. 15:8; 18:16; Neh. 11:30; Jer. 7:31–32).

Hinnom, Valley of (hin'om). A narrow valley southwest of Jerusalem (Josh. 15:8; 18:16; 2 Chron. 28:3).

Hirah (hī'ra). 1900 B.C. A friend of Judah (Gen. 38:1, 12).

Hiram [Huram] (hī'ram [hū'ram]; abbreviated form of Ahiram, *My brother is exalted*). **[1]** 975 B.C. A king of Tyre who befriended David and Solomon (2 Sam. 5:11; 1 Kings 5; 9:11; 10:11). **[2]** The skillful worker in brass whom Solomon secured from King Hiram (1 Kings 7:13, 40, 45; 2 Chron. 4:11, 16).

Hizki [Hezeki] (hiz'kī [hez'e-kī]; *Jehovah is strength*). A son of Elpaal and descendant of Benjamin (1 Chron. 8:17).

Hizkiah [Hizkijah] (hiz-kī'a [hiz-ki'ja]; *Jehovah is strength*). *See* Hezekiah **[4]**.

Hobab (hō'bab; *beloved*). The father-in-law or brother-in-law of Moses (Num. 10:29; Judg. 4:11). The phrase "father-in-law" in Judges 4:11 may possibly mean nothing more than "in-law," or perhaps Jethro was also named Hobab; but the identity is uncertain. *See also* Jethro.

Hobah (hō'ba; *hiding place*). The town north of Damascus that was the farthest point to which Abraham pursued the defeated eastern kings (Gen. 14:15).

Hobaiah (hō-bī'ah). A form of Habaiah.

Hod (hod; *glory*). One of the sons of Zophah (1 Chron. 7:37).

Hodaiah (hō-dā'ya). A form of Hodaviah.

Hodaviah (hō-da-vī'a; *give honor to Jehovah*). **[1]** An ancestor of returning captives (Ezra 2:40). He is also called Hodevah (*Jehovah is honor*). in Nehemiah 7:43. **[2]** 750

B.C. A chief of the tribe of Manasseh (1 Chron. 5:24). **[3]** A descendant of Benjamin (1 Chron. 9:7). **[4]** A son of Eloenai and descendant of Zerubbabel and David (1 Chron. 3:24).

Hodesh (hō′desh; *new moon*). A wife of Shaharaim (1 Chron. 8:9).

Hodevah (ho-dē′va). *See* Hodaviah.

Hodiah (ho-dī′a; *splendor of Jehovah*). A brother-in-law of Naham (1 Chron. 4:19). The KJV incorrectly identifies him as the "wife" of Naham.

Hodijah (hō-dī′jah; *splendor of Jehovah*). **[1]** 450 B.C. A Levite in the time of Nehemiah. (Neh. 8:7; 10:10, 13). **[2]** 450 B.C. One who sealed the new covenant with God after the Exile (Neh. 10:18).

Hoglah (hog′la; *partridge*). 1400 B.C. A daughter of Zelophehad (Num. 26:33; 27:1; Josh. 17:3).

Hoham (hō′ham). 1400 B.C. An Amorite king slain by Joshua (Josh. 10:1–27).

Holon (hō′lon; *sandy*). **[1]** A Moabite town (Jer. 48:21); possibly modern Horon. **[2]** A town in the hill country of Judah west of Hebron (Josh. 15:51). Also called Hilen (1 Chron. 6:58).

Homam [Hemam] (hō′mam [hē′mam]; *raging*). 1950 B.C. A Horite descendant of Esau (1 Chron. 1:39). He is called Hemam in Genesis 36:22 (probably a copyist's error).

Hophni (hof′nī). 1100 B.C. The unholy son of Eli slain at the battle of Aphek (1 Sam. 1:3; 2:22–24, 34).

Hophra (haph′ra; *the heart of Ra endures*). Ruled 589–570 B.C. A king of Egypt who marched against Nebuchadnezzar II to aid Zedekiah. His campaign failed when he retreated to Egypt and the Babylonians laid siege to Jerusalem (Jer. 37:5–8; 44:30).

Hor, Mount (hōr; *hill*). **[1]** A mountain on the boundary of Edom (Num. 20:22; 33:37); tradition identifies it as modern Jebel Harun, but Jebel Madeirch is more likely the location. **[2]** A mountain between the Mediterranean Sea and the entrance of Hamath **[2]**, possibly in the Lebanon range (Num. 34:7–8).

Horam (hō′ram; *height*). 1400 B.C. A king of Gezer defeated by Joshua (Josh. 10:33).

Horeb, Mount (hō′reb; *waste*). The mountain in the Sinai Peninsula where Moses heard God speak to him through the burning bush. (Exod. 3:1, 17:6).

Horem (hō′rem; *sacred*). A fortress of the tribe of Naphtali (Josh. 19:38); modern Hurah at the southern end of the Wadi el-Ain.

Horesh (hō′resh; *forest*). A place in the wilderness of Ziph where David hid from King Saul (1 Sam. 23:15).

Hor Hagidgad (hōr′ ha-gid′gad; *cleft mountain*). A place where the wandering Israelites camped (Num. 33:32); probably located on what is now called the Wadi Ghadaghed. It is perhaps identical with Gudgodah (q.v.).

Hori (hō′rī; *noble*). **[1]** 1950 B.C. A descendant of Esau (Gen. 36:22; 1 Chron. 1:39). **[2]** 1475 B.C. The father of one of the men sent to spy out the Promised Land (Num. 13:5).

Hormah (hor′ma; *complete destruction*). A Canaanite city located near Ziklag; originally called Zephath (1 Sam. 30:30); perhaps the same as modern Tell el-Milk, east-southeast of Beersheba.

Horonaim (hor′o-nā′im; *two caves*). A sanctuary town of Moab, near Zoar (Isa. 15:5; Jer. 48:3).

Hosah (hō′sa; *refuge*). 1000 B.C. One of the first doorkeepers of the ark of the covenant (1 Chron. 16:38; 26:10–11, 16).

Hosah (hō′sa; *refuge*). A landmark city of the tribe of Asher on the boundary near Tyre (Josh. 19:29).

Hosea [Osee] (ho-zē′a [ō′zē]; *deliverance*). 750 B.C. A prophet of Israel; he denounced the idolatries of Israel and Samaria (Hos. 1:1–2).

Hoshaiah (ho-shā′ya; *Jehovah has saved*). [1] 625 B.C. The father of Jezaniah or Azariah (Jer. 42:1; 43:2). [2] 450 B.C. A man who led half of the princes of Judah in procession at the dedication of the walls (Neh. 12:32).

Hoshama (ho-shā′ma; *Jehovah has heard*). 550 B.C. A son or descendant of Jeconiah or Jehoiakim (1 Chron. 3:18).

Hoshea [Hosea] (ho-shē′a [hō-sā′a]; *salvation*). [1] 1000 B.C. A chief of the tribe of Ephraim in the days of David (1 Chron. 27:20). [2] 732–723 B.C. The last king of Israel; he was imprisoned by Sargon of Assyria (2 Kings 15:30; 17:1, 4, 6; 18:1). [3] 450 B.C. One who sealed the covenant with Nehemiah (Neh. 10:23). [4] The original name of Joshua (q.v.).

Hotham [Hothan] (hō′tham [hō′than] [1] A descendant of Asher (1 Chron. 7:32). [2] 1025 B.C. Father of two of David's best men (1 Chron. 11:44).

Hothan (hō′than). A form of Hotham.

Hothir (hō′thir; *abundance*). 975 B.C. Son of Heman in charge of the twenty-first course of the tabernacle service (1 Chron. 25:4, 28).

Hozai (hō′zā-ī). An unknown prophet who recorded some events of King Manasseh's life (2 Chron. 33:19).

Hukkok (huk′ok; *ditch*). A place on the border of Naphtali (Josh. 19:34); probably modern Yakuk.

Hukok (huk′ok; *hewn*). A city marking the boundary of Asher (1 Chron. 6:75). It is identical with Helkath (q.v.).

Hul (hul; *circle*). Grandson of Shem (Gen. 10:23; 1 Chron. 1:17). Possibly an Aramean tribe is referred to; some have suggested the people of Hūlīa near Mount Masius.

Huldah (hul'da; *weasel*). 625 B.C. A prophetess in the days of King Josiah (2 Kings 22:14; 2 Chron. 34:22).

Humtah (hum'tah; *place of lizards*). A city in the mountains of Judah near Hebron (Josh. 15:54).

Hupham (hū'fam; *coast inhabitant*). The head of a family descendant from Benjamin (Num. 26:39). In Genesis 46:21 and First Chronicles 7:12, his name is listed as Huppim (*coast people* or *protection*).

Huppah (hup'a; *covering*). 1000 B.C. A priest in the time of David who had charge of one of the courses of service in the sanctuary (1 Chron. 24:13).

Huppim (hup'ēm). *See* Hupham.

Hur (hur; *noble*). **[1]** 1500 B.C. A son of Caleb (Exod. 31:2; 35:30; 38:22; 1 Chron. 2:19, 50; 4:1, 4). **[2]** 1450 B.C. One of the men who held up Moses' arms during the battle with Amalek (Exod. 17:10, 12; 24:14). **[3]** 1400 B.C. A Midianite king slain by Israel (Num. 31:8; Josh. 13:21). **[4]** An officer of Solomon on Mouint Ephraim (1 Kings 4:8). **[5]** 475 B.C. Father of Rephaiah, who helped rebuild the wall of Jerusalem in Nehemiah's time (Neh. 3:9). **[6]** A son of Judah (1 Chron. 4:1).

Hurai (hū'ra-ī; *noble*). One of David's thirty mighty men (1 Chron. 11:32). Also called Hiddai (2 Sam. 23:30).

Huram (hū'ram; *lofty brother*). **[1]** 1825 B.C. A descendant of Bela and a grandson of Benjamin (1 Chron. 8:5). **[2]** A king of Tyre who formed an alliance with David and Solomon. **[3]** 950 B.C. A skilled craftsman from

Tyre employed by Solomon (2 Chron. 4:16). Also called Hiram (1 Kings 7:13).

Huri (hū'rī; *linen weaver*). A descendant of Gad (1 Chron. 5:14).

Hushah (hū'sha; *haste*). A descendant of Judah (1 Chron. 4:4).

Hushai (hu'sha-ī; *quick*). 975 B.C. A friend and counselor of David (2 Sam. 15:32, 37; 16:16–18; 17:5–15). Probably the father of Baana (1 Kings 4:16).

Husham (hū'sham; *hastily*). A descendant of Esau who became king of Edom (Gen. 36:34–35; 1 Chron. 1:45–46).

Hushim (hū'shim; *hastily*). [1] 1875 B.C. A son of Dan (Gen. 46:23); in Numbers 26:42, his name is Shuham [2] A descendant of Benjamin (1 Chron. 7:12). [3] One of the two wives of Shaharaim (1 Chron. 8:8, 11).

Huz [Uz] (huz [uz]; *firmness*). The oldest son of Nahor and Milcah (Gen. 22:21).

Hymenaeus (hi-men-ē'us). A.D. 65. An early Christian who fell into apostasy and error (1 Tim. 1:20; 2 Tim. 2:17).

I

Ibhar (ib'har; *Jehovah chooses*). 975 B.C. One of David's sons born at Jerusalem (2 Sam. 5:15; 1 Chron. 3:6).

Ibleam (ib'le-am; *he destroys the people*). A city of the tribe of Manasseh (Josh. 17:11; Judg. 1:27); generally believed to be another name for Bileam (q.v.).

Ibneiah (ib-nē'ya; *Jehovah builds*). 450 B.C. A son of Jeroham. Head of a Benjamite family that returned from the Captivity (1 Chron. 9:8).

Ibnijah (ib-nī′ja; *Jehovah builds*). Father of Reuel (1 Chron. 9:8).

Ibri (ib′rē). 1000 B.C. A descendant of Merari in the time of David (1 Chron. 24:27).

Ibzan (ib′zan; *swift*). Ruled 1078–1072 B.C. A Bethlehemite who judged Israel for seven years (Judg. 12:8–10).

Ichabod (ik′a-bod; *inglorious*). 1050 B.C. Son of Phinehas, born after his father's death and after the ark was taken (1 Sam. 4:19–22).

Iconium (ī-kō′ni-um). Capital of the province of Lycaonia in Asia Minor (Acts 13:51; 14:1).

Idalah (id′a-la; *memorial of God*). A city of the tribe of Zebulun (Josh. 19:15); modern Khirbet el-Huvara.

Idbash (id′bash; *corpulent*). One of the sons of the father of Etam (1 Chron. 4:3).

Iddo (id′ō; *festa*). [1] A descendant of Gershon (1 Chron. 6:21); called Adaiah in First Chronicles 6:41. [2] 1000 B.C. Captain of the tribe of Manasseh in Gilead (1 Chron. 27:21). [3] 975 B.C. Father of Abinadab (1 Kings 4:14). [4] 900 B.C. A prophet who wrote about the kings of Israel (2 Chron. 9:29; 12:15). [5] 575 B.C. Grandfather of the prophet Zecharaiah (Ezra 5:1; Zech. 1:7). [6] 525 B.C. A priest who returned to Jerusalem with Zerubbabel (Neh. 12:4); perhaps the same as [4]. [7] 450 B.C. The official of Casiphia who provided Levites for Ezra (Ezra 8:17).

Idumea (id-u-mē′a; *land of the Edomites*). An area in southwestern Palestine. After the fall of Jerusalem in 586 B.C. many Edomites migrated into this area thus giving it the name Idumea (the Greek form of the Hebrew Edom (Mark 3:8).

Igal [Igeal] (ī'gal [i'ge-al]; *Jehovah redeems*). **[1]** 1450 B.C. One of the twelve spies sent to search out Canaan (Num. 13:7). **[2]** 1000 B.C. One of David's heroes (2 Sam. 23:36). **[3]** A descendant of the royal house of Judah (1 Chron. 3:22).

Igdaliah (ig-da-lī'a; *Jehovah is great*). Ancestor of persons who had a "chamber" in the temple (Jer. 35:4).

Igeal (i'ge'al). A form of Igal.

Iim [Ijim; Iyim] (ī'im [ī'im; ī'im]; *heaps*). **[1]** A town in extreme southern Judah (Josh. 15:29); modern Deir el-Ghawi. **[2]** A town east of the Jordan River, perhaps the Moabite fortress of Mahaiy (Num. 33:45); probably the same as Ije Abarim.

Ije Abarim (ī'je ab'a-rim; *ruins*). A place where the Israelites camped in the territory of Moab (Num. 33:45). *See also* Iim [2].

Ijon (ī'jon; *ruin*). A city of northern Palestine belonging to the tribe of Naphtali (1 Kings 15:20); modern Merj 'Ayun, a few kilometers northwest of Dan.

Ikkesh (ik'kesh; *subtle*). 1025 B.C. Father of Ira, one of David's mighty men (2 Sam. 23:26; 1 Chron. 11:28; 27:9).

Ilai (ī'la-ī; *elevated*). 1000 B.C. One of David's mighty men (1 Chron. 11:29). Also called Zalmon (2 Sam. 23:28).

Illyricum (i-lir'i-kum). A Roman province on the east coast of the Adriatic Sea, stretching from Italy on the north to Macedonia on the south (Rom. 15:19). It was later renamed Dalmatia (q.v.).

Imla [Imlah] (im'la; *God fulfills*). 900 B.C. Father of Micaiah (2 Chron. 18:7–8).

Immer (im'er; *prominent*). A family of priests who gave their name to the sixteenth course of the temple service (1 Chron. 9:12, 24:14; Ezra 2:37; Neh. 7:40).

Immer (im'er; *prominent*). A person or place in Babylonia (Ezra 2:59; Neh. 7:61); its exact location is unknown.

Imna (im'na; *may he preserve*). A descendant of Asher (Gen. 46:17; 1 Chron. 7:35).

Imnah [Jimna; Jimnah] (im'na [jim'na; jim'na]; *good fortune*). [1] 1875 B.C. A son of Asher (Num. 26:44; 1 Chron. 7:30). [2] 1725 B.C. Father of Kore in Hezekiah's reign (2 Chron. 31:14).

Imrah (im'ra; *stubborn*). A descendant of Asher (1 Chron. 7:36).

Imri (im'rī; *Jehovah has promised*). [1] A descendant of Judah (1 Chron. 9:4). [2] 475 B.C. Father of Zaccur, one of Nehemiah's assistants (Neh. 3:2).

India (in-dē'ah). A land on the eastern limit of the Persian Empire, surrounding the Indus River (Esther 1:1; 8:9).

Iob (ī'ob). A form of Jashub [1].

Iphdeiah [Iphedeiah] (if-dē'ya [if-e-dē-ya]; *Jehovah redeems*). A descendant of Benjamin (1 Chron. 8:25).

Iphtah (if'tah). A form of Jiphtah.

Iphtahel (if'ta-hel). A form of Jiphthah El.

Ir (ir; *donkey's colt*). A descendant of Benjamin (1 Chron. 7:12); possibly the same as Iri (v. 7). Not to be confused with Ir Nahash.

Ir-nahash (ir-nā'hash; *serpent city*). A person or a town of the tribe of Judah (1 Chron. 4:12).

Ir Shemesh (ir-she'mesh; *city of the sun*). A city of the tribe of Dan (Josh. 19:41); probably another name for Beth Shemesh (q.v.).

Ira (Ī′ra; *young donkey*). **[1]** 1000 B.C. A priest to David (2 Sam. 20:26). **[2]** 1000 B.C. One of David's thirty mighty men (1 Chron. 11:28; 2 Sam. 23:38) and a captain of the temple guard (1 Chron. 27:9). **[3]** 1000 B.C. Another of David's thirty (1 Chron. 11:40; 2 Sam. 23:26).

Irad (Ī′rad; *wild donkey*). A descendant of Enoch (Gen. 4:18).

Iram (Ī′ram). A duke of Edom (Gen. 36:43).

Iri (Ī′ri; *Jehovah is watcher*). A descendant of Benjamin (1 Chron. 7:7); possibly the same as Ir (v. 12).

Irijah (i′rī′ja; *Jehovah sees*). 600 B.C. A captain of the gate who arrested Jeremiah (Jer. 37:13–14).

Iron (Ī′ron; *place of terror*). A city of the tribe of Naphtali (Josh. 19:38); probably modern Yarun, 16 km. (10 mi.) west of Hula Lake.

Irpeel (ir′pe-el; *God heals*). A city of the tribe of Benjamin (Josh. 18:27); perhaps the same as modern Rafat, 10 km. (6 mi.) northwest of Jerusalem.

Iru (Ī′rū; *young donkey*). 1425 B.C. A son of Caleb (1 Chron. 4:15).

Isaac (Ī′zak; *laughter*). 2066 B.C. The son of Abraham and Sarah, born to them in their old age. He was the father of Jacob and Esau and an ancestor of Christ (Gen. 21—25; Matt. 1:2).

Isaiah [Esaias] (Ī-zā′ya [e-zā′yas]; *salvation of Jehovah*). 739–701 B.C. Called the "prince of prophets"; his career lasted over sixty years. He foretold the coming of Christ (Isa. 1:1; 7:14; 9:6; 52:12–53).

Iscah (is′ka). 2075 B.C. Daughter of Haran, sister of Milcah, and niece of Abraham (Gen. 11:29).

Iscariot (is-kar′i-ot; *man of Kerioth*). The surname of Judas, the apostle who betrayed Jesus (John 6:71; 12:4; 13:2, 26). *See* Judas Iscariot.

Ishbah (ish´ba). A descendant of Judah (1 Chron. 4:17).

Ishbak (ish´bak; *free*). 2000 B.C. Son of Abraham and father of a northern Arabian tribe (Gen. 25:2; 1 Chron. 1:32).

Ishbi-benob (ish´bī-bē´nob; *dweller on the mount*). 1000 B.C. One of the sons of Rapha the Philistine; he attacked David but was killed by Abishai (2 Sam. 21:15–22).

Ishbosheth (ish-bō´sheth; *man of shame*). 1000 B.C. Son and successor of King Saul. He reigned two years before being defeated by David (2 Sam. 2:8–15; 3:8, 14–15; 4:5–12). He also was known as Esh-baal (1 Chron. 8:33; 9:39).

Ishi (ish´ī; *God has saved*). [1] A member of the family of Jerahmeel (1 Chron 2:31). [2] A descendant of Judah (1 Chron. 4:20). [3] A descendant of Simeon (1 Chron. 4:42). [4] 750 B.C. A chief of the tribe of Manasseh (1 Chron. 5:24).

Ishiah (ī-shī´a). *See* Isshiah.

Ishijah [Isshijah] (ish-ī´ja [ish-shī´ja]; *Jehovah exists*). 450 B.C. A son of Harum who divorced his foreign wife (Ezra 10:31).

Ishma (ish´ma; *may God hear*). A brother of Jezreel and Idbash, all descendants of Caleb (1 Chron. 4:3).

Ishmael (ish´ma-el; *God hears*). [1] 2050 B.C. Son of Abraham and Hagar; his descendants are the Arabian nomads (Gen. 16:11–16; 17:18–26; 25:9–17; 28:9; 36:3). [2] A descendant of Benjamin (1 Chron. 8:38). [3] 900 B.C. Father of Zebadiah (2 Chron. 19:11). [4] 850 B.C. A captain in the time of Jehoiada and Joash (2 Chron. 23:1). [5] 575 B.C. The cunning son of Nethaniah and traitor of Israel (Jer. 40:8–41:18). [6] 450

B.C. A Levite who married a foreign wife during the Exile (Ezra 10:22).

Ishmaiah [Ismaiah] (ish-ma´ya [is-ma´ya]; *Jehovah hears*). **[1]** 1000 B.C. A chief of Zebulun in David's time (1 Chron. 27:19). **[2]** 1000 B.C. A chief of Gibeon who joined David at Ziklag (1 Chron. 12:4).

Ishmerai (ish´me-rī; *Jehovah is protector*). A descendant of Benjamin (1 Chron. 8:18).

Ishhod [Ishod] (ī´shod [ī´shod]; *man of vitality*). A man of Manasseh (1 Chron. 7:18).

Ishpan (ish´pan; *strong*). A chief man of Benjamin (1 Chron. 8:22).

Ish-tob (ish´tob; *man of Tob*). A small area east of the Jordan River (2 Sam. 10:6).

Ishuah [Ishvah; Isuah] (ish´u-al [ish´vah; is´u-a]; *to be like*). 1875 B.C. Second son of Asher (Gen. 46:17; 1 Chron. 7:30).

Ishvi [Ishuai; Isui; Ishyo; Jesui; Jishui] (ish´vī [ish´yū-ī; is´yū-ī; ish´yō; jes´ū-ī, jish´ū-ī]; *equal*). **[1]** 1875 B.C. Third son of Asher (Gen. 46:17; Num. 26:44; 1 Chron. 7:30). **[2]** Ruled 1005–1003 B.C. A son of King Saul by Ahinoam (1 Sam. 14:49). Some believe he is identical with Ishbosheth.

Ismachiah (is-ma-kī´a; *Jehovah supports*). 725 B.C. An overseer under King Hezekiah (2 Chron. 31:13).

Ismaiah (is-mā´ya). *See* Ishmaiah.

Ispah [Ishpah] (is´pa [ish´pa]; *strong*). A descendant of Benjamin (1 Chron. 8:16).

Israel (iz´ra-el; *he struggles with God*). The name given to Jacob after he wrestled with God at Peniel (Gen. 32:28; 35:10).

Israel (iz´ra-el; *he struggles with God*). The northern kingdom of the Hebrews in Palestine, inhabited by the ten tribes that followed Ishbosheth and Jeroboam. The cities of Jericho and Gezer marked its southern boundary (2 Chron. 35:18; cf. Gen. 32:32). *See also* Jacob.

Issachar (is'a-kar; *reward*). [1] 1900 B.C. Ninth son of Jacob and ancestor of one of the twelve tribes of Israel (Gen. 30:17–18; 49:14–15). [2] 975 B.C. A tabernacle porter (1 Chron. 26:5).

Isshiah [Ishijah] (is-shī'a [ish-ī'ja]; *may Jehovah forget*). [1] A Levite who was head of the house of Rehabiah (1 Chron. 24:21). [2] A Levite of the house of Uzziel (1 Chron. 24:25).

Isuah (is'u-a). *See* Ishuah.

Isui (is'u-ī). *See* Ishvi.

Italy (it'a-li). The peninsula jutting from the Alps into the Mediterranean Sea, bounded on the south by the straits of Messina (Acts 18:2; 27:1).

Ithai (ith'a-ī). A form of Ittai.

Ithamar (ith'a-mar; *oasis of palms*). 1400 B.C. A son of Aaron (Exod. 6:23; 28:1); Eli was high priest of his line (1 Chron. 24:6).

Ithiel (ith'i-el; *God is with me*). [1] A man of the tribe of Benjamin (Neh. 11:7). [2] A person to whom the proverbs of Agur were directed (Prov. 30:1).

Ithmah (ith'ma; *orphan*). 1000 B.C. A Moabite, one of David's guards (1 Chron. 11:46).

Ithnan (ith'nan; *constant*). A town in extreme southern Judah (Josh. 15:23).

Ithra (ith'ra). A form of Jithra.

Ithran (ith'ran; *excellent*). [1] 1900 B.C. A descendant of Seir (Gen. 36:26). [2] A son of Zophah of Asher (1 Chron. 7:37).

Ithream (ith're-am; *remnant of the people*). 975 B.C. A son of David probably by Eglah (2 Sam. 3:5).

Ittah Kazin (it'a kā'zin). A form of Eth Kazin.

Ittai (it'a-ī; *timely*). [1] 975 B.C. A Philistine friend and general of David (2 Sam. 15:11–22; 18:2, 4, 12). [2] 1000 B.C. One of David's mighty men (2 Sam. 23:29). Also called Ithai (1 Chron. 11:31).

Iturea (it-u-rē'a; *pertaining to Jetur*). A small province on the northwest boundary of Palestine at the base of Mount Hermon (Luke 3:1). It probably derived its name from Jetur, a son of Ishmael.

Ivah [Ivvah] (ī'va [iv'vah]; *sky*). A city located on the Euphrates River (2 Kings 18:34; 19:13); perhaps the same as Ava.

Iye-abarim (ī'ēē-a'bur-ēēm). A form of Ije Abarim.

Iyim (ī'yim). A form of Ijim.

Izehar [Izhar] (īz'e-har [īz'har]; *may the deity shine*). [1] A Levite, the father of Korah (Exod. 6:18–21; Num. 3:19). [2] *See* Zohar [3].

Izrahiah (iz-ra-hī'a; *Jehovah will appear*). A descendant of Issachar (1 Chron. 7:3).

Izri (iz'rī). A form of Jizri.

Izziah (iz'ī'uh). A form of Jeziah.

J

Jaakan [Jakan] (jā'a-kan [jā'kan]; *intelligent*). A son of Ezer, son of Seir (Deut. 10:6; 1 Chron. 1:42). In Genesis 36:27, he is called Akan. Many scholars believe the reference in the Deuteronomy passage is to a city. *See* Beeroth.

Jaakobah (jā-a-kō'ba; *to Jacob*). A descendant of Simeon (1 Chron. 4:36).

Jaalah [Jaala] (jā'a-la [jā'a-la]; *elevation*). A servant of Solomon whose descendants returned from the Exile (Ezra 2:56; Neh. 7:58).

Jaalam [Jalam] (jā-a-lam [jā'lam]; *hidden*). A chief of Edom (Gen. 36:5, 14, 18; 1 Chron. 1:35).

Jaanai [Janai] (jā'a-ni [ja'nī]; *Jehovah answers*). A chief of a family descended from Gad (1 Chron. 5:12).

Jaare-oregim (jā'a-re-or'e-jim; *foresters*). Father of Elhanan, slayer of Goliath the Gittite (2 Sam. 21:19). Some suggest this is a copyist's error for Jair (cf. 1 Chron. 20:5), the *oregim (weavers)* being a mistaken repetition of the last word in the verse.

Jaasau [Jaasai, Jaasu] (jā'a-so [jā'a-sī, jā'a-su]; *Jehovah is maker*). One who married a foreign wife (Ezra 10:37) **J** after the Babylonian exile.

Jaasiel [Jasiel] (jā-ā'si-el [jā'si-el]; *God is maker*). **[1]** One of David's mighty men (1 Chron. 11:47). **[2]** Leader of the tribe of Benjamin during David's reign (1 Chron. 27:21). *See* **David**.

Jaazaniah [Jezaniah] (jā-az-a-nī'a [jez-a-nī'a]; *Jehovah is hearing*). **[1]** A captain of the forces who joined Gedaliah (2 Kings 25:23). He is the Jezaniah *(Jehovah determines; Jehovah hears)* of Jeremiah 40:8; 42:1, and possibly the Azariah of Jeremiah 43:2. **[2]** A chief of the tribe of Rechabites, a son of a certain man named Jeremiah but not the prophet (Jer. 35:3). **[3]** A leader of elders who were enticing the people to idolatry (Ezek. 8:11). **[4]** A wicked prince of Judah seen in Ezekiel's vision (Ezek. 11:1).

Jaazer [Jazer] (jā'a-zer [jā'zer]; *God helps*). A fortified, Amorite city east of the Jordan River, in or near the region of Gilead (Num. 21:32; 32:1).

Jaaziah (jā-a-zī́-a; *Jehovah is determining*). A descendant of Merari living in Solomon's day (1 Chron. 24:26–27).

Jaaziel (jā-ā́zi-el; *God is determining*). A temple musician in David's time (1 Chron. 15:18). He is called Aziel in verse 20.

Jabal (jā́bal; *moving*). Son of Lamech, a nomad (Gen. 4:20).

Jabbok (jab́ok; *flowing*). An eastern tributary of the Jordan River, which served as the western border of Ammon (Gen. 32:22; Deut. 2:37).

Jabesh (jā́besh; *dry place*). Father of Shallum, who killed Zechariah and reigned in his place (2 Kings 15:10–14). *See also* Jabesh-gilead.

Jabesh-gilead (jā́besh-giĺe-ad; *dry*). A city of Gilead (Judg. 21:8; 1 Sam. 11:1). It may have been located at a site now called Wadi Yabis, about 23 km. (20 mi.) south of the Sea of Galilee.

Jabez (jā́bez; *height*). Head of a family of Judah (1 Chron. 4:9–10).

Jabez (jā́bez; *sorrow*). A dwelling place of scribes, probably in Judah (1 Chron. 2:55).

Jabin (jā́bin; *intelligent; observed*). [1] A king of Hazor defeated by Joshua (Josh. 11:1). [2] Another king of Hazor who oppressed Israel and was defeated by Deborah (Judg. 4).

Jabneel [Jabneh] (jab́ne-el [jab́ne]; *building of God*). [1] A city marking the northern border of Judah (Josh. 15:11); modern Yebnah, about 6 km. (4 mi.) inland from the Mediterranean Sea and 14.5 km. (9 mi.) north-northeast of Ashdod (2 Chron. 26:6). [2] A border town of the tribe of Naphtali (Josh. 19:33); probably modern Khirbet Yeman, 11 km. (7 mi.) southwest of Tiberias.

Jabneh (jab'ne). *See* Jabneel.

Jachan (jā'kan; *afflicting*). A descendant of Gad (1 Chron. 5:13).

Jachin (jā'kin; *founding* or *he will establish*). **[1]** A son of Simeon (Gen. 46:10); Exod. 6:15; Num. 26:12). He is called Jarib in First Chronicles 4:24. **[2]** A priest in Jerusalem after the Babylonian Captivity (1 Chron. 9:10; Neh. 11:10). **[3]** Head of a family of Aaron (1 Chron. 24:17). *See* Jarib.

Jachin (jā'kin; *God establishes*). The right hand pillar of Solomon's porch on the temple of Jerusalem (1 Kings 7:21). *See* Boaz.

Jachinites (jā'kin-ītes). Descendants of Jachin.

Jacob (jā'kob; *supplanter; following after*). **[1]** Son of Isaac, twin of Esau, and an ancestor of Christ. He bought Esau's birthright and became known as **Israel,** the father of the Jewish nation (Gen. 25—50; Matt. 1:2). God changed his name from Jacob to Israel (*God strives;* Gen. 32:28; 35:10), after he wrestled with a mysterious stranger at the ford of the Jabbok river. **[2]** The father of Joseph, the husband of Mary (Matt. 1:15–16). *See also* Heli, Jabbok.

Jacob Testament of. An ancient book written anonymously which describes legendary events leading up to the death of Jacob. Jacob's Well. The well where Jesus talked to the Samaritan woman (John 4:1–26), ½ mile S.E. of Shechem. *See* Schechem.

Jada (jā'da; *knowing*). A son of Onam and grandson of Jerahmeel (1 Chron. 2:28, 32).

Jadau (jā'do; *friend*). One who married a foreign wife (Ezra 10:43).

Jaddai [Jadau] (ja'dī; *friend*). A Judahite who divorced his foreign wife in order to follow the instructions of

Ezra and turn back God's wrath after the return from Babylonian exile.

Jaddua (ja-dū'a; *very knowing; known*). [1] A Levite who sealed the covenant (Neh. 10:21). [2] The last high priest mentioned in the Old Testament (Neh. 12:11, 22).

Jadon (jā'don; *judging*). A Judahite who helped repair the walls of Jerusalem after the Exile (Neh. 3:7).

Jael (jā'el; *a wild goat*). Wife of Heber who killed Sisera, the mighty enemy of Israel (Judg. 4:17–22; 5:6, 24).

Jagur (jā'ger; *husbandman*). A town in extreme southern Judah (Josh. 15:21); probably modern Tell Ghurr.

Jahaleleel [Jehallelel, Jehaleleel] (jaha'le-leel [jeha'le-lel, jeha'le-leel]; *may God shine forth*). A descendant of Judah through the ancestry of Caleb (1 Chron. 4:16). *See* Caleb.

Jahath (jā'hath; *comfort; revival*). [1] A descendant of Judah, son of Reaiah (1 Chron. 4:2). [2], [3], [4], Three descendants of Levi: a son of Libni (1 Chron. 6:20, 43); a son of Shimei (1 Chron. 23:10, 11); a son of Shelmoth (1 Chron. 24:22). [5] A Levite who helped oversee temple repair (2 Chron. 34:12).

Jahaz [Jahaza, Jahazah, Jahzah] jā'haz [(jā'ha-za; ja-hā'za)]; *a place trodden under foot*). A battlefield on the wastelands of Moab (Num. 21:23); its exact location is unknown.

Jahaziah [Jahzeiah] (jā-ha-zī'a [ja'zee-a]; *Jehovah reveals*). A son of Tikvah. One of four men who opposed Ezra's condemnation of marriage to foreign women (Ezra 10:15). *See* Ezra.

Jahaziel (ja-hā'zi-el; *God reveals*). A Benjamite warrior who joined David at Ziklag (1 Chron. 12:4). [2] A priest who helped bring the ark of the covenant into the temple (1 Chron. 16:6). [3] A Levite, son of Hebron (1 Chron. 23:19; 24:23). [4] A Levite who encouraged Jehoshaphat's army against the Moabites (2 Chron. 20:14–17). [5] A tribal leader whose son returned from Babylon (Ezra 8:5).

Jahdai (ja'da-ī; *Jehovah leads* or *leader; guide*). One of the family of Caleb the spy (1 Chron. 2:47).

Jahdiel (ja'di-el; *union of God; God gives joy*). Head of a family of Manasseh east of the Jordan (1 Chron. 5:24).

Jahdo (ja'do; *union*). Descendant of Gad (1 Chron. 5:14).

Jahleel (ja'le-el; *God waits; wait for God*). A son of Zebulun (Gen. 46:14; Num. 26:26), ancestor of the Jahleelites (Num. 26:26).

Jahleelites (jā'leel-ites). Descendants of Jahleel.

Jahmai (ja'ma-ī; *Jehovah protects*). Tribal leader of Issachar (1 Chron. 7:2).

Jahzeel [Jahziel] (ja'ze-el; *God apportions*). A son of Naphtali listed three times (Gen. 46:24; Num. 26:48; 1 Chron. 7:13).

Jahzerah (ja'ze-ra; *Jehovah protects*). A priest of the family of Immer whose descendants dwelt in Jerusalem after the Babylonian exile (1 Chron. 9:12). Perhaps another name for Ahasai (Neh. 11:13).

Jahziel (ja'ze-el). *See* Jahzeel.

Jair (jā'ir; *Jehovah enlightens*). [1] A descendant of Judah through his father and of Manasseh through his mother (Num. 32:41; Deut. 3:14; 1 Kings 4:13; 1 Chron. 2:22). [2] Judge of Israel for twenty-two years (Judg. 10:3–5). [3] The father of Mordecai, Esther's cousin (Esther 2:5). [4] *See* Jaare-oregim.

Jairite (jā'ir-īte). A descendant of Jair No. 1 (2 Sam. 20:26).

Jairus (jā'ī-rus; *enlightened*). A ruler of a synagogue near Capernaum whose daughter Jesus raised from the dead (Mark 5:21–23, 35–43; Luke 8:41).

Jakan (jā'kan). *See* Jaakan.

Jakeh (jā'ke; *hearkening*). The father of Agur, the wise man (Prov. 30:1).

Jakim (jā'kim; *May God establish*). [1] Descendant of Benjamin (1 Chron. 8:19). [2] Head of a priestly family descended from Aaron (1 Chron. 24:12).

Jalon (jā'lon; *Jehovah abides*). A descendant of Caleb the spy (1 Chron. 4:17).

Jambres (jam'brēz; *he who is rebellious*). According to late Jewish tradition used by the apostle Paul (2 Tim. 3:8), one of the Egyptian magicians who opposed Moses (Exod. 7:9–13; cf. Exod. 7:9–13). *See* Jannes.

James (jāmz; Greek form of Jacob). [1] The son of Zebedee and brother of John called to be one of the twelve. He was slain by Herod Agrippa I (Matt. 4:21; Mark 5:37; Luke 9:54; Acts 12:2). [2] The son of Alpheus, another of the twelve apostles. He is probably the same as James *the less,* the son of Mary. By *the less* is meant his age or height in relation to James the son of Zebedee or James the less well-known. (Matt. 10:3; Mark 15:40; Acts 1:13). [3] The brother of Jesus (Matt. 13:55). After Christ's resurrection, he became a believer (1 Cor. 15:7) and a leader of the church at Jerusalem (Acts 12:17; Gal. 1:19; 2:9). He wrote the Epistle of James (James 1:1). [4] Unknown person mentioned as "the brother of Judas." Most view this as an incorrect translation and would render ". . . Judas, the son of James" (Luke 6:16; Acts 1:13).

Jamin (jā'min; *right hand; favor*). [1] A son of Simeon (Gen. 46:10; Exod. 6:15; Num. 26:12; 1 Chron.

4:24). **[2]** A descendant of Ram (1 Chron. 2:27). **[3]** A priest who explained the Law (Neh. 8:7).

Jaminites (jā′min-ītes). Descendants of Jamin [1].

Jamlech (jam′lek; *Jehovah rules*). A prince of Simeon (1 Chron. 4:34, 41).

Janna [Jannai] (jan′a [jan′ī]). An ancestor of Christ (Luke 3:24).

Jannes (jan-ez; *he who seduces*). An Egyptian magician who opposed Moses (2 Tim. 3:8–9; cf. Exod. 7:9–13). *See* Jambres.

Janoah [Janohah] (ja-nō′a [ja-nō′ha]; *resting*). **[1]** A city of the tribe of Naphtali, north of Galilee (2 Kings 15:29); possibly modern Yanuh, 10.5 km. (6.5 mi.) southeast of Tyre. **[2]** A town on Ephraim's border (Josh. 16:6); possibly modern Yanun, 11 km. (7 mi.) southeast of Shechem.

Janum [Janim] (jā′num [Ja′nim]; *sleeping*). A town in the mountains of Judah, west-southwest of Hebron (Josh. 15:53).

Japheth (jā′feth; *the extender; fair; enlarged*). One of the three sons of Noah, usually mentioned after his two brothers Shem and Ham, and thus presumed to be the youngest. Considered the father of the Indo-European races (Gen. 5:32; 6:10; 7:13; 9:18, 23, 27; 1 Chron. 1:4–5).

Japhia (jā-fī′a; *may God enlighten*). **[1]** Amorite king of Lachish defeated by Joshua (Josh. 10:3). **[2]** A son of David (2 Sam. 5:15; 1 Chron. 3:7; 14:6).

Japhia (jā-fī′a; *may God enlighten*). A boundary town of Zebulun, 3 km. (2 mi.) southwest of Nazareth (Josh. 19:12).

Japhlet (jaf′let; *may God deliver*). A descendant of Asher (1 Chron. 7:32–33).

Japhletites [Japhleti] (jaf′le′-tites [jaf′le-ti]. The descendants of Japhlet who lived near the southern border of Ephraim (Josh. 16:3). Apparently not the Japhlet of 1 Chron. 7:32–33.

Japho (jā′fo; *beautiful*). A Palestinian city on the Mediterranean coast 56 km. (34 mi.) northwest of Jerusalem (Josh. 19:46). It was later called Joppa (q.v.).

Jarah (jā′ra; *unveiler; honey*). A son of Ahaz of the family of Saul (1 Chron. 9:42). He is called Jehoadah in First Chronicles 8:36.

Jareb (jā′reb; *contender; avenger*). A king of Assyria (Hos. 5:13; 10:6); surely a nickname.

Jared [Jered] (jā′red [je′red]; *servant*). A descendant of Seth and ancestor of Christ (Gen. 5:15–20; 1 Chron. 1:2; Luke 3:37).

Jaresiah [Jaareshiah] (jar-e-sī′a [ja-ar-e-shī′a]; *Jehovah plants*). A descendant of Benjamin son of Jehoram (1 Chron. 8:27).

Jarha (jar′ha). An Egyptian servant who married his master's daughter (1 Chron. 2:34–35).

Jarib (jā′rib; *may God strive*). [1] A tribal leader in the time of Ezra (Ezra 8:16). [2] A priest who divorced his foreign wife after the Exile (Ezra 10:18). [3] *See* Jachin [1].

Jarmuth (jar′muth; *height*). [1] A city in the lowlands of Judah (Josh. 10:3); modern Khirbet Yarmuk. [2] A city of the tribe of Issachar assigned to the Levites (Josh. 21:29); the same as Ramoth [3].

Jaroah (ja-rō′a; *new moon*). A descendant of Gad (1 Chron. 5:14).

Jashen (jā′shen *shining*). The father of some, or one, of David's mighty men (2 Sam. 23:32). But the text probably should read thus: ". . . Jashen, Jonathan the son of

Shammah the Hararite." Thus, Jashen would be one of the mighty men, and Shage (1 Chron. 11:34) is the same as Shammah (2 Sam. 23:33). *See also* Hashem.

Jasher [Jasher] (jā'sher [ja'shar]; *upright*). One who wrote a now lost book (Josh. 10:13; 2 Sam. 1:18).

Jashobeam (ja-shō-be-am; *the people return*). [1] One of David's mighty men (1 Chron. 11:11; 27:2). [2] One who joined David at Ziklag (1 Chron. 12:6). *See* Adino.

Jashub (jā'shub; *turning back*). [1] A son of Issachar and founder of a tribal family, the Jashubites (Num. 26:24). [2] One who divorced his foreign wife (Ezra 10:29). *See* Jashubi-lehem. [2] *See* Job [2].

Jashubi-lehem (je-shū'bi-lē'hem; *turning back to Bethlehem*). A descendant of Judah (1 Chron. 4:22).

Jashubites (jā'shu-bītes). Descendants of Jasute.

Jasiel (jā'si-el). *See* Jaasiel.

Jason (jā'sun; *healing*). [1] Paul's host during his stay at Thessalonica (Acts 17:5–9). [2] A Jewish Christian kinsman of Paul who sent salutations to Rome (Rom. 16:21). Both are possibly identical.

Jathniel (jath'ni-el; *God is giving*). A gatekeeper of the tabernacle (1 Chron. 26:2).

Jattir (jat'ir; *preeminence*). A town in the mountains of Judah, assigned to the Levites (Josh. 15:48; 21:14); possibly modern Khirbet 'Atti, 21 km. (13 mi.) south-southwest of Hebron.

Javan (jā'van). Fourth son of Japheth (Gen. 10:2, 4; 1 Chron. 1:5, 7). The name corresponds etymologically with Ionia and may denote the Greeks (cf. Isa. 66:19).

Javan (jā'van; *Ionians*). A trading post in southern Arabia (Ezek. 27:13).

Jazer (jā'zer; *fortified*). A fortified Amorite city east of the

Jordan river (Josh. 13:25). Captured by Israel and rebuilt by Gad.

Jaziz (jā'ziz; *shining*). David's chief shepherd (1 Chron. 27:31).

Jearim (jē'a-rim; *woods*). Mountains marking the boundary of Judah about 13 km. (8 mi.) northeast of Beth-shemesh (Josh. 15:10).

Jeaterai [Jeatherai] (je-at'e—rī [je-ath'-e-rī]; *steadfast*). A descendant of Gershon (1 Chron. 6:21).

Jeberechiah (je-ber-e-kī'a; *Jehovah is blessing*). The father of the Zechariah whom Isaiah took as a witness (Isa. 8:2).

Jebus (jē'bus; *manager*). An early name for Jerusalem (Judg. 19:10–11).

Jebusites (jē'bu-sītes). Original inhabitants of the city of Jebus. King David's army defeated the Jebusites after Joab apparently snuck into the city through an underground water shaft to lead the conquest (2 Sam. 5:69; 1 Chron. 11:4–8). David then renamed the former Jebusite stronghold, "the city of David" and made it the capital of his kingdom.

Jecamiah [Jekamiah] (jek-a-mī'a; *may Jehovah establish*). **[1]** A descendant of Judah (1 Chron. 2:41). **[2]** A son of King Jeconiah (Jehoiachin; 1 Chron. 3:18).

Jecholiah [Jecoliah; Jechiliah; Jecoliah] (jek-o-lī'a, [jeki-lī-a; jek-ō-lī-a]; *Jehovah is able*). Mother of Uzziah (or Azariah), king of Judah (2 Kings 15:2; 2 Chron. 26:3).

Jechonias (jek-o-nī'as). Greek form of Jeconiah. *See* Jehoiachin.

Jecoliah (jek-o-lī'a). *See* Jecholiah.

Jeconiah (jek-o-nī'a). *See* Jehoiachin.

Jedaiah (je-dā′ya; *Jehovah is praise*). [1] A descendant of Simeon (1 Chron. 4:37). [2] One who helped repair the wall (Neh. 3:10).

Jedaiah (je-dā′ya; *Jehovah has favored*). [1] A son of Shimri (1 Chron. 4:37). [2] A priest of Jerusalem (1 Chron. 9:10; 24:7; Ezra 2:36; Neh. 7:39). [3] A priest whose descendants returned from Babylonian exile (Neh. 7:39). [4] A Judahite who helped repair the walls of Jerusalem (Neh. 3:10). [5] A priest who returned with Zerubbabel (Neh. 11:10; 12:6, 19). [6] Another priest who came up with Zerubbabel (Neh. 12:7, 21). [7] One who brought gifts to the temple (Zech. 6:10, 14).

Jediael (je-dī′a-el; *known by God*). [1] A son of Benjamin (1 Chron. 7:6, 10–11). Possibly the same as Ashbel (1 Chron. 8:1). [2] One of David's mighty men (1 Chron. 11:45). [3] One who joined David at Ziklag (1 Chron. 12:20). [4] A descendant of Korah, son of Meshelemiah (1 Chron. 26:2).

Jedidah (je-dī′da; *beloved*). Mother of King Josiah (2 Kings 22:1).

Jedidiah (je-di-dī-a; *beloved of Jehovah*). The name God gave Solomon through Nathan (2 Sam. 12:25).

Jeduthun (je-dū′thun; *the praising one*). [1] One of the three chief musicians of the service of song (1 Chron. 9:16; 25:1–6; Neh. 11:17). He was also named Ethan (1 Chron. 6:44; 15:17, 19). [2] The father of Obed-edom (1 Chron. 16:38). Some believe him identical with [1].

Jeezer (je-ē′zer; contracted form of Abiezer, *father of help*). A descendant of Manasseh (Num. 26:30). Probably the same as the Abiezer of Joshua's time (Josh. 17:2; 1 Chron. 7:18).

Jeezerites (je-ē'zer-ītes). Descendants of Jeezer.

Jegar-sahadutha [Galeed] (jē'gar-sa-had-ū'tha [gal'e-ed]; *heap of witness*). A pile of stones erected by Laban to memorialize his pact with Jacob; near Mount Gilead north of the Jabbok River (Gen. 31:47). Galeed is Hebrew and Jegar-sahadutha is Aramaic; both mean the same thing.

Jehaleleel [Jehalelel; Jehallelel] (je-hai-ē'le-el [je-hal'e-lel]; *may God shine forth*). [1] A descendant of Judah through Caleb the spy (1 Chron. 4:16). [2] A descendant of Merari in the time of Hezekiah (2 Chron. 29:12).

Jehdeiah (je-dē'ya; *may Jehovah rejoice*). [1] A descendant of Levi in David's time (1 Chron. 24:20). [2] An overseer of David's donkeys (1 Chron. 27:30).

Jehezekel [Jehezkel] (je-hez'e-kel [je-hez'-kel]; *Jehovah strengthens*). A priest with sanctuary duty (1 Chron. 24:16).

Jehiah (je-hī'a; *Jehovah is living*). A Levite gatekeeper of the ark (1 Chron. 15:24). He was also called Jeiel (1 Chron. 15:18; 2 Chron. 20:14).

Jehiel [Jehuel] (je-hī'el [je-hū'el]; *God is living*). [1] A singer in the tabernacle in David's time (1 Chron. 15:18; 16:5). [2] A descendant of Gershon (1 Chron. 23:8; 29:8). [3] A companion of the sons of David (1 Chron. 27:32). [4] A son of Jehoshaphat (2 Chron. 21:2). [5] A son of Heman the singer (2 Chron. 29:14). [6] A Levite in charge of the dedicated things in the temple (2 Chron. 31:13). [7] A chief priest in Josiah's day (2 Chron. 35:8). [8] Father of one who returned from the Exile (Ezra 8:9). [9] Father of the one who first admitted taking a foreign wife during the Exile (Ezra 10:2).

[10], [11] Two who divorced their foreign wives after the Babylonian exile (Ezra 10:21, 26).

Jehieli (je-hī′e-lī; *Jehovah lives*). A Levite set over the treasures of the sanctuary in David's time (1 Chron. 26:21–22). *See* Jehiel.

Jehizkiah (jē-hiz-kī′a; *Jehovah is strong* or *Jehovah strengthens*). An opponent of those who would have made fellow Jews slaves (2 Chron. 28:12). *See* Hezekiah.

Jehoadah [Jehoaddah] (je-hō′a-da [je-hō′a-da]; *Jehovah unveils; Jehovah has numbered*). *See* Jarah.

Jehoaddan [Jehoaddin] (je-ho-ad′an [je-ho-ad′an]; *Jehovah gives delight*). Mother of King Amaziah and wife of King Joash (2 Kings 14:2; 2 Chron. 25:1).

Jehoahaz (je-hō′a-haz; *Jehovah upholds*). **[1]** Son and successor of Jehu on the throne of Israel. His reign was one of disaster (2 Kings 10:35; 13:2–25). **[2]** The son of Josiah and ruler of Judah for three months before he was deposed by Pharaoh Necho (2 Kings 23:30–34; 2 Chron. 36:1–4). He was also called Shallum before becoming king (1 Chron. 3:15; Jer. 22:11). **[3]** *See* Ahaziah [2].

Jehoash [Joash] [je′hō-ash [jō′ash]; *Jehovah has given; Jehovah supports*). **[1]** The father of Gideon (Judg. 6:11). **[2]** A man commanded by King Ahab to imprison the prophet Micaiah (1 Kings 22:26). **[3]** The eighth king of Judah. Until the time of Jehoiada the priest's death, Jehoash followed God; afterwards, he brought idolatry and disaster to his country (2 Kings 11:21–12:21). He is more frequently called by the shortened form of his name, Joash. **[4]** The thirteenth king of Israel; he was successful in many military campaigns (2 Kings 13:9–14:16). He is most frequently called Joash, an abbreviated form of his name. **[5]** A descendant of Shelah, the family of Judah (1 Chron. 4:22). **[6]** A descendant of Becher, of the family of Benjamin (1 Chron. 7:8). **[7]** A commander of the warriors who left Saul and joined David's army at Ziklag (1 Chron. 12:3). **[8]** An officer in charge of David's olive oil supplies (1 Chron. 27:28).

Jehohanan (je-hō-hā′nan; *Jehovah is gracious*). **[1]** A gatekeeper of the tabernacle in David's time (1 Chron. 26:3). **[2]** A chief captain of Judah (2 Chron. 17:15). **[3]** Father of Ishmael (2 Chron. 23:1). **[4]** One who divorced his foreign wife after the Exile (Ezra 10:28). **[5]** A priest who returned to Jerusalem with Zerubbabel (Neh. 12:13). **[6]** A singer at the purification of the wall of Jerusalem (Neh. 12:42). **[7]** Son of Tobiah the Ammonite (Neh. 6:17–18). **[8]** A son of Eliashib [Johanan] (Ezra 10:6).

Jehoiachin [Jechonias, Jeconiah] (je-hoi′a-kin [jek-o-nī′as; jek-o-nī-a]; *Jehovah establishes*). Ruler of Judah when it was captured by Nebuchadnezzar. He was an ancestor of Christ (2 Kings 24:8–16; 2 Chron. 36:9–10; Matt. 1:11–12). Jeconiah [Jechonias] ("Jehovah is able") is an altered form of his name (1 Chron. 3:16–17; Jer. 24:1) as is Coniah ("Jehovah is creating"; Jer. 22:24, 28; 37:1).

Jehoiada (je-hoi′a-da; *Jehovah knows*). **[1]** The father of Benaiah, one of David's officers (2 Sam. 8:18; 1 Kings 1:8, 26). **[2]** The chief priest of the temple for many years of the monarchy. He hid Joash from Athaliah for 6 years (2 Kings 11–12:9). **[3]** One who joined David at Ziklag (1 Chron. 12:27). **[4]** A counselor of David (1 Chron. 27:34). **[5]** One who helped to repair a gate of Jerusalem (Neh. 3:6). **[6]** A priest replaced by Zephaniah (Jer. 29:26). *See* Joiada.

Jehoiakim (je-hoi′a-kim; *Jehovah sets up* or *Jehovah has established*). The name given to Eliakim by Pharaoh Necho when he made him king of Judah. The name probably means that Necho claimed Jehovah had authorized him to put Eliakim on the throne (2 Kings 23:34—24:6). Not to be confused with Joiakim.

Jehoiarib (je-hoi′a-rib; *Jehovah contends*). [1] Head of a family of Aaron (1 Chron. 24:7). [2] *See* Joiarib [3].

Jehonadab [Jonadab] (je-hon′a-dab [jon′a-dab]; *Jehovah is liberal*). [1] Descendant of Rechab, who forbade his followers and descendants to drink wine and live in houses (Jer. 35:6–19; 2 Kings 10:15, 23). [2] The sly son of David's brother, Shimeah (2 Sam. 13:3, 5, 32, 35).

Jehonathan (je-hon′a-than; *Jehovah gives*). [1] An overseer of David's storehouses (1 Chron. 27:25). [2] One sent by Jehoshaphat to teach the Law (2 Chron. 17:8). [3] A priest (Neh. 12:18). He is called Jonathan in Nehemiah 12:35.

Jehoram [Joram] (je-hō′ram [jō′ram]; *Jehovah is exalted*). Joram is a shortened form of the name. [1] Son of Toi, king of Hamath (2 Sam. 8:9–10). [2] The fifth king of Judah. Son and successor of Jehoshaphat and an ancestor of Christ (2 Kings 8:16–24; Matt. 1:8). [3] The tenth king of Israel, slain by Jehu (2 Kings 1:17; 3:1–6; 9:24). [4] A priest commissioned to teach the people (2 Chron. 17:8).

Jehoshabeath [Jehosheba] (je-hō-shab′e-ath [je-hosh-e-ba]; *Jehovah is her oath*). A daughter of Jehoram, king of Judah, who helped conceal Joash (2 Chron. 22:11). In Second Kings 1:2, she is called Jehosheba.

Jehoshaphat [Josaphat] [Joshaphat] (je-hosh′a-fat [jos′a-fat] [josh′a-fat]; *Jehovah is judge*). [1] The recorder

J

of David (2 Sam. 8:16; 20:24; 1 Kings 4:3). **[2]** An officer of Solomon (1 Kings 4:17). **[3]** Father of Jehu, who conspired against Joram (2 Kings 9:2, 14). **[4]** A priest who helped to bring the ark of the covenant from Obed-edom (1 Chron. 15:24). **[5]** Faithful king of Judah and an ancestor of Christ (1 Kings 22:41–50; Matt. 1:8).

Jehoshaphat (je-hosh′a-fat; *Jehovah is judge*). The valley where the Last Judgment will take place (Joel 3:2); tradition identifies it as the Kidron Valley (q.v.).

Jehosheba (je-hosh′e-ba). *See* Jehoshabeath.

Jehoshua (je-hosh′u-a). *See* Joshua.

Jehovah [Yahweh] (je-hō′va [ya′wā]). One of the most important names for God in the Old Testament. Derived from the verb *to be,* its meaning is most often rendered, *I am who I am,* and *I will be who I will be.* This divine name was revealed to Moses in the burning bush (Exod. 3:14) and is expressed in Hebrew simply by the four consonants, YHWH. *See* YHWH.

Jehovah-jireh (je-hō′va-jī′re; *Jehovah will provide*). The place where Abraham attempted to offer Isaac as a sacrifice (Gen. 22:14); its exact location is unknown.

Jehovah-nissi (je-hō′va-nis′ī; *Jehovah is my banner*). The altar that Moses built at Rephidim in honor of Israel's victory over Amalek (Exod. 17:15).

Jehovah-shalom (je-hō′va-sha′lom; *Jehovah will send peace*). An altar that Gideon built at Ophrah [2] (Judg. 6:24).

Jehozabad (je-hoz′a-bad; *Jehovah endows*). **[1]** A servant who killed Jehoash (2 Kings 12:21; 2 Chron. 24:26). **[2]** A gatekeeper descended from Korah (1 Chron. 26:4). **[3]** A chief captain of Jehoshaphat (2 Chron. 17:18). Not to be confused with Jozabad.

Jehozadak (je-hoz'a-dak). *See* Josedech.

Jehu (jē'hū; *Jehovah is he*). [1] The prophet who brought tidings of disaster to Baasha of Israel (1 Kings 16:1–12; 2 Chron. 19:2). [2] The eleventh king of Israel (1 Kings 19:16–17; 2 Kings 9–10). His corrupt leadership weakened the nation. [3] A descendant of Hezron (1 Chron. 2:38). [4] A descendant of Simeon (1 Chron. 4:35). [5] One who joined David at Ziklag (1 Chron. 12:3).

Jehubbah (je-hūb'a; *Jehovah is hidden*). A descendant of Asher (1 Chron. 7:34).

Jehucal [Jucal] (je-hū'kal [joo'kal]; *Jehovah is able*). A messenger of Zedekiah (Jer. 37:3; 38:1).

Jehud (jē'hud; *honorable*). A town of the tribe of Dan located between Baalath and Bene-berak (Josh. 19:45); probably modern el-Yehudiyeh.

Jehudi (je-hū'dī; *Judahite, a Jew*). A man who brought Baruch to the princes and read the king Jeremiah's prophecies (Jer. 36:14, 21, 23).

Jehudijah (je-hu-dī'ja; *the Jewess*). The wife of Ezra and descendant of Caleb (1 Chron. 4:18).

Jehuel. *See* Jehiel.

Jehush [Jeush] (jē'hush [jē'ush]; *collector*). [1] A son of Esau and Aholibamah (Gen. 36:5, 14, 18). [2] A Benjaminite, son of Bilhan (1 Chron. 7:10). [3] A man of the family of Saul (1 Chron. 8:39). [4] A son of Shimei and a Gershonite Levite (1 Chron. 23:10–11). [5] A son of King Rehoboam and grandson of King Solomon (2 Chron. 11:19).

Jeiel [Jehiel] (je-ī'el [je-hī'el]; *God snatches away*). [1] A chief of the tribe of Reuben (1 Chron. 5:7). [2] An ancestor of Saul (1 Chron. 9:35). [3] One of David's mighty men (1 Chron. 11:44). [4] A singer and gatekeeper of the tabernacle (1 Chron. 15:18, 21; 16:5). [5]

A descendant of Asaph (2 Chron. 20:14). **[6]** A scribe or recorder of Uzziah (2 Chron. 26:11). **[7]** A Levite in Hezekiah's time (2 Chron. 29:13). **[8]** A chief Levite in the days of Josiah (2 Chron. 35:9). **[9]** One who returned to Jerusalem with Ezra (Ezra 8:13). **[10]** One who married a foreign wife during the Exile (Ezra 10:43).

Jekabzeel (je-kab´ze-el; *congregation of God*). See Kabzeel.

Jekameam (jek-a-mē´am; *raise up*). A descendant of Levi (1 Chron. 23:19; 24:23).

Jekamiah (jek-a-mī´a). See Jecamiah.

Jekuthiel (je-kū´thi-el; *may God nourish*). A descendant of the spy Caleb (1 Chron. 4:18).

Jemima (je-mī´ma; *little dove*). First daughter of Job to be born after his restoration from affliction (Job 42:14).

Jemuel (jem´u-el; *God is light*). See Nemuel.

Jephthae (jef´the). Greek form of Jephthah (q.v.).

Jephthah [Jephthae] (jef´tha [jef´the]; *God will set free*). The ninth judge of Israel who delivered his people from Ammon (Judg. 11—12:7).

Jephunneh (je-fun´e; *appearing*). **[1]** A man of Judah and father of Caleb the spy (Num. 13:6; 14:6; Deut. 1:36). **[2]** Head of a family of the tribe of Asher (1 Chron. 7:38).

Jerah (jē´ra; *moon*). A son of Joktan (Gen. 10:26; 1 Chron. 1:20). Possibly an Arabian tribe is intended.

Jerahmeel (je-ra´me-el; *God is merciful*). **[1]** A son of Hezron, grandson of Judah (1 Chron. 2:9, 25–27, 33, 42). **[2]** A son of Kish (1 Chron. 24:29). **[3]** An officer of Jehoiakim (Jer. 36:26).

Jerjhmeelites (je-ra-meel´ites). Descendants of Jerahmeel (1 Sam. 27:10; 30:29).

Jered (jē′red; *low; flowing*). **[1]** A son of Ezra, a descendant of Caleb (1 Chron. 4:18). **[2]** *See* Jared.

Jeremai (jer′e-mī; *Jehovah is high*). One who divorced his foreign wife after the Exile (Ezra 10:33).

Jeremiah [Jeremias; Jeremy] (jer-e-mī′a [jer-e-mī′as; jer′e-mī]; *Jehovah is high*). **[1]** The father of Hamutal (Jer. 52:1). **[2]** A woman of Libnah whose daughter married King Josiah (2 Kings 23:31; Jer. 52:1). **[3]** Head of a family of the tribe of Manasseh (1 Chron. 5:24). **[4]** One who joined David at Ziklag (1 Chron. 12:4). **[5]** A man of Gad who joined David at Ziklag (1 Chron. 12:10). **[6]** Another who joined David at Ziklag (1 Chron. 12:13). **[7]** A priest who sealed the new covenant with God after the Exile (Neh. 10:2; 12:1, 12). **[8]** A descendant of Jonadab (Jer. 35:3). **[9]** A prophet whose activity covered the reigns of the last five kings of Judah. He denounced the policies and idolatries of his nation (Jer. 1; 20; 26; 36).

Jeremias (jer-e-mī′as). Greek form of Jeremiah (q.v.).

Jeremoth [Jerimoth, Ramoth] (jer′e-mōth [jer′i-moth] [ra′mōth]; *elevation*). **[1]** A son of Becher, of the tribe of Benjamin (1 Chron. 7:8). **[2]** A son of Beriah (1 Chron. 8:14). **[3], [4]** Three who married foreign wives (Ezra 10:26–27, 29). **[5]** A son of Mushi, descendant of Levi (1 Chron. 23:23). He is called Jerimoth in First Chronicles 24:30. **[6]** One appointed by David to the song service of the temple (1 Chron. 25:22). He is called Jerimoth in First Chronicles 25:4. **[7]** A son of Azriel and chief officer of the tribe of Naphtali during David's reign (1 Chron. 27:19).

Jeriah [Jerijah] (jer-ī′a [jer-ī′ja]; *Jehovah sees*). A descendant of Hebron in the days of David (1 Chron. 23:19; 24:23; 26:31).

Jeribai (jer′i-bī; *Jehovah contends*). One of David's mighty men (1 Chron. 11:46).

Jericho (jer′i-kō; *his sweet smell*). A fortified city of Canaan located about 8 km. (5 mi.) from the north end of the Dead Sea and 16 km. (10 mi.) northwest of the Jordan River (Num. 22:1; Deut. 32:49). Founded as early as 8000 B.C. Today it is the oldest continually inhabited city in the world.

Jeriel (jer′i-el; *God sees*). A descendant of Issachar (1 Chron. 7:2).

Jerijah (jer-ī′ja). *See* Jeriah.

Jerimoth (jer′i-moth; *elevation*). [1] A son of Bela (1 Chron. 7:7). [2] A son of Becher, son of Benjamin (1 Chron. 7:8). [3] One who joined David at Ziklag (1 Chron. 12:5). [4] A ruler of the tribe of Naphtali (1 Chron. 27:19). [5] A son of David (2 Chron. 11:18). [6], [7] *See* Jeremoth [5], [6]. [8] A Levite overseer in the temple during the reign of King Hezekiah of Judah (2 Chron. 31:13).

Jerioth (je′ri-oth; *tent curtains*). A wife or concubine of Caleb (1 Chron. 2:18).

Jeroboam (jer-o-bō′am; *enlarger; he pleads the people's cause*). [1] The first king of Israel after the division of the kingdom. He reigned for 22 years (1 Kings 11:26–40; 12:1–14:20). [2] The thirteenth king of Israel; his Israel was strong but overtly idolatrous (2 Kings 14:23–29).

Jeroham (je-rō′ham; *loved*). [1] A Levite, the grandfather of Samuel (1 Sam. 1:1; 1 Chron. 6:27). [2] A descendant of Benjamin (1 Chron. 9:8). [3] Head of a family of Benjamin (1 Chron. 8:27). [4] A priest whose son lived in Jerusalem after the Exile (1 Chron. (9:12; Neh. 11:12). [5] Father of two who joined David at Ziklag

(1 Chron. 12:7). **[6]** Father of Azareel, prince of Dan (1 Chron. 27:22). **[7]** Father of one who helped Jehoiada to set Joash on the throne of Judah (2 Chron. 23:1). **[8]** Father of Adaiah the priest (Neh. 11:12). May be the same as [4].

Jerubbaal (jer-ub-bā'al; *let Baal contend* or possibly *let Baal show himself great*). The name given to Gideon by his father (Judg. 6:32; 7:1; 8:29).

Jerubbesheth (jer-ub-bē'sheth; *contender with the idol*). Name given to Jerubbaal (Gideon) by those who wanted to avoid pronouncing Baal (2 Sam. 11:21).

Jeruel (je-rū'el; *founded by God*). A wilderness area in Judah near the cliff of Ziz and En-gedi (2 Chron. 20:16).

Jerusalem (je-rū'sa-lem; *possession of peace*). Capital of the southern kingdom of Judah until its destruction by Nebuchadnezzar in 586 B.C. Located 48 km. (30 mi.) from the Mediterranean Sea and 27 km. (18 mi.) west of the Jordan River (Josh. 10:1; 2 Sam. 5:5).

Jerusalem, The New (je-rū'sa-lem). The holy city described by John in Revelation 21—22. Not built by human hands, the New Jerusalem is a heavenly city built and provided for by God (Rev. 21:2).

Jerusha [Jerushah] (Je-rū'sha [je-rū'sha]; *taken in marriage*). The wife of King Uzziah (2 Kings 15:33; 2 Chron. 27:1).

Jesaiah [Jeshaiah] (je-sā'ya [je-shā'ya]; *Jehovah is helper*). **[1]** A grandson of Zerubbabel (1 Chron. 3:21). **[2]** One appointed to the song service (1 Chron. 25:3, 15). **[3]** A grandson of Moses (1 Chron. 26:25). **[4]** One who returned from the Babylonian Captivity (Ezra 8:7). **[5]** A descendant of Merari who returned from Exile (Ezra 8:19). **[6]** One whose descendants dwelled in Jerusalem (Neh. 11:17).

JERUSALEM AND HISTORY

The most famous city in Bible lands is Jerusalem. From early times it was an important center. For example, Abram gave gifts to Melchizedek, who was the "king of Salem" (Gen. 14:18). This "Salem" was most likely the city of Jerusalem.

When the Israelites conquered the Promised Land, Benjamin's tribe was assigned the territory that included Jerusalem. But the invading armies were not strong enough to capture the city, and it was not until King David's time that Jerusalem finally became Hebrew territory (2 Sam. 5:6–7). David made the city his capital. He brought the ark of the covenant there, pitched a suitable tent for it, and began planning a temple to house the ark. His son Solomon completed the job (2 Sam. 7:12–16 and 1 Kings 5–6).

Later kings neglected both the temple and the city of Jerusalem. But at the height of its glory, Jerusalem was a showplace of the nation and the temple was world-famous. The greatest era in the history of the city and temple was under Solomon.

The city was protected by God when the national leaders worshiped Him and trusted Him. When Sennacherib attempted to destroy it, the Assyrian army was destroyed by a miracle from God (2 Kings 19:35–37).

In 587 B.C. Nebuchadnezzar of Babylon invaded Palestine, overran the city, and took the people away as slaves. The expensive treasures that were housed in the city and the many skilled craftsmen who maintained the valuable works of art and architectural design are described in 2 Kings 24:10–17.

For fifty years the city of Jerusalem lay in waste, but in 537 B.C. Zerubbabel and 50,000 followers were allowed to return and start rebuilding (Ezra 2:64–65; 3:8). Nehemiah rebuilt the walls of Jerusalem in about 444 B.C. (Neh. 6:15). Slowly, the Hebrews returned from their captivity and worked at rebuilding other sections of their city.

Other strong nations arose—the Greeks under Alexander the Great, the Egyptians, and the Persians. In 198 B.C., Jerusalem became a part of the Seleucid Empire. Judas Maccabee, one of Israel's greatest heros, retook the city in 165 B.C. and purified the temple.

In 63 B.C., Roman armies swept through Palestine and captured Jerusalem, ruining what was left of Zerubbabel's attempts to rebuild the temple. However, in 37 B.C., Herod the Great began rebuilding the temple on a grand scale; his work was so complex that the temple wasn't complete when Jesus was taken there as a baby (Luke 2:21–39). The end of Jerusalem's history in biblical times came when Titus, the Roman emperor, leveled the city and temple in A.D. 70.

Despite the troubled history of the "holy city," it still stands as a symbol of the Jewish people. "Zion" is one name given to it (although this really refers to one of the several hills around Jerusalem). The Bible calls the city by various names of honor: "city of David" (2 Sam. 5:7); "city of God" (Psa. 46:4); "city of truth" (Zec. 8:3); "holy city" (Neh. 11:1); "throne of the Lord" (Jer. 3:17) and many more.

The Egyptian pharaoh's daughter visited Solomon there (1 Kings 3:1); the Queen of Sheba also visited (1 Kings 10:1–2). Many events of Jesus' earthly ministry occurred there: Palm Sunday, the meal in an upper room, the trials and death of Christ, and His appearance after the Resurrection (Luke 24:33ff.).

In both Hebrews and Revelation, Jerusalem symbolizes the future hope of Christians who are faithful. The fact that heaven is called the "New Jerusalem" (Rev. 21:2) shows that eternal life will be beautiful and wonderful, even as a perfect Jerusalem would be (Heb. 12:22; Rev. 21:10; 22:19).

Even today, Jerusalem is a center for historical study and international struggle. Three world religions claim it as a holy city—Islam, Judaism, and Christianity.

Jeshanah (jesh′ā-na; *old*). [1] A city in the hill country of Ephraim (2 Chron. 13:19); variously identified as modern 'Ain Sinya, 6 km. (4 mi.) north of Bethel, or Burj el-Isanah, about 10 km. (6 mi.) north of Bethel. [2] The Old Gate in the northwest corner of Jerusalem at the time of Nehemiah (Neh. 3:6; 12:39).

Jesharelah (jesh-a-rē′la). *See* Asarelah.

Jeshebeab (je-sheb′e-ab; *may the father endure*). Head of the fourteenth course of priests (1 Chron. 24:13).

Jesher (jē-sher; *rightness*). A son of Caleb (1 Chron. 2:18).

Jeshiah [Jesshiah] (je-shī′a [je-shī′a]; *Jehovah exists*). The second son of Uzziel (1 Chron. 23:20). Also called Ishiah (1 Chron. 24:25).

Jeshimon (jesh′i-mon; *wasteland*). [1] A wilderness area lying west of the Dead Sea a few kilometers south of Hebron (1 Sam. 23:19; 26:1, 3). [2] A wilderness on the northeast end of the Dead Sea, near Pisgah and Peor (Num. 21:20).

Jeshishai (je-shi′sha-i; *Jehovah is ancient or aged*). A descendant of Gad (1 Chron. 5:14).

Jeshohaiah (je-sho-hā′ya; *humbled by Jehovah*). A descendant of Simeon (1 Chron. 4:36).

Jeshua [Jeshuah] (jesh′u-a [jesh′u-a]; *Jehovah is deliverance*). [1] A priest of the sanctuary (1 Chron. 24:11; Ezra 2:36; Neh. 7:39). [2] A Levite in charge of various offerings to the temple (2 Chron. 31:15). [3] A priest who returned to Jerusalem with Zerubbabel (Ezra 2:2; 3:2–9; 4:3; Neh. 7:7; 12:1–26). [4] Father of Jozabad the Levite (Ezra 8:33). [5] One whose descendants returned from the Exile (Ezra 2:6; Neh. 7:11). [6] Father of one who repaired the wall of Jerusalem (Neh. 3:19). [7] A Levite who explained the Law to the people (Neh. 8:7; 9:4–5). [8] One who sealed the new covenant with God after the Exile (Ezra 2:40; Neh. 7:43; 10:9). Some believe he is identical with [6]. [9] *See* Joshua.

Jeshua (jesh′u-a; *a savior*). A town in southern Judah that was repopulated by Jews returning from the Babylonian Captivity (Neh. 11:26); probably modern Tell es-

Sa'roeh, about 19 km. (12 mi.) eastnortheast of Beer-sheba.

Jeshurun [Jesurun] (jesh'u-run [jes'oo-run]; *beloved*). A symbolic name for Israel (Deut. 32:15; Isa. 44:2).

Jesiah [Isshiah] [Jesshiah] (je-sī'a [ish-ī'-a] [je-shī'a]; *Jehovah exists*). **[1]** One who joined David at Ziklag (1 Chron. 12:6). **[2]** A descendant of Uzziel and a Levite (1 Chron. 23:20). He is called Isshiah in First Chronicles 24:25.

Jesimiel (je-sim'i-el; *God sets*). A descendant of Simeon (1 Chron. 4:36).

Jesse (jes'e; *Jehovah exists; wealthy*). Father of David and an ancestor of Christ (Ruth 4:17, 22; 1 Sam. 17:17; Matt. 1:5–6).

Jesshiah (je-shī'a). *See* Jeshiah.

Jesui (jes'u-ī). *See* Ishui.

Jesuites (jez'ū-ites). Descendants of Jesui, of the tribe of Asher (Num. 26:44).

Jesurun (jes'oo-run). *See* Jeshurun.

Jesus [Jose] (jē'zus [jō'-zē]; *Greek form of Joshua*). **[1]** Jesus Barabbas, a prisoner released by Pontius Pilate before the crucifixion of Jesus of Nazareth (Mt. 27:16–17). **[2]** A Christian who, with Paul, sent greetings to the Colossians (Col. 4:11); he was also called Justus. **[3]** *See* Joshua.

Jesus Christ (jē'zus krīst; Jesus—*Jehovah is salvation*, Christ—*the anointed one*). The son of the Virgin Mary who came to earth to fulfill the prophecies of the King who would die for the sins of His people. The account of His ministry is found in the Gospels of Matthew, Mark, Luke, and John.

Jesus Justus *See* Justus.

Jesus, son of Sirach. Author of the apocryphal book of Ecclesiasticus.

Jether [Jithran] (jē'ther [jith'ran]; *abundance*). [1] The firstborn son of Gideon (Judg. 8:20). [2] A son of Jerahmeel (1 Chron. 2:32). [3] A descendant of Caleb the spy (1 Chron. 4:17). [4] A descendant of Asher (1 Chron. 7:38). [5] *See* Ithra.

Jetheth (jē'theth; *subjection*). A duke of Edom (Gen. 36:40; 1 Chron. 1:51).

Jethlah [Ithlah] [Jithlah] (jeth'la [ith'la] [jith'la]; *a hanging place*). A town of Dan (Josh. 19:42).

Jethro (jeth'ro; *excellence*). The father-in-law of Moses. He advised Moses to delegate the time-consuming administration of justice (Exod. 3:1; 4:18; 18:1–12). He is called Reuel in Exodus 2:18. In Numbers 10:29, the KJV calls him Raguel; but the Hebrew text reads Reuel.

Jetur (jē'tur). A son of Ishmael (Gen. 25:15; 1 Chron. 1:31).

Jeuel (je-ū'el; *God has healed*). A descendant of Judah (1 Chron. 9:6).

Jeush [Jehush] (jē'ush [jē'hush]; *collector*). [1] A son of Esau (Gen. 36:5, 14, 18; 1 Chron. 1:35). [2] A descendant of Benjamin (1 Chron. 7:10). [3] A son of Eshek and a descendant of King Saul (1 Chron. 8:39). [4] A descendant of Gershon and the head of a clan (1 Chron. 23:10–11). [5] A son of Rehoboam (2 Chron. 11:19).

Jeuz (jē'uz; *counselor*). Son of Shaharaim, a descendant of Benjamin (1 Chron. 8:10).

Jews. A name first applied to the people living in Judah after the division of the monarchy into North (Israel) and South (Judah). Applied to all the descendants of Abraham after the Babylonian exile. *See* Hebrews.

Jezaniah (jez-a-nī′a). *See* Jaazaniah [1].

Jezebel (jez′e-bel; *unexalted; unhusbanded*). [1] The wicked, idolatrous queen of Israel (1 Kings 16:31; 18:4–21:25; 2 Kings 9:7–37). [2] A false prophetess at Thyatira (Rev. 2:20). Possibly the name is symbolic and not the prophetess's real name.

JEZEBEL'S IDOLATRY

Jezebel, daughter of King Ethbaal of Sidon, was raised in Sidon, a commercial city on the coast of the Mediterranean Sea. Sidon was considered to be a center of vice and ungodliness. When Jezebel married King Ahab of Israel, she moved to Jezreel, a city that served Jehovah. Jezebel soon decided to turn Jezreel into a city similar to her native town.

Jezebel tried to convince her husband to begin serving the golden calf, under the pretense that such worship would really be a service to Jehovah. Actually, the calf was a central idol in the worship of Baal, a sungod who was important to ancient Phoenicians. Because Baal was believed to have power over crops, flocks, and the fertility of farm families, the golden calf was often linked with him. As the worship of Baal spread to countries bordering Phoenicia, more peoples adopted the religion's lascivious rites, which included human sacrifice, self-torture, and kissing the image. The practices of the Baal cult offended pious Jews, but because King Ahab was easily manipulated by Jezebel, beautiful temples honoring Baal were soon erected throughout Israel.

The priests of Jehovah opposed Jezebel; many of them were murdered. Even the great prophet Elijah fled from her wrath (1 Kings 18:4–19).

In her effort to erase the mark of Jehovah throughout Israel, Jezebel became the first female religious persecutor in Bible history. She so effectively injected the poison of idolatry into the veins of Israel that the nation suffered.

Elijah said, "The dogs shall eat Jezebel by the wall of Jezreel" (1 Kings 21:23). This prophesy came true; only Jezebel's skull, feet, and the palms of her hands were left to bury (2 Kings 9:36–37).

The hearts of the Israelites must have been ripe for idolatry, or Jezebel would not have been able to so pervert their religion. King Ahab committed a grave sin against God by marrying her, because Jezebel worshiped Baal (1 Kings 21:25–26).

Jezer (jē′zer; *purpose*). The third son of Naphtali (Gen. 46:24; Num. 26:49; 1 Chron 7:13).

Jezentes (jē′zer-ites). Descendants of Jezer (Num. 26:49).

Jeziah (je-zī′a; *Jehovah unites*). One who took a foreign wife (Ezra 10:25).

Jeziel (jē′zi-el; *God unites*). Man of valor who joined David at Ziklag (1 Chron. 12:3).

Jezliah [Jizliah] (jez-lī′a [jiz-lī′a]; *Jehovah delivers*). A descendant of Benjamin (1 Chron. 8:18).

Jezoar (je-zō′er). A descendant of Caleb, the son of Hur (1 Chron. 4:7). *See* Zohar [3].

Jezrahiah (jez-ra-hī′a; *Jehovah is shining*). An overseer of the singers at the purification of the people (Neh. 12:42). *See* Izrahiah.

Jezreel (jez′re-el; *God scatters*). [1] A descendant of Etam (1 Chron. 4:3). [2] The symbolic name of a son of Hosea (Hos. 1:4).

Jezreel (jez′re-el; *seed of God*). [1] A city on the Plain of Jezreel between Mount Gilboa and Mount Carmel (Josh. 19:18; 1 Kings 21:1). [2] A town in Judah's hill country (Josh. 15:56); probably modern Khirbet Terrama on the Plain of Dibleh. [3] Name of the entire valley that separates Samaria from Galilee (Josh. 17:16). A major battlefield of nations throughout history. Also *see* Armageddon.

Jezreelite (jez′reel-īte). A name applied to Naboth, who had a vineyard in Jezreel (1 Kings 21:1, 4, 6–7, 15–16).

Jezreelitess (jez'reel-ī-tes). A female inhabitant of Jezreel was one of the first two wives of David (1 Sam. 27:3; 1 Chron. 3:1).

Jibsam [Ibsam] (jib'sam [ib'sam]; *lovely scent*). A son of Tola (1 Chron. 7:2).

Jidlaph (jid'laf; *melting away*). Son of Nahor and nephew of Abraham (Gen. 22:22).

Jimna (jim'na). *See* Imna.

Jiphtah (jif'ta; *breaking through*). A city in Judah near Ashnah and Nezib (Josh. 15:43).

Jiphthah-el [Jiphthah El] (jif'tha-el [jif'tha el]; *God opens*). A valley that served as the boundary between the territories of Zebulun and Asher (Josh. 9:14, 27).

Jishui [Ishui] [Ishvi] [Ishyo] (jish'ūī [ish'ū-ī] [ish'vē] [ish'yō]; *man of Jehovah*). A son of King Saul and his wife Ahinoam (1 Sam. 19:49), also called Abinadab (1 Sam. 31:2).

Jisshiah [Isshiah] [Jeshia] (jish'ī-a) [ish'ī-a] [jesh'ī-a] *Jehovah exists*). One of David's mighty men (1 Chron. 12:6).

Jithra [Ithra] [Jether] (jith'ra) [ith'ra] [jeth'er]; *excellence*). An Israelite who fathered Amassa by David's sister or half-sister, Abigail (2 Sam. 17:25). *See* Amasa.

Jithran (jith'ran; *abundance*). A son of Zophan (1 Chron. 7:37). Apparently the same person as Jether (1 Chron. 7:38).

Jizliah [Izliah] [Jezliah] (jiz'lī-a) [iz'lī-a] [jez'lī-a]; *Jehovah delivers*). A son of Elpaal (1 Chron. 8:18).

Jizri [Izri] (jiz'rī [iz'rī]; *creator*). A Levite and head musician for the sanctuary (1 Chron 25:11). Also called Zeri (1 Chron. 25:3).

Joab (jō'ab; *Jehovah is father*). **[1]** A son of Zeruiah, David's sister. He was captain of David's army (2 Sam.

2:13–32; 3:23–31; 18; 1 Kings 2:22–23). **[2]** A descendant of Judah (1 Chron. 2:54). Some scholars believe a city of Judah is referred to here. The name would include the four words that follow in the KJV and be written: Atroth-beth-joab. **[3]** One of the tribe of Judah (1 Chron. 4:14). **[4]** An ancestor of returned captives (Ezra 2:6; 8:9; Neh. 7:11).

Joah (jō'a; *Jehovah is brother*). **[1]** A son of Asaph, the recorder in the time of Hezekiah (2 Kings 18:18, 26: Isa. 36:3, 11, 22). **[2]** A descendant of Gers (1 Chron. 6:21; 2 Chron. 29:12). **[3]** A porter in the tabernacle (1 Chron. 26:4). **[4]** A Levite commissioned to repair the Lord's house (2 Chron. 34:8).

Joahaz (jō'a-haz; *Jehovah helps*). Father of Joah, Josiah's recorder (2 Chron. 34:8).

Joanna (jō-an'a; *God-given*). **[1]** An ancestor of Christ (Luke 3:27). **[2]** The wife of Chuza, Herod's steward, who ministered to Christ and the apostles (Luke 8:3; 24:10).

Joannas [Joanan] [Joanna] [Johanan] [jō-an'an] [jō-an'a] [jō-han'an]; *God-given*). Son of Rhesa and the father of Judah in the genealogy of Jesus (Luke 3:27).

Joash (jō'ash; abbreviated form of Jehoash). *See* Jehoash.

Joatham (jō'a-tham). Greek form of Jotham (q.v.)

Job (jōb; *foe* or *hostile one*). **[1]** A pious man of Uz. His endurance in fierce trial resulted in marvelous blessing (Job 1–3; 42; Ezek. 14:14, 20). **[2]** The third son of Issachar (Gen. 46:13); he is also called Jashub (Num. 26:24; 1 Chron. 7:1).

Jobab (jō'bab). **[1]** A son of Joktan (Gen. 10:29; 1 Chron. 1:23). The name may possibly refer to an unknown Arabian tribe. **[2]** A king of Edom (Gen. 36:33–34; 1 Chron. 1:44–45). **[3]** A king of Canaan conquered by Joshua (Josh. 11:1). **[4]** A descendant of Benjamin (1 Chron. 8:9). **[5]** Another descendant of Benjamin (1 Chron. 8:18).

Jochebed (jok′e-bed; *Jehovah is honor* [*or glory*]). A descendant of Levi and mother of Moses (Exod. 6:20; Num. 26:59).

Joed (jō′ed; *Jehovah is witness*). A son of Pedaiah, a descendant of Benjamin (Neh. 11:7).

Joel (jō′el; *Jehovah is God*). **[1]** The firstborn son of Samuel the prophet (1 Sam. 8:2; 1 Chron. 6:33; 15:17). *See also* Vashni. **[2]** A descendant of Simeon (1 Chron. 4:35). **[3]** The father of Shemaiah, a descendant of Reuben (1 Chron. 5:4, 8). **[4]** A chief of the tribe of Gad (1 Chron. 5:12). **[5]** An ancestor of the prophet Samuel (1 Chron. 6:36). **[6]** A descendant of Tola (1 Chron. 7:3). **[7]** One of David's mighty men (1 Chron. 11:38). **[8]** A Levite in David's time (1 Chron. 15:7, 11; 23:8). **[9]** A keeper of the treasures of the Lord's house (1 Chron. 26:22). **[10]** A prince of Manasseh west of the Jordan (1 Chron. 27:20). **[11]** A Levite who aided in cleansing the temple (2 Chron. 29:12). **[12]** One who married a foreign wife during the Exile (Ezra 10:43). **[13]** An overseer of the descendants of Benjamin in Jerusalem (Neh. 11:9). **[14]** A prophet in the days of Uzziah (Joel 1:1; Acts 2:16).

Joelah (jo-ē′la; *God is snatching; may he avail!*). One who joined David at Ziklag (1 Chron. 12:7).

Joezer (jo-ē′zer; *Jehovah is help*). A warrior who joined David at Ziklag (1 Chron. 12:6).

Jogbehah (jog′be-ha; *high*). A city east of the Jordan River, inhabited by the tribe of Gad (Num. 32:35); present-day Jubeihat, located 10 km. (6 mi.) northwest of Rabbath-ammon.

Jogli (jog-li; *may God reveal*). A prince of Dan (Num. 34:22).

Joha (jō′ha; *Jehovah is living*). [1] A descendant of Benjamin (1 Chron. 8:16). [2] One of David's valiant men (1 Chron. 11:45).

Johanan (jō′hā′nan; *Jehovah is gracious*). [1] A captain who allied with Gedaliah after the fall of Jerusalem (2 Kings 25:23; Jer. 40:8, 13). [2] Eldest son of Josiah, king of Judah (1 Chron. 3:15). [3] A son of Elionai (1 Chron. 3:24). [4] Father of a priest in Solomon's time (1 Chron. 6:9–10). [5], [6] Two valiant men who joined David at Ziklag (1 Chron. 12:4, 12). [7] One who opposed making slaves of Judean captives in Ahaz's time (2 Chron. 28:12). [8] A returned exile (Ezra 8:12). [9] A priest who beckoned the exiles to Jerusalem (Ezra 10:6). [10] A son of Tobiah the Ammonite (Neh. 6:18). [11] A priest in the days of Joiakim (Neh. 12:22–23).

John (jon; a contraction of Jehohanan, *gift of God*). [1] The son of Zacharias and Elizabeth who came to prepare the way for the Messiah. He was called John the Baptist and was beheaded by Herod (Matt. 3; 11:7–18; 14:1–10; Luke 1:13–17). [2] A son of Zebedee and one of the twelve apostles. He is traditionally accorded the authorship of the Revelation, the Fourth Gospel, and the three epistles bearing his name (Matt. 4:21; 10:2; Acts 1:13; Gal. 2:9; Rev. 1:1). [3] A relative of the high priest Annas, who sat in judgment on Peter (Acts 4:6). [4] A missionary better known by his surname, Mark (q.v.). *See also* Jehohanan; Johanan.

John Mark (jon mark). See John [4].

Joiada (joi′a-da; *Jehovah knows*). An ancestor of the priest Jeshua (Neh. 12:10-11, 22; 13:28). *See* Jehoiada.

Joiakim (joi'a-kim; *Jehovah sets up*). The son of Jeshua who returned from the Babylonian Captivity (Neh. 12:10, 12, 26). Not to be confused with Jehoiakim.

Joiárib (joi'a-rib; *Jehovah contends*). [1] One whom Ezra sent to persuade ministers to return to the land of Israel (Ezra 8:16). [2] An ancestor of a family living in Jerusalem (Neh. 11:5). [3] A priest who returned from captivity (Neh. 11:10; 12:6, 19). He is called Jehoiarib in First Chronicles 9:10.

Jokdeam (jok'de-am; *anger of the people*). A city in the mountains of Judah south of Hebron (Josh. 15:56).

Jokim (jō'kim; *Jehovah sets up*). A descendant of Judah (1 Chron. 4:22).

Jokmeam (jok'mē-am; *standing of the people*). A city of the tribe of Ephraim, given to the Levites. It stood nearly opposite the mouth of the Jabbok River (1 Chron. 6:68); probably the same as Kibzaim (q.v.).

Jokneam (jok'nē-am; *building up of the people*). [1] A city in Zebulun allotted to the Levites (Josh. 21:34). It stood on or near Mount Carmel, probably Tell Kaimun, about 11.3 km. (7 mi.) northwest of Megiddo. [2] A city in Ephraim (1 Kings 4:12). We should probably read Jokmeam (q.v.).

Jokshan (jok'shan; *fowler*). A son of Abraham by Keturah (Gen. 25:2–3; 1 Chron 1:32).

Joktan (jok'tan; *little*). A son of Eber of Shem's line (Gen. 10:25–26; 1 Chron. 1:19–20, 23). Perhaps the reference is to an Arabian tribe from whom many other Arabian groups sprang.

Joktheel (jok'the-el; *subdued by God*). [1] A city located in the lowlands of Judah (Josh. 15:38). [2] The name given to Sela [now Petra], capital of the Edomites (2 Kings 14:7).

Jona [Jonah; Jonas] (jō'na; [jō'na; jō'nas]; *a dove*). [1] The father of Simon Peter (John 1:42; 21:15–17). [2] A Hebrew prophet sent to preach to Nineveh in the days of Jeroboam II. He was the first Hebrew prophet sent to a heathen nation (2 Kings 14:25; Jon. 1:1, 3, 5, 17; 2:10; Matt. 12:39–41).

Jonadab (jon'a-dab). *See* Jehonadab.

Jonah (jō'na). *See* Jona.

Jonam (jō'nam). *See* Jonán.

Jonan [Jonam] (jō'nan [jō'nam]; *grace*). An ancestor of Christ (Luke 3:30).

Jonas (jō'nas). Greek form of Jonah.

Jonathan (jon'a-than; *Jehovah has given*). [1] A priest of an idol shrine in the territory of Ephraim (Judg. 18:30). [2] A son of Abiathar the high priest (2 Sam. 15:27, 36; 17:17; 1 Kings 1:42). [3] A son of Shimea, David's brother (2 Sam. 21:21; 1 Chron. 20:7). [4] One of David's mighty men (2 Sam. 23:32; 1 Chron. 11:34). [5] A grandson of Onam (1 Chron. 2:32–33). [6] An uncle of David (1 Chron. 27:32). [7] Father of one who returned with Ezra (Ezra 8:6). [8] One involved with the foreign wife controversy (Ezra 10:15). [9] A descendant of Jeshua the high priest (Neh. 12:11). [10] A priest (Neh. 12:14). [11] A scribe in whose house Jeremiah was kept prisoner (Jer. 37:15, 20; 38:26). [12] One who joined Gedaliah after the fall of Jerusalem (Jer. 40:8). [13] A son of Saul and close friend of David (1 Sam. 14: 18:1–4; 31:2). [14] *See* Jehonathan [3].

Joppa (jop'pa; *beauty*). A town on the coast of Palestine (2 Chron. 2:16; Acts 9:36). *See* Japho.

Jorah (jō'ra; *autumn rain*). *See* Hariph [2].

Jorai (jō'ra-ī; *Jehovah has seen*). A chief of the tribe of Gad (1 Chron. 5:13).

Joram (jō'ram; shortened form of Jehoram). [1] A descendant of Moses (1 Chron. 26: 25). [2] *See* Hadoram [2]. [3] *See* Jehoram [2], [3].

Jordan (jor'daa; meaning uncertain). The major river of Palestine. It rises in a valley between Mount Lebanon and Hermon. It follows a twisting route to enter the north end of the Dead Sea (Gen. 13:10; Josh. 2:7).

Jorim (jō'rim; a shortened form of Jehoram). An ancestor of Christ (Luke 3:29).

Jorkoam (jor'kō'am; *spreading the people*). A son of Raham, or a city he founded (1 Chron. 2:44).

Jorkoam (jor'kō'am; *paleness*). A place belonging to the tribe of Judah (1 Chron. 2:44). It may be identical with Jokdeam (q.v.)

Josabad (jos'a-bad). *See* Jozabad.

Josaphat (jos'a-fat). Greek form of Jehoshaphat (q.v.).

Jose (jō'se; *Jehovah is saviour*). An ancestor of Christ (Luke 3:29). Not to be confused with Joses.

Josech (jō'sek; *may God increase*).

Josedech (jos'e-dek; *Jehovah is righteous*). A priest and father of Jeshua the high priest (Hag. 1:1, 12, 14; Zech 6:11). He is also called Jozadak (Ezra 3:2, 8; 5:2; 10:18; Neh. 12:26). and Jehozadak (1 Chron. 6:14–15).

Joseph (jō'zef; *may Jehovah increase*). [1] The son of Jacob and Rachel. He was sold into slavery but became the prime minister of Egypt (Gen. 37; 39–50). [2] Father of one of the spies sent into Canaan (Num. 13:7). [3] A son of Asaph (1 Chron. 25:2, 9). [4] One who married a foreign wife during the Exile (Ezra 10:42). [5] A priest of the family of Shebaniah (Neh. 12:14). [6] The husband of Mary, mother of Jesus (Matt. 1:16–24; 2:13;

Luke 1:27; 2:4). **[7]** A converted Jew of Arimathea in whose tomb Jesus was laid (Matt. 27:57, 59; Luke 15:43). **[8]** An ancestor of Christ (Luke 3:24). **[9]** Another ancestor of Christ (Luke 3:26). **[10]** Yet another ancestor of Christ (Luke 3:30). **[11]** A disciple considered to take the place of Judas Iscariot (Acts 1:23). He was also known as Barsabas and Justus.

Joses (jō′sez; *helped*). **[1]** One of the brothers of Christ (Matt. 13:55; Mark 6:3). **[2]** The son of Mary, the wife of Cleophas (Matt. 27:56; Mark 15:40, 47). **[3]** The original name of Barnabas (Acts 4:36), also called Joseph. Not to be confused with Jose.

Joshah (jō′sha; *Jehovah's gift*). A descendant of Simeon (1 Chron. 4:34).

Joshaphat (josh′a-fat; *Jehovah judges*). **[1]** One of David's valiant men (1 Chron. 11:43). **[2]** A priest who preceded the Ark when it was moved to Jerusalem (1 Chron. 15:24).

Joshaviah (josh-a-vī′a; *Jehovah is equality*). One of David's valiant men (1 Chron. 11:46).

Joshbekashah (josh-be-kā′sha; *seat of hardness*). A son of Heman, David's song leader (1 Chron. 25:4, 24).

Josheb Basshebeth (jo-shu-bī′a ba-she-beth′). A form of Jashobeam.

Joshibiah (jo-she-bī′a). Son of Seraiah.

Joshua [Jehoshua; Jeshua] (josh′u-a [je-hosh′u-a; jesh′u-a]; *Jehovah is salvation*). **[1]** The successor of Moses; the general who led the conquest of the Promised Land (Exod. 17:9–14; 24:13; Deut. 31:1–23; 34:9). Moses changed his name from Hoshea ("Jehovah is help") to Joshua. Oshea is another form of Hoshea (Num. 13:8, 16: Deut. 32:44). Joshua and Jehoshua are forms of the same name. He is also called Jeshua

(Neh. 8:17). [2] A native of Beth-shem in the days of Eli (1 Sam. 6:14, 18). [3] The governor of Jerusalem under Josiah (2 Kings 23:8). [4] High priest at the rebuilding of the temple (Hag. 1:1, 12, 14; 2:2, 4; Zech 3:1, 3, 6).

Joshua (josh'u-a; *Jehovah is salvation*). A gate in the city wall of Jerusalem (2 Kings 23:8).

Josiah [Josias] (jō- sī'a [jō-sī'as]; *Jehovah supports*). [1] Godly king of Judah during whose reign the Book of the Law was found (1 Kings 13:2; 2 Kings 22:1–23:30). He was an ancestor of Christ (Matt. 1:10–11). [2] A son of Zephaniah living in Jerusalem (Zech. 6:10). *See also* Hen.

Josias (jō-sī'as). Greek form of Josiah (q.v.).

Josibiah (jo-si-bī'a; *Jehovah causes to dwell*). A descendant of Simeon (1 Chron. 4:35).

Josiphiah (jos-i-fī'a; *Jehovah abides*). Father of one who returned from the Exile (Ezra 8:10).

Jotbah (jot'ba; *pleasantness*). The home of Haruz, whose daughter was the mother of King Amon of Judah (2 Kings 21:19).

Jotbathah (jot'ba-tha; *pleasantness*). An encampment of the Israelites in the wilderness. Apparently it was near Eziongeber (Num. 33:33: Deut. 10:7); it is possibly modern el-Taba.

Jotham [Joatham] (jō'tham [jō'a-tham]; *Jehovah is perfect*). [1] The son of Gideon who managed to escape from Abimelech (Judg. 9:5, 7, 21, 57). [2] A son of Jahdai (1 Chron. 2:47). [3] The eleventh king of Judah and an ancestor of Christ (2 Kings 15:5–38; Isa. 1:1; 7:1; Matt. 1:9).

Jozabad [Josabad] (joz'a-bad [jos'a-bad]; *Jehovah endows*). [1] One who joined David at Ziklag (1 Chron.

12:4). **[2]**, **[3]** Two descendants of Manasseh who joined David at Ziklag (1 Chron. 12:20). **[4]** An overseer of the dedicated things of the temple under Hezekiah (2 Chron. 31:13). **[5]** A chief of the Levites in Josiah's time (2 Chron. 35:9). **[6]** One who helped weigh the sanctuary vessels (Ezra 8:33). **[7]**, **[8]** Two who had married foreign wives (Ezra 10:22–23). **[9]** One who interpreted the Law (Neh. 8:7). **[10]** A chief Levite after the Exile (Neh. 11:16). Not to be confused with Jehozabad.

Jozachar (joz'a-kar; *Jehovah remembers*). The servant and murderer of King Joash of Judah (2 Kings 12:21). He is called Zabad in Second Chronicles 24:26.

Jozadak (joz'a-dak). *See* Josedech.

Jubal (joo'bal; *playing; nomad*). Son of Lamech; he was skilled with musical instruments (Gen. 4:21).

Jucal (joo'kal). *See* Jehucal.

Juda [Judah; Judas; Jude] (joo'da [joo'da; joo'das; jood]; *praise*). **[1]** A son of Jacob by Leah and an ancestor of Christ. He acquired the birthright Reuben lost. His descendants became one of the twelve tribes of Israel (Gen. 29:35; 37:26–28; 43:3–10; Matt. 1:2–3; Luke 3:33). **[2]** An ancestor of one who helped to rebuild the temple (Ezra 3:9). **[3]** One who married a foreign wife during the Exile (Ezra 10:23). **[4]** Second in authority over Jerusalem after the Exile (Neh. 11:9). **[5]** One who came up to Jerusalem with Zerubbabel (Neh. 12:8). **[6]** A prince of Judah (Neh. 12:34). **[7]** A priest and musician (Neh. 12:36). **[8]** One of the twelve apostles. He betrayed his Lord and hanged himself (Matt. 10:4; 26:14, 25, 47; 27:3; Luke 6:16; 22:3, 47–48). He was called Iscariot, apparently meaning "a man of Kerioth," a town 19 km. (12 mi.) from Hebron. **[9]** One of the brothers of Jesus (Matt. 13:55; Mark 6:3). He wrote the epistle bearing his name (Jude 1). **[10]** A Galilean who caused a rebellion against Rome (Acts 5:37). **[11]** One with whom Paul stayed at Damascus (Acts 9:11). **[12]** A prophet sent to Antioch with Silas (Acts 15:22, 27); he was surnamed Barsabas. **[13]** *See* Thaddeus. **[14]**, **[15]** Two ancestors of Christ (Luke 3:26, 30).

Judah [Joda] (joo´da [jo´da]; *praise*). The territory of one of the original twelve tribes. Judah, along with Benjamin, formed the southern kingdom after Solomon's death. The uncertain border between Israel and Judah ran between Bethel in Israel and Ramah in Judah. Jerusalem was its capital (2 Chron. 13:18; 15:8).

Judaizers (joo-dee-ī´zerz). Early Christian converts who insisted that believers should adopt Jewish customs as a condition of salvation (Acts 15:1).

Judas Maccabeus (joo´das mak-a-bē´us). *See* Maccabees.

Judea [Judaea] [Jewry] (joo-dē´a [joo-dē´a] [joo´rī]; *praise*). First mentioned as a Persian province (Ezra 3:8). Later it became a Roman province (Matt.2:1). Its northern boundary was Joppa on the west to a point 16.1 km. (10 mi.) north of the Dead Sea on the east. Its southern boundary was about 7 miles southwest of Gaza, through Beer-sheba, to the southern end of the Dead Sea.

Judges. Military heroes who led Israelites against their enemies from about 1380–1050 B.C. Their sometimes short-lived careers are explored in the book of Judges.

Judith (joo´dith; *Jewess*). A wife of Esau (Gen. 26:34). *See* Esau's Wives.

Julia (joo´li-a; *soft-haired*). A Christian woman to whom Paul sent greetings (Rom. 16:15).

Julius (joo'li'us; *soft-haired*). A centurion who delivered Paul to Rome (Acts 27:1, 3).

Junia (joo'ni-a; *youth*). A man or woman (probably a man) to whom Paul sent greetings (Rom. 16:7).

Jushab-hesed (joo'shab-hē'sed; *kindness is returned*). A son of Zerubbabel (1 Chron. 3:20).

Justus (jus'tus; *just*). **[1]** A believer in Corinth with whom Paul lodged (Acts 18:7). **[2]** *See* Jesus [2]. **[3]** *See* Joseph [11].

Juttah (jut'a; *extended*). A city in the mountains of Judah. It is near Maon, Carmel, and Ziph (now Yatta), 8.8 km. (5.5 mi.) southwest of Hebron (Josh. 15:55; 21:16).

K

Kabzeel (kab'ze-el; *God gathers*). A city in Judah (Josh. 15:21; 2 Sam. 23:20); probably modern Khirbet Hora. In Nehemiah 11:25 the city was also known as Jekabzeel (q.v.).

Kadesh (kā'desh). *See* Kadesh Barnea; also Meribah [2].

Kadesh Barnea (kā'desh bar'ne-a; *consecrated*). A wilderness on Palestine's southern frontier. It was on the border between the wilderness of Paran on the south and the wilderness of Zin on the north of the Sinai Peninsula (Num. 32:8; 34:4). It is also called simply Kadesh (Num. 13:26; 20:1). In Genesis 14:7 the region is called Enmishpat.

Kadmiel (kad'mi-el; *God is first* or *before God*). **[1]** One whose descendants returned from Exile (Ezra 2:40; Neh. 7:43). **[2]** One who helped rebuild the temple

(Ezra 3:9). **[3]** Levite who led the devotions of the people (Neh. 9:4–5; 10:9).

Kadmonites (kad´ma-nītes). A nomadic Canaanite tribe that inhabited Palestine in Abraham's time (Gen. 15:19).

Kain (kān) (*smith*). A tribe mentioned in Balaam's fourth prophecy (Num. 24:22).

Kain [Cain] (kān [kān]; *smith*). A town in the mountain country of Judah (Josh. 15:57).

Kallai (kal´a-ī; *swift*). A priest who returned with Zerubbabel (Neh. 12:20).

Kamon (kā´man). *See* Camon.

Kanah (kā´na; *of reeds*). **[1]** A stream that divided the territories of Ephraim and Manasseh; perhaps Wadi Kanah which enters the Mediterranean 6.4 km. (4 mi.) north of Joppa (Josh. 16:8; 17:9). **[2]** A city in Asher not far from Sidon, presently known as Ain Kanah (Josh. 19:28).

Kareah [Careah] (ka-rē´a [ka-rē´a]; *bald head*). The father of Johanan and Jonathan (Jer. 40:8). The KJV spells the name Careah in Second Kings 25:23.

Karkaa [Karka] (kar´ka-a [kar´ka]; *floor; deep ground*). An unknown site on the southern boundary of the tribe of Judah (Josh. 15:3).

Karkor (kar´kor; *even [or deep] ground*). A city in Gad, east of the Jordan. The site of Gideon's victory over Zebah and Zalmunna (Judg. 8:10). It is present-day Karkar.

Karnaim (kar-na´am). A city in northern Transjordan (Amos 6:13). Probably the same place as Ashteroth Karnaim (Gen. 14:5).

Kartah (kar´ta; *city*). A city in Zebulun given to the Merarite Levites (Josh. 21:34). The site has been identified

K

with Ailit on the seacoast 14.5 km. (9 mi). south of the point where Carmel reaches the sea.

Kartan (kar'tan; *town; city*). City of Naphtali given to the Gershonite Levites (Josh. 21:32); it is the same as Kirjathaim in First Chronicles 6:76 and is modern Khirbet el-Kureiyeh.

Kattath (kat'ath; *small*) A town in Zebulun (Josh. 19:15). It is probably identical with the Kitron in Judges 1:30.

Kebar (kē'bar). *See* Chebar.

Kedar (kē'der; *powerful* or *dark*). [1] Second son of Ishmael (Gen. 25:13; 1 Chron. 1:29). [2] The tribe which sprang from Kedar, as well as the territory which they inhabited in the northern Arabian desert (Is. 21:16–17).

Kedemah (ked'e-ma; *eastward*). A son of Ishmael, head of a clan (Gen. 25:13; 1 Chron. 1:31).

Kedemoth (ked'e-moth; *antiquity; old age*). A Levitical town east of the Dead Sea (Josh. 13:18; 21:37; 1 Chron. 6:79).

Kedesh (kē'desh; *holy*). [1] A city of the Canaanites near the northern border, defeated by Joshua (Josh. 12:22; 19:37). [2] Levitical city of refuge in Naphtali. It was sometimes called Kedesh Naphtali (Josh. 20:7; Judg. 4:6, 9). It is probably modern Kades, about 7.2 km. (4.5 mi.) northwest of Lake Huleh. [3] A Levitical city in Issachar (1 Chron. 6:72). [4] A city of Judah near Hazor and Ithan (Josh. 15:23).

Kedesh-Napthali (kē'desh naf'ta-li). A form of Kedesh [1].

Kehelathah (ke-he-lā'tha; *congregation*). A desert encampment of the Israelites (Num. 33:22–23). It is probably Krintilet Krayeh, also called Ajrud.

Keilah (ke-ī′la; *fortress*). A descendant of Caleb (1 Chron. 4:19).

Keilah (ke-ī′la; *fortress*). A town in the lowlands of Judah (1 Sam. 23:1, 13; Josh. 15:44). It is 8.5 mi. north of Hebron at Khirbet Kila.

Kelaiah (ke-lā′ya; *"Jehovah is light; swift for Jehovah"*). One of the priests who divorced his foreign wife after the Exile (Ezra 10:23). Possibly the same as Kelita (q.v.).

Kelita (kel′i-ta; *littleness*). [1] A priest who explained the Law when it was read by Ezra (Neh. 8:7). [2] One of those who sealed the covenant (Neh. 10:10); possibly the same as [1]. One or both of these may be identical with each other and/or Kelaiah (q.v.).

Keluhi (ke-lū′hī). *See* Chelluh.

Kemuel (kem′u-el; *helper of God*). [1] A son of Nahor and a nephew of Abraham (Gen. 22:21). [2] A prince of Ephraim (Num. 34:24). [3] A Levite (1 Chron. 27:17).

Kenan (kē′nan). *See* Cainan.

Kenath (kē′nath; *possession*). A town on the extreme northeastern border of Israelite territory, the easternmost of the ten cities of the Decapolis (Num. 32:42). It is identified with Kanawat.

Kenaz [Kenez] (kē′naz [kē′nez]; *side* or *hunting*). [1] A duke of Edom (Gen. 36:42; 1 Chron. 1:53). [2] The fourth son of Eliphaz (Gen. 36:11, 15; 1 Chron. 1:36); perhaps the same as [1]. [3] Father of Othniel the judge (Josh. 15:17; Judg. 1:13). [4] A grandson of Caleb (1 Chron. 4:15).

Kenezzites [Kenizzites] (kē′nez-ītes [kē′nez-ites]). An Edomite tribe of Canaan in the time of Abraham (Gen. 15:19).

Kenites (ken′ītes; *metalsmiths*). A wandering tribe of people associated with the Midianites (Judg. 1:16) and later with the Amalekites (1 Sam. 15:6). The Kenites lived in the desert regions of Sinai, Midian, Edom, Amalek, and the Negev.

Keren-Happuch (ker′en-hap′uk; *horn of antimony*). The third daughter of Job to be born after his restoration to health (Job 42:14).

Kerioth [Kerioth-Hezron] [Kirioth] (kē′ri-oth [kē′ri-oth hez′ran] [ki′ri-oth]; *the cities*). **[1]** A town in extreme southern Judah (Josh. 15:25). **[2]** A city of Moab (Jer. 48:24, 41; Amos 2:2); possibly the same as Ar.

Kerith [Cherith](ker′ith ker′ith]). A ravine east of the Jordan where Elijah was fed by ravens (1 Kings 17:3, 5.

Keros (kir′os; *crooked*). Ancestor of a clan who returned from Exile to the land of Israel (Ezra 2:44; Neh. 7:47).

Kerub [Cherub] (ker′ub [ker′ub]). An unidentified place in Babylonia from which some Jews were unable to establish their Israelite ancestry after returning to Judah (Ezra 2:59; Neh. 7:61).

Kesalon [Chesalon] (kes′a-lan [kes′a-lan]). A town on the slopes of Mt. Jearim, about 9 mi. (15 km.) north of Jerusalem (Josh. 15:10).

Kesil (kē′sil; *fool*). A town in the extreme south of Judah (Josh. 15:30).

Kesulloth [Chesulloth] (ke-sul′ath [ke-sul′ath]; *loins*). A town in the territory of Issachar, north of Jezreel (Josh. 19:18). Identified as modern Iksal, about 3 mi. (5 km.) north of Nazareth.

Keturah (ke-tū′ra; *fragrance*). A wife of Abraham (Gen. 25:1, 4; 1 Chron. 1:32).

Keziah (ke-zī′a; *cinnamon*). The second daughter of Job to be born after his restoration from affliction (Job 42:14).

Keziz (kē'ziz; "the angle; border; cassia tree"). A valley and town of Benjamin (Josh. 18:21). *See* Emek Keziz.

Kibroth-Hattaavah (kib'roth-ha-ta'a-va; *the graves of gluttony*). A campsite on the Sinai Peninsula where the Israelites grew tired of manna (Num. 11:34–35). This may be Rueis el-Ebeirig, northeast of Jebel Mesa.

Kibzaim (kib'zā'im; *double gathering*). A city of Ephraim given to the Levites (Josh. 21:22). It may be the same as Jokmeam.

Kidon [Chidon] (kē'dan [kē'dan]). The site where Uzzah reached out to steady the ark of the covenant and was struck dead (1 Chron. 13:9. Called Nacon in 2 Sam. 6:6.

Kidron [Cedron] (kid'ron [kē'dron]; *obscure; gloomy*). A valley in Jerusalem between the Mount of Ophel and the Mount of Olives (2 Sam. 15:23; John 18:1). Today it is called Wadi Sitti Maryan.

Kilmad [Chilmad] (kil'mad). A place in Mesopotamia that traded with Tyre. Location unknown (Ezek. 27:23).

Kinah (kī'na; *dirge; lamentation*). A city on the extreme southern boundary of Judah (Josh. 15:22).

King's Highway. A major trade route from the gulf of Aqabah through the Transjordan to Damascus, in use long before 2,000 B.C. (Num. 20:17; 21:22).

King's Valley. The valley of Shaveh, east of Jerusalem where Abraham met Melchizedek. Absalom raised a pillar to himself here (Gen. 14:17; 2 Sam. 18:18).

Kinnereth [Chinnereth, Chinneroth, Cinneroth] (kin'a-roth [kin'a-reth, kin'a-roth, kin'a-roth]; *harps*). [1] Ancient name of the Sea of Galilee (Num. 34:11; Deut. 3:17). [2] An ancient fortified city of Naphtali

(Josh. 19:35). **[3]** A fertile plain that surrounds the city of Kinnereth (1 Kings 15:20), known as the Plain of Gennesaret in Roman times.

Kios [Chios] (kē'os) [kē'os). An island in the Mediterranean about 12 mi. (19 km.) west of Smyrna.

Kir (kir; *a city; wall; meeting*). **[1]** An eastern country whose location has not been determined (2 Kings 16:9; Amos 9:7). The Arameans migrated from this place to Syria. It may have been the area between the Caspian and Black Seas, the modern Georgia. **[2]** See Kir-haraseth.

Kir-haraseth [Kir-hareseth, Kir-haresh, Kir-heres, Kir of Moab] (kir-har'a-seth [kir-har'e-seth, kir-har'esh, kir-her'es, [kir av mō'ab]]; *city of pottery*). A fortified city, probably the same as Kir (2 Kings 3:25; 16:9; Isa. 16:7, 11; Jer. 48:31). Its modern name is Kerak and it is located about 17.7 km. (11 mi.) east of the south bay of the Dead Sea.

Kir-heres (kir-her'es). *See* Kir-haraseth.

Kiriath-Baal (kir'i-ath ba-al'). A form of Kirjath-Jearim.

Kirioth (kir'i-oth). *See* Kerioth.

Kirjath (kir'jath; *city*). A city belonging to the tribe of Benjamin (Josh. 18:28). It is probably Kirjath-jearim (q.v.).

Kirjathaim [Kiriathaim] (kir-jath-thā'im; *double city*). **[1]** A Moabite city on the east of the Jordan (Num. 32:37); probably Khirbet-el-Kureiyat, north of the Arnon. **[2]** *See* Kartan.

Kirjath-arba (kir'jath-ar'ba; *fourth city*). An early name for the city of Hebron (Gen. 23:2; Josh. 14:15). *See* Hebron.

Kirjath-arim (kir'jath-a-rim'). *See* Kirjath-jearim.

Kirjath-baal (kir'jath-bā'al). *See* Kirjath-jearim.

Kirjath-huzoth [Kiriath-huzoth] (kir′jath-hū′zoth [kir′ē-ath-hū′zoth]; *city of streets*). A town of Moab (Num. 22:39). Its location is unknown, but Kirjathaim and Kerioth are possibilities.

Kirjath-jearim [Kiriath-jearim] (kir′jath-jē′a-rim [kir′ē-ath-jē′a-rim]; *city of woods*). Originally one of the cities of the Gibeonites located at the northwestern boundary of Judah (Josh. 9:17; Judg. 18:14). It is identical with Baalah (Josh. 15:9), Kirjath-arim (Ezra 2:25), Kirjath-baal (Josh. 18:14), and Baale-judah (2 Sam. 6:2). It is thought to be modern Deir el-Azhar, about 13.4 km. (8.3 mi.) northwest of Jerusalem.

Kirjath-sannah (kir′jath-sa′na; *city of instruction*). *See* Debir [1].

Kirjath-sepher (kir′jath-sēf′er; *city of books*). *See* Debir [1].

Kirjathaim [Kiriathaim] (kir-jath′ī-am [kir-yath′ī-am]; *double cities*). [1] An ancient city of the Emim occupied and rebuilt by the tribe of Reuben. [2] A city of refuge in the territory of Naphtali given to the Levites.

Kish [Cis] (kish [sis]; *bow; power*). [1] A son of Gibeon (1 Chron. 8:30; 9:36). [2] A Levite in David's time (1 Chron. 23:21; 24:29). [3] A descendant of Levi who assisted in the cleansing of the temple under Hezekiah (2 Chron. 29:12). [4] Great-grandfather of Mordecai (Esther 2:5) [5] The father of King Saul (1 Sam. 9:1, 3; 14:51; Acts 13:21).

Kishi (kish′ī; *a gift*). Father of Ethan, also known as Kushaiah (1 Chron. 6:44; 15:17).

Kishion [Kishon] (kish′i-on [kī′shon]; *hardness*). A city on the boundary of the tribe of Issachar (Josh. 19:20; 21:28). It is probably modern Tel el-Ajjul, 20.1 km. (12.5 mi.) northeast of Megiddo.

Kishon [Kison] (kī'shon [kī'son]; *bending; crooked*). A river in central Palestine which rises in Mount Tabor and, flowing westward, drains the valley of Esdraelon [Jezreel] (Judg. 4:7, 13; 1 Kings 18:40; Psa. 83:9). Next to the Jordan, it is the most important river in Palestine. *See* Kishion.

Kisloth Tabor [Chisloth-tabor] (kis'lath tā'bor [kis'lath tā'bor]; *loins of Tabor*). A bordertown of Zebulun near Mt. Tabor (Josh. 19:12). Probably identified with Kesulloth.

Kithlish [Kitlish] (kith'lish [kit'lish]; *a man's wall*). A city located in the lowlands of Judah, perhaps the same as Dilean (Josh. 15:40); identified with Khirbet el-Mak-haz.

Kitron (kit'ron; *shortened*). One of the towns of Zebulum (Judg. 1:30); perhaps the same as Kattath. It is identified with modern Tell el-Far, about 9.7 km. (6 mi.) southeast of Haifa.

Kittim (kit'im; *knotty*). [1] A son of Javan (Gen. 10:4; 1 Chron. 1:7). [2] Hebrew name for Cyprus (Jer. 2:10; Ezek. 27:6). Later became a symbol of Rome (Dan. 11:30).

Koa (kō'a; *male camel*). A prince or people dwelling between Egypt and Syria; named as enemy of Jerusalem (Ezek. 23:23).

Kohath (kō'hath; *assembly*). The second son of Levi and beginning of a priestly clan (Gen. 46:11; Exod. 6:16, 18).

Kohathites (kō'hath-ites). The descendants of Kohath, son of Levi (Exod. 6:16).

Koheleth (kō-hel'eth). Hebrew title of the book of Ecclesiastes, usually translates as *preacher* in most English versions of the Bible (Eccl. 1:1). The Hebrew word actually means *gatherer* or *assembler.*

Kolaiah (ko-lā′ya; *voice of Jehovah*). **[1]** A descendant of Benjamin (Neh. 11:7). **[2]** Father of the false prophet Ahab (Jer. 29:21).

Korah [Core] (kō′ra [ko′re]; *baldness*). **[1]** A son of Esau by Aholibamah (Gen. 36:5, 14, 18; 1 Chron. 1:35). **[2]** A son of Eliphaz (Gen. 36:16). **[3]** A son of Hebron (1 Chron. 2:43). **[4]** Grandson of Kohath and ancestor of some sacred musicians (1 Chron. 6:22; Psa. 42; 45–46 titles). He was one of the leaders of the rebellion against Moses and Aaron; the earth swallowed them up (Num. 16:1–35).

Korahites [Korhites] (kōr′a-hītes [kōr′hītes]). Part of the Kohathite Levites descended from Korah. Many held responsible positions in the tabernacle (Exod. 6:24). Also spelled as Korathites (Num. 26:58).

Korazin [Chorazin] (kōr′a-zin) [kor′a-zin]. Town on the Sea of Galilee, condemned by Christ for its failure to repent (Mk. 11:21; Luke 10:13). Identified with modern Kerazeh, about 2 mi. (3 km.) north of Capernaum.

Kore (kō′re; *one who proclaims*). **[1]** A Levite in charge of the freewill offerings in Hezekiah's time (2 Chron. 31:14). **[2]** A son of Asaph whose descendants were gatekeepers at the tabernacle (1 Chron. 9:19; 26:1, 19).

Koz (koz; *thorn*). **[1]** The ancestor of a priestly family returning from captivity (Ezra 2:61; Neh. 7:63). In the Hebrew text, the name appears as *Hakkoz;* the KJV considers the *Ha-* of the name to be the prefixed Hebrew definite article—here denoting a *certain* family. Others take all the word as a name (i.e., *Hakkoz*). If this be the case, the Hakkoz of First Chronicles 24:10 probably also refers to this person. [2] An ancestor of one who helped to repair the walls of Jerusalem (Neh. 3:4, 21).

Kve (kwē). A Kingdom identified as East Glicia in Southeast Asia Minor. Its king paid tribute to Tiglath-Pileser III of Assyria (1 Kings 10:28).

Kushaiah (ku-shā'ya; *bow of Jehovah*). See Kishi.

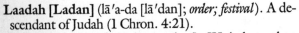

L

Laadah [Ladan] (lā'a-da [lā'dan]; *order; festival*). A descendant of Judah (1 Chron. 4:21).

Laadan (lā'a-dan; *festive-born; ordered*). [1] A descendant of Ephraim (1 Chron. 7:26). [2] A Levite from the family of Gershon (1 Chron. 23:7–9; 26:21). Also known as Libni (Exod. 6:17; Num. 3:18).

Laban (lā'ban; *white*). The brother of Rebekah and father of Rachel and Leah. Jacob served him for seven years in order to marry Rachel, but Laban tricked him by substituting Leah at the wedding festivals (Gen. 24–31).

Laban (lā'ban; *white*). An obscure place in the Sinai Peninsula (Deut. 1:1); perhaps the same as Libnah [1].

Lachish (lā'kish; *who exists of himself*). A southern city of Judah midway between Jerusalem and Gaza (Josh. 10:3, 5; 2 Kings 18:17). The modern site of this Amorite city is Tell-ed-Duweir.

Lael (lā'el; *belonging to God*). A descendant of Gershon (Num. 3:24).

Lahad (lā'had; *sluggish*). A descendant of Judah (1 Chron. 4:2).

Lahai-roi (la-hī'roi). See Beer-lahai-roi.

Lahmam (la'mam; *their bread*). A city located in the lowlands of Judah (Josh. 15:40); probably Khirbet el-Lahm.

Lahmi (la'mī; *warrior*). Brother of Goliath, the giant (1 Chron. 20:5).

Laish (lā'ish; *lion*). Father of Phalti, who became the husband of Michal (1 Sam. 25:44; 2 Sam. 3:15).

Laish [Leshem] (lā'ish [lē'shem]; *a lion*). **[1]** The northern limit of the tribe of Dan (Judg. 18:7–29; Isa. 10:30; Josh. 19:47). The Danites changed its name to Dan (q.v.). **[2]** A place named in Isaiah 10:30 with Gallim and Anathoth.

Laishah [lā'ish-a]. A city of Benjamin in the path of the Assyrians approach to Jerusalem from the north (Isa. 10:30).

Lake of Gennesaret. See Gennesaret.

Lakum [Lakkum] (lāk'am [lāk'am]; *fortress*). One of the landmarks on the boundary of Naphtali (Josh. 19:33); probably modern Mansura near the head of Wadi Pejjas.

Lamech (lā'mek; *strong youth; overthrower*). **[1]** Father of Noah and ancestor of Christ (Gen. 5:25–31; Luke 3:36). **[2]** Father of Jabal and Jubal; he is the first recorded polygamist (Gen. 4:18–26).

Laodicea (lā-od-i-sē'a; *just people*). A chief city of Phrygia in Asia Minor (Col. 2:1; 4:15; Rev. 1:11). It is located on the Lycous River, a tributary of the Meander.

Lapidoth [Lappidoth] (lap'i-doth [lap'i-doth]; *flames; torches*). The husband of Deborah, the prophetess (Judg. 4:4).

Lasea (la-sē'a; *wise*). A seaport of Crete (Acts 27:8). It is about 8 km. (5 mi.) east of Fair Havens.

Lasha (lā′sha; *to anoint*). A Canaanite boundary somewhere in the southeast of Palestine (Gen. 10:19). It has been identified with Callirhoe, a ravine east of the Dead Sea known for its hot springs. Now called Wadi Zerka Ma'in, it enters the Dead Sea about 17.7 km. (11 mi.) east of the mouth of the Jordan.

Lasharon (la-shā′ron; *of or to Sharon*). A town belonging to the Canaanites (Josh. 12:18). It may be the same as Aphek [3].

Lazarus (laz′a-rus; abridged form of Eleazar, *God has helped*). [1] The brother of Mary and Martha whom Jesus raised from the dead (John 11:1–12: 17). [2] A believing beggar who was carried to Abraham's bosom (Luke 16:19–31).

Leah (lē′a; *weary*). Jacob's wife through the deception of her father, Laban (Gen. 29–31).

Lebana [Lebanah] (le-ba′na [leb′a-na]; *white*). Chief of a family of returning exiles (Ezra 2:45; Neh. 7:48).

Lebanah (leb′a-na). *See* Lebana.

Leb Kamai [Chaldea, Leb-gamai]. Code name for Chaldea, or Babylonia (Jer. 51:1).

Lebanon (leb′a-non; *white*). One of two ranges of mountains in northern Palestine (Deut. 1:7; Josh. 1:4). The second is called the Anti-Lebanons; Mount Hermon is its highest peak. Running for about 161 km. (100 mi.), the chain begins about 24.1 km. (15 mi.) southeast of Sidon and runs north to about 19.3 km. (12 mi.) north-northeast of Tripolis in Syria.

Lebaoth (le-bā′oth; *lioness*). One of the towns of southern Judah in Simeon (Josh. 15:32). It is the same as Beth-lebaoth and perhaps identical with Beth-birei (q.v.).

Lebbaeus (le-bē′us). *See* Thaddeus.

Lebo Hamath (lēbo hā′math; *entrance of Hamath*). A city on the northern boundary of Palestine. Identified with Lebwe, located at the north end of the valley of Lebanon. The actual borders of Israel extended to Lebo Hamath only during the reigns of David, Solomon, and Jeroboam II (Num. 34:8; 1 Kings 8:65; 2 Kings 14:25; Ezek. 47:15, 20; 48:1).

Lebonah (le-bō′na; *incense*). A place 12.9 km. (8 mi.) north of Bethel (Judg. 21:19).

Lecah (lē′ka; *walking; addition*). A descendant of Judah (1 Chron. 4:21).

Lehabim (le-hā′bim; *flame, red*). A descendant of Mizraim (Gen. 10:13; 1 Chron. 1:11). Possibly a reference to a tribe of Egyptians.

Lehi (lē′hī; *jawbone*). The location in Judah where Samson slew many Philistines (Judg. 15:9, 14, 19). The site is unknown. In verse 17 it is called Ramath-lehi ("elevation of the jawbone").

Lemuel (lem′u-el; *Godward; dedicated*). An unknown king often supposed to be Solomon or Hezekiah, whose words are recorded in Proverbs 31:1–9.

Leshem (lē′shem). *See* Laish.

Letushim (le-tū′shim; *hammered*). A son of Dedan (Gen. 25:3).

Leummim (le-um′im; *nations*). A son of Dedan (Gen. 25:3).

Levi (lē′vī; *joined*). [1] The third son of Jacob who avenged Dinah's wrong (Gen. 34:25–31), and went to Egypt with his father (Gen. 39:34; Exod. 6:16). His descendants became the priests of Israel. [2] An ancestor of Christ (Luke 3:24). [3] An ancestor of Christ (Luke 3:29). [4] Another name of Matthew (q.v.). [5] The tribe descended from Levi (Exod. 6:19).

Levitical cities (la-vit′a-cal). 43 cities assigned to the tribe of Levi, scattered throughout the land of Palestine (Num. 35:1–8).

Libnah (lib′na; *white*). [1] An encampment of the Israelites during their journey in the wilderness (Num. 33:20–21). It may be identical with Laban. [2] A Levitical city of Jerusalem (Josh. 10:29–31; 2 Kings 19:8). It is now alled Tel-el-safieh.

Libni (lib′nī; *whiteness; distinguished*). [1] A son of Merari (1 Chron. 6:29). [2] *See* Laadan.

Libnites (lib′nites). Descendants of Libni, a son of Gershon and the grandson of Levi (Num. 3:21; 26:58; Exod. 6:17; 1 Chron. 6:17).

Libya (lib′ya; *heart of the sea*). The Greek name for the continent of Africa, west of Egypt (Acts 2:10). The Hebrews called this region Phut [Put]. Even though the Hebrew text of Ezekiel 30:5 and 38:5 read Phut, the KJV rendered the word *Libya*. *See also* Lubim.

Libyans [Lubim] (lib′yans) [lū-brēm′]. The inhabitants of Libya (Jer. 46:9; Nah. 3:9).

Likhi (lik′hī; *learned*). A descendant of Benjamin (1 Chron. 7:19).

Linus (lī′nus; *net*). A Roman friend of Paul (2 Tim. 4:21).

Lo-ammi (lō-am′ī; *not my people*). Symbolic name of Hosea's son (Hos. 1:9).

Lod (lod; *nativity*). A city of Benjamin in the Plain of Sharon (1 Chron. 8:12; Ezra 2:33). Today it is Ludd, about 17.7 km. (11 mi.) southeast of Joppa. In New Testament times it was called Lydda.

Lo-debar (lo-dē′bar; *barren*). A place east of the Jordan River (2 Sam. 9:4); probably the same as Debir [3].

Lois (lō'is; *pleasing; desirable*). The pious grandmother of Timothy (2 Tim. 1:5).

Lo-ruhamah (lō-roo-ha'ma; *receiving no compassion*). A figurative name of Hosea's daughter, indicating God's rejection of Israel (Hos. 1:6).

Lot (lot; *veiled*). Abraham's nephew who escaped from wicked Sodom (Gen. 13:1–14; Gen. 19).

Lotan (lō'tan; *hidden*). An Edomite duke (Gen. 36:20–29).

Lubim (lū'bim; *dwellers in a thirsty land*). The North African continent west of Egypt (Neh. 3:9). *See also* Libya.

Lucas (lū'kas). *See* Luke.

Lucifer (loo'si-fer; Latin, *light-bearer*). An epithet for the king of Babylon (Isa. 14:12). Lucifer translates a Hebrew word meaning "light-bearer." The title came to be applied to Satan.

Lucius (lū'shi-us; *morning born; luminous*). [1] A prophet or teacher from Cyrene ministering at Antioch (Acts 13:1). [2] A Jewish Christian who saluted the community at Rome (Rom. 16:21). Perhaps the same as [1].

Lud (lud). Fourth son of Shem (Gen. 10:22). Possibly the Lydians are intended.

Ludim (lū'dim). A son of Mizraim (Gen. 10:13). Possibly a reference to the inhabitants of an unknown country connected with the Egyptians.

Luhith (lu'hith; *tablets*). A town in Moab, between Aeropolis and Zoar (Isa. 15:5; Jer. 48:5).

Luke [Lucas] (lūk [lu'kas]; *light-giving*). Evangelist, physician, and author of the Third Gospel and Acts (Col. 4:14; 2 Tim. 4:11; Philem. 24).

Luz (luz; *almond tree*). [1] A city 17.7 km. (11 mi.) north of Jerusalem. In later times it was called Beth-el (Gen. 28:19; Josh. 16:2). [2] A town of the Hittites (Judg.

1:22–26). The ruin Luweiziyeh, about 4.5 miles northwest of Baniyas, has been proposed as the site.

Lycaonia (lik-a-ō′ni-a; *she-wolf*). An inland district of Asia Minor. Paul twice visited in the cities of Derbe and Lystra here (Acts 14:6–11). It was bordered on the north by Galatia and on the south by Cilicia.

Lycia (li′shi-a; *land of Lycus*). A region in southwestern Asia Minor (Acts 27:5); the place juts into the Mediterranean Sea.

Lydda (lid′a; *a standing pool*). A town located on the Plains of Sharon (Acts 9:32). It is identical with Lod (q.v.).

Lydia (lid′i-a; *native of Lydia*). A woman convert of Thyatira (Acts 16:14–15).

Lydia (lid′i-a *Lydus land*). A country and people in Northern Africa, west of Egypt (Ezek. 30:5).

Lydians [Men of Lydia, Men of Lud] (lid′i-ans). Men who fought with the Egyptians at the battle of Carchemish (Jer. 46:9).

Lysanias (li-sā′ni-us; *that drives away sorrow*). The tetrarch of Abilene (Luke 3:1).

Lysias (lis′i-as). *See* Claudius Lysias.

Lystra (lis′tra; *that dissolves*). A city of Lycaonia in central Asia Minor. Paul was stoned here (Acts 14:6–21).

M

Maachah [Maacah] (mā′a-ka [mā′a-ka]; *oppression*). **[1]** The son of Nahor, Abraham's brother (Gen. 22:24). **[2]** One of David's wives and mother of Absalom (2 Sam. 3:3; 1 Chron. 3:2). **[3]** A king of Maachah (2 Sam.

10:6). Some translate "the king of Maacah." **[4]** Father of Achish, king of Gath (1 Kings 2:39). He is called Maoch in First Samuel 27:2. **[5]** The mother of Asa, king of Judah (1 Kings 15:10, 13; 2 Chron. 15:16). She is called Michaiah (2 Chron. 13:2). **[6]** Concubine of Caleb (1 Chron. 2:48). **[7]** Wife of Machir, son of Manasseh (1 Chron. 7:15–16). **[8]** Wife of Jehiel (1 Chron. 8:29; 9:35). **[9]** Father of one of David's warriors (1 Chron. 11:43). **[10]** Father of Shephatiah, ruler of Simeon (1 Chron. 27:16).

Maachathi [properly Maacah] (ma-ak′a-thi [mā′a-ka]). A small kingdom that adjoined Geshur on the western border of Bashan (Deut. 3:14), the inhabitants of which were called Maachathites or Maacathites (Josh. 12:5; 13:13).

Maadai (ma-a-dā′ī; *God promises*). One who married a foreign wife (Ezra 10:34; Neh. 12:5).

Maadiah (ma-a-dī′a; *God promises*). A priest who returned from the Babylonian Captivity (Neh. 12:5). He is called Moadiah in Nehemiah 12:17.

Maai (ma-ā′ī; *God is compassionate*). A priest who helped to purify the people who returned from the Exile (Neh. 12:36).

Maaleh-acrabbim [Akrabbim] (ma-al′e-a-krab′im [a-krab′bim] *ascent of scorpions*). A high place which marks part of the boundary of Judah between Kedish and the Dead Sea (Josh. 15:3; Num. 34:4). Akrabbim is a shortened form of the name.

Maarath (mā′a-rath; *den*). A town located in the mountains of Judah (Josh. 15:59). It is near Beth-aron and is now called Umman.

Maasai [Maasiai] (mā′a-sī [mā′a-sī-ī]; *work of Jehovah*).

An Aaronite priest whose family lived in Jerusalem after the Babylonian exile (1 Chron. 9:12).

Maaseiah (mā-a-sī'ya; *Jehovah is a refuge*). [1] A Levite of the praise service (1 Chron. 15:18, 20). [2] A captain who helped to make Joash king (2 Chron. 23:1). [3] Officer of King Uzziah (2 Chron. 26:11). [4] A son of Ahaz, king of Judah (2 Chron. 28:7). [5] Governor of Jerusalem under Josiah's reign (2 Chron. 34:8). [6], [7], [8], [9] Four men who took foreign wives during the Exile (Ezra 10:18, 21–22, 30). [10] Father of Azariah, who repaired part of the wall of Jerusalem (Neh. 3:23). [11] A priest who stood with Ezra while he read the Law (Neh. 8:4). [12] A priest who explained the Law (Neh. 8:7); possibly the same as [11]. [13] One who sealed the new covenant with God after the Exile (Neh. 10:25).[14] A descendant of Pharez living in Jerusalem (Neh. 11:5). [15] One whose descendants lived in Jerusalem (Neh. 11:7). [16], [17] Two priests who took part in the purification of the wall of Jerusalem (Neh. 12:41–42). [18] A priest whose son was sent by King Zedekiah to inquire of the Lord (Jer. 21:1; 29:25). [19] Father of a false prophet (Jer. 29:21). [20] An officer of the temple (Jer. 35:4). [21] Grandfather of Baruch, Jeremiah's scribe (Jer. 32:12).

Maasiai (ma-as'i-ī; *work of Jehovah*). *See* Maasai.

Maath (mā'ath; *small*). An ancestor of Christ (Luke 3:26).

Maaz (mā'az; *counselor*). Oldest son of Ram (1 Chron. 2:27).

Maaziah (ma-a-zī'a; *Jehovah is a refuge*). [1] Priest to whom certain sanctuary duties were charged (1 Chron. 24:18). [2] A priest who sealed the new covenant with God after the Exile (Neh. 10:8).

Maccabees (mak´a-bēs). Members of the ruling Hasmonean family of Jewish leaders and rulers who reigned in Judea from 167 to 37 B.C. Applied especially to Judas Maccabeus and his brothers who defeated the Syrians under Antiochus IV Epiphanies about 165 B.C. and who rededicated the Jerusalem Temple.

Macedonia (mas-e-dō´ni-a; meaning unknown). A nation lying to the north of Greece proper (Acts 16:9; 18:5).

Macedonians (mas-e-dō´ni-ans). Natives or residents of Macedonia, a region of northern Greece (Acts 19:29; 2 Cor. 9:2).

Machaerus (ma-kā´rus). The place where John the Baptist apparently was imprisoned and put to death, according to the Jewish historian, Josephus.

Machbanai [Machbannai, Macbannai] (mak´ba-nī [mak´ba-nī, mak´ba-nī]; *thick*). Warrior who joined David at Ziklag (1 Chron. 12:13).

Machbenah (mak-bē´na; *knob, lump*). [1] A descendant of Caleb (1 Chron. 2:49). [2] Possibly a place identical with Cabbon (q.v.).

Machi (mā´kī; *decrease*). Father of one of the spies sent into Canaan (Num. 13:15).

Machir (mā´kir; *salesman; sold*). [1] A son of Manasseh (Gen. 50:23; Num. 26:29; Josh. 13:31). [2] A descendant of Manasseh living near Mahanaim (2 Sam. 9:4–5; 17:27).

Machirites (mā´kir-ītes). The descendants of Makir [1].

Machnadebai (mach-na-dē´bī; *liberal; gift of the noble one*). One who had married a foreign wife (Ezra 10:40).

Machpelah (mak-pē´la; *double*). The place where the burial cave of Abraham is located, near Hebron (Gen. 23:17; 25:9).

Madaba. A form of Medeba.

Madai (ma-dā′ī). Son of Japheth (Gen. 10:2; 1 Chron. 1:5). The name possibly refers to the inhabitants of Media.

Madian (mā′di·an). *See* Midian.

Madmannah (mad-man′a; *dunghill*). A town near Gaza in southern Judah (Josh. 15:31). It is perhaps the same as Beth-marcaboth, which is Umm pemneh, about 19.3 km. (12 mi.) northeast of Beer-sheba.

Madmen (mad′men; *dunghill*). A location in Moab (Jer. 48:2). It may be modern Khirbet Dimneh, 4 km. (2.5 mi.) northwest of Rabba.

Madmenah (mad-mē′na; *dung heap*). A village north of Jerusalem in the territory belonging to Benjamin (Isa. 10:31).

Madon (mā′don; *strife*). A city of northern Canaan (Josh. 11:1; 12:19). The name still exists in Khirbet Madin, 5 km. (3 mi.) south of Hattin.

Magadon. A form of Magdala.

Magbish (mag′bish; *fortress*). An unidentified town in Benjamin (Ezra 2:30).

Magdala (mag′da-la; *tower*). A village located on the western edge of the Sea of Galilee (Matt. 15:39). It is present-day el-Mejdel, 4.8 km. (3 mi.) north-northwest of Tiberias.

Magdalene (mag′da-lēn; *of Magdala*. The designation given to a woman named Mary, one of Jesus' most prominent Galilean female disciples. (Luke 8:2; Matt. 27:55; Mark 15:40; John 19:25). She was the first of any of Jesus' followers to see him after his resurrection (Mark 16:9; John 20:11–18).

Magdiel (mag′di-el; *renowned of God*). A duke of Edom (Gen. 36:43; 1 Chron. 1:54).

Magi (mā′jī). *See* Wise Men.

Magog (mā′gog; *land of Gog*). **[1]** The second son of Japheth (Gen. 10:2; 1 Chron. 1:5). Possibly a people inhabiting the north land. The name may denote the Scythians or be a comprehensive term for northern barbarians.

Magog (mā′gog; *land of Gog*). A country of undetermined location, generally described as being in a northerly direction from Palestine (Ezek. 38:2; 39:6). The first-century Jewish historian Josephus identified the land with the Scythians.

Magor-missabib (mā′gor-mis′a-bib; *terror is about*). Symbolic name given to Pashur by Jeremiah (Jer. 20:1–3).

Magpiash (mag′pi-ash; *collector of a cluster of stars; moth-killer*). One who sealed the new covenant with God after the Exile (Neh. 10:20).

Mahalab (ma-hā′lab). A town in the territory of Asher (Josh. 19:29).

Mahalah (ma-hā′la; *weak one*). Descendant of Manasseh (1 Chron. 7:18). *See* Mahlah.

M

Mahalaleel [Maleleel] (ma-hā′la-lē′el [ma-lē′le-el]; *God is splendor*). **[1]** Son of Cainan and an ancestor of Christ (Gen. 5:12–13, 15; Luke 3:37). **[2]** One whose descendants lived at Jerusalem (Neh. 11:4).

Mahalath (mā′ha-lath; *mild*). **[1]** One of Esau's wives (Gen. 28:9). *See* Esau's Wives. **[2]** Wife of Rehoboam (2 Chron. 11:18).

Mahali (mā′ha-lī). *See* Mahli.

Mahanaim (ma-ha-nā′im; *two armies*). A place on the boundary between Reuben and Gad (Gen. 32:2; Josh. 21:38). It is east of the Jordan and south of the Jabbok. The exact site is undetermined.

Mahaneh-dan (mā′ha-ne-dan; *camp of Dan*). A campsite

between Zorah and Eshtaol (Judg. 18:12). It is west of Kirjath-jearim.

Maharai (ma-har'a-ī; *swift*). One of David's warriors (2 Sam. 23:28; 1 Chron. 11:30; 27:13).

Mahath (mā'hath; *snatching*). [1] A descendant of Kohath who helped to purify the sanctuary (1 Chron. 6:35; 2 Chron. 29:12). [2] A Levite overseer of dedicated things during Hezekiah's reign (2 Chron. 31:13).

Maharite (mā'ha-rīt). The family name of Eliel, one of David's mighty men (1 Chron. 11:46).

Mahazioth (ma-hā'zi-oth; *visions*). One set over the song service of the temple (1 Chron. 25:4, 30).

Maher-Shalal-Hash-Baz (mā'her-shal'al-hash'baz; *the spoil hastens, the prey speeds*). Symbolic name of Isaiah's son (Isa. 8:1–4).

Mahlah (ma'la; *weak one*). Eldest daughter of Zelophehad allowed a share of the land because her father had no sons (Num. 26:33; 27:1; Josh. 17:3). *See* Mahalah.

Mahli [Mahali] (ma'lī [mā'la-lī]; *mild; sickly*). [1] A son of Merari (Exod. 6:19; Num. 3:20; 1 Chron. 6:19, 29; Ezra 8:18). [2] A descendant of Levi 1 Chron. 6:47; 23:23; 24:30).

Mahlites (ma'līts). A tribal family of Levites descended from Mahli, the son of Merari (Num. 3:33, 26:58).

Mahlon (ma'lon; *mild; sickly*). The first husband of Ruth who died in Moab (Ruth 1:2–5).

Mahol (mā'hol; *dancer*). Father of renowned wise men (1 Kings 4:31).

Mahseiah [Maaseiah] (ma-sī-a [ma-asī'a]; *Jehovah is a refuge*). The father of Neriah (Jer. 32:12; 51:59).

Makaz (ma'kaz; *a boundary*). A place mentioned in First Kings 4:9; it is thought to be Khirbet el-Mukheigin, south of Ekron.

Makheloth (mak-ē'loth; *congregations*). A desert encampment of the Israelites (Num. 33:25); probably modern Kuntilet Krayeh or Ajurd.

Makkedah (mak-ē'da; *place of shepherds*). A city of the Canaanites located on the Plain of Judah (Josh. 10:10; 12:16). It is 19.3 km. (12 mi.) southwest of Jerusalem in the plain country of Judah, and is now called Mughar.

Maktesh (mak'tesh; *mortar*). A section of Jerusalem where merchants gathered (Zeph. 1:11); probably the northern portion of the city.

Malachi (mal'a-kī; *my messenger*). The last of the prophets recorded in the Old Testament; he was contemporary with Nehemiah (Mal. 1:1).

Malcham [Milcam] (mal'kam [mil'kum]; *their king*). **[1]** A descendant of Benjamin (1 Chron. 8:9). **[2]** *See* Molech.

Malchiah [Malchijah; Malkyah; Melchiah] (mal-kī'a [mal-kī'ja; mal-kī'ja; mel-kī'a]; *Jehovah is king*). **[1]** A leader of singing under David's reign (1 Chron. 6:40). **[2]** An Aaronite whose descendants dwelled in Jerusalem after the Captivity (1 Chron. 9:12; Neh. 11:12). **[3]** Head of a priestly family (1 Chron. 24:9). **[4]**, **[5]**, **[6]** Three who married foreign wives during the Exile (Ezra 10:25, 31). **[7]**, **[8]**, **[9]** Three who helped to rebuild the wall of Jerusalem (Neh. 3:11, 14, 31). **[10]** A prince or Levite who stood beside Ezra as he read the Law (Neh. 8:4). **[11]** A priest who helped to purify the wall of Jerusalem (Neh. 10:3; 12:42). **[12]** Father of Pashur (Jer. 21:1; 38:1).

Malchiel (mal'ki-el; *God is king*). A descendant of Asher (Gen. 46:17; Num. 26:45; 1 Chron. 7:31).

Malchielites (mal'ki-el-īts). Descendants of Malchiel (Num. 26:45).

Malchijah (mal´kī-ja). *See* Malchiah.

Malchiram (mal-kī´ram; *my king is exalted*). A descendent of King Jehoiakim (1 Chron. 3:18).

Malchi-shua (mal´kī-shoo´a). *See* Melchi-shua.

Malchus (mal´kus; *counselor; ruler*). A servant of the high priest whose ear Peter cut off (John 18:10).

Maleleel (ma-lē´le-el). Greek form of Mahalaleel (q.v.).

Mallothi (mal´lo-thi; *Jehovah is speaking*). One who was set over the song service of the temple (1 Chron. 25:4, 26).

Malluch [Malluchi] (mal´uk [mal´uk-ī]; *counselor; ruling*). **[1]** A descendant of Levi (1 Chron. 6:44). **[2]**, **[3]** Two who took foreign wives during the Exile (Ezra 10:29, 32). **[4]** A priest who sealed the covenant (Neh. 10:4). **[5]** A leader who sealed the new covenant with God after the Exile (Neh. 10:27). **[6]** One of the priests who returned with Zerubbabel (Neh. 12:2); he is called Melicu in verse 14.

Malta (mal´ta; *refuge*). A small island in the Mediterranean Sea between Sicily and Africa, about 90 mi. (140 km.) southwest of Syracuse. The apostle Paul was shipwrecked there (Acts 28:1).

Mamre (mam´re; *firmness; vigor*). An Amorite chief who allied with Abraham (Gen. 14:13, 24).

Mamre (mam´re; *firmness; vigor*). A place in the Hebron district, west of Machpelah (Gen. 23:17, 19; 49:30). The site has been identified at Râmet el-Khalil, 2 mi. north of Hebron.

Manaen (man´a-en; *comforter*). A teacher or prophet at Antioch (Acts 13:1).

Manahath (man´a-hath; *resting place; rest*). A descendant of Seir (Gen. 36:23; 1 Chron. 1:40).

Manahath (man'a-hath; *resting place; rest*). A city of Benjamin (1 Chron. 8:6).

Manahathites [Manahethites; Manuhoth; Menuhoth] (man'a-hath-īts [man'a-heth-īts; man'ū-hōth; men'ū-hoth]). Descendants of a man or the inhabitants of a place named Manahath, presumably belonging to the tribe of Judah (1 Chron. 2:54).

Manasseh [Manasses] (ma-nas'e [ma-nas'ez]; *causing forgetfulness*). **[1]** The first son of Joseph (Gen. 41:51). His descendants became one of the twelve tribes of Israel and occupied both sides of the Jordan (Josh. 16:4–9; 17). **[2]** The idolatrous successor of Hezekiah to the throne of Judah. He was an ancestor of Christ (2 Kings 21:1–18; Matt. 1:10). **[3]** One whose descendants set up graven images at Laish (Judg. 18:30). Most scholars suggest that we should read Moses here instead. Perhaps a scribe felt an idolatrous descendant would cast reproach on the great lawgiver. A few manuscripts of the Septuagint, Old Latin, and the Vulgate read Moses here. **[4], [5]** Two who had taken foreign wives (Ezra 10:30, 33).

Manasses (ma-nas'ez). Greek form of Manasseh (q.v.).

Manassites (man'a-sīts). Descendants of Manasseh **[1]** (Deut. 4:43; Judg. 12:4).

Manoah (ma-nō'a; *quiet*). The father of Samson the judge (Judg. 13:1–23).

Manuhoth (man'ū-hōth). *See* Manahathites.

Maoch (mā'ok; *poor*). *See* Maachah **[4]**.

Maon (mā'on; *abode*). **[1]** A son of Shammai or a city he founded (1 Chron. 2:45). **[2]** A mountain city of Judah (Josh. 15:55; 1 Sam. 23:24). It is modern Tell Main, about 13.8 km. (8.5 mi.) south of Hebron. **[3]** A wilderness east of the city, Maon, and west of the Dead Sea

(1 Sam. 23:24–25) where David and his men hid from King Saul.

Maonites (mā′ōn-īts) A people who oppressed Israel but whose exact identification is uncertain. They may be identical to the Meunites (2 Chron. 26:7), an Arab tribe south of the Dead Sea.

Mara (ma′ra; *bitter*). Name assumed by Naomi after the death of her husband (Ruth 1:20).

Marah (ma′ra; *bitter*). The fountain of bitter water in the wilderness of Shur where the Israelites first halted after crossing the Red Sea (Exod. 15:23; Num. 33:8). The traditional site is 'Ain Hawarah, about 75.6 km. (47 mi.) from Suez.

Maralah [Mareal] (mar′a-la [mar′i-al]; *sleep*). A boundary village of Zebulun (Josh. 19:11). It is probably Tell Ghalta in the Plain of Kishon.

Marcus (mar′kus). *See* Mark.

Mareal (mar′i-al). See Maralah.

Mareshah (ma-rē′sha; *summit*). **[1]** Father of Hebron (1 Chron. 2:42). **[2]** Son of Laadah (1 Chron. 4:21).

Mareshah (ma-rē′sha; *summit*). A city in the lowlands of Judah (Josh. 15:44; 2 Chron. 11:8). Its ruins are placed at 1.6 km. (1 mi.) southest of Beit Jibrin.

Mari (ma′rē). An ancient Mesopotamian city on the west bank of the Euphrates river. It was the center of the Amorite kingdom that flourished about 1800–1700 B.C. Although not mentioned in the Bible, archaeological finds at Mari have yielded much information about legal, economic and diplomatic matters in the ancient world.

Mark [Marcus] (mark [mar′kus]; *polite; shining*). A Christian convert and missionary companion of Paul (Acts 12:12, 25; 15:37, 39; Col. 4:10). Mark is his Latin name, John his Hebrew name. He wrote the Gospel bearing his name.

Mark, John. *See* Mark.

Maroth (mā′roth; *bitterness*). A town in the lowlands of Judah (Mic. 1:12); possibly the same as Maarath (q.v.).

Marsena (mar′se-na; *forgetful man*). A prince of Persia (Esther 1:14).

Mars Hill. *See* Areopagus.

Martha (mar′tha; *lady*). Sister of Mary and Lazarus in Bethany (Luke 10:38, 40–41; John 11:1–39).

Mary (mā′ri; Greek form of Miriam, *strong*). **[1]** The mother of Jesus Christ; her song of faith (Luke 1:46–55) reveals her deep faith (Matt. 1:16–20; cf. John 2:1–11). **[2]** Mary the sister of Martha. She anointed the Lord with ointment and received His approval (Luke 10:39, 42; John 11:1–45). **[3]** A woman of Magdala in Galilee. She had been converted after having "seven devils" cast out of her (Matt. 27:56, 61; 28:1; Luke 8:2; John 19:25). **[4]** The mother of John Mark (Acts 12:12). **[5]** A Roman Christian to whom Paul sent greetings (Rom. 16:6). **[6]** Mary, the mother of Joses (Mark 15:47) and James (Luke 24:10), the "other Mary" (Matt. 28:1), and the Mary, wife of Cleophas (John 19:25), are possibly to be identified as the same person (Mark 15:40).

Mash (mash; *drawn out*). Son or grandson of Shem (Gen. 10:23). In First Chronicles 1:18 he is called Meshech. Possibly an Aramean people dwelling near Mount Masius in northern Mesopotamia is meant.

Mashal (ma′shal; *parable*). A city in Asher given to the Levites (1 Chron. 6:74). It is probably located on the plain south of Accho. It is identical with Mishal (q.v.).

M

Masrekah (mas're-ka; *whistling*). An ancient city in Edom (Gen. 36:36; 1 Chron. 1:47). It is Jebel el-Mushrat, about 35.4 km. (22 mi.) south-southwest of Maan.

Massa (mas'a; *burden; oracle*). A son of Ishmael (Gen. 25:14; 1 Chron. 1:30).

Massah (mas'a; *temptation*). The name of a spot in the vicinity of Horeb where the Israelites tempted God (Exod. 17:7; Deut. 6:16). *See also* Meribah [1].

Mathusala (ma-thū'sa-la). Greek form of Methuselah (q.v.).

Matred (mā'trid; *expulsion*). Mother of Mehetabel, wife of Hadar (Gen. 36:39; 1 Chron. 1:50).

Matri (mā'trī; *Jehovah is watching* or *rainy*). Ancestor of a tribe of Benjamin to which Saul belonged (1 Sam. 10:21).

Mattan (mat'an; *gift*). [1] A priest of Baal slain by the Jews (2 Kings 11:18; 2 Chron. 23:17). [2] Father of a prince of Judah (Jer. 38:1).

Mattanah (mat'a-na; *gift*). An encampment during the latter part of Israel's wandering (Num. 21:18–19). It was north of the Arnon River and west of the wilderness of Kedemoth.

Mattaniah (mat-a-nī'a; *gift*). [1] The original name of King Zedekiah (2 Kings 24:17). [2] A descendant of Asaph whose family dwelt at Jerusalem (1 Chron. 9:15; 2 Chron. 20:14; Neh. 11:17, 22; 13:13). [3] A son of Heman the singer (1 Chron. 25:4, 16). [4] One who helped to cleanse the temple (2 Chron. 29:13). [5], [6], [7], [8] Four who married foreign wives during the Exile (Ezra 10:26–27, 30, 37). [9] One of the gatekeepers (Neh. 12:25).

Mattatha (mat′a-tha; *gift*). Ancestor of Jesus (Luke 3:31). Not to be confused with Mattathah.

Mattathah [Mattattah] [mat′a-ta]; *gift*). One who divorced his foreign wife after the exile (Ezra 10:33). Not to be confused with Mattatha.

Mattathias (mat-a-thī′as [mat-a-thī′a]; *God's gift*). **[1]** An ancestor of Jesus (Luke 3:25). **[2]** Another ancestor of Jesus (Luke 3:26).

Mattenai (mat-te-nā′i; *gift of Jehovah*). **[1]**, **[2]** Two who married foreign wives during the Exile (Ezra 10:33, 37). **[3]** A priest who returned from the Exile (Neh. 12:19).

Matthan (mat′than; *gift*). An ancestor of Jesus (Matt. 1:15).

Matthat (mat′that; *gift*). **[1]** Grandfather of Joseph and ancestor of Jesus (Luke 3:24). **[2]** Another ancestor of Jesus (Luke 3:29).

Matthew (math′ū; *gift of God*). One of the twelve apostles; he was a tax collector before his call. He was also known as Levi (Matt. 9:9; 10:3; Mark 2:14). He wrote the Gospel bearing his name.

Matthias (ma-thī′as; *God's gift*). A Christian chosen to become an apostle to fill the place of Judas (Acts 1:23, 26). He was surnamed Justus.

Mattithiah (mat-i-thī′a; *gift of Jehovah*). **[1]** A Levite in charge of "things made in pans" (1 Chron. 9:31). **[2]** A Levite singer and gatekeeper (1 Chron. 15:18, 21; 16:5). **[3]** A son of Jeduthun (1 Chron. 25:3, 21). **[4]** One who took a foreign wife during the Exile (Ezra 10:43). **[5]** One who stood with Ezra when he read the Law (Neh. 8:4).

Meah (mē′a; *hundred*). A tower at Jerusalem not far from the Sheep Gate (Neh. 3:1; 12:39).

Mearah (me-ā′ra; *den*). A place, possibly a cavern, in Sidon in northern Canaan (Josh. 13:4).

Mecherathite [me-kē′ra-thīt; *dweller in Mecherah*). A name applied to Hepher, one of David's mighty men (1 Chron. 11:36).

Mebunnai (me-bun′ī; *built up*). *See* Sibbechai.

Meconah [Mecona; Mekona] (me-kō′na) [me-kō′na; me-kō′na]; *foundation*). A city in southern Judah, between Ziklag and En Rimmon (Neh. 11:28). Inhabited by Judahites after the Babylonian Exile.

Medad (mē′dad; *love, friend*). One of the elders of the Hebrews on whom the spirit fell (Num. 11:26–27).

Medan (mē′dan; *judgment*). A son of Abraham by Keturah (Gen. 25:2; 1 Chron. 1:32).

Medeba (med′e-ba; *waters of quiet*). A Moabite town on the Jordan River in the territory of Reuben east of the Arnon (Num. 21:30; Josh. 13:9). It is now Madaba, 9.7 km. (6 mi.) south of Heshbon.

Media (mē′di-a; *middle land*). A country of Asia located south of the Caspian Sea, west of Parthia, north of Elam, and east of the Yagros Mountains. During the 400's B.C. the Persians and Medes had a powerful empire here (Esther 1:3, 14, 18; Dan. 8:20).

Mediterranean Sea (med-i-ter-rā′ne-an). A large sea bordered by many important nations of the ancient world, including Palestine. The Hebrews referred to it by several different names: "the Great Sea" (Num. 34:6); "the Western Sea" (Deut. 34:2); "the Sea of the Philistines" (Exod. 23:31); and simply "the sea" (Josh 16:8; Jon. 1:4).

Megiddo [Megiddon] (me-gid′ō [me-gid′on]; *place of troops*). A city on the southern edge of the Plain of Esdraelon (Jezreel) at the northeast of Mount Carmel (Josh 12:21; 17:11; Zech. 12:11).

Megiddon (me-gid′on). *See* Megiddo.

Mehetabel [Mehetabeel] (me-het′e-bel [me-het′a-bel]; *God is doing good*). **[1]** Wife of King Hadar of Edom (Gen. 36:39; 1 Chron. 1:50). **[2]** Father of Delaiah who defied Nehemiah (Neh. 6:10).

Mehida (me-hī′da; *famous*). An ancestor of returned captives (Ezra 2:52; Neh. 7:54).

Mehir (mē′her; *price*). A descendant of Caleb of Hur (1 Chron. 4:11).

Meholah (me-hō′la). Shortened form of Abel Meholah.

Meholathite (me-hō′la-thīt). A native or inhabitant of Meholah, a city in the Jordan River Valley near Beth Shean (1 Sam. 18:19).

Mehujael (me-hū′ja-el; *smitten by God*). A descendant of Cain (Gen. 4:18).

Mehuman (me-hū′man; *true*). One of the chamberlains of Ahasuerus (Esther 1:10).

Mehunim (mē-hū′nim). A form of Meunim.

Me-jarkon (me-jar′kon; *the waters of Jordan*). A city in the territory of Dan near Joppa (Josh. 19:46).

Mekonah [Meconah] (me-kō′na [me-ko′na]; *provision*). A town of Judah named in connection with Ziklag and other towns of the far south (Neh. 11:28).

Melatiah (mel-a-tī′a; *Jehovah delivers*). An assistant wall-builder (Neh. 3:7).

Melchi (mel′kī; *my King*). **[1]** An ancestor of Jesus (Luke 3:24). **[2]** Another ancestor of Jesus (Luke 3:28).

Melchiah (mel-kī′a). *See* Malchiah.

Melchisedec (mel-kis′e-dek). Greek form of Melchizedek (q.v.).

Melchi-shua [Malchi-shua] (mel-kī-shoo′a [mal-kī-shoo'a; *my king is salvation*]). The third son of King Saul (1 Sam. 14:49; 31:2; 1 Chron. 8:33).

Melchizedek [Melchisedec] (mel-kis'e-dek [mel-kis'e-dek]; *king of righteousness*). King and high priest of Salem. He was a prophetic symbol or "type" of Christ (Gen. 14:18–20; Ps. 110:4; Heb. 5–7.)

Melea (mēl'ē-a; *full*). Ancestor of Christ (Luke 3:31).

Melech (me'lek; *king*). Great-grandson of Saul (1 Chron. 8:35; 9:41).

Melicu (mel'i-kū). *See* Malluch [4].

Melita (mel'i-ta; A form of Malta.

Melzar (mel'zar; *the overseer*). One to whom Daniel and his companions were entrusted (Dan. 1:11, 16); this is possibly a title, rather than a proper name.

Memphis (mem'fis; *abode of the good*). An ancient Egyptian city located on the western bank of the Nile in the central portion of the country (Hos. 9:6). It was also called Noph (Jer. 2:16).

Memucan (me-mū'kan; *sorceror*). A Persian prince (Esther 1:14–21).

Menahem (men'a-hem; *comforter*). The idolatrous and cruel usurper of the throne of Israel who killed Shallum (2 Kings 15:14–23).

Menan (mē'nan). An ancestor of Christ (Luke 3:31).

Menuhoth (men-ū'hoth). See Manuhoth.

Meonenim (me-on'e-nim; *regardless of time*). A place near Shechem in Ephraim (Judg. 9:37).

Meonothai (me-on'o-thī; *dwelling of the Lord*). A descendant of Judah (1 Chron. 4:14).

Mephaath (mef'a-ath; *force of waters*). A city allotted to Reuben and assigned to the Levites (Josh 13:18). It was near Kedemoth or Kirjath-aim.

Mephibosheth (me-fib'o-sheth; *idol breaker*). **[1]** Son of

Saul by his concubine Rizpah (2 Sam. 21:8). **[2]** A grandson of Saul. He was loyal to David, even though Ziba told David he was a traitor (2 Sam. 4:4; 9:6–13). He was also called Merib-baal ("Baal contends") (1 Chron. 8:34; 9:40).

Merab (mē′rab; *increase*). Daughter of Saul promised to David but given to Adriel (1 Sam. 14:49; 18:17, 19). Apparently she was a sister of Michal.

Meraiah (me-rī′ya; *revelation of Jehovah*). A priest of Jerusalem in the days of Joiakim (Neh. 12:12).

Meraioth (me-rā′yoth; *revelations*). **[1]** A descendant of Aaron and ancestor of Azariah (1 Chron. 6:6–7, 52; Ezra 7:3). **[2]** Another priest of the same line (1 Chron. 9:11; Neh. 11:11). **[3]** Another priest at the end of the Exile (Neh. 12:15); possibly the same as Meremoth [1] or [3].

Merari (me-rā′rī; *bitter; excited*). The third son of Levi and founder of a priestly clan (Gen. 46:11; Exod. 6:16, 19; Num. 3; 4:29–45).

Merarites (me-rā′rīts). Descendants of Merari (Num. 26:57). During the wilderness journey, they had the responsibility of transporting tabernacle materials and were stationed on its north side (Num. 26:51; 3:35–37).

Merathaim (mer-a-thā′im; *double rebellion*). Symbolic name for the country of the Chaldeans, also known as Babylon (Jer. 50:21).

Mered (mē′red; *rebellious*). Son of Ezra, descendant of Judah (1 Chron. 4:17–18).

Meremoth (mer′e-moth; *heights*). **[1]** A priest who weighed the gold and silver vessels of the temple (Ezra 8:33; Neh. 3:4, 21). **[2]** One who divorced his foreign wife after the Exile (Ezra 10:36). **[3]** One who sealed the

M

New Covenant with God after the Exile (Neh. 10:5; 12:3). **[4]** A priest who returned with Zerubbabel from the Babylonian Exile (Neh. 12:3).

Meres (mē'rez; *forgetful*). One of the seven princes of Persia (Esther 1:14).

Meribah (mer'i-ba; *quarrel*). **[1]** The desert location where Moses smote the rock (Exod. 17:7). **[2]** Another name for Kadesh Barnea in the wilderness of Zin, where the Hebrew people rebelled against Moses (Num. 20:13). In Deuteronomy 32:51 the place is called Meribah-Kadesh.

Meribah-Kadesh [Meribath] (mer'i-ba-kā'desh [mer'i-bath]). *See* Meribah [2].

Merib-baal (mer'ib-bā'al). *See* Mephibosheth.

Merodach-baladan (me-rō'dak-bal'a-dan; Babylonian, *Marduk-baladan—[the god] Marduk has given a son*). A king of Babylon in the days of Hezekiah (Jer. 50:2). Also called Berodach-baladan (2 Kings 20:12).

Merom (mē'rom; *elevations*). A lake 16.1 km. (10 mi.) north of the Sea of Galilee (Josh 11:5, 7).

Meronoth (me-ra'nath). A place near Gibeon (Neh. 3:70).

Meronathite (me-ran'a-thīt). An inhabitant of Meronoth (1 Chron. 27:30; Neh. 3:7).

Meroz (mē'roz; *refuge*). A place near Kishon (Judg. 5:23). Its exact location is unknown, but may be modern Khirbet Marus, about 12.1 km. (7.5 mi.) south of Kedesh of Naphtali.

Mesech. *See* Meshech.

Mesha (mē'sha; *freedom*). **[1]** A king of Moab who rebelled against Ahaziah (2 Kings 3:4). **[2]** Eldest son of Caleb (1 Chron. 2:42). **[3]** A descendant of Benjamin (1 Chron. 8:9).

Mesha (mē′sha; *refuge*). A boundary marker of the descendants of Joktan (Gen. 10:30). It seems to be west of Sephar.

Meshach (mē′shak; *the shadow of the prince; who is this?*). The name given to Mishael after he went into Babylonian captivity. He was delivered from the fiery furnace (Dan. 1:7; 3:12–30).

Meshech [Mesech] (mē′shek [mē′sek]; *long; tall*). [1] A son of Japheth (Gen. 10:2; 1 Chron. 1:5). [2] Possibly a people inhabiting the land in the mountains north of Assyria, known as Moschi, Moschoi, or Musku (Ezek. 27:13). [3] *See* Mash. [4] A tribe mentioned in association with Kedar (Ps. 120:5).

Meshelemiah (me-shel-e-mī′a; *Jehovah recompenses*). A descendant of Levi (1 Chron. 9:21; 26:1–2, 9). He is also called Shelemiah (1 Chron. 26:14).

Meshezabeel [Meshezabel] (me-shez′a-bēl [me-shez′a-bel]; *God is deliverer*). [1] A priest who helped rebuild the wall (Neh. 3:4). [2] One who signed the covenant (Neh. 10:21). [3] A descendant of Judah (Neh. 11:24).

Meshezabel. *See* Meshezabeel.

Meshillemith (me-shil′e-mith; *retribution*). A priest whose descendants lived in Jerusalem (1 Chron. 9:12). He is called Meshillemoth in Nehemiah 11:13.

Meshillemoth (me-shil′e-moth; *retribution*). [1] A descendant of Ephraim (2 Chron. 28:12). [2] *See* Meshillemith.

Meshobab (me-shō′bab; *restored*). A prince of Simeon (1 Chron. 4:34).

Meshullam (me-shul′am; *associate; friend*). [1] Grandfather of Shaphan, a scribe (2 Kings 22:3). [2] A descendant of King Jehoiakim (1 Chron. 3:19). [3] Head of a family of Gad (1 Chron. 5:13). [4] A descendant of

Benjamin (1 Chron. 8:17). **[5]** One whose son lived in Jerusalem (1 Chron. 9:7). **[6]** One who lived in Jerusalem (1 Chron. 9:8). **[7]** A descendant of Aaron and an ancestor of Ezra (1 Chron. 9:11; Neh. 11:11). He is also called Shallum (1 Chron. 6:12–13; Ezra 7:2). **[8]** A priest (1 Chron. 9:12). **[9]** An overseer of the temple work (2 Chron. 34:12). **[10]** A chief man who returned with Ezra to Jerusalem (Ezra 8:16). **[11]** One who assisted in taking account of those who had foreign wives after the Exile (Ezra 10:15). **[12]** One who took a foreign wife during the Exile (Ezra 10:29). **[13], [14]** Two who rebuilt part of the wall of Jerusalem (Neh. 3:4, 6, 30; 6:18). **[15]** A prince or priest who stood with Ezra while he read the Law (Neh. 8:4). **[16]** A priest who sealed the New Covenant with God after the Exile (Neh. 10:7). **[17]** One who sealed the New Covenant with God after the Exile (Neh. 10:20). **[18]** One whose descendants lived in Jerusalem (Neh. 11:7). **[19]** A priest who assisted in the dedication of the wall of Jerusalem (Neh. 12:13, 33). **[20]** A descendant of Ginnethon (Neh. 12:16). **[21]** A Levite and gatekeeper after the Exile (Neh. 12:25).

Meshullemeth (me-shul′e-meth; *restitution*). Wife of Manasseh and mother of Amon (2 Kings 21:19).

Mesopotamia (mes-o-po-tā′mi-a; *between two rivers*). A region located between the Tigris and Euphrates Rivers (Gen. 24:10; Deut. 23:4), excluding the mountain regions where the rivers take their rise and the low-lying plains of Babylon.

Metheg-ammah (mē′theg-am′a; *bridle of bondage*). A stronghold of the Philistines captured by David (2 Sam. 8:1). Many scholars believe that the name refers to Gath.

Methusael (me-thū′sa-el; *man of God*). The father of Lamech (Gen. 4:18).

Methuselah [**Mathusala**] (me-thū′ze′la [ma-thū′sa-la]; *man of the dart*). The longest living human recorded in the Bible, the grandfather of Noah and an ancestor of Christ (Gen. 5:21–27; Luke 3:37).

Meunim [**Mehunim**], **Meunites** (me-ū′nem [mē-hū′nem; me-ū-nīts]; *habitations*). An Arabian tribe that lived in and around their capital at Maon (Josh. 15:55), about 12 mi. (19 km.) southeast of Petra.

Mezahab (mez′a-hab; *waters of gold*). Grandfather of Mehetabel, wife of Hadar, the eighth king of Edom (Gen. 36:39; 1 Chron. 1:50).

Miamin (mī′a-min). *See* Mijamin.

Mibhar (mib′har; *elite*). One of David's mighty men (1 Chron. 11:38).

Mibsam (mib-sam; *sweet odor*). [1] A son of Ishmael (Gen. 25:13; 1 Chron. 1:29). [2] A son of Simeon (1 Chron. 4:25).

Mibzar (mib′zar; *fortified*). Chief of Edom (Gen. 36:42; 1 Chron. 1:53).

Mica [**Micah, Micha, Michah**] (mī′ka; all probably contractions of Micaiah). [1] Owner of a small private sanctuary (Judg. 17:1–5). [2] A descendant of Reuben (1 Chron. 5:5). [3] A son of Merib-baal, Mephibosheth in Second Samuel 4:4 (1 Chron. 8:34). [4] A descendant of Kohath, son of Levi (1 Chron. 23:20; 24:24). [5] The father of Abdon (2 Chron. 34:20). He is called Michaiah in Second Kings 22:12. [6] A prophet (Jer. 26:18; Mic. 1:1). [7] The son of Zichri (1 Chron. 9:15; Neh. 11:17). [8] One who signed the covenant (Neh. 10:11).

Michael (mī′ka-el; *who is like God?*). [1] One sent to spy out the land of Canaan (Num. 13:13). [2] A descendant of Gad (1 Chron. 5:13). [3] Another descendant of Gad (1 Chron. 5:14). [4] An ancestor of Asaph (1 Chron. 6:40). [5] A chief of the tribe of Issachar (1 Chron. 7:3). [6] One residing in Jerusalem (1 Chron. 8:16). [7] A warrior who joined David at Ziklag (1 Chron. 12:20). [8] Father of Omri, a prince of Issachar (1 Chron. 27:18). [9] A son of Jehoshaphat (2 Chron. 21:2). [10] An ancestor of one who returned from the Exile (Ezra 8:8). [11] An archangel, or an angel of high rank, who served as prince or guardian of the nation of Israel (Dan. 10:21; 12:1).

Michah (mī'ka). *See* Mica.

Michaiah [Micaiah] (mī-kā'ya [mī'kā'ya]; *who is like Jehovah?*). [1] Wife of Rehoboam (2 Chron. 13:2). She is also called Maachah (1 Kings 15:2; 2 Chron. 11:20). *See* Maachah [5]. [2] *See* Mica [5]. [3] A prince of Judah (2 Chron. 17:7). [4] The son of Zaccur (Neh. 12:35). [5] One present at the dedication of the wall (Neh. 12:41). [6] A prophet who predicted Ahab's downfall (1 Kings 22:8–28; 2 Chron. 18:7–27).

Michal (mī'kel; *who is like God?*). The youngest daughter of Saul whom David married (1 Sam. 14:49). Michal "had no child unto the day of her death" (2 Sam. 6:23). Yet Second Samuel 21:8 states she had five sons. The KJV rendering, "whom she brought up for Adriel," is not a permissible translation—the Hebrew text states she bore them. A few Hebrew, Greek, and Syriac manuscripts read: "the five sons of Merab" instead of Michal, which seems a plausible solution to the problem. See First Samuel 18:19.

Michmash [Michmas] [Micmash] (mik'mash [mik'-mas; mic'mash]; *hidden place*). A town of Benjamin

(1 Sam. 13:5; Isa. 10:28; Ezra 2:27). The pass of Mukkmas retains the name. The town is 12.1 km. (7.5 mi.) northeast of Jerusalem and east of Bethaven.

Michmethah [Micmethath] (mik´me-tha [mik´methath]; *the gift of a striker*). A landmark boundary of Manasseh on the western side of the Jordan, east of Sehechm (Josh. 17:7).

Michri (mik´rī; *purchase price*). An ancestor of a clan of Benjamin in Jerusalem (1 Chron. 9:8).

Middin (mid´in; *judgment*). A village in the wilderness of Judah (Josh. 15:61). It is probably modern Khirbet Abu Tabak in the Valley of Achor.

Middle Gate. A gate in the city wall of Jerusalem or the Temple area (Jer. 39:3). Exact location unknown due to expansion, destruction, rebuilding, and renaming through the centuries.

Midian (mid´i-an; *contention*). A son of Abraham by Keturah and founder of the Midianites (Gen. 25:2, 4; 36:35; 1 Chron. 1:32).

Midian [Madian] (mid´i-an [mā´di-an]; *contention*). The land of the descendants of Midian beyond the Jordan. It included Edom, the Sinai Peninsula, and Arabian Petra (Exod. 2:15–16; Judg. 6:1; Acts 7:29).

Midianites (mid´i-a-nīts). A nomadic people who were enemies of the Ancient Israelites. Distantly related to the Israelites through Midian, one of the sons of Abraham. Sent by Abraham "to the country of the east" (Gen. 25:6), they are known thereafter in the Old Testament as the "people of the east" (Judg. 6:3, 33).

Migdal Eder [Edar] (mig´dul ē´dur [e´dur]; *tower of the Eder*). A watchtower between Hebron and Bethlehem where Jacob once camped (Gen. 35:21). Identified with

Siyar El-Ghanam, about 5 mi. 18 km. south of Jerusalem.

Migdalel (mig′dal-el; *tower of God*). A fortified city of Naphtali (Josh. 19:38). It may be modern Mujeidil 20.1 km. (12.5 mi.) northwest of Kedesh [Kades].

Migdalgad (mig′dal-gad; *tower of fortune*). A lowland city of Judah (Josh. 15:37); probably modern Khirbet el-Mejdeleh 8 km. (5 mi.) south of Beit Jibrin.

Migdol (mig′dol; *tower*). [1] A location in the extreme northeast of Egypt (Jer. 44:1; 46:14). [2] An encampment of the Israelites west of the Red Sea (Exod. 14:2; Num. 33:7).

Migron (mig′ron; *fear*). [1] A Benjamite village north of Michmash (Isa. 10:28). It may be modern Makrum. [2[If there were two Migrons, the second was located at the outermost part of Gibeah and considerably south of Michmash (1 Sam. 14:2). Tell Miryam has been suggested as the site.

Mijamin [Miamin; Minjamin] (mij′a-min; *on the right hand*). [1] A priest in the time of David (1 Chron. 24:9). *See also* Miniamin [2]. [2] One who sealed the new covenant (Neh. 10:7). [3] One who divorced his foreign wife after the Babylonian Exile (Ezra 10:25). [4] A chief of the priests who returned with Zerubbabel from Babylon (Neh. 12:5), also called Minjamin (Neh. 12:17).

Mikloth (mik′loth; *twigs; sticks*). [1] A descendant of Benjamin living in Jerusalem (1 Chron. 8:32; 9:37–38). [2] A chief military officer under David (1 Chron. 27:4).

Mikneiah (mik-nē′ya; *possession of Jehovah*). A Levite musician (1 Chron. 15:18, 21).

Milalai (mil-a-lā′i; *eloquent*). A priest who aided in the purification of the wall (Neh. 12:36).

Milcah (mil′ka; *queen*). **[1]** A daughter of Haran, Abraham's brother, and wife of Nahor (Gen. 11:29; 22:20, 23). **[2]** A daughter of Zelophehad (Num. 26:33; 27:1).

Milcom. *See* Molech.

Miletus [Miletum] (mī-lē′tus [mī-lē′tum]; *scarlet*). A coastal city of Ionia (Acts 20:15; 2 Tim. 4:20). It was 57.9 km. (36 mi.) south of Ephesus.

Millo (mil′ō; *mound*). **[1]** A bastion in Jerusalem built in anticipation of an Assyrian siege (2 Sam. 5:9; 1 Kings 9:15). **[2]** An acropolis of Shechem, a high platform of artificial fill (Judg. 9:6, 20).

Miniamin [Minjamin] (min′ya-min [min′ja-min]; *on the right hand*). **[1]** A Levite who apportioned the tithes (2 Chron. 31:15). **[2]** A priest in the days of Joiakim (Neh. 12:17). He is possibly the same as Mijamin in First Chronicles 24:9. *See* Mijamin [1]. **[3]** A priest who helped dedicate the wall (Neh. 12:41).

Minni (min′ī; *prepared*). A portion of the land of Armenia (Jer. 51:27). It was directly south of Lake Urmia and next to the Kingdom of Ararah of the Araxes River.

Minnith (min′ith; *distribution*). A location east of the Jordan where Jephthah slaughtered the Ammonites (Judg. 11:33; Ezek. 27:17). It may be modern Khirbet Hamzeh 6.4 km. (4 mi.) northeast of Hebron.

Miphkad Gate (mif′kad; *appointment; census*). A gate in or near the northern end of the east wall of Jerusalem (Neh. 3:31).

Miriam (mir′i-am; *bitterness*). **[1]** The sister of Moses and Aaron. She rebelled against Moses with Aaron at Hazeroth (Exod. 2:4–10; Num. 12:1–15; 20:1). **[2]** A descendant of Judah (1 Chron. 4:17).

Mirma [Mirmah] (mir´ma [mir´ma]; *height*). Descendant of Benjamin (1 Chron. 8:10).

Misgab (mis´gab; *height, stronghold*). An unidentified location in Moab (Jer. 48:1). It may not be a proper name.

Mishael (mish´a-el; *who is what God is?*). One who carried away the dead Nadab and Abihu (Exod. 6:22; Lev. 10:4). [2] One who stood with Ezra at the reading of the Law (Neh. 8:4). [3] One of the companions of Daniel in Babylon (Dan. 1:6–7, 11, 19). *See* Meshach.

Mishal [Misheal] (mī´shal [mī´she-al]; *requiring*). A territorial town of Asher (Josh. 19:26; 21:30); not to be confused with Mashal.

Misham (mī´sham; *impetuous; fame*). A descendant of Benjamin (1 Chron. 8:12).

Mishma (mish´ma; *fame*). [1] A son of Ishmael (Gen. 25:14; 1 Chron. 1:30). [2] A descendant of Simeon (1 Chron. 4:25).

Mishmannah (mish-man´a; *strength; vigor*). One who joined David at Ziklag (1 Chron. 12:10).

Mishraites (mish´ra-ītes). One of the four families of Kiriath Jearim, from whom the Zorathites and Eshtaolites descended (1 Chron. 2:53).

Mispar [Mizpar] (mis´par [miz´par]). *See* Mispereth.

Mispereth (mis´pe-reth; *writing*). One who returned from captivity (Neh. 7:7). He is called Mispar in Ezra 2:2.

Misrephoth-maim (mis´re-foth-mā´im; *hot waters*). A location in northern Palestine (Josh. 11:8; 13:6). It was on the frontier of the country of the Sidonians. It is identified with modern Khirbet el-Musheir-efeh 17.7 km. (11 mi.) north of Accho and 8 km. (5 mi.) from the Mediterranean.

Mithcah [Mithkah] (mith´ka [mith´ka]; *sweetness*). An

unidentified encampment of the Israelites in the wilderness (Num. 33:28).

Mithnite (mith´nīt). A term used to describe Joshaphat, one of David's mighty men (1 Chron. 11:43).

Mithredath (mith´re-dath; *given by [the god] Mithra*). **[1]** The treasurer of Cyrus through whom he restored the temple vessels (Ezra 1:8). **[2]** One who wrote to the king of Persia protesting the restoration of Jerusalem (Ezra 4:7).

Mitylene (mit-i-lē´ne; *purity*). The principal city of the Island of Lesbos off the western coast of Asia Minor (Acts 20:14).

Mizar (mī´zar; *little*). A hill east of the Jordan, probably within sight of Mount Hermon on Lebanon's eastern slope (Psa. 42:6).

Mizpah [Mizpeh] (miz´pa [miz´pe]; *a watchtower*). **[1]** A mound of stones on Mount Gilead (Gen. 31:49). **[2]** A Hivite settlement in northern Palestine at the foot of Mount Hermon (Josh. 11:3). **[3]** A city in the lowlands of Judah (Josh 15:38). It was just north of Eleutheropolis [Beit Jibrin]. **[4]** A town in Gilead east of the Jordan (Judg. 11:34). It is possibly identical with Ramath-Mizpeh. **[5]** A town of Benjamin just north of Jerusalem (Josh. 18:26; 1 Kings 15:22). The exact site is uncertain. **[6]** A place in Moab (1 Sam. 22:3); perhaps modern Rujm el-Meshrefeh west-southwest of Madaba.

Mizpar (miz´par). *See* Mispar; Mispereth.

Mizraim (miz´ra-im). The second son of Ham (Gen. 10:6, 13; 1 Chron. 1:8, 11). Possibly the Egyptian people are intended.

Mizzah (miz´a; *terror; joy*). A duke of Edom (Gen. 36:13, 17; 1 Chron. 1:37).

Mnason (nā´son; *remembering*). A Cyprian convert who

M

accompanied Paul from Caesarea on Paul's last visit to Jerusalem (Acts 21:16).

Moab (mō'ab; *from my father*). The son of Lot by his daughter and an ancestor of the Moabites (Gen. 19:34–37).

Moab (mō'ab; *from my father*). A land that consisted of the plateau east of the Dead Sea between the wadis Arnon and Zered, though at certain periods extending to the north of the Arnon (Deut. 1:5; Num. 22–25).

Moabites (mō'a-bīts). Natives or inhabitants of the land of Moab (Num. 22:4).

Moabitess (mō'a-bī-tes). A description of several women from Moab. [1] Ruth, wife of Boaz (Ruth 1:22; 2:2, 21; 4:5, 10). [2] Some of Solomon's wives (1 Kings 11:11). [3] Shimrith, the mother of Jehozabad (2 Chron. 24:26).

Moabite Stone. A black basalt memorial stone discovered in Moab in 1868. Containing 34 lines in an alphabet similar to Hebrew, it was probably erected about 850 B.C. The story on the stone celebrated King Mesha's overthrow of the nation of Israel (see 2 Kings 3:4–27).

Moadiah (mo-a-dī'a). *See* Maadiah.

Moladah (mol'a-da; *origin*). A southern city of Judah (Josh. 15:26; Neh. 11:26).

Molech [Malcham; Milcan; Moloch] (mō'lek [mal'-kum; mil'kum; mō'lek]). National god of the Ammonites whose worship involved child sacrifice (Lev. 18:21; Zeph. 1:5; Acts 7:43).

Molid (mō'lid; *begetter*). A descendant of Judah (1 Chron. 2:29).

Morasthite [mō'ras-thīt]. A native of Moresheth-gath.

Mordecai (mor'de'kī; *related to Marduk*). [1] A Jewish

exile who became a vizier of Persia. He helped save the Jews from destruction (Esther 2—10). **[2]** A leader who returned from the Babylonian Captivity (Ezra 2:2; Neh. 7:7).

Moreh (mō're; *diviner*). **[1]** The first stopping place of Abraham after he entered Canaan (Gen. 12:6). It was near Shechem. **[2]** A hill lying at the foot of the valley of Jezreel (Judg. 7:1). It is probably modern Jebel Dahy or Little Hermon about 12.9 km. (8 mi.) northwest of Mount Gilboa.

Moresheth-gath (mō'resh-eth-gath; *possession of Gath*). The hometown of Micah (Mic. 1:14). It may be modern Tel ej-Judeiyeh about 3.2 km. (2 mi.) north of Eleutheropolis.

Moriah (mo-rī'a; *Jehovah provides*). **[1]** An elevation in Jerusalem on which Solomon built the temple (2 Chron. 3:1). Probably the same hilltop was used as the threshing floor of Araunah. The name Moriah was possibly ascribed by the Chronicler because of its traditional meaning (2 Sam. 24:18; 2 Chron. 3:1). **[2]** The hill on which Abraham was prepared to sacrifice Isaac (Gen. 22:2). The site is uncertain, but Samaritans identify Moriah with Moreh [1]. This seems unlikely.

Morsera [Moserah] (mo-sē'ra [mo-sē'ra]; *bonds*). The location of an Israelite wilderness encampment near Mount Hor on the border of Edom (Deut. 10:6).

Moseroth (mō-sē'roth; *bands*). A desert encampment of the Hebrews (Num. 33:30). Some identify it with Mosera (q.v.).

Moses (mō-zez; *drawn out*). The great prophet and lawgiver of Israel. He led his people from Egyptian bondage. The Book of Exodus tells his story. The first five books of the Bible are traditionally attributed to him.

Mount Baal Hermon (bā´ul-hur-mun). A mountain from which the Israelites were unable to expel the Hivites (Judg. 3:3).

Mount of the Beatitudes. A slope on the northwest shore of Galilee where Jesus is believed to have delivered the Sermon on the Mount. (Matt. 5:1—7:29), also known as the Sermon on the Plain (Luke 6:20—49).

Mount of the Congregation. A mountain in Babylonian mythology in the far north where the gods congregated (Isa. 14:13).

Mount of Corruption. A hill on the southern ridge of the Mount of Olives. The place where Solomon built places of worship *(high places)* to accommodate his foreign wives. These places destroyed in King Josiah's reformation (2 Kings 23:13).

Mount Ephraim. *See* Ephraim **[5].**

Mount Heres (hē´rēz; *mountain of the sun*). A mountain near Aijalon and Shaalbin on the border between Judah and Dan (Judg. 1:35).

Mount of Olives. A north-to-south ridge of hills east of Jerusalem. A prominent feature of Jerusalem's landscape where Jesus was betrayed on the night before his crucifixion (Matt. 26:36; Mark 14:32).

Mountain of the Valley. A mountain east of the Jordan river valley in the territory of Reuben (Josh. 13:19).

Mountains of the Amalekites. A place in the land of Ephraim connected with Pirathon, a town where Abdon died (Judg. 12:15).

Mountains of the Amorites. The hill country of Judah and Ephraim (Deut. 1:7, 20).

Moza (mō´za; *origin; offspring*). **[1]** A son of Caleb (1 Chron. 2:46). **[2]** A descendant of Saul (1 Chron. 8:36—37; 9:42—43).

Mozah (mō'za; *unleavened*). A city allotted to Benjamin (Josh. 18:26); probably Kalunya 7.6 km. (4.7 mi.) northwest of Jerusalem on the road to Jaffa.

Muppim (mup'im; *obscurities*). A son of Benjamin (Gen. 46:21). He is also called Shuppim (1 Chron. 7:12, 15; 26:16), Shupham (Num. 26:39), Shephuphan (1 Chron. 8:5). These last three names mean "serpent." While this individual may have borne many names, probably copyists' errors account for some of the diversity.

Mushi (mū'shī; *drawn out; deserted*). A son of Merari, son of Levi (Exod. 6:19); Num. 3:20; 1 Chron. 6:19, 47).

Mushites (mū'shītes). Descendants of Mushi (Num. 3:33; 26:58). A son of Merari and grandson of Levi (Exod. 6:19; 1 Chron. 6:19, 47).

Myra (mī'ra; *weep*). A town of Lycia where Paul changed ships on his way to Rome (Acts 27:5). It is now called Dembre.

Mysia (mish'i-a; *abominable*). A province in northwestern Asia Minor (Acts 16:7). Lydia is to the south and the Aegean Sea to the west of this province.

N

Naam (nā'am; *pleasantness*). A son of Caleb (1 Chron. 4:15).

Naamah (nā'a-ma; *lovely, beautiful*). [1] Daughter of Lamech and Zillah (Gen. 4:22). [2] A wife of Solomon and mother of Rehoboam (1 Kings 14:21; 2 Chron. 12:13).

Naamah (na'a-ma; *lovely, beautiful*). A town in the southwestern lowlands of Judah (Josh. 15:41). It is probably modern Khirbet Fered near Arak Ma'aman.

Naaman (nā′a-man; *pleasantness*). **[1]** A Syrian general who was healed of leprosy by bathing in the Jordan (2 Kings 5; Luke 4:27). **[2]** Grandson of Benjamin (Gen. 26:38, 40). **[3]** A son of Benjamin and founder of a tribal family (Gen. 46:21).

Naamathite (nā′am-a-thīte; *dweller in Naamah*). A native or inhabitant of Naameh, perhaps Djebel-el-Na'ameh in northwestern Arabia. Zophor one of Job's three friends, was a Naamathite.

Naamites (nā′am-ītes). Descendants of Naaman, of the tribe of Benjamin (Num. 26:40).

Naarah (nā′a-ra; *a girl* or *mill*). A wife of Ashur (1 Chron. 4:5–6).

Naarai (nā′a-rī; *youthful*). One of David's valiant men (1 Chron. 11:37). Probably the same as Paarai (2 Sam. 23:35).

Naaran [Naarath] (nā′a-ran [nā′a-rath]; *youthful*). A border town of Ephraim (1 Chron. 7:28). It was east of Bethel and near Jericho, and was also called Naarath (Josh. 16:7).

Naarath (nā′a-rath). *See* Naaran.

Naashon (nā′a-shon). *See* Nahson.

Naasson (nā′a-son). Greek form of Nahshon (q.v.).

Nabajoth (nab-a-jōth). The first-born son of Ishmael (1 Chron. 1:29), also called Nebajoth.

Nabal (nā′bal; *empty person*). A wealthy Carmelite who refused David and his men food (1 Sam. 25).

Nabatea (nab-a-tē′a). An Arabic territory situated between the Dead Sea and the Gulf of Aqaba. Nebajoth, the son of Ishmael and brother-in-law of Edom (Gen.

25:13; 28:9) was possibly an ancestor of the Nabateans.

Nabonidus (na-bō-nī′dus; [the God] *Nabonidus is exalted*). The last king of the Neo-Babylonian, or Chaldean, Empire (556–539 B.C.). He is not mentioned in the Bible.

Naboth (nā′both; *a sprout*). The owner whom Jezebel had killed in order to obtain his vineyard (1 Kings 21:1–18).

Nachon (nā′kon; *firm, prepared*). Scripture refers to the threshing floor of Nachon/Chidon (1 Sam. 6:6; 1 Chron. 13:9). This is either the combined name of two individuals, or two place names, or a combination of both. *Chidon* possibly means *destruction* or a *javelin*.

Nachon (nā′kon). *See* Chidon.

Nachor (nā′kor). Greek form of Nahor (q.v.).

Nadab (nā′dab; *liberal*). [1] Firstborn son of Aaron, struck dead for offering "strange fire" to God (Exod. 6:23; Lev. 10:1–3). [2] A descendant of Jerahmeel (1 Chron. 2:28, 30). [3] A brother of Gibeon (1 Chron. 8:30). [4] Son of Jeroboam I; he ruled Israel for two years (1 Kings 15:25–31).

Nagge [**Naggal**] (na′gē [na′gī]; *splendor*). Ancestor of Jesus (Luke 3:25). *See also* Neariah.

Nag Hammadi (nag hamma′di). A town in Upper Egypt where an astonishing number of Coptic translations of ancient Gnostic writings were found in 1945.

Nahalal [**Nahallal; Nahalol**] (nā′ha-lal [nā′hal-al; nā′ha-lol]; *pasture*). A city of Zebulun assigned to the Levites (Josh. 19:15; 21:35; Judg. 1:30). It is probably modern Khirbet el-Teim, south of Accho.

Nahaliel (na-hā′li-el; *brook of God*). An Israelite encampment north of the Arnon River and east of Moab (Num.

N

21:19). It may be modern Wadi el-Waleh or Wadi Zerka Ma'in.

Nahallal (nā′hal-al). *See* Nahalal.

Nahalol (nā′ha-lol). *See* Nahalal.

Naham (nā′ham; *comfort*). A descendant of Judah, a chieftain (1 Chron. 4:19).

Nahamani (na-ha-mā′ni; *comforter*). One who returned with Zerubbabel (Neh. 7:7).

Naharai [Nahari] (nā′ha-rī; *intelligent*). Joab's armor-bearer (1 Chron. 11:39; 2 Sam. 23:37).

Nahari (nā′ha-rī). *See* Naharai.

Nahash (nā′hash; *oracle* or *serpent*). [1] The father of Abigail and Zeruiah (2 Sam. 17:25). [2] An Ammonite king that was defeated by Saul (1 Sam. 11:1–2; 12:12). [3] Another king of Ammon (2 Sam. 10:2; 17:27; 1 Chron. 19:1–2). Not to be confused with Ir-nahash.

Nahath (nā′hath; *quietness*). [1] A descendant of Esau (Gen. 36:13; 1 Chron. 1:37). [2] An overseer of the offerings at the temple (2 Chron. 31:13). [3] *See* Toah.

Nahbi (nā′bī; *fainthearted*). The spy of Naphtali whom Moses sent out to explore Canaan (Num. 13:14).

Nahor [Nachor] (nā′hor [nā′kor]; *piercer*). [1] Grandfather of Abraham and ancestor of Christ (Gen. 11:22–25; Luke 3:34). [2] A brother of Abraham (Gen. 11:26–27, 29; 22:20, 23; Josh. 24:2).

Nahor (nā′hor). A city mentioned in Genesis 24:10. This is possibly Haran so-called after Abraham's brother, Nahor.

Nahshon [Naashon; Naasson] (na′shon [nā′a-shon; nā′a-shon]; *oracle*). A descendant of Judah and ancestor of Christ. Perhaps Aaron's brother-in-law (Exod. 6:23; Num. 1:7; Matt. 1:4).

Nahum [Naum] (nā′hum [nā′um]; *compassionate*). [1]

One of the later prophets; he prophesied against Nineveh (Nah. 1:1). **[2]** An ancestor of Jesus (Luke 3:25).

Nain (nā′in; *delightful*). A village in Galilee where Christ resurrected a widow's son (Luke 7:11). It is located 3.2 km. (2 mi.) south of Mount Tabor and a little southwest of the Sea of Galilee.

Naioth (nā′oth; *habitations*). The place in Ramah where a community of prophets gathered around Samuel (1 Sam. 19:18–23; 20:1). Its location is not clearly identified. *See also* Ramah [2].

Naomi (na-ō′mi; *my joy*). Mother-in-law to Ruth (Ruth 1:2—44:17).

Naphath-Dor [Naphoth] (nā′fath dōr [nā′fōth]). A form of Dor (Josh. 17:11).

Naphish (nā′fish; *numerous*). Son of Ishmael (Gen. 25:15; 1 Chron. 1:31).

Naphtali (naf′ta-lī; *my wrestling*). The sixth son of Jacob (Gen. 30:7–8). His descendants became one of the twelve tribes.

Naphtali [Nephthalim] (naf′ta-lī [nef′tha-lim]; *my wrestling*). A territory assigned to the tribe of Naphtali, located in mountainous northern Palestine (Josh. 19:32–39; Matt. 4:13). It was bounded on the east by the Upper Jordan River and the Sea of Galilee and on the west by the territories of Zebulun and Asher.

Naphtuhim (naf-tu′him). A son of Mizraim (Gen. 10:13; 1 Chron. 1:11). Many think this refers to a district in Egypt, possibly a designation for the people of the Egyptian Delta.

Narcissus (nar-sis′us; meaning unknown). A Roman Christian (Rom. 16:11).

Nathan (nā′than; *gift*). **[1]** Prophet and royal advisor to

David (2 Sam. 7:2–17; 12:1–25). [2] A son of King David and ancestor of Christ (2 Sam. 5:14; 1 Chron. 3:5; Luke 3:31). [3] Father of Igal (2 Sam. 23:36). [4] A descendant of Jerahmeel (1 Chron. 2:36). [5] A companion of Ezra (Ezra 8:16). [6] One of those who had married a foreign wife (Ezra 10:39). [7] Brother of Joel, one of David's valiant men (1 Chron. 11:38). [8] Father of Solomon's chief officer (1 Kings 4:5). [9] A chief man of Israel (Zech. 10:10). *See* Nathan-melech.

Nathanael (na-than´a-el; *God has given*). A Galilean called by Christ to be a disciple. He is probably to be identified with Bartholomew (John 1:45–49; 21:2; Acts 1:13). *See also* Bartholomew.

Nathan-Melech (nā´than-mel´ek; *King's gift*). An officer under Josiah (2 Kings 23:11).

Naum (nā´um; *comforter*). *See* Nahum.

Nazarene (naz-a-rēn). An inhabitant or native of Nazareth. Used in the Gospels to identify Jesus (Mark 1:23, 24; Matt. 2:23).

Nazareth (naz´a-reth; *watchtower*). The hometown of Jesus in lower Galilee, north of the Plain of Esdraelon [Jezreel] (Matt. 4:13; Mark 1:9). It is 8 km. (5 mi.) west-southwest of Tiberias, 32.2 km. (20 mi.) southwest of modern Tell Hum [Capernaum] and 141.6 km. (88 mi.) north of Jerusalem.

Nazirite (naz´a-rite; *separated, consecrated*). A person who took a vow to consecrate himself or herself to God through separation from certain worldly things (Num. 6:1–8).

Neah (nē´a; *the settlement*). A landmark boundary of Zebulun (Josh. 19:13). It is probably modern Tell el-wawiyat.

Neapolis (ne-ap´o-lis; *new city*). A seaport of Philippi in

Macedonia (Acts 16:11; cf. 20:6). It is on the Strymonian Gulf 16.1 km. (10 mi.) east-southeast of Philippi.

Neariah (ne-a-rī′a; *attendant of Jehovah*). [1] A descendant of David (1 Chron. 3:22). [2] A descendant of Simeon who smote the Amalekites in Mount Seir (1 Chron. 4:42).

Nebai (nē′bī; *projecting*). A co-covenantor with Ezra (Neh. 10:19).

Nebaioth [Nebajoth] (ne-ba′yoth [ne-bā′joth]; *husbandry*). [1] Oldest son of Ishmael (Gen. 25:13; 28:9; 36:3; 1 Chron. 1:29). [2] An Israelite tribe descended from Nebaioth. Possibly to be identified with the later Naboteans (Isa. 60:7).

Nebajoth (ne-bā′joth). *See* Nebaioth.

Neballat (ne-bal′at; *blessed with life*). A town of Benjamin repopulated after the Babylonian Captivity (Neh. 11:34). It is now Beit Nabala 6.4 km. (4 mi.) northeast of Lydda.

Nebat (nē′bat; *God has regarded*). Father of Jeroboam I (1 Kings 11:26).

Nebo (nē′bō; *height*). An ancestor of Jews who divorced their foreign wives after the Exile (Ezra 10:43). This reference quite possibly refers to a city.

Nebo (nē′bō; *height*). [1] The mountain from which Moses saw the Promised Land (Deut. 32:49; 34:1). It is a peak in the Abarim Mountains east of the Jordan, opposite Jericho; probably modern Jebel en Neba, 12.9 km. (8 mi.) east of the mouth of the Jordan. On a clear day, all of Palestine can be seen from this peak. [2] A city of Reuben that fell again to the Moabites (Num. 32:3, 38; 33:47). It is probably modern Khirbet el-Mekhayyet, south of Mount Nebo. [3] A city in Judah

(Ezra 2:29; Neh. 7:33), probably modern Beth-Nube, near Lydda.

Nebuchadnezzar [Nebuchadrezzar] (neb-u-kad-nez′er [neb-u-kad-rez′er]; Babylonian, *Nabur-kudurri-utsur— may* [*the god*] *Nabu protect my son*). Great king of the Babylonian Empire; he captured Jerusalem three times and carried Judah into captivity (2 Kings 24:1, 10–11; 25:1, 8, 22; Dan. 1–4).

Nebushasban [Nebushazban] (neb′ū-shaz′ban; *Nabu delivers me*). A Babylonian prince (Jer. 39:13).

Nebuzaradan (neb-u-zar-ā′dan; Babylonian, [*the god*] *Nabu has given seed*). A Babylonian captain of the guard at the siege of Jerusalem (2 Kings 25:8, 11, 20).

Necho [Nechoh, Neco, Necoh] (nē′ko). Pharaoh of Egypt who fought Josiah at Megiddo (2 Chron. 35:20).

Nedabiah (ned-a-bī′a; *moved of Jehovah*). A descendant of Jehoiakim king of Judah (1 Chron. 3:18).

Neger [Negeb] (neg′er [neg′eb]; *dry, parched*). The southern desert region of Palestine which includes about 4,500 square miles. Abraham (Gen. 12:9; 13:1) and the 12 spies journeyed through the Neger (Num. 13:17, 22). The prophet Isaiah described the Neger as a land of trouble, anguish, and hardship (Isa. 30:6) which would be made to "blossom as a rose" (Isa. 35:1).

Nehelam (ne-hel′am). A form of Nehelamite.

Nehelamite (ne-hel′a-mīte; *dweller of Nehelam*). The designation of Shemaiah, a false prophet who went with captive Judahites to Babylon (Jer. 29:24, 31–32).

Nehemiah (nē′he-mī-a; *God is consolation*). [1] Governor of Jerusalem; he helped rebuild the fallen city (Neh. 1:1; 8:9; 12:47). [2] A chief man who returned from the Exile (Ezra 2:2; Neh. 7:7). [3] One who repaired the wall of Jerusalem (Neh. 3:16).

Nehum (nē'hum). *See* Rehum.

Nehushta (ne-hush'ta; *serpent*). Wife of Jehoiakim; mother of Jehoiachin (2 Kings 24:8).

Nehushtan (ne-hūsh'tan; *serpent*). The name given to the fiery serpent made by Moses and set on a pole so that persons bitten could look at it and live (Num. 21). Destroyed during the later reforms of King Hezekiah because it had become an object of worship (2 Kings 13:4).

Neiel (ne-ī'el; *dwelling place of God*). A landmark boundary of Asher (Josh. 19:27). It is probably modern Khirbet Ya'hin on the edge of the Plain of Acre [Accho].

Nekeb (nē'keb; *cave*). A town on the boundary of the territory of Naphtali (Josh. 19:33); perhaps the same as Adami (q.v.).

Nekoda (ne-kō'da; *speckled*). [1] Head of a family of Nethinim (Ezra 2:48; Neh. 7:50). [2] The head of a family without genealogy after the Exile (Ezra 2:60; Neh. 7:62).

Nemuel (nem'u-el; *God is speaking*). [1] A descendant of Reuben (Num. 26:9). [2] A son of Simeon (Num. 26:12; 1 Chron. 4:24). In Genesis 46:10; Exodus 6:15, he is called Jemuel.

Nemuelites (nem'u-el-ītes). The family or clan descended from Nemuel [2].

Nepheg (nē'feg; *boaster*). [1] A brother of Korah (Exod. 6:21). [2] A son of David (2 Sam. 5:15; 1 Chron. 3:7; 14:6).

Nephilim (nef'i-lēm; *giants*). A word of uncertain meaning. Perhaps the Nephilim were the offspring of the polygamous marriages of famous rulers and mighty warriors before the flood (Gen. 6:4; Num. 13:33).

Nephishesim [Nephusim, Nephisim, Nephish] (ne-fish′e-sim [ne′fu-zim, ne-fish′im, ne-fish′]; *expansions*). Ancestor of returned captives (Neh. 7:52). He is called Nephusim in Ezra 2:50. This man is possibly identical with Naphish.

Nephthalim (nef′tha-lim). *See* Naphtali.

Nephtoah (nef-tō′a; *open*). A spring that marks the boundary between Judah and Benjamin (Josh. 15:9). It is identified with modern Lifta, 3.2 km. (2 mi.) north-west of Jerusalem.

Nephusim (ne-fū′sim). *See* Nephishesim.

Nephussim (ne-fū′sim). A form of Nephishesim.

Ner (nur; *light*). **[1]** Father of Abner, Saul's commander-in-chief (1 Sam. 14:50). **[2]** Grandfather of Saul (1 Chron. 8:33; 9:39). These relationships are unclear. Abner may have been Saul's uncle. If so, Ner [1] and [2] and the same. He is also called Abiel (1 Sam. 9:1). It is also possible that Ner [2] (Abiel) had sons named Ner [1] and Kish, the father of Saul.

Nereus (nē′re-us; *roose*). A Roman Christian (Rom. 16:15).

Nergal-sharezer (nur′gal-sha-rē′zer; *May the god Nergal defend the prince*). A Babylonian officer who released Jere-miah (Jer. 39:3, 13–14).

Neri (nē′rī; *lamp is Jehovah*). Ancestor of Christ (Luke 3:27).

Neriah (ne-rī′a; *Jehovah is a lamp*). Father of Baruch (Jer. 32:12, 16; 36:4, 8, 32).

Nero (nē′rō). Fifth emperor of Rome who ruled from 54–68 A.D. He vowed that he would return to the poli-cies of the great emperor Augustus and managed to ex-pand the borders and solidify certain territories of the Roman Empire. Nero became a kind of apocalyptic figure sometimes identified with the beast in Rev. 13:3, 12. Other possible references to Nero in the New Testament include Acts 25:11–12; 26:32; and Phil. 4:22.

Netaim (ni-tā′im; *plants*). A place in Judah where some royal potters lived (1 Chron. 4:23).

Nethaneel [Nethaneal, Nethanel] (ne-than′e-el [ne-than′e-al, ne-than′el]; *God gives*). **[1]** Chief of Issachar whom Moses sent to spy out the land of Canaan (Num. 1:8; 2:5; 7:18, 23; 10:15). **[2]** Fourth son of Jesse (1 Chron. 2:14). **[3]** One of the trumpet blowers when the ark of the covenant was brought up (1 Chron. 15:24). **[4]** A Levite (1 Chron. 24:6). **[5]** A son of Obed-edom and gatekeeper of the tabernacle (1 Chron. 26:4). **[6]** A prince commissioned by Jehoshaphat to teach the people (2 Chron. 17:7). **[7]** A Levite in the days of Josiah (2 Chron. 35:9). **[8]** A priest who married a foreign wife (Ezra 10:22). **[9]** A priest in the days of Joiakim (Neh. 12:21). **[10]** Levite musician at the purification ceremony (Neh. 12:36).

Nethaniah (neth-a-nī′a; *Jehovah gives*). **[1]** A musician in David's worship services (1 Chron. 25:2, 12). **[2]** A Levite whom Jehoshaphat sent to teach in Judah's cities (2 Chron. 17:8). **[3]** Father of Jehudi (Jer. 36:14). **[4]** Father of Ishmael, the murderer of Gedaliah (Jer. 40:8, 14–15; 41:11).

Nethinim (neth′a-nēm). A group of people of non-Jewish background who served as temple servants. Some of the Nethinim returned to Jerusalem with Ezra after the Babylonian Exile (Ezra 7:7).

Netophah (ne-tō′fa). A city in Judah (Ezra 2:22). A Netophathite is one from this city (1 Chron. 2:54).

Neziah (ne-zī′a; *faithful*). Head of a Nethinim family

that returned to Jerusalem with Zerubbabel (Ezra 2:54; Neh. 7:56).

Nezib (nē′zib; *standing-place*). A city in the lowlands of Judah (Josh. 15:43). It is now Beit Nasib, near Ashna.

Nibhaz (nib′haz). An idol worshipped by the Arites (2 Kings 17:31).

Nibshan (nib′shan; *prophecy*). A wilderness town of Judah (Josh. 15:62); possibly modern Khirbet el-Makari south of Jericho between Beth-araban and En-gev.

Nicanor (ni-kā′nor; *conqueror*). One of the seven chosen in the ministry to the poor (Acts 6:5).

Nicodemus (nik-o-dē′mus; *conqueror of the people*). A Pharisee and ruler of the Jews who assisted in Christ's burial (John 3:1–15; 7:50–52; 19:39–42).

Nicolaitans (nik-ō-lā-i-tans). An early sectarian group of Christians led by Nicolas who was possibly the deacon of Acts 6:5. Mentioned explicitly in Rev. 2:6, 14–15 as a group holding "the doctrine of Balaam" and teaching sacrifice to idols and sexual immorality.

Nicolaus [Nicolas] (nik-o-lā′us [nik′o-las]; *conqueror of the people*). One of the seven chosen to aid in the ministration to the poor (Acts 6:5).

Nicopolis (ni-kop′o-lis; *city of victory*). [1] A town in Epirus in western Greece about 6.4 km. (4 mi.) north of Actium. [2] A city on both sides of the Nestus River, the boundary between Thrace and Macedonia. Paul referred to one of the above in Titus 3:12; the first is preferred.

Niger (nī′jer). Surname of Simeon (q.v.).

Nile (nīl; *dark blue*). The greatest river of Egypt and the world's longest. It is simply referred to in Scripture as "the river" (Gen. 13:1; Exod. 2:3; 7:21). The Nile is about 6,669.3 km. (4,145 mi.) long.

Nimrah (nim'ra). *See* Beth-Nimrah.

Nimrim (nim'rim; *basins of clear water*). A brook in Moab (Isa. 15:6; Jer. 48:34). The name still exists in Wadi en-Nemeirah near the southeast end of the Dead Sea.

Nimrod (nim'rod; *valiant; strong*). A son of Cush (Gen. 10:8–9; 1 Chron. 1:10). His kingdom included Babel, Erech, Accad, and Calneh, cities in Shinar, but also included Assyria.

Nimshi (nim'shi; *weasel*). An ancestor of Jehu (1 Kings 19:16; 2 Kings 9:2, 14).

Nineveh [Nineve] (nin'e-ve; meaning unknown). The capital of the Kingdom of Assyria (Nah. 1:1; cf. 3:1; Zeph. 2:13; Luke 11:32). It was located east of the Tigris River in the area north of the point the Tigris joins the Upper Zab. The ruins are now called Tell Kuyunjik and Tell Nebi Yunus.

Ninevites (nin'e-vītes). Residents of Nineveh, the capital of Assyria. Jesus spoke favorably of the repentance of the Ninevites centuries after the preaching of the prophet Jonah (Jon. 3:2–7; 4:11).

Nisan (nī'san). [1] The name given to Abib after the Babylonian Exile (Esth. 3:7). [2] The first month of the Jewish sacred year.

Nisroch (nis'rok). An Assyrian god with a temple in Nineveh (Isa. 37:33).

No [No Amon] (nō [nō' a-man]; *stirring up*). An Egyptian city better known as Thebes (Ezek. 30:14–16; Jer. 46:25). It was the capital of Upper Egypt.

Noadiah (nō-a-dī'a; *Jehovah has met*). [1] Son of Binnui to whom Ezra entrusted the sacred vessels of the temple (Ezra 8:33). [2] A prophetess opposed to Nehemiah (Neh. 6:14).

Noah [Noe] (nō′a [nō′e]; *rest*). Son of Lamech; the patriarch chosen to build the ark. Only his family survived the flood (Gen. 5:28–32; 6:8–22; 7–10). He was an ancestor of Christ (Luke 3:36).

Noah (nō′a; *rest*). A daughter of Zelophehad (Num. 26:33; Josh. 17:3).

Nob (nōb; *prophecy*). A city of the tribe of Benjamin located northeast of Jerusalem, within sight of the city (1 Sam. 21:1; 22:19).

Nobah (nō′ba; *howling*). A descendant of Manasseh who conquered Kenath (Num. 32:42).

Nobah (nō′ba; *howling*). [1] A town of Gad east of the Jordan (Judg. 8:11). Its site is a tell near Safut. [2] A city in Gilead, location unknown (Num. 32:42).

Nod (nod; *vagabond*). An unidentified land east of Eden to which Cain fled after the murder of Abel (Gen. 4:16). Some suppose it to be China, but this is speculation.

Nodab (nō′dab; *nobility*). An Arabian tribe of the Syrian desert, east of the Jordon River (1 Chron. 5:19).

Noe (nō′e). Greek form of Noah (q.v.)

Nogah (nō′ga; *splendor*). A son of David (1 Chron. 3:7; 14:6).

Nohah (nō′ha; *rest*). A son of Benjamin (1 Chron. 8:2).

Non (non). *See* Nun.

Noph (nōf). *See* Memphis.

Nophah (nō′fa; *blast*). A city in Moab (Num. 21:30). It is not referred to elsewhere and may not be a place name. However, it may be another name for Nobah (q.v.).

Nun [Non] (nun [non]; *fish*). [1] A descendant of Ephraim (1 Chron. 7:27); possibly the same as [2]. [2] The father of Joshua (Exod. 33:11; 1 Kings 16:34).

Nuzi (nu′ze). An ancient Mesopotamian city which flourished from 2000–1000 B.C. Now located 10 mi.

(16 km.) southwest of Kirkuk, in the northern part of Iraq. It was excavated in 1925–31 by the American School of Oriental Research. Some 20,000 small clay tablets were discovered which describe an ancient civilization, perhaps partly contemporary with Abraham.

Nymphas (nim 'fas; *gift of the Nymphs*). A Christian of Laodicea to whom Paul sends greetings (Col. 4:15). Some manuscripts read Nympha, which would make this individual a woman.

O

Obadiah (ō-ba-dī'a; *servant of Jehovah*). **[1]** The governor or prime minister of Ahab who tried to protect the prophets against Jezebel (1 Kings 18:3–16). **[2]** A descendant of David (1 Chron. 3:21). **[3]** A chief of the tribe of Issachar (1 Chron. 7:3). **[4]** A descendant of King Saul (1 Chron. 8:38; 9:44). **[5]** A man of the tribe of Zebulun (1 Chron. 27:19). **[6]** A chief of the Gadites who joined David at Ziklag (1 Chron. 12:9). **[7]** One of the princes whom Jehoshaphat commissioned to teach the Law (2 Chron. 17:7–9). **[8]** A Levite overseer in work done on the temple (2 Chron. 34:12). **[9]** The chief of a family that returned to Jerusalem (Ezra 8:9). **[10]** One who sealed the covenant with Nehemiah (Neh. 10:5). **[11]** A gatekeeper for the sanctuary of the temple (Neh. 12:25). **[12]** The fourth of the "minor prophets." His message was directed against Edom (Obad. 1). **[13]** *See* Abda [2].

Obal (ō'bal). *See* Ebal.

Obed (ō'bed; *worshipper*). [1] A son of Boaz and Ruth, father of Jesse, and ancestor of Christ (Ruth 4:17; Matt. 1:5; Luke 3:32). [2] A descendant of Judah (1 Chron. 2:37–38.) [3] One of David's warriors (1 Chron. 11:47). [4] A Levite gatekeeper in David's time (1 Chron. 26:7). [5] Father of Azariah, who helped make Joash king of Judah (2 Chron. 23:1).

Obed-edom (ō'bed-ē'dom; *servant of [the god] Edom*). [1] A man who housed the ark for three months (2 Sam. 6:10–12; 1 Chron. 13:13–14). [2] One of the chief Levitical singers and doorkeepers (1 Chron. 15:18, 21, 24; 16:5, 38; 26:4, 8, 15). [3] A temple treasurer or official, or perhaps the tribe that sprang from [2] (2 Chron. 25:24). [4] A Levite musician who ministered before the ark when it was placed in the tabernacle (1 Chron. 16:5, 38). He may be identical with Obed-Edom [2].

Obil (ō'bil; *tender*). A descendant of Ishmael who attended to David's camels (1 Chron. 27:30).

Oboth (ō'both; *water skins*). An encampment of the Israelites east of Moab (Num. 21:10; 33:43). It is probably modern 'Ain el-Weiba.

Ocran [Ochran] (ok'ran; *troubler*). A descendant of Asher (Num. 1:13; 2:27).

Oded (ō'ded; *canter*). [1] Father of Azariah the prophet (2 Chron. 15:1). [2] A prophet of Samaria who persuaded the northern army to free their Judean slaves (2 Chron. 28:9–15).

Og (og; *giant*). The giant king of Bashan, defeated at Edrei (Num. 21:33–35; Deut. 3:1–13).

Ojad (ō'had; *strength*). A son of Simeon (Gen. 46:10; Exod. 6:15).

Ohel (ō'hel; *tent*). A son of Zerubbabel (1 Chron. 3:20).

Oholah [Aholah] (ō-hō'la [a-hō'la]; *her own tent*). A symbolic name for Samaria, capital of the Northern Kingdom, and its ten tribes (Ezek. 23:4–5, 36, 44).

Oholiab (ō-hōl'i-ab). A form of Aholiab.

Oholibah (ō-hōl'i-ba; *my tent is in her*). A symbolic name given to Jerusalem by the prophet Ezekiel to signify its unfaithfulness to God. (Ezek. 23:4–44).

Oholibamah (ō-hōl'i-ba-ma). A form of Aholibamah.

Olives, Mount of [Mount of Corruption; Olivet]. A ridge east of Jerusalem and separated from Jerusalem by the Kidron Valley (2 Sam. 15:30; Mark 11:1; Acts 1:12). It is called the Mount of Corruption in Second Kings 23:13.

Olympas (ō-lim'pas; meaning unknown). A Roman Christian (Rom. 16:15).

Omar (ō'mar; *commander*). A grandson of Esau and a duke of Edom (Gen. 36:15).

Omri (om'ri; *pilgrim of God*). [1] The sixth king of Israel and founder of the third dynasty. He founded Samaria and made it Israel's capital (1 Kings 16:15–28). [2] A descendant of Benjamin, the son of Becher (1 Chron. 7:8). [3] A descendant of Perez living at Jerusalem (1 Chron. 9:4). [4] A prince of Issachar in the days of David (1 Chron. 27:18).

On (on; *strength*). A Reubenite who rebelled against Moses and Aaron (Num. 16:1).

On (on; *strength*). An ancient city of Lower Egypt situated on the Nile Delta (Gen. 41:45, 50). It is identical with Beth-Shemesh [4], 30.6 km. (19 mi.) north of Memphis.

Onam (ō'nam; *vigorous*). [1] A grandson of Seir (Gen.

36:23; 1 Chron. 1:40). **[2]** A son of Jerahmeel of Judah (1 Chron. 2:26, 28).

Onan (ō'nan; *vigorous*). The second son of Judah. He was slain by God for disobedience (Gen. 38:44–10; Num. 26:19).

Onesimus (o-nes'i-mus; *useful*). A slave on whose behalf Paul wrote an epistle to his master, Philemon (Col. 4:9; Philem. 10, 15).

Onesiphorus (on-e-sif'o-rus; *profit-bringer*). A loyal friend of Paul's who often refreshed him in prison (2 Tim. 1:16; 4:19).

Ono ō'no; *grief*). A city of Benjamin (1 Chron. 8:12; Ezra 2:33). It is probably modern Kafr 'Ana 11.3 km. (7 mi.) southeast of Joppa.

Ophel (ō'fel; *knoll*). A hill in southeastern Jerusalem (2 Chron. 27:3; Neh. 3:26; 11:21). It was near the Water Gate, Horse Gate, Pool of Siloam, the east court of the temple, and the Kidron Valley.

Ophir (ō'fer; *fruitful; rich*). A son of Joktan (Gen. 10:29; 1 Chron. 1:23). The name may possibly refer to a tribe who inhabited modern Somaliland.

Ophir (ō'fer; *fruitful; rich*). A region where Solomon mined gold (1 Kings 9:28; 1 Chron. 29:4). The location is highly uncertain. Josephus thought it was India, but the African coast in modern Somaliland is more probable.

Ophni (of'nī; *the high place*). A city of Benjamin (Josh. 18:24). It was 4.8 km. (3 mi.) north-northwest of Bethel.

Ophrah (of'ra; *fawn*). A descendant of Judah (1 Chron. 4:14).

Ophrah (of'ra; *fawn*). **[1]** A city of Benjamin (Josh. 18:23; 1 Sam. 13:17). It is probably modern el Taiyibeh, about 6.4 km. (4 mi.) east-northeast of Bethel. [2] A city in Manasseh (Judg. 6:11, 24; 9:5). It is now called Arrabeh.

Oreb (ō′reb; *raven*). One of two Midianite chieftains defeated by Gideon and beheaded by the Ephraimites (Judg. 7:25; 8:3; Ps. 83:11). Also *see* Zeeb.

Oreb (ō′reb *raven*). The rock east of Jordan near Beth-bareh where the Midianite chieftain Oreb died (Judg. 7:25; Isa. 10:26). It is now called Ash-el-Ghorab.

Oren (ō′ren; *cedar*). A son of Jerahmeel of Judah (1 Chron. 2:25).

Ornan (or′nan; *prince*). A Jebusite from whom David bought a piece of land, on which Solomon's temple was erected (1 Chron. 21:15–25). He is called Araunah in Second Samuel 24:16.

Orontes (ō-ran′tez). The chief river of Syria in southwest Asia on which three important cities in the Old Testament were situated: Riblah (2 Kings 23:33–35), Hamath (1 Kings 8:65), and Ka′desh. The Orontes River itself is not mentioned in the Bible.

Orpah (or′pa; *neck*). Daughter-in-law of Naomi (Ruth 1:4–14).

Osee (ō′ze). Greek form of Hosea (q.v.)

Oshea (o-shē′a). *See* Joshua.

Othni (oth′ni; *Jehovah is power*). A Levite, son of Shemaiah and tabernacle gatekeeper in David's time (1 Chron. 26:7).

Othniel (oth′ni-el; *God is power*). Caleb's younger brother who liberated Israel from foreign rule (Judg. 1:13; 3:8–11; 1 Chron. 27:15).

Ozem (ō′zem; *irritable*). [1] A brother of David (1 Chron. 2:15). [2] A son of Jerahmeel of Judah (1 Chron. 2:25).

Ozias (o-zī′as). Greek form of Uzziah (q.v.).

Osnapper (ōz-nap′pur). The biblical name for Ashur-banipal, a king of Assyria.

Ozni (oz′ni). *See* Ezbon [1].

P

Paarai (pā′a-rī; *revelation of Jehovah* or *devotee of Peor*). One of David's mighty men (2 Sam. 23:35); probably the same as Naarai (1 Chron. 11:37).

Padan-aram [Padan, Paddan] (pā′dan-ā′ram [pā′dan]; *plain [tableland] of Aram*). The plain region of Mesopotamia from the Lebanon Mountains to beyond the Euphrates, and from the Taurus Mountains on the north to beyond Damascus on the south (Gen. 25:20; 28:2; 31:18). It is called simply Padan in Genesis 48:7.

Padon (pā′don; *redemption*). One who returned with Zerubbabel (Ezra 2:44; Neh. 7:47).

Pagiel (pā′gi-el; *God's intervention*). A chief of Asher (Num. 1:13; 2:27).

Pahath-Moab (pā′hath-mō′ab; *ruler of Moab*). A Jewish family named after an ancestor of the above name or title (Ezra 2:6; Neh. 3:11). The one who sealed the covenant bearing this name is either another Jew or else the above family is intended (Neh. 10:1, 14).

Pai [Pau] (pā′ī [pā′u]; *howling*). The capital of Hadar, King of Edom (Gen. 36:39; 1 Chron. 1:50). Its location is unknown.

Palal (pā′lal; *God judges*). One who helped rebuild the wall (Neh. 3:25).

Palestine [Palestina] (pal-es-tīn [pal-es-tin´a]; *which is covered*). An ill-defined region consisting of the west coast of Canaan between the Jordan River and the Dead Sea on the east and the Mediterranean on the west (Gen. 15:18; Exod. 15:14; Joel 3:4). Its northern border is roughly the Lebanon Mountain range. It stretches in a southwesterly triangle to the Gulf of Aqaba on the Red Sea.

Pallu [Phallu] (pal´u [fal´u]; *distinguished*). A son of Reuben (Gen. 46:9; Exod. 6:14; 1 Chron. 5:3).

Palluites (pal´u-ītes). A tribal family descended from Pallu (Num. 26:5).

Palti (pal´tī; *delivered*). [1] The man selected from Benjamin to spy out the land (Num. 13:9). [2] *See* Paltiel [2].

Paltiel [Phaltiel, Phalti] (pal´ti-el [fal´ti-el, fal´ti]; *delivered*). [1] A prince of the tribe of Issachar (Num. 34:26). [2] The man who married David's wife (2 Sam. 3:15). He is called Phalti in First Samuel 25:44.

Paltite (pal´tite). [1] A family name of Helez, one of David's mighty men (2 Sam. 23:26). [2] A native of Beth Pelet, a city in southern Judah (Josh. 15:27).

Pamphylia (pam-fil´i-a; *a nation made up of every tribe*). A southern coastal area in Asia Minor; its main city is Perga (Acts 13:13; 14:24; 27:5).

Paphos (pa´fos; *that which boils*). A town on the southwest extremity of Cyprus; it was visited by Paul and Barnabas (Acts 13:6–13). It is modern Baffa.

Paradise (par´a-dīs; *pleasure ground; park*). Figurative name for the place where God dwells (2 Cor. 12:3) and the abode of the righteous (Luke 23:43; Rev. 2:7).

Parah (pa´ra; *young cow*). A town of Benjamin (Josh.

18:23). It is probably modern Wadi el-Farah 5.5 miles northeast of Jerusalem.

Paran (pā'ran; *beauty*). A wilderness seven days' march from Mount Sinai (Gen. 21:21; Num. 10:12; 1 Sam. 25:1). It is located east of the wilderness of Beer-sheba and Shurj, and it merges with the Wilderness of Sin with no clearly marked boundary. The area borders on Edom and Midian; it is sometimes called Mount Paran (Hab. 3:3) and El-Paran (Gen. 14:6).

Parbar (par'bar; *a suburb*). An area on the west side of the temple containing officials' chambers and cattle stalls (1 Chron. 26:18).

Parmashta (par-mash'ta; *strong-fisted*). A son of Haman (Esther 9:9).

Parmenas (par'me-nas; *steadfast*). One of the seven deacons (Acts 6:5).

Parnach (par'nak; *gifted*). A descendant of Zebulun (Num. 34:25).

Parosh [Pharosh] (pā'rosh [fā'rosh]; *a flea*). [1] One whose descendants returned from the Exile (Ezra 2:3; Neh. 7:8). [2] Another whose family returned from the Exile (Ezra 8:3). [3] One whose descendants had taken foreign wives during the Exile (Ezra 10:25). [4] One who sealed the covenant (Neh. 10:14). [5] The father of one who helped repair the wall of Jerusalem (Neh. 3:25). All of these are possibly the same.

Parshandatha (par-shan-dā'tha; *inquisitive*). A son of Haman slain by the Jews (Esther 9:7).

Parthians (par'thi-uns). A tribal group from Parthia, a region southeast of the Caspian Sea in ancient Persia (modern day Iran). Mentioned in Acts 2:9 as one of the many national and language groups gathered in Jerusalem for the Feast of Pentecost.

Paruah (pa-roo'a; *blooming*). Father of Jehohsaphat (1 Kings 4:17).

Parvaim (par-vā'im; *eastern*). A place where gold was obtained for the decoration of Solomon's temple (2 Chron. 3:6). It may be modern Sak el-Farwain in southern Arabia.

Parzites [Perezite, Pharzite] (par'zītes [per'ez-ītes, phar'zītes]). A tribal family descended from Perez, son of Judah (Num. 26:20).

Pasach (pā'sak; *divider*). A descendant of Asher (1 Chron. 7:33).

Pas-dammim (pas-dam'im). *See* Ephes-dammim.

Paseah [Phaseah] (pa-sē'a [fa-sē'a]; *limping*). **[1]** A descendant of Judah through Caleb (1 Chron. 4:12). **[2]** One whose family returned from Babylonian Exile. (Ezra 2:49; Neh. 7:51). **[3]** Father of Jehoiada, who helped repair the wall (Neh. 3:6).

Pashur [Pashhur] (pash'er; *splitter; cleaver*). **[1]** Head of a priestly family (Ezra 2:38; 10:22; Neh. 7:41). **[2]** A priest who sealed the covenant with God after the Exile (Neh. 10:1, 3). Possibly identical with [1]. **[3]** A son of Immor the priest (Jer. 20:1–6) who put Jeremiah in stocks because Jeremiah's prophecies were so unpopular. **[4]** A priest, the "chief governor in the house of the Lord," who persecuted Jeremiah (Jer. 20:1–6). **[5]** Son of Melchiah, whose family returned to Jerusalem (1 Chron. 9:12; Neh. 11:12; Jer. 21:1; 38:1).

Patara (pat'a-ra; *trodden under foot*). A seacoast city of southwest Lycia in Asia Minor (Acts 21:1).

Pathros (path'ros; *the southern land*). The country of Upper Egypt inhabited by the Pathrusim (Isa. 11:11; Jer. 44:1–12), one of the seven peoples coming out of Egypt.

Pathrusim (path-roo´sim; *southerners*). A descendant of Mizraim (Gen. 10:14; 1 Chron. 1:12). Possibly the inhabitants of Pathros.

Patmos (pat´mos; *mortal*). A barren island to which John was banished (Rev. 1:9). It is in the Greek archipelagos and is now called Patino.

Patrobas (pat´ro-bas; *paternal*). A Roman Christian (Rom. 16:14).

Pau (pā´u). *See* Pai.

Paul (pol; Latin, *Paulus—little*). A Pharisee who studied Jewish law under Gamaliel (Acts 21:39). He was converted and made an apostle to the Gentiles (Acts 26:12–20). Perhaps he used his Roman name in humility. The Book of Acts tells of his missionary journeys.

Pedahel (ped´a-hel; *God delivers*). A prince of Naphtali (Num. 34:28).

Pedahzur (pe-da´zer; *the rock delivers*). Father of Gamaliel (Num. 1:10; 2:20).

Pedaiah (pe-dī´ya; *Jehovah delivers*). [1] Father of Joel (1 Chron. 27:20). [2] A descendant of Jeconiah (1 Chron. 3:18–19) and the father of Zerubbabel (1 Chron. 3:19). [3] Grandfather of King Josiah (2 Kings 23:36). [4] Son or grandson of Jeconiah (1 Chron. 3:18–19). [5] One who helped to rebuild the wall of Jerusalem (Neh. 3:25). [6] One who stood with Ezra when he read the Law (Neh. 8:4; 13:13). [7] A descendant of Benjamin (Neh. 11:7).

Pekah (pē´ka; *opening*). A usurper of the throne of Israel; he ruled for twenty years (2 Kings 15:25–31).

Pekahiah (pek-a-hī´a; *Jehovah opens*). Son and successor of Menahem on the throne of Israel. He was murdered by Pekah (2 Kings 15:22–26).

Pekod (pē'kad; *visited by judgment*). A minor Aramean tribe in eastern Babylonia. Jeremiah applied the name to the entire land of Babylonia to indicate symbolically that they would be judged by God (Jer. 50:21).

Pelaiah (pe-lā'ya; *Jehovah is wonderful*). [1] A son of Elioenai (1 Chron. 3:24). [2] A Levite who explained the Law when Ezra read it (Neh. 8:7). [3] A Levite who sealed the covenant (Neh. 10:10); he may be the same as [2].

Pelaliah (pel-a-lī'a; *Jehovah intervenes*). A priest whose grandson dwelled in Jerusalem after the Exile (Neh. 11:12).

Pelatiah (pel-a-tī'a; *Jehovah delivers*). [1] One who sealed the new covenant with God after the Exile (Neh. 10:22). [2] A descendant of David (1 Chron. 3:21). [3] A captain of Simeon (1 Chron. 4:42–43). [4] A wicked prince seen in Ezekiel's vision (Ezek. 11:1, 13).

Peleg [Phalec] (pē'leg [fā'lek]; *division*). Son of Eber and ancestor of Christ (Gen. 10:25; 1:16; Luke 3:35).

Pelet (pē'let; *deliverance*). [1] A son of Jahdai of the family of Caleb (1 Chron. 2:47). [2] One who joined David at Ziklag (1 Chron. 12:3).

Peleth (pē'leth; *flight; haste*). [1] Father of On (Num. 16:1). [2] A son of Jonathan and a descendant of Pharez (1 Chron. 2:33).

Pella (pel'a). A city of the Decapolis in Transjordan. Not mentioned in the Bible but referred to by the Jewish historian Josephus as one of the "Ten Cities" in what the Romans called *Decapolis* (Matt. 4:25; Mark 5:20; 7:31).

Pelonite (pel'a-nīte). A designation for Helez (1 Chron. 11:27) and Ahijah (1 Chron. 11:36), two of David's mighty men. Also called the Paltite (2 Sam. 23:26), or a native of Beth Pelet.

Pleusium (pe-lu′sē-um; *city of mud*). Greek name for the Egyptian city of Sin. Identified with a fortress located about a mile (1.5 km.) from the Mediterranean in the northeast Nile Delta.

Peniel (pe-nī′el). *See* Penvel.

Peninnah (pe-nin′na; *coral; pearl*). Second wife of Elkanah, father of Samuel (1 Sam. 1:2, 4).

Penuel (pe-nū′el; *face of God*). [1] A descendant of Benjamin (1 Chron. 8:25). [2] A chief or father of Gedar (1 Chron. 4:4).

Penuel [Peniel] (pe-nu′el [pe-nī′el]; *face of God*). An encampment of the Hebrews east of Jordan (Gen. 32:30–31; Judg. 8:8, 17). It derived its name from the fact that Jacob had seen God face-to-face there.

Peor (pē′or; *opening*). A mountain peak near Pisgah in Moab (Num. 23:28). It stood across the Jordan River from Jericho.

Perath [Euphrates] (per′ath [ū-fra′tēs]). A place where Jeremiah was instructed to go and hide in a crevice in the rocks (Jer. 13:4–7).

Perazim (pe-rā′zim). *See* Baal-perazim.

Perea (pe-rē′a; *the land beyond*). The Greek term for Transjordan. Though the term appears in the New Testament only in a variant reading of Luke 6:17, it is used regularly by the Jewish historian Josephus.

Peresh (per′esh; *separate*). Son of Machir, son of Manasseh (1 Chron. 7:16).

Perez [Phares; Pharez] (pē′rez [fā′rez]; *bursting through*). Eldest son of Judah and an ancestor of Christ (1 Chron. 27:3; Neh. 11:4). He is also called Pharez (Gen. 38:29; 46:12; Luke 3:33).

Perez-Uzzah [Uzza] (pē'rez-uz'a [uz'a]; *breech of Uzzah*). The name David gave to the place Uzzah was struck by God (2 Sam. 6:8).

Perezites (per'e-zītes). A form of Parzites.

Perga (pur'ga; *very earthy*). The capital of Pamphylia in Asia Minor during the Roman period (Acts 13:13).

Pergamos [Pergamum] (pur'ga-mos [pur'ga-mum]; *elevation*). A city of Mysia in northwest Asia Minor and the site of one of the seven churches of Asia (Rev. 2:12–17).

Perida [Peruda] (pe-rī'da [pe-roo'da]; *unique*). One whose descendants returned from the Exile (Neh. 7:57: Ezra 2:55).

Perizzites (per'a-zites; *villagers*). Inhabitants of the "forest country" (Josh. 17:15) in the territory of the tribes of Ephraim, Manasseh, and Judah (Judg. 1:4–5).

Persepolis (per-sep'ō-lis; *city of Persia*). The ceremonial capital of the Persian Empire under Darius the Great (522–486 B.C.), his son Xerxes (486–465 B.C.), and their successors. It is mentioned in the apocryphal book of 2 Maccabees (2 Macc. 9:1–2).

Persia (per'sha; *cuts* or *divides*). A great empire including all of western Asia and parts of Europe and Africa (Ezra 1:8; Ezek. 38:5). Persia proper corresponded to what is now the province of Fars in Iran.

Persis (pur'sis; *Persian*). A Christian woman at Rome (Rom. 16:12).

Peruda (pe'roo'da). *See* Perida.

Peter (pē'ter; *stone; rock*). A fisherman called to be an apostle of Christ. He became one of the leaders of the early church (Matt. 4:18–20; 16:15–19; Acts 2). Christ changed this man's name from Simon to a name meaning "rock" (*Cephas* in Aramaic, *Peter* in Greek).

Pethahiah (peth-a-hī'a; *Jehovah opens up*). **[1]** A chief Levite in the time of David (1 Chron. 24:16). **[2]** A Levite having a foreign wife (Ezra 10:23). **[3]** A descendant of Judah (Neh. 11:24). **[4]** A Levite who regulated the devotions of the people after Ezra had finished reading the Law (Neh. 9:5).

Pethor (pē'thor; *soothsayer*). The residence of Balaam (Num. 22:5; Deut. 23:4). The town was near the Euphrates River and the mountains of Aram. It was a few kilometers south of Carchemish.

Pethuel (pe-thū'el; *God's opening*). Father of Joel the prophet (Joel 1:1).

Petra (pet'ra; *rock*). The capital of Edom and later of Nabatea, situated about 170 mi. (275 km.) southwest of modern Amman and about 50 mi. (80 km.) south of the Dead Sea. Many scholars identify it with Sela (Judg. 1:36; 2 Kings 14:7).

Peullethai [Peulthai] (pē-ūl'e-thī [pē-ūl'thī]; *wages of the Lord*). A son of Obed-edom and gatekeeper in the time of David (1 Chron. 26:5).

Phalec (fā'lek). Greek form of Peleg (q.v.).

Phallu (fal'oo). *See* Pallu.

Phalti (fal'tī). *See* Paltiel [2].

Phaltiel (fal'ti-el). *See* Paltiel.

Phanuel (fa-noo'el; *face of God*). Father of Anna (Luke 2:36).

Pharaoh (fār'ō; *inhabitant of the palace*). Royal title of Egyptian kings, equivalent to our word *king* (Gen. 12:15; 37:36; Exod. 2:15; 1 Kings 3:1; Isa. 19:11).

Phares (fā'rez). Greek form of Perez (q.v.).

Pharez (fā'rez). *See* Perez.

Pharisees (fār'a-sees; *separated ones*). A religious and political party in New Testament times. They were known for their insistence on observing the Law of God, especially purity (Matt. 23:23–26; Mark 7:1–13; Luke 11:37–42; 18:12).

Pharosh (fā′rosh). *See* Parosh.

Pharpar (far′par; *produces fruit*). One of the two rivers of Damascus (2 Kings 5:12). It is probably the modern Nahr el-'A'waj.

Pharzites (far′zites). A form of Parzites.

Phaseah (fa-sē′a). *See* Paseah.

Phebe [Phoebe] (fē′be; *shining*). A servant of the church at Corinth or Cenchrea who helped Paul (Rom. 16:1).

Phenice [Phoenix] (fē′nis [fē′nix]; *date palm*). [1] A harbor in southern Crete (Acts 27:12). [2] *See* Phoenicia.

Phenicia (fa-nē-sha). A form of Phoenicia.

Phichol [Phicol] (fī′kol; *dark water*). A captain or captains of the army of Abimelech, king of the Philistines (Gen. 21:22; 26:26). Some scholars think this is not a proper name (nor Abimelech), but a Philistine military title. Abraham and Isaac journeyed to Gerar many years apart but yet both encountered an Abimelech and Phichol residing there. If these names are titles, that would help explain this puzzling situation; *See* Abimelech.

Philadelphia (fĭl-a-del′fĭ-a; *love of a brother*). A town of Lydia in Asia Minor. It was the site of one of the seven churches of Asia (Rev. 1:11; 3:7–13). It was 45.5 km. (28.3 mi.) southeast of Sardis.

Philemon (fī-lē′mon; *friendship*). A convert at Colossae to whom Paul wrote an epistle on behalf of his runaway servant, Onesimus (Philem. 1, 5–7).

Philetus (fī-le′tus; *beloved*). A convert who was condemned by Paul because of his stand on the Resurrection (2 Tim. 2:17).

Philip (fil'ip; *lover of horses*). **[1]** One of the twelve apostles of Christ (Matt. 10:3; John 1:44–48; 6:5–9). **[2]** An evangelist mentioned several times in Acts (Acts 6:5; 8:5–13). **[3]** *See* Herod [3], [4]. **[4]** A son of Herod the Great and Marianne; first husband of Herodias (Matt. 14:3; Luke 3:19).

Philippi (fi-lip'ī; *city of Philip*). A city of Macedonia founded by Philip the Great and named for him (Acts 16:12; 20:3–6). It lies inland about 16.1 km. (10 mi.) northwest of its seaport, Neapolis.

Philippians (fi-lip'ē-ans). Natives or inhabitants of Philippi (Phil. 4:15), a city of Macedonia situated about 113 km. (70 mi.) northeast of Thessalonica (Acts 16:12; Phil. 1:1).

Philistia (fil-is'ti-a; *land of sojourners*). An area on the southwest coast of Palestine (Psa. 60:8; 87:4; 108:9). This land, which was the home of traditional enemies of Israel, was 80 km. (50 mi.) long and only 24 km. (15 mi.) wide.

Philistines [Philistim] (fi'is-tēns [fil-is'tim]). An aggressive tribal group that occupied part of southwest Palestine from about 1200 to 600 B.C. The Hebrew word *pelishti* actually refers to the territory they occupied, Philistia. From this the name Palestine has been derived, the land promised to and occupied by the covenant people of Jehovah. The Philistines were a continual threat to Israel, often occupying Israelite settlements (1 Sam. 10:5). However, by the end of David's reign, their power began to decline significantly.

Philo Judaeus (fi'lo ju-dē'as). A Jewish philosopher and teacher who is known for his allegorical interpretation of Scripture. He is also known as Philo of Alexandria. Born into an influential Jewish family in Egypt around 20 B.C., he taught and wrote during the time of Jesus and died in A.D. 50.

Philologus (fi-lol'o-gus; *talkative*). A Roman Christian to whom Paul sent greetings (Rom. 16:15).

Phinehas (fin'e-as; *the nubian*). [1] Grandson of Aaron and high priest (Exod. 6:25; Num. 25:6–18; 1 Chron. 6:4; 9:20). [2] Younger son of Eli; he was a priest who abused his office (1 Sam. 1:3; 2:22–24, 34). [3] Father of Eleazar (Ezra 8:33).

Phlegon (flē'gon; *zealous*). A Roman Christian (Rom. 16:14).

Phoenicia [Phenice] (fe-nish'i-a [fē'nis]; *land of palm trees*). A thin strip of territory between the Mediterranean Sea on the west and on the east the mountains of Lebanon (Acts 21:2; 11:19; 15:3). It included the hills running south from those mountains.

Phoenicians (fō-nē'shi-uns). Inhabitants of Phoenicia, the ancient nation northwest of Palestine along the Mediterranean Sea. Conquered by the Israelites around 1380 B.C., they became noted shipbuilders and eventually one of the most distinguished seafaring peoples in history (see Ezek. 27:9; 1 Kings 5:6).

Phoenix (fē'nix). *See* Phenice.

Phrygia (frij'i-a; *barren*). A large and important inland province of Asia Minor (Acts 2:10; 16:6).

Phurah [Puran] (fū'ra [pū'ra]; *beauty*). A servant of Gideon (Judg. 7:10–11).

Phut [Put] (fut [put]; *bow*). The third son of Ham (Gen. 10:6; 1 Chron. 1:8). Possibly a reference to a people related to the Egyptians. Many consider the reference to be to a people related to the Libyans.

Phut (fut). *See* Libya.

Phuvah [Pua; Puah; Puvah] (fū'va [pū'al; pū'va]; *girl*). **[1]** Second son of Issachar (Gen. 46:13; Num. 26:23; 1 Chron. 7:1). **[2]** Father of Tola the judge (Judg. 10:1). **[3]** One of two midwives whom Pharaoh ordered to kill Hebrew males at their birth (Exod. 1:15). The midwives courageously disobeyed Pharaoh's command.

Phygellus (fi-gel'us; *fugitive*). One who deserted Paul in Asia (2 Tim. 1:15).

Pibeseth (pi-bē'seth; *house of Bast*). An Egyptian town located on the west bank of the Pelusiac branch of the Nile (Ezek. 30:17). It is now called Tell Basta, about 72.4 km. (45 mi.) east-northeast of Cairo.

Pi-hahiroth (pī-ha-hī'roth; *the mouth*). The location of the final Israelite encampment prior to crossing the Red Sea (Exod. 14:2, 9; Num. 33:7–8). The site is uncertain, but it may be the swamps of Jeneffel at the edge of the pass between Baal-zephon and the Great Bitter Lake.

Pilate (pī'lat). *See* Pontius Pilate.

Pildash (pil'dash; *flame of fire*). A son of Nahor, Abraham's brother (Gen. 22:22).

Pileha [Pilha] (pil'e-ha [pil'ha]; *worship*). One who sealed the covenant (Neh. 10:24).

Piltai (pil'tī; *my deliverance*). A priest in Jerusalem in the days of Joiakim (Neh. 12:17).

Pinon (pī'non; *darkness*). A chief of Edom (Gen. 36:41; 1 Chron. 1:52).

Piram (pī'ram; *indomitable* or *wild*). An Amorite king slain by Joshua (Josh. 10:3).

Pirathon (pir′a-thon; *princely*). The town where Abdon the judge was buried (Judg. 12:15). It is now called Ferata and is 12 km. (7.5 mi.) southwest of Shechem.

Pirathonite (pir′a-tha-nīte). A native or inhabitant of Pirathon (Judg. 12:13; 1 Chron. 11:31).

Pisgah (pis′ga; *fortress*). The mountain ranges from which Moses viewed the Promised Land (Num. 21:20; Deut. 3:27). This part of the Abarim Range is near the northeast end of the Dead Sea.

Pisidia (pi-sid′i-a; *pitch*). An island district of Asia Minor with Antioch as its capital (Acts 13:14).

Pisidian Antioch (pi-sid′e-an an′tē-ak). *See* Antioch.

Pison [Pison] (pī′son [pī′san]; *freely flowing*). A river of Eden (Gen. 2:11). It has traditionally been identified with the Phasis (modern Rion) or the Kur, a tributary of the Araxes. The Palla Copas canal has been suggested also.

Pispah [Pispa] (pis-pa; *expansion*). A descendant of Asher (1 Chron. 7:38).

Pithom (pī′thom; *temple of Tem*). An Egyptian store-city built by the Israelites (Exod. 1:11). It was located in the valley connecting the Nile and Lake Timsha. The ruins are at Tell el-Maskhutah.

Pithon (pī′thon; *harmless*). A son of Micah and great-grandson of Saul (1 Chron. 8:35).

Pochereth-Zebaim (pok′e-reth-ze-bā′im; *binder of gazelles*). One whose children returned (Ezra 2:57; Neh. 7:59)

Pontius Pilate (pon′shus pī′lat; Latin, *Pontius Pilatus—marine dart-carrier*). A Roman procurator of Judea. When Christ was brought before him for judgment, Pilate, fearing the Jews, turned Him over to the people even though he found Him not guilty (Matt. 27:2–24; John 18:28–40).

Pontus (pon′tus; *the sea*). A district in northeastern Asia Minor on the Pontus Euxinum (Acts 2:9; 1 Pet. 1:1).

Poratha (pō′r′a-tha; *bounteous*). A son of Haman slain by the Jews (Esther 9:8).

Porcius Festus (por′shi-us fes′tus). *See* Festus.

Potiphar (pot′i-fer; *belonging to the sun-god*). Egyptian captain of the guard who became the master of Joseph (Gen. 37:36; 39).

Potipherah (po-tif′er-a; *given of the sun-god*). A priest of On; father-in-law of Joseph (Gen. 41:45, 50).

Potter's Field. *See* Aceldama.

Praetorium (pre-tō′ri-um). The Praetorium was originally the headquarters of a Roman camp, but in the provinces the name was used to designate the official residence. Jesus was brought to Pilate's Praetorium in Jerusalem (Mark 15:16).

Prisca (pris′ka). Shortened form of Priscilla (q.v.)

Priscilla [Prisca] (pri-sil′a [pris′ka]; *ancient one*). The wife of Aquila; a Jewish Christian deeply loyal to her faith (Acts 18:2, 18, 26; Rom. 16:3).

Prison, Gate of the. A gate in the city wall of Jerusalem or the Temple area (Neh. 12:39). Exact location unknown because of the history of expansion, destruction, and rebuilding of the walls of Jerusalem.

Prochorus (prok′o-rus; *choir leader*). One of the seven deacons (Acts 6:5).

Psalmist. A writer or composer of a psalm. Used to refer to David as the "sweet psalmist of Israel" (2 Sam. 23:1).

Ptolemais (tol-e-mā′is). *See* Acco.

Pua (pū′a). *See* Phuvah.

Puah (pū′a). *See* Phuvah.

Publius (pub'li-us; *common; first*). Governor of Malta who courteously received Paul and his company when they were shipwrecked (Acts 28:1–10).

Pudens (pū'denz; *modest*). A Roman Christian (2 Tim. 4:21).

Puhites (pu'hītes). A form of Puthites.

Pul (pul). *See* Tiglath-pileser.

Pul (pul; *Lord*). A country of undetermined location (Isa. 66:19), sometimes considered to be Libya.

Punites (pu'nītes). The descendants of Puah, of the tribe of Isachar (Num. 26:23).

Punon (pū'non; *ore pit*). An Israelite encampment during the last portion of the wilderness wandering (Num. 33:42). It is probably modern Feeinan on the east side of the Aravah.

Purah [Phurah] (pū'ra [fūr'a]; *beauty*). One of Gideon's servants who went with him to scout the enemy camp of the Midianites (Judg. 7:10–11).

Purim (pur'im; *lots*). A Jewish holiday observed a month before Passover in commemoration of Jewish deliverance from massacre led by Esther and Mordecai (Esth. 3:7; 9:24–32).

Put (put). *See* Phut.

Put (put). *See* Libya.

P

Puteoli (pu-tē'o-lī; *sulphurous wells*). A seaport on the northern shore of the Bay of Naples (Acts 28:13). The modern city of Pozzuoli stands there.

Puthites [Puhites] (pū'thites [pū'hītes]). A family of the tribe of Judah in Kiriath-Jearim (1 Chron. 2:53).

Putiel (pū'ti-el; *God enlightens*). Father-in-law of Eleazer, son of Aaron (Exod. 6:25).

Puvah (pu'va). A form of Puah.

Pyrrhus (pir´as; *flame-colored*). The father of Sopater of Berea (Acts 20:4), though some ancient Greek manuscripts do not contain his name.

Q

Quartus (kwor´tus; *fourth*). A Corinthian Christian who sent greetings to the church in Rome (Rom. 16:23).

Queen of Heaven. A fertility goddess worshipped in Judah before its collapse. (Jer. 7:13; 44:17–19, 25). This term may refer to the goddess Ishtar, or the Canaanite goddess Anat.

Queen of Sheba. *See* Sheba.

Quicksands, the. *See* Syrtis.

Quirinius Cyrenius (kwī-ren´i-us [sī-ren´-i-us]). Roman governor of Syria at the time of Jesus' birth (Luke 2:1–5).

Qumran, Khirbet(fir´bet kum´ran). An ancient ruin on the northwestern shore of the Dead Sea where several ancient scrolls were discovered in 1947. These became known as the Dead Sea scrolls and were connected with a Jewish community active from 130 B. C. to A. D. 135.

R

Raamah [Raama] (rā´a-ma; *trembling*). A son of Cush (Gen. 10:7; 1 Chron. 1:9). Possibly a reference to the inhabitants of a place in southwest Arabia.

Raamah (rā´a-ma; *trembling*). A place near Ma'in in

southwest Arabia (Ezek. 27:22). It is called Regma in inscriptions from that area.

Raamiah (rā-a-mī′a; *Jehovah causes trembling*). A chief who returned to the land (Neh. 7:7). In Ezra 2:2, he is called Reelaiah *(Jehovah causes trembling)*.

Raamses (ram′sēz). A form of Rameses.

Rabbah [Rabbath] (rab′a [rab′ath]; *great*). [1] The chief city of the Ammonites (Deut. 3:11; Josh. 13:25). It was located 37 km. (23 mi.) east of the Jordan River at the headwaters of the Jabbok. [2] A city in Judah near Kirjath-jearim (Josh. 15:60).

Rabbith (rab′ith; *great*). A boundary town of Issachar (Josh. 19:20). It is perhaps the present village of Raba 12.9 km. (8 mi.) south of Mount Gilboa.

Rabmag (rab′mag; *chief magician* or *priest*). This is not a proper name, but an official position of some sort. It is unclear whether it is a high religious or governmental position (Jer. 39:3, 13). Nergal-sharezer of Babylonia bore this title.

Rabsaris, The. (rab′sa-ris). Not a proper name, but an official position in the Babylonian and Assyrian governments. Its precise nature is unknown. [1] One of three officials sent from Lachish by Sennacherib, king of Assyria (2 Kings 18:17). [2] An official under Nebuchadnezzar, King of Babylon, who possibly ordered the release of Jeremiah (Jer. 39:3, 13).

Rabshakeh, The (rab′sha-ke). The title of an office in the Assyrian government. Its precise function is unknown, but suggestions include that of a field marshal or governor of the Assyrian provinces east of Haran (2 Kings 18:17–28; 19:4, 8).

Racal (rā′kal). A form of Rachal.

Rachab (rā′kab). Greek form of Rahab (q.v.).

Rachal [Racal] (rā'kal; *trade*). A town in Judah (1 Sam. 30:29). Some believe the text should read Carmel and would be identical with Carmel [2].

Rachel [Rahel] (rā'chel [rā'hel]; *ewe*). The younger daughter of Laban, wife of Jacob, and mother of Joseph and Benjamin (Gen. 29–35).

Raddai (rad'ā'ī; *Jehovah subdues*). Brother of David (1 Chron. 2:14).

Ragau (rā'go). Greek form of Reu (q.v.).

Raguel (ra'gū'el). *See* Jethro.

Rahab [Rachab] (rā'hab [rā'kab]; *broad*). The harlot of Jericho who helped the Hebrew spies and who became an ancestor of Christ (Josh. 2:1–21; 6:17–25; Matt. 1:5).

Rahab-Hem-Shebeth (rā'hab-hem-shi-beth; *Rahab sits idle*). A name given by the prophet Isaiah to Egypt (Isa. 30:7), comparing Egypt to Rabab the Dragon, a mythological sea monster of chaos.

Rahab the Dragon (rā'hab; *agitated*). A mythological sea monster representing the evil forces of chaos subdued by God's creative power. The name is not connected with Rahab of Jericho. References in Job (9:13; 26:12), Psalms (87:4; 89:10) and (Isaiah 51:9) speak of an evil power overcome by God.

Raham (rā'ham; *pity*). A descendant of Caleb (1 Chron. 2:44).

Rahel (rā'hel). *See* Rachel.

Raken (rā'kem; *friendship*). A descendant of Manasseh (1 Chron. 7:16).

Rakkath (rak'ath; *empty*). A fortress city in Naphtali on the western shore of the Sea of Galilee (Josh 19:35); probably Tell ellatiyeh.

Rakkon (rak'on; *narrow place*). A place near Joppa in the territory of Dan (Josh. 19:46).

Ram [Aram] (ram [a'ram]; *exalted*). [1] An ancestor of David and of Christ (Ruth 4:19; Matt. 1:3–4; Luke 3:33). [2] Son of Jerahmeel of Judah (1 Chron. 2:27). [3] Head of the family of Elihu (Job 32:2).

Ramah [Rama] (rā'ma [rā'ma]; *elevated*). [1] A town in Benjamin near Gibeah, Geba, and Bethel (Josh. 18:25; Judg. 4:5; Isa. 10:29; Matt. 2:18). It has been identified as modern Er-Ram 8 km. (5 mi.) north of Jerusalem. [2] The town where Samuel was born (1 Sam. 1:1). It is also called Ramathaim-Zophim (1 Sam. 1:11). Its location is uncertain but has been identified with Ramah [1] and modern-day Rentis, about 14.5 km. (9 mi.) northeast of Lydda. It may be Arimathea. [3] A frontier town of Asher (Josh. 19:29). If not the same as Ramah [4] it may be Rameh, about 20.9 km. (13 mi.) south-southeast of Tyre. [4] A fortified city of Naphtali (Josh. 19:36). The site may be modern Rameh, 27.4 km. (17 mi.) east-northeast of Accho. [5] *See* Ramoth-gilead. [6] *See* Ramath.

Ramath [Ramoth] (rā'math [rā'moth]; *height, elevation*). A city of Simeon called "Ramath of the South" (Josh. 19:8). It is now Kurnab. It is also called "Ramoth" in First Samuel 30:27.

Ramathaim-Zophim (rā'ma-thā'im-zō'fim). *See* Ramah [2].

Ramath-Lehi (rā'math-lē'hī; *elevation of the jawbone*). *See* Lehi.

Ramath-Mizpeh [Ramath-Mizpah, Ramoth-Mizpah] (rā'math-miz'pe; [rā'math-miz'pa, rā'moth-miz'pa]; *place of the watchtower*). A city of Gad in Gilead (Josh. 13:26). It was 24 km. (15 mi.) northwest of Rab-

R

bath of Ammon, at the Jabbok. It may be identical with Mizpeh [4].

Ramath-Nebeb (rā'math neg'eb). A form of Ramah.

Ramath of the South. (ra'math). A form of Ramah.

Ramathite (rā'ma-thīte). A native or inhabitant of Ramah. Shimei the Ramathite was overseer of the vineyards of David (1 Chron. 27:27).

Rameses [Raamses] (ram'e-sēz [ram'sēz]; *child of the sun*). The royal city of the Egyptian King Ramses II which the ancestors of Israel were forced to help build around 1300–1100 B.C. (Exod. 1:11). The "land of Ramses" is used to describe the fertile district of Egypt where the Israelites settled (Gen. 47:11; Exod. 12:37). It was almost certainly the Land of Goshen, in the northeastern Nile Delta (Gen. 47:11).

Ramiah (ra-mī'a; *Jehovah is high*). One who married a foreign wife during the Exile (Ezra 10:25).

Ramoth (rā'moth; "heights"). One who had divorced his foreign wife (Ezra 10:29). *See* Jeremoth.

Ramoth (rā'moth; *high places* or *heights*). [1] A Levitical city of Gilead in Gad (Deut. 4:43; Josh. 20:8). It is identical with Ramoth-gilead. [2] A city of Levi in Issachar (1 Chron. 6:37). It is identical with Jarmuth [2] and Remeth (q.v.). [3] *See* Ramath.

Ramoth-gilead [Ramoth] (rā-moth-gil'e-ad [rā'moth]; *heights of Gilead*). The chief city of Gad. It was a city of refuge ascribed to the Levites (1 Kings 4:13; 22:4). Sometimes it is called simply Ramoth (Deut. 4:43; Josh. 20:8). It has been identified with both Tell Ramith and Tell el-Hush.

Ramoth-Mizpah (rā'moth-miz'pa). A form of Ramath-mizpah.

Ramoth-Negeb (rā'moth-neg'eb). A form of Ramah.

Rapha [Raphah] (ra'fa; *God has healed*). **[1]** The fifth son of Benjamin (1 Chron. 8:2). He is called Rephaiah in First Chronicles 9:43. **[2]** A descendant of King Saul (1 Chron. 8:37).

Raphu (ra'fū; *healed*). Father of a spy sent into Canaan (Num. 13:9).

Ras Shamra (ras sham'ra; *fennel mand*). The modern name of the mound (Minet el-Beida) which marks the site of the ancient city Ugarit. The site is on the coast of Syria, opposite the island of Cyprus.

Reaia [Reaiah] (re-ā'ya [re-aā'ya]; *Jehovah sees*). **[1]** A descendant of Reuben (1 Chron. 5:5). **[2]** One whose descendants returned from the Exile (Ezra 2:47; Neh. 7:50). **[3]** A descendant of Judah (1 Chron. 4:2); perhaps the same as Haroeh (1 Chron. 2:52).

Reba (rē'ba; *fourth part; sprout;* or *off-spring*). One of the Midianite chieftains slain by the Israelites under Moses (Num. 31:8; Josh 13:21).

Rebecca (re-bek'a). Greek form of Rebekah (q.v.).

Rebekah [Rebecca] (re-bek'a [re-bek'a]; *cow*). Wife of Isaac and mother of Jacob and Esau (Gen. 22:23; 24–28).

Rechab (rē'kab; *charioteer*). **[1]** A descendant of Benjamin who murdered Ish-bosheth (2 Sam. 4:2, 5–9). **[2]** Founder of a tribe called Rechabites (2 Kings 10:15; Jer. 35). **[3]** A descendant of Hemath (1 Chron. 2:55). **[4]** One who helped to build the wall of Jerusalem (Neh. 3:14).

Rechabites (rē'kab-ītes). A Kenite tribe founded by Jonadlab, the son of Rechab (Jer. 35:1–9).

Rechah (rē'ka; *uttermost part*). A village in Judah (1 Chron. 4:12). Its location is not known.

Red Sea. A sea that divides Egypt and Arabia. It was across this body of water that the Israelites escaped from Egypt (Exod. 10:19). The Hebrews called it the Sea of Deliverance; others called it the "Sea of Reeds."

Reelaiah (re-el-ā′ya). *See* Raamiah.

Refuge, Cities of. *See* Cities of Refuge.

Refuse Gate. One of the gates in the city wall of Jerusalem or the Temple area (Neh. 2:13; 3:13–14; 12:31).

Regem (rē′gem; *a friend*). A descendant of Caleb (2 Chron. 2:47). *See* Regem-melech.

Regem-melech (rē′gem-mē′lek; *royal friend*). A messenger sent out by some Jews. Some authorities do not take this as a proper name but read: ". . . Sherezer, the friend of the king" (Zech. 7:2).

Rehabiah (rē-ha-bī′a; *Jehovah is a widener*). Eldest son of Eliezer, son of Moses (1 Chron. 23:17; 24:21).

Rehob (rē′hob; *breadth; width*). **[1]** Father of Hadadezer, king of Zobah (2 Sam. 8:3, 12). **[2]** A Levite who sealed the covenant (Neh. 10:11).

Rehob (rē′hob; *breadth; width*).**[1]***See* Beth-rehob. **[2]**, **[3]** Two towns of Asher (Josh. 19:28, 30). One of them was given to the Levites and one remained in the hands of the Canaanites (Judg. 1:31; Josh. 21:31).

Rehoboam [Roboam] (re′ho-bō′am [ro′bō′am]; *freer of the people*). The son of Solomon; when he was king, ten tribes revolted from him and he set up the southern kingdom of Judah (1 Kings 11:43; 12; 14). He was an ancestor of Christ (Matt. 1:7).

Rehoboth (re-hō′both; *broad places*). **[1]** A well dug by Isaac in the Valley of Gerar (Gen. 26:22). It is probably modern Wadi Ruheibeh, 30.6 km. (19 mi.) southwest of Beer-sheba. **[2]** A suburb of Nineveh (Gen. 10:11).

[3] A city somewhere in northern Edom (Gen. 36:37; 1 Chron. 1:48). Its location is unidentified.

Rehoboth by the River (re-hō′both; *broad places*). A city located somewhere in northern Edom (Gen. 36:37; 1 Chron. 1:48). The home of Saul, an early king of Edom.

Rehoboth Ir (re-hō′both ēr; *broad places of the city*). Outlying area of the city of Nineveh (Gen. 10:11) in Assyria.

Rehum (rē′hum; *pity*). **[1]** A chief man that returned from Exile with Zerubbabel (Ezra 2:2). He is called Nehum ("comfort") in Nehemiah 7:7. **[2]** A chancellor of Artaxerxes (Ezra 4:8, 17). **[3]** A Levite who helped to repair the wall of Jerusalem (Neh. 3:17). **[4]** One who sealed the covenant (Neh. 10:25). **[5]** One who went up with Zerubbabel (Neh. 12:3).

Rei (rē′i; *friendly*). A friend of David (1 Kings 1:8).

Rekem (rē′kem; *friendship*). **[1]** A Midianite king slain by the Israelites (Num. 31:8; Josh. 13:21). **[2]** A son of Hebron (1 Chron. 2:43–44).

Rekem (re′kem; *friendship*). A city of Benjamin (Josh. 18:27). It is probably modern Ar Kalandujeh.

Remaliah (rem-a-lī′a; *Jehovah increases*). Father of Pekah (2 Kings 15:25–37). This is perhaps not a proper name, but a slur on Pekah's impoverished background.

Remeth (rē′meth; *height*). A city of the tribe of Issachar (Josh. 19:21); not to be confused with Ramath.

Remmon (rem′on). *See* Rimmon.

Remmon-methoar (rem′on-meth′o-ar). *See* Rimmon [3].

Remphan [Rephan, Rompha] (rem′fan [re′fan; rom′-fuh]). An idol worshiped by Israel in the wilderness (Acts 7:43), perhaps the same as Chiun (Amos 5:26).

Rephael (rē′fa-el; *God has healed*). Firstborn son of

Obed-edom and tabernacle gatekeeper (1 Chron. 26:7).

Rephah (rē′fa; *agreeable*). A descendant of Ephraim (1 Chron. 7:25).

Rephaiah (re-fā′ya; *Jehovah is healing*). [1] Head of a family of the house of David (1 Chron. 3:21). [2] A captain of Simeon (1 Chron. 4:42). [3] A son of Tola (1 Chron. 7:2). [4] One who helped to rebuild the wall of Jerusalem (Neh. 3:9). [5] *See* Rapha [1].

Rephaim, Valley of (ref′a-im; *lofty men*). [1] The site in Judah where David defeated the Philistines (Isa. 17:5; 2 Sam. 5:18). It lies between Jerusalem and Bethlehem, southwest of Jerusalem and the Valley of Hinnom. It is probably the present-day Valley el-Bukka. [2] A race of giants who lived in Palestine before the time of Abraham (Gen. 14:5; 15:20). The last known survivor of the rephaim was Og, king of Bashan (Deut. 3:11).

Rephidim (ref′i-dim; *refreshments*). An Israelite encampment between the Wilderness of Sin and Mount Sinai (Exod. 17:1, 8). It may be the Wadi Refayid, northwest of Jebel Musa.

Resen (rē′sen; *bride*). A city between Nineveh and Calah in Assyria (Gen. 10:12).

Resheph (rē′shef; *a flame*). [1] A descendant of Ephraim (1 Chron. 7:25). [2] A Canaanite deity worshiped as lord of the underworld.

Reu [Ragau] (rē′ū [rā′go]; *friend*). Son of Peleg and ancestor of Christ (Gen. 11:18–21; Luke 3:35).

Reuben (roo′ben; *behold, a son*). Eldest son of Jacob and Leah; he lost his birthright through sin against his father (Gen. 29:32; 35:22; 37:29). His descendants became one of the twelve tribes of Israel.

Reuel (roo′el; *God is his friend*). [1] A son of Esau by Bashemath (Gen. 36:4; 1 Chron. 1:35, 37). [2] Descendant of Benjamin (1 Chron. 9:8). **[3]** *See* Jethro. **[4]** *See* Deuel.

Reumah (roo'ma; *coral*). Nahor's concubine (Gen. 22:24).

Rezeph (rē'zef; *glowing coal*). A city of Syria taken by Sennacherib (2 Kings 19:12; Isa. 37:12). It is perhaps the modern Rusafah several kilometers west of the Euphrates toward Palmyra.

Rezia [Rizia] (re-zī'a [ri-zī'a]; *delight*). A descendant of Asher (1 Chron. 7:39).

Rezin (rēz'in; *dominion*). **[1]** The last king of Syria who, along with Pekah, fought Judah (2 Kings 15:37; 16:5–10). **[2]** One whose descendants returned from the Babylonian Captivity (Ezra 2:48; Neh. 7:50).

Rezon (rē'zon; *prince; noble*). A Syrian rebel who set up his own government in Damascus (1 Kings 11:23). Many scholars think Rezon simply is a title denoting a prince and identify him with Hezion (q.v.).

Rhegium (rē'jē-um; *fracture*). A town located in southern Italy (Acts 28:13). It was opposite Messina in Sicily and is now called Reggio.

Rhesa (rē'a; *prince*). An ancestor of Christ (Luke 3:27).

Rhoda (rō'da; *rose*). A maid in the house of Mary (Acts 12:12–15).

Rhodes (rōdz; *rose*). An island located off the coast of Caria in southwest Asia Minor (Acts 21:1).

Ribai (rī'bī; *Jehovah contends*). Father of Ittai, one of David's valiant men (2 Sam. 23:29; 1 Chron. 11:31).

Riblah (rib'la; *fertility*). **[1]** A city on the Orontes where the sons of Zedekiah were slain (Jer. 39:5–7; 2 Kings 23:33). It was 80 km. (50 mi.) south of Hamath. It may be modern Ribleh in the Plain of Coelesyria. **[2]** A border city of the Promised Land (Num. 34:11). It is perhaps modern Harmel northeast of the source of the Orontes.

Rimmon (rim′on; *pomegranate*). Father of Ishbosheth's murderers (2 Sam. 4:2–9).

Rimmon [Remmon] rim′on [rem′on]; "pomegranate"). **[1]** A town in southern Judah (Josh. 15:32; 1 Chron. 4:32; Zech. 14:10). It is identified with Khirbet Umm er-Ramānīn, about 9 mi. from Beersheba. **[2]** A rock near Gibeah (Judg. 20:45–47; 21:13). It is possibly a limestone projection 3.5 mi. east of Bethel. **[3]** A border town of Zebulun (1 Chron. 6:77). The town is called Dimnah in Joshua 21:35, a reading many scholars consider a corruption of Rimmon. The site is referred to in Joshua 19:13 as Remmon-methoar. Many translate verse 13: . . . [the border] goes out to Ittah-Kazin and goes to Kemmon and bends [methoar] to Neah. **[4]** A Syrian god whose temple was at Damascus. Worshipped by Naaman the Syrian and the King of Syria (2 Kings 5:18).

Rimmon-Methoar (rim′on me-thō′ar). A form of Rimmon.

Rimmon-parez (rim′on-pē′rez; *pomegranates of the breach*). The fifteenth encampment of the Israelites (Num. 33:19). It is somewhere between Rithmah and Libnah and is possibly Nakt el-Biyar.

Rimmon, Rock of (rim′on). A form of Rimmon **[2]**.

Rimmono (rim mō′no). A Levitical city of Zebulun (1 Chron. 6:77).

Rinnah (rin′a; *a loud cry*). A descendant of Judah (1 Chron. 4:20).

Riphath (ri′fath; *spoken*). A son of Gomer (Gen. 10:3). A copyist's mistake makes him Diphath in First Chronicles

1:6. Possibly a reference to the Paphlagonians on the Black Sea.

Rissah (ris′a; *heap of ruins*). An encampment in the wilderness (Num. 33:21–22). It is probably modern Kuntilet el-Jerafi.

Rithmah (rith′ma; *wild broom bush*). The fourteenth encampment of Israel in the wilderness (Num. 33:18). It is perhaps the same as Kadesh.

Rizia (ri-zī-a). *See* Rezia.

Rizpah (riz′pa; *glowing stone*). A concubine of Saul (2 Sam. 3:7; 21:8–11).

Roboam (ro-bō′am). Greek form of Rehoboam.

Rodanim (rō′da-nim). *See* Dodanim.

Rogelim (rō′ge-lim; *place of fullers*). The dwelling place of Barzillai (2 Sam. 17:27). It was located in Gilead and is probably Bersiniya 8.8 km. (5.5 mi.) southwest of Irbid.

Rohgah (rō′ga; *outcry; alarm*). A chief of Asher (1 Chron. 7:34).

Romamti-ezer (ro-mam′ti-ē′zer; *I have exalted help*). Son of Heman appointed over the service of song (1 Chron. 25:4, 31).

Roman Empire. The powerful pagan empire that controlled most of the known world during New Testament times. It reached the height of its power from about A.D. 100 to 175.

R

Rome (rōm; *city of Romulus*). The capital of the great Roman Empire (Acts 23:11). It is located in Italy on the Tiber River.

Rosh (rosh; *head*). [1] A descendant of Benjamin (Gen. 46:21). [2] A northern people mentioned with Meshech and Tubal (Ezek. 38: 2–3; 39:1).

Rufus (roo′fus; *red*). [1] A son of Simon of Cyrene (Mark 15:21). He was probably well-known to those to whom Mark wrote his gospel. **[2]** A Roman Christian (Rom. 16:13); some identify him with **[1]**.

Ruhamah (ru-ha'ma; *mercy is shown*). A symbolic name given to Israel by the prophet Ibsea to indicate the return of God's mercy (Hos. 2:1).

Rumah (rū'ma; *exalted*). A town whose locality is uncertain (2 Kings 23:36). Perhaps it is Arumah near Shechem or Rumah [Khirbet Rumeh] in Galilee, 9.7 km. (6 mi.) north of Nazareth.

Ruth (rooth; *friendship; companion*). Moabite wife of Mahlon and Boaz; she was the great-grandmother of David and an ancestor of Christ (Ruth 1:4–5, 14–16; 4:10; Matt. 1:5).

S

Sabeans (sa-bē'ans). The inhabitants of Sheba, an ancient country of southwest Arabia, was known as Yemen (Job. 1:15).

Sabta [Sabtah] (sab'ta; *striking*). The third son of Cush (Gen. 10:7; 1 Chron. 1:9). Possibly a people of southern Arabia is intended.

Sabtecha [Sabtechah, Sabteca] (sab'te-ka; *striking*). The fifth son of Cush (Gen. 10:7; 1 Chron. 1:9). Possibly a reference to a people of south Arabia.

Sacar (sā'kar; *reward*). **[1]** The father of one of David's mighty men (1 Chron. 11:35). He is called Sharar ("strong") in Second Samuel 23:33. **[2]** A Levite tabernacle gatekeeper in the days of David (1 Chron. 26:4).

Sachia [Sachiah, Sakia] (sa-kī'a; *captive of the Lord*). A descendant of Benjamin (1 Chron. 8:10).

Sadoc (sā'dok; Greek form of Zadok—*righteous*). An ancestor of Christ (Matt. 1:14).

Sadducees (saj'u-sēz). Members of a Jewish faction that opposed Jesus. Known for their denial of a bodily resurrection.

Sala [Salah] (sā'la; *petition; sprout*). A son of Arphaxad and ancestor of Christ (Gen. 10:24; 11:12; Luke 3:35). He is called Shelah in First Chronicles 1:18, 24.

Salamis (sal'a-mis; *shaken*). A town located on the east end of Cyprus (Acts 13:5). It is 4.8 km. (3 mi.) northwest of modern Famagusta.

Salathiel (sa-lā'thi-el). Greek form of Shealtiel (q.v.).

Salcah [Salchah] [Salechah] (sal'ka; *wandering*). A city located at the extreme limits of Bashan (Deut. 3:10; Josh. 12:5). It is now Salkhad 106.2 km. (66 mi.) east of the Jordan, opposite Beth-shean in Samaria.

Salem (sā'lem; *peaceful*). The city of Melchizedek (Gen. 14:18; Psa. 76:2). It is possibly modern Salim; however, many believe it to be Jerusalem.

Salim (sa'lim; *peaceful*). The place where John baptized (John 3:23). It is near the waters of Aenon which were probably north of Shechem, although the site is uncertain.

Sallai (sal'a-ī; *rejecter*). [1] A chief man of the tribe of Benjamin (Neh. 11:8). [2] A priest who returned with Zerubbabel from the Exile (Neh. 12:20). He is called Sallu in Nehemiah 12:7.

Sallu (sal'u; *contempt*). [1] A descendant of Benjamin dwelling in Jerusalem (1 Chron. 9:7; Neh. 11:7). [2] *See* Sallai [2].

Salmai [Shalmai; Shamlai] (sal'mī [shal'mī; sham'lī]). A Temple servant whose descendants returned to Jerusalem after the Babylonian Exile (Neh. 7:48; Ezra 2:46).

Salma [Salmon] (sal'ma [sal'mon]; *strength*). [1] A son of Caleb, son of Hur (1 Chron. 2:51, 54). [2] Father of Boaz and ancestor of Christ (Ruth 4:20–21; Matt. 1:4–5; Luke 3:32). Not to be confused with Zalmon.

Salmon (sal'mon). *See* Zalmon.

Salmone (sal-mō'ne; *peace*). The easternmost point of the island of Crete (Acts 27:7). It is now known as Cape Sidero.

Salome (sa-lō'me; *peace*). [1] One of the women who saw the Crucifixion (Mark. 15:40; 16:1). Matthew 27:56 mentions that the mother of the sons of Zebedee was present; she is probably to be identified with Salome. John 19:25 lists the sister of Jesus' mother among those near the cross; some scholars identify her with Salome, but others deny this. [2] The daughter of Herodias who danced before Herod (Matt. 14:6; Mark 6:22).

Salt, City of. *See* City of Salt.

Salt Sea [Dead Sea; East Sea]. The body of water at the southern end of the Jordan Valley, which contains no marine life because of its heavy mineral contents (Gen. 14:3; Num. 34:12). Its modern name is the Dead Sea.

Salt, Valley of. A plain traditionally located at the lower end of the Dead Sea (2 Sam. 8:13). Another such valley, the Wadi el-Milh (salt), is east of Beer-sheba, and may be the site of the defeat of the Edomites.

Salu (sā'lu; *miserable; unfortunate*). Father of Zimri, who was slain (Num. 25:14).

Samaria (sa-mā'ri-a; *watch mountain*). [1] The capital of the northern kingdom of Israel (1 Kings 20:1; 2 Chron. 18:2; Jer. 41:5). It was 67.6 km. (42 mi.) north of Jerusalem. **[2]** Another name for the kingdom of Israel (1 Kings 13:32; 2 Kings 17:24). **[3]** A territory in the uplands of central Palestine that corresponded roughly with the lands allotted to the tribe of Ephraim and the western portion of Manasseh. It consisted of about 1400 square miles of attractive, fertile land which enabled both commerce and invasion from neighboring nations. **[4]** A district of Palestine in Christ's time (Luke 17:11–19). Galilee was on its north and Judea on the south.

Samaritans (sa-mar′i-tans). Natives or inhabitants of Samaria. Samaria became the new capital of Israel during the reigns of Omri and Ahab until its capture by the Assyrians in 722–721 B.C. Its leading citizens were deported and replaced by foreign colonists (2 Kings 17:4) who intermarried among the Israelites. The Samaritans were known for their worship of the God of Israel in addition to the pagan gods imported from foreign lands (2 Kings 17:29).

Samgar-nebo (sam′gar-nē′bo). A Babylonian officer who sat with other officials in the middle gate of Jerusalem (Jer. 39:3). Some take this as a proper name (perhaps meaning "be gracious, Nebo"). Others view it as a title of Nergal-sharezer.

Samlah (sam′la; *garment*). King of Edom (Gen. 36:36; 1 Chron. 1:47–48).

Samos (sā′mos; *lofty place*). An island of Greece (Acts 20:15). It is off the eastern coast of Asia Minor southwest of Ephesus.

Samothracia [Samothrace] (sam-o-thrās′ē-a [sam′o[thrās]; *of the Samians and Thracians*). A small island in the Aegean Sea off the southern coast of Thrace (Acts 16:11).

S

Samson (sam'son; *distinguished; strong*). Judge of Israel for 20 years. His great strength and moral weakness have made him famous (Judg. 13:24; 14–16).

Samuel [Shemuel] (sam'ū-el [she-mū'el]; *name of God*). Prophet and last judge of Israel. He anointed Saul and later David as king (1 Sam. 1:20; 3–13; 15–16; 19; 25:1; Heb. 11:32).

Sanballat (san-bal'at; *the god, Sin, has given life*). A leading opponent of the Jews at the time they were rebuilding the walls of Jerusalem (Neh. 2:10; 4:1, 7; 6:1–14).

Sanhedrin (san'hē-dran; *a council* or *assembly*). The highest ruling body and court of justice among the Jewish people in the time of Jesus. The Sanhedrin was granted limited authority over certain religious, civil, and criminal matters by the foreign nations that dominated the land of Israel at various times in its history.

Sansannah (san-san'a; *thorn bush*). A village in extreme southern Judah (Josh. 15:31). It is probably modern Khirbet esh-Shamsaniyat about 16.1 km. (10 mi.) north-northeast of Beer-sheba.

Saph (saf; *preserver*). A descendant of Rapha the giant (2 Sam. 21:18). He is called Sippai ("Jehovah is preserver") in First Chronicles 20:4.

Saphir [Shaphir] (sā'fer [shā'fer]; *beautiful*). A town in Judah (Mic. 1:11). It was west of Hebron and may be Khirbet el-Kom.

Sapphira (sa'fi'ra; *beautiful; sapphire*). The dishonest wife of Ananias, who was struck dead by God (Acts 5:1–10).

Sara (sā'ra). Greek form of Sarah (q.v.).

Sarah [Sara; Sarai] (sā'ra [sā'ra; sā'rī]; *princess*). The wife of Abraham and mother of Isaac (Gen. 17–18; 20–21; Heb. 11:11; 1 Pet. 3:6). Her name was changed from Sarai ("Jehovah is prince") to Sarah ("princess") because she would be the progenitor of a great nation (Gen. 17:15). *See* Serah.

Sarai (sā′rī). *See* Sarah.

Saraph (sā′raf; *burning*). A descendant of Judah (1 Chron. 4:22).

Sardis (sar′dis; *prince of joy*). The capital city of Lydia where a church was located (Rev. 1:11; 3:1, 4). It was on the east bank of the Pactolus River about 80.5 km. (50 mi.) east of Smyrna.

Sardites [Seredites] (zar′dītes [sēr′e-dītes]). A tribal family founded by Sered (Num. 26:26; Gen. 46:14).

Sargon (sar′gon; *the king is legitimate*). An important king of Assyria and Babylonia (722–705 B.C.) who finished the siege of Samaria and carried away Israel. He is called by name only once in Scripture (Isa. 20:1).

Sarid (sā′rid; *survivor*). A landmark in the territory of Zebulun (Josh. 19:10, 12). It is modern Tell Shadud in the northern portion of the Plain of Esdraelon [Jezreel] about 8 km. (5 mi.) southwest of Nazareth.

Saron (sā′ron). The Greek form of Sharon (q.v.).

Sarsechim (sar′se-kim; *chief of the eunuchs*). A prince of Babylon who sat at the gate (Jer. 39:3).

Saruch (sā′ruk). Greek form of Serug (q.v.).

Satan (sā′ton; *adversary*). The great opposer, or adversary of God and humanity; the devil. The Hebrew word for Satan sometimes refers to human enemies (1 Sam. 29:4; Ps. 109:6). Once it refers to the angel who opposed Balaam (Num. 22:22). However when used as a proper name, it refers to the superhuman enemy of God, humanity, and good (1 Chron. 21:1; Job 1–2). This use of the word also occurs frequently in the New Testament.

Satan, Synagogue of. A phrase used by John to describe Jews who opposed the Church (Rev. 2:9; 3:9).

Satrap (sā′trap). The title of a governor in the province of ancient Persia (Ezra 8:36; Esth. 3:12).

Saul [Shaul] (sol [shol]; *asked*). **[1]** The first king of Israel; God eventually gave him up. He tried several times to slay David, but was killed himself at Gilboa (1 Sam. 9–31). **[2]** The original name of Paul (q.v.). **[3]** *See* Shaul [1].

Sceva (sē′va; *fitted*). A Jewish priest at Ephesus whose sons attempted to cast out a demon, but were wounded by it instead (Acts 19:14–16).

Scythians (sith′ē-ans). A barbaric race of people who lived in Scythia, an ancient region of southeastern Europe and southwestern Asia, now generally identified as the area known (until recently) as the Soviet Union.

Sea of Galilee. *See* Galilee, Sea of.

Sea of Glass. A symbolic sea which stood for God's holiness and purity in the book of Revelation (Rev. 4:6).

Sea, the Great. Another name for the Mediterranean Sea (Josh. 15:47).

Sea of Jazer. (jā′zer). A lake in Gilead, east of the Jordan River (Jer. 43:32).

Sea, Salt. *See* Dead Sea.

Sea, Tiberius. *See* Tiberius.

Seba (sē′ba; meaning unknown). Eldest son of Cush (Gen. 10:7; 1 Chron. 1:9). Not to be confused with Sheba. Possibly the name refers to a people of southern Arabia.

Seba (sē′ba; meaning unknown). An African nation bordering the land of Cush (Psa. 72:10; Isa. 43:3). There is some confusion between Sheba and Seba, but they are probably two distinct locations.

Secacah (se-kā′ka; *thicket*). A city of Judah near the Dead Sea (Josh. 15:61). It was situated in the Valley of Achor.

Sechu [Secu] (sē'kū; *watchplace*). A location with a well on the route from Gibeah to Ramah (1 Sam. 19:22).

Second Quarter, The. A district in Jerusalem formed by the west wall of the Temple and the ancient wall of the city. The district in which Huldah the prophetess lived (2 Kings 2:14).

Secundus (se-kun'dus; *second*). A Thessalonian Christian and friend of Paul (Acts 20:4).

Segub (sē'gub; *might; protection*). [1] Younger son of Hiel who rebuilt Jericho in the days of Ahab (1 Kings 16:34). [2] A grandson of Judah (1 Chron. 2:21–22).

Seir (sē'ir; *hairy, rough*). [1] The valley and mountains of Aravah from the Dead Sea south to the Elanitic Gulf (Gen. 14:6; 32:3). Seir was the name of the mountain range in Edom and the name came to include the entire territory. [2] A ridge on Judah's border west of Kirjath-jearim (Josh. 15:10).

Seir (sē'ir; *hairy, rough*). The grandfather of Hori, ancestor of the Horites (1 Chron. 1:39).

Seirath [Seirah] (se-ī'rath [se-ī'ra]; *tempest*). A place in Mount Ephraim to which Ehud fled after he murdered Eglon (Judg. 3:26).

Sela [Selah] (sē'la; *a rock*). [1] The capital of Edom, located between the Dead Sea and the Gulf of Aqaba (2 Kings 14:7; Isa. 16:1). It is also called Petra. [2] A rock formation about 1,160 m. (3,800 ft.) above sea level, which dominates the city of Petra (cf. Judg. 1:36). It is now called Ummel-Bizarah.

Sela-hammahlekoth (sē'la-ha-ma'le-koth; *rock of divisions*). A cliff in the wilderness near Moan where David escaped from Saul (1 Sam. 23:28).

Seled (sē'led; *exultation*). A descendant of Judah (1 Chron. 2:30).

Seleucia (sē-lū'shi-a; *beaten by the waves*). A Syrian seaport from which Paul and Barnabas began their first missionary journey (Acts 13:4). It is located 8 km. (5 mi.) north of the mouth of the Orontes River.

Sem (sem). Greek form of Shem (q.v.).

Semachiah (sem-a-kī'a; *Jehovah supports*). A gatekeeper of the tabernacle in David's day (1 Chron. 26:7).

Semei [Semein] (sem'e-i [sem'e-in]; Greek form of Shimei). An ancestor of Christ (Luke 3:26).

Senaah (se-nā'a). *See* Hassenaah.

Seneh (sē'ne; *thornbush*). The more southerly of two rocks in the passage between Michmash and Geba (1 Sam. 14:4–5). It is 10.5 km. (6.5 mi.) northeast of Jerusalem.

Senir (sē'nir). *See* Shenir.

Sennacherib (se-nak'er-ib; Babylonian, *Sin-ahi-eriba—[the moon-god] Sin has compensated me with brothers*). An Assyrian king who killed his brother to usurp the throne. He unsuccessfully invaded Judah. The amazing story of the destruction of his army is told in Second Kings 19 (2 Kings 18:13; Isa. 36:1; 37:17, 21, 37).

Senuah (se-nū'a; *hated one*). A descendant of Benjamin (Neh. 11:9). Possibly the same as Hasenuah (q.v.).

Seorim (sē-ōr'im; *fear; distress*). A priest in the days of David (1 Chron. 24:8).

Sephar (sē'far *border country*). An area in the southeastern portion of Arabia (Gen. 10:30).

Sepharad (se-fa'rad; *descending*). A place where the Jerusalem exiles lived (Obad. 20). It is probably Sardis in Asia Minor (q.v.).

Sepharvaim (se-far-va'yim; *the two scribes*). A city formerly identified with Sippar on the east bank of the Euphrates;

it is now believed to be the Syrian city Shabara (Isa. 37:13).

Sepharites (se'fer-vītes). Natives or inhabitants of Sepharvaim (2 Kings 17:31).

Serah (sē' ra; *extension*). A daughter of Asher (Gen. 46:17; 1 Chron. 7:30). Numbers 26:46 should read Serah, not Sarah.

Seraiah (se-rā'ya; *Jehovah is prince; Jehovah has prevailed*). [1] A scribe of David (2 Sam. 8:17). In Second Samuel 20:25, he is called Sheva and Shavsha in First Chronicles 18:16. He is also called Shisha in First Kings 4:3. [2] Chief priest of Jerusalem (2 Kings 25:18; 1 Chron. 6:14; Ezra 7:1). [3] One whom Gedaliah advised to submit to Chaldea (2 Kings 25:23; Jer. 40:8). [4] The brother of Othniel (1 Chron. 4:13–14). [5] A descendant of Simeon (1 Chron. 4:35). [6] A priest that returned to Jerusalem with Zerubbabel (Ezra 2:2, probably identical with Seraiah of Neh. 10:2. [7] A leader sent to capture Jeremiah (Jer. 36:26). [8] A prince of Judah who went to Babylon (Jer. 51:59, 61). [9] A son of Hilkiah dwelling in Jerusalem after the Exile (Neh. 11:11). [10] A chief of the priests who returned from Babylon (Neh. 12:1, 7).

Seraphim (ser'a-fim; *fiery, burning ones*). Angelic or heavenly beings associated with Isaiah's prophetic call and vision of God in the Temple (Isa. 6:1–7).

Sered (sē'red; *escape; deliverance*). Eldest son of Zebulun (Gen. 46:14; Num. 26:26).

Seredites (sē'red-ītes). *See* Sardites.

Sergius Paulus (sur'jē-us po'lus). The Roman deputy of Cyprus who was converted because Elymas was struck blind (Acts 13:7).

Serpent Well. A well, fountain, or spring between the

Valley Gate and the Refuse (Dung) Gate in Jerusalem in Nehemiah's time (Neh. 2:13; dragon well, KJV; Jackal's Well, RSV).

Serug [Saruch] (sē'rug [sā'ruk]; *strength; firmness*). Father of Nahor and ancestor of Christ (Gen. 11:20–21; Luke 3:35).

Seth [Sheth] (seth [sheth]; *compensation*). Son of Adam and Eve, and an ancestor of Christ (Gen. 4:25–26; 1 Chron. 1:1; Luke 3:38).

Sethur (sē'thur; *hidden*). One sent to spy out the land (Num. 13:13).

Shaalabbin [Shaalbim] (sha-a-lab'in [sha-al'bim]; *place of foxes*). A city of the tribe of Dan (Josh. 19:42; Judg. 1:35). It may be modern Silbit 4.8 km. (3 mi.) north-west of Aijalon.

Shaalbon (shā-al'ban). The home of Eliahaba, one of David's mighty men (2 Sam. 23:32). It may be the same as Shaalabin.

Shaalbonite (shā-al'ban-īte). A native of inhabitant of Shaalbon (2 Sam. 23:32).

Shaalim [Shalim] (shā'a-lim [shā'lim]; *foxes*). An unidentified region, perhaps in the region of Ephraim or Benjamin, where Saul searched for his father's donkeys (1 Sam. 9:4).

Shaaph (shā'af; *union, friendship*). **[1]** A descendant of Judah (1 Chron. 2:47). **[2]** A son of Caleb (1 Chron. 2:49).

Shaaraim [Sharaim] (sha-a-rā'im [sha-rā'im]; *two gates*). **[1]** A town in lowland Judah west of Socoh (1 Sam. 17:52; Josh. 15:36). **[2]** A town of Simeon (1 Chron. 4:31). It is identified with Tell el-Far'ah about 24.9 km. (15.5 mi.) south-southeast of Gaza.

Shaashgaz (shā-ash′gaz; *lover of beauty*). A chamberlain of Ahasuerus (Esther 2:14).

Shabbethai (shab′e-thī; *sabbath-born*). [1] An assistant to Ezra (Ezra 10:15). [2] One who explained the Law to the people (Neh. 8:7). [3] A chief Levite in Jerusalem (Neh. 11:16). All three may be identical.

Shachia [Sachia] (sha-kī′a [sa-kī′a]; *fame of Jehovah*). A descendant of Benjamin (1 Chron. 8:10).

Shaddai (shad′ī; *almighty*). Prefixed by El (God), signifies God as the source of blessing. The name with which God appeared to Abraham, Isaac, and Jacob (Exod. 6:3).

Shadrach (shā′drak; *command of Aku*). The name given to Hananiah at Babylon. He was cast into a fiery furnace and rescued (Dan. 1:7; 3).

Shage [Shagee, Shageh] (sha′ge [sha′gē; sha′ge]; *erring; wandering*). Father of one of David's mighty men (1 Chron. 11:34). Possibly another name of Shammah (q.v.) or Agee (2 Sam. 23:11).

Shaharaim (shā-ha-rā′im; *double dawn*). A descendant of Benjamin who went to Moab (1 Chron. 8:8).

Shahazimah [Shahazumah] (shā-ha-zi′ma [shā-ha-zū′ma]; "heights"). A city of Issachar (Josh. 19:22). It is between Mount Tabor and the Jordan, and is probably modern Tell el-Mekarkash [Mukarkash].

Shalem (shā′lem; *peaceful; secure*). Possibly a town near Shechem (Gen. 33:18) but most modern translations do not regard the word as a proper name. They translate the word for Shalem as "peace": "And Jacob came in peace [Shalem] to the city of Shechem."

Shalim (shā′lim). *See* Shaalim.

Shalisha [Shalishah] (sha-lī′sha; *the third*). An area near Mount Ephraim through which Saul passed when searching for his father's livestock (1 Sam. 9:4). It was probably northeast of Lydda.

Shalleketh [Shallecheth] (shal'e-keth). The west gate of the Temple of Solomon in Jerusalem (1 Chron. 26:16).

Shallum [Shallun] (shal'um [shal'un]; *recompenser*). **[1]** The youngest son of Naphtali (1 Chron. 7:13). He is also called Shillem (Gen. 46:24; Num. 26:49). **[2]** A descendant of Simeon (1 Chron. 4:25). **[3]** A descendant of Judah (1 Chron. 2:40–41). **[4]** One who usurped the throne of Israel and reigned for one month (2 Kings 15:10–15). **[5]** Husband of Huldah the prophetess (2 Kings 22:14; 2 Chron. 34:22). **[6]** *See* Jehoahaz [2]. **[7]** *See* Meshullam [7]. **[8]** A gatekeeper of the tabernacle (1 Chron. 9:17–19, 31; Ezra 2:42; Neh. 7:45). **[9]** Father of Jehizkiah (2 Chron. 28:12). **[10]**, **[11]** Two who married foreign wives during the Exile (Ezra 10:24, 42). **[12]** One who helped to repair the wall of Jerusalem (Neh. 3:12). **[13]** One who helped to repair the gate of Jerusalem (Neh. 3:15). **[14]** An uncle of Jeremiah (Jer. 32:7). **[15]** Father of one who was a temple officer in the days of Jehoiakim (Jer. 35:4).

Shalmai (shal'mī; *Jehovah is recompenser*). Ancestor of returned exiles (Ezra 2:46; Neh. 7:48).

Shalman (shal'man). The king who sacked Beth-arbel (Hos. 10:14). Perhaps he was either Shalmaneser V of Assyria or Shalman king of Moab.

Shalmaneser (shal-man-ē'zer; Babylonian, *Shulmaner-asharidu*—[*the god*] *Shulmanu is chief*). The king of Assyria to whom Hoshea became subject was Shalmaneser V (2 Kings 17:3). Either Shalmaneser or Sargon, his successor, was the king to whom Samaria fell after a long siege (2 Kings 17:6; 18:9).

Shama (shā'ma; *hearer*). One of David's heroes (1 Chron. 11:44).

Shamariah (sham-a-rī'a). *See* Shemariah.

Shamed [Shemed] (sha'med [she'med]; *destroyer*). A son of Elpaal (1 Chron. 8:12).

Shamer [Shemer] (shā'mer [she'mer]; *preserver*). **[1]** A descendant of Merari (1 Chron. 6:46). **[2]** A descendant of Asher (1 Chron. 7:34). He is called Shomer in First Chronicles 7:32.

Shamgar (sham'gar; *cupbearer; fleer*). Judge of Israel who rescued his people from the Philistines (Judg. 3:31; 5:6).

Shamhuth (sham'huth; *desolation*). A captain of David's army (1 Chron. 27:8).

Shamir (shā'mir; *hardstone*). A son of Micah, a Levite (1 Chron. 24:24).

Shamlai (sham'lī). A form of Salmai.

Shamir (shā'mir; *hardstone*). **[1]** A city in the mountainous district of Judah (Josh. 15:48). It is probably modern el-Bireh. **[2]** A town in Mount Ephraim (Judg. 10:1–2). Sanur between Samaria and Engannim have been suggested as sites.

Shamma (sham'a; *fame; renown*). A descendant of Asher (1 Chron. 7:37). *See* Shammah.

Shammah (sham'a; *fame; renown*). **[1]** A grandson of Esau (Gen. 36:13, 17; 1 Chron. 1:37). **[2]** A son of Jesse (1 Sam. 16:9; 17:13). He is also called Shimeah or Shimea (2 Sam. 13:3; 21:21; 1 Chron. 20:7), and Shimma (1 Chron. 2:13). **[3]** One of David's mighty men or the father of one of David's mighty men (2 Sam. 23:11). **[4]** Another of David's mighty men (2 Sam. 23:33), called Shammoth in First Chronicles 11:27. **[5]** Yet another of David's mighty men (2 Sam. 23:25).

Shammai (sham'ī; *celebrated*). **[1]** A descendant of Judah (1 Chron. 2:28, 32). **[2]** A descendant of Caleb, son of Hezron (1 Chron. 2:44–45). **[3]** A son or grandson of Ezra (1 Chron. 4:17).

Shammoth (sham'oth). *See* Shammah [4].

Shammua [Shammuah] (sha-mū'a; *heard by God*). **[1]** One sent to spy out the land of Canaan (Num. 13:4). **[2]** One of David's sons (2 Sam. 5:14; 1 Chron. 14:4). In First Chronicles 3:5, he is called Shimea. **[3]** A Levite who led the temple worship after the Exile (Neh. 11:17). He is also called Shemaiah (1 Chron. 9:16). **[4]** The head of a priestly family in Nehemiah's day (Neh. 12:18).

Shamsherai (sham'she-rī; *heroic*). A descendant of Benjamin (1 Chron. 8:26).

Shapham (shā'fam; *youthful; vigorous*). A chief of Gad (1 Chron. 5:12).

Shaphan (shā'fan; *rock badger*). **[1]** A scribe of Josiah who read him the Law (2 Kings 22:3; 2 Chron. 34:8–21). **[2]** Father of a chief officer under Josiah (2 Kings 22:12; 2 Chron. 34:20). **[3]** Father of Elasah (Jer. 29:3). **[4]** Father of Jaazaniah whom Ezekiel saw in a vision (Ezek. 8:11). **[5]** The father of Gemariah (Jer. 36:10–12), in whose house Baruch the scribe read Jeremiah's scroll to the people. Many scholars consider all of the above to be identical.

Shaphat (shā'fat; *judge*). **[1]** One sent to spy out the land of Canaan (Num. 13:5). **[2]** Father of Elisha the prophet (1 Kings 19:16, 19; 2 Kings 3:11; 6:31). **[3]** One of the family of David (1 Chron. 3:22). **[4]** A chief of Gad (1 Chron. 5:12). **[5]** An overseer of David's herds in the valley (1 Chron. 27:29).

Shapher [Shepher] (shā'fer [she'fer]; *bright*). A mountain encampment during the Hebrews' wanderings in the wilderness (Num. 33:23). Jebel 'Araif en-Nakah, south of Kadesh, has been suggested as the site.

Shaphir [Saphir] (shā'fir [sā'fir]; *beautiful*). A place, probably a city, which Micah prophesied against (Mic. 1:11).

Sharai (shā'ra-i; *Jehovah is deliverer*). One who took a foreign wife (Ezra 10:40).

Sharaim (sha-rā'im. *See* Shaaraim) [1].

Sharar (shā'rar). *See* Sacar [1].

Sharezer [Sherezer] (sha-rē'zer [she-rē'zer]; Babylonian, "Sharutsur"—*he has protected the king*). [1] A son of the Assyrian king Sennacherib who, with his brother, killed their father (2 Kings 19:37; Isa. 37:38). [2] One sent to consult the priests and prophets (Zech. 7:2).

Sharon [Saron] (shar-un [sar'un]; *his song*). [1] A region that lies between the Mediterranean Sea from Joppa to Carmel and the central portion of Palestine (1 Chron. 27:29; Acts 9:35). [2] A district east of the Jordan occupied by the tribe of Gad (1 Chron. 5:16).

Sharonite, The (shar'a-nīte; *of Sharon*). A term applied to Shitrai, King David's chief herdsman in the plain of Sharon (1 Chron. 27:29).

Sharuhen (sha-roo'hen; *gracious house*). A city in Simeon near Beth-lebaoth (Josh. 19:6). It is perhaps identical with Shaaraim [2].

Shashai (shā'shī; *noble; free*). One who married a foreign wife during the Exile (Ezra 10:40).

Shashak (shā'shak; *runner*). A descendant of Benjamin (1 Chron. 8:14, 25).

Shaul [Saul] (shā'ul [sol]; *asked of God*). [1] The sixth king of Edom (Gen. 36:37–38; 1 Chron. 1:48–49). [2] A descendant of Levi (1 Chron. 6:24). [3] A son of Sim-

S

eon found in several lists (Gen. 46:10; Exod. 6:15; 1 Chron. 4:24).

Sharlites (shar'ītes). A tribal family descended from Shaul (Num. 26:13).

Shaveh (shā've; *plain*). A place near Salem mentioned as the King's Valley (Gen. 14:17; 2 Sam. 18:18). It may be the same as the Kidron Valley.

Shaveh-kiriathaim (shā've-kir-ya-thā'im; *plain of Kiriathaim*). A plain near Kirjathaim [1], the dwelling place of the Emim (Gen. 14:5).

Shavsha (shav'sha). *See* Seraiah [1].

Sheal (shē'al; *request*). An Israelite who divorced his foreign wife after the Babylonian Exile (Ezra 10:29).

Shealtiel [Salathiel] (she-al'ti-el [sa-la'thi-el]; *asked of God*). Father of Zerubbabel and an ancestor of Christ (Ezra 3:2, 8; 5:2; Hag. 1:1, 12; Matt. 1:12).

Sheariah (she-a-rī'a; *esteemed of Jehovah*). A descendant of Saul (1 Chron. 8:38; 9:44).

Shearing House. The location where the royal family of King Ahaziah of Judah was slaughtered (2 Kings 10:12–14). The Hebrew name is *Beth 'eked;* the site is probably Beit Kad, about 25.7 km. (16 mi.) north-northeast of Samaria.

Shear-jashub (shē'ar-ja'shub; *a remnant returns*). Symbolic name given a son of Isaiah (Isa. 7:3) in the days of King Ahaz of Judah.

Sheba (shē'ba; *oath; covenant*). [1] A chief of Gad (1 Chron. 5:13). [2] One who rebelled against David and was beheaded for it (2 Sam. 20). [3] A grandson of Abraham (Gen. 25:3; 1 Chron. 1:32). [4] A descendant of Shem (Gen. 10:28; 1 Chron. 1:22). Some scholars identify [5] with [4]. They believe Sheba is a tribe or people and stress that close genealogical ties account for the occurrence of the name in both Ham's and Shem's genealogy. [5] A descendant of Ham (Gen. 10:7; 1 Chron. 1:9).

Sheba (shē′ba; *oath, covenant*). [1] A country in southwest Arabia (1 Kings 10:1–13; 2 Chron. 9:1–12). Its capital was Ma′rib, which was about 60 miles east-northeast of San′a, the present capital of Yemen. [2] A town of Simeon mentioned after Beer-sheba (Josh. 19:2). Its location is uncertain.

Sheba, Queen of. A queen who came to visit King Solomon. She tested him with "hard questions" and found that Solomon's wisdom and prosperity exceeded his fame (1 Kings 10:1–13).

Shebah [Shibah] (shē′ba [shī′ba]; *well of seven*). The well at Beer-sheba where Isaac made a covenant with Abimelech (Gen. 26:33).

Shebam (shē′bam; *fragrance*). A city east of the Jordan given to the tribes of Reuben and Gad (Num. 32:3). It is located 8 km. (5 mi.) from Heshbon. It is identical with Sibmah (q.v.).

Shebaniah (sheb-a-nī′a; *Jehovah is powerful*). [1] A priest who aided in bringing the ark of the covenant to the temple (1 Chron. 15:24). [2] A Levite who guided the devotions of the people (Neh. 9:4–5; 10:10). [3], [4] Two priests who sealed the covenant (Neh. 10:4, 12, 14).

Shebarim (she′ba-rim; *broken places*). A place to which the Israelites ran on their flight from Ai (Josh. 7:5). The location of the site is unknown.

Sheber (shē′ber; *breach*). A descendant of Jephunneh (1 Chron. 2:48).

Shebna (sheb′na; *youthfulness*). The scribe or secretary of

Hezekiah replaced by Eliakim (2 Kings 18:18; Isa. 22:15–25; 36:3–22).

Shebuel (she-bū′el; *God is renown*). [1] A son of Gershom (1 Chron. 23:16; 26:24). [2] A son of Haman, chief singer in the sanctuary (1 Chron. 24:4). He is called Shubael in verse 20.

Shechaniah [Shecaniah] (shek-a-nī′a; *Jehovah is a neighbor*). [1] Head of a family of the house of David (1 Chron. 3:21–22. [2], [3] Two whose descendants returned from the Babylonian Captivity (Ezra 8:3, 5). [4] One who took a foreign wife during the Exile (Ezra 10:2). [5] Father of one who repaired the wall of Jerusalem (Neh. 3:29). [6] Father-in-law to one who opposed Nehemiah (Neh. 6:18). [7] A priest who returned from the Exile (Neh. 12:3). [8] A priest in the time of David (1 Chron. 24:11). [9] A priest in Hezekiah's day (2 Chron. 31:15).

Shechem [Sychem] (shē′kem [sī′kem]; *shoulder*). [1] Son of Hamor who defiled Dinah; he and his family were soon destroyed for that act (Gen. 33:19; 34). [2] A descendant of Manasseh (Num. 26:31; Josh 17:2). [3] Another descendant of Manasseh (1 Chron. 7:19).

Shechem [Sichem; Sychem] (she′kem [sī′kem; sī′kem]; *shoulder*). An ancient city in central Palestine (Gen. 12:6; 33:18; Josh 24:32; Acts 7:16) in the hill country of Ephraim. It is present-day Nablus, located about 66 km. (41 mi.) north of Jerusalem between Mount Ebal and Mount Gerizim.

Shechemites (shek′em-ītes). The descendants of Shechem a son of Gilead of the tribe of Manasseh (Num. 26:31; Josh. 17:2).

Shedeur (shed′e-er; *shedder of light*). One who helped number the people (Num. 1:5; 2:10; 7:30, 35).

Sheep Gate. A gate in the city wall of Jerusalem or Temple area (Neh. 3:1, 32; 12:39; John 5:2).

Sheerah [Sherah] (shē'a-ra [shē'ra]; *blood relationship*). A female descendant of Ephraim (1 Chron. 7:24) who built or fortified three villages.

Shehariah (she-ha-rī'ah; *Jehovah is the dawn*). A descendant of Benjamin (1 Chron. 8:26).

Shelah (shē'la; *prayer*). [1] The youngest son of Judah (Gen. 38:5–26; 1 Chron. 2:3; 4:21). [2] *See* Sala. [3] *See* Siloam.

Shelanites (shē'la-nītes). The descendants of Shelah, son of Judah (Num. 26:20).

Shelemiah (shel-e-mī'a; *Jehovah has recompensed*). [1] *See* Meshelemiah. [2], [3] Two who married foreign wives during the Exile (Ezra 10:39, 41). [4] Father of Hananiah (Neh. 3:30). [5] A priest over the treasury (Neh. 13:13). [6] An ancestor of one who was sent by the princes to get Baruch (Jer. 36:14). [7] One ordered to capture Baruch and Jeremiah (Jer. 36:26). [8] Father of one sent to Jeremiah to ask for prayers (Jer. 37:3; 38:1). [9] Father of the guard who apprehended Jeremiah (Jer. 37:13).

Sheleph (shē'lef; *drawn out*). A son of Joktan (Gen. 10:26; 1 Chron. 1:20). A Semitic people dwelling in Arabia is possibly intended.

Shelesh (shē'lesh; *triplet*). A descendant of Asher (1 Chron. 7:35).

Shelomi (she-lō'mē; *God is my peace*). Father of a prince of Asher (Num. 34:27).

Shelomith (she-l'ō-mith; *peacefulness*). [1] Mother of one stoned for blasphemy in the wilderness (Lev. 24:11). [2] Daughter of Zerubbabel (1 Chron. 3:19). [3] A descendant of Gershon (1 Chron. 23:9). [4] A descendant of

Levi and Kohath (1 Chron. 23:18). **[5]** One over the treasures in the days of David (1 Chron. 26:25–28). **[6]** Child of Rehoboam (2 Chron. 11:20). **[7]** An ancestor of a family that returned from the Exile (Ezra 8:10). Not to be confused with Shelomoth.

Shelomoth (shel′o-moth; *peacefulness*). A descendant of Izhar (1 Chron. 24:22). Many identify him with Shelomith **[4]**.

Shelumiel (she-lū′mi-el; *God is peace*). A chief of Simeon appointed to assist Moses (Num. 1:6; 2:12; 7:36).

Shem [Sem] (shem [sem]; *name; renown*). Son of Noah and ancestor of Christ (Gen. 5:32; 6:10; 10:1; Luke 3:36).

Shema (shē′ma; *fame; repute*). **[1]** A son of Hebron (1 Chron. 2:43–44). **[2]** A descendant of Reuben (1 Chron. 5:8). **[3]** A chief of the tribe of Benjamin (1 Chron. 8:13). **[4]** One who stood with Ezra when he read the Law (Neh. 8:4).

Shema (shē′ma; *fame; repute*). A city of Judah in the Negeb (Josh. 15:26).

Shemaah (she-mā′a; *fame*). Father of two valiant men who joined David (1 Chron. 12:3).

Shemaiah (she-mā′ya; *Jehovah hears*). **[1]** A prophet who warned Rehoboam against war (1 Kings 12:22; 2 Chron. 11:2). **[2]** A descendant of David (1 Chron. 3:22). **[3]** Head of a family of Simeon (1 Chron. 4:37). **[4]** Son of Joel (1 Chron. 5:4). **[5]** A descendant of Merari (1 Chron. 9:14; Neh. 11:15). **[6]** One who helped to bring the ark of the covenant to the temple (1 Chron. 15:8, 11). **[7]** A Levite who recorded the allotment in David's day (1 Chron. 24:6). **[8]** A gatekeeper for the tabernacle (1 Chron. 26:4, 6–7). **[9]** A Levite whom Jehoshaphat sent to teach the people (2 Chron. 17:8).

[10] One who helped to cleanse the temple (2 Chron. 29:14). [11] A Levite in Hezekiah's day (2 Chron. 31:15). [12] A chief Levite in Josiah's day (2 Chron. 35:9). [13] One who returned with Ezra (Ezra 8:13). [14] A person sent to Iddo to enlist ministers (Ezra 8:16). [15], [16] Two who married foreign wives during the Exile (Ezra 10:21, 31). [17] One who helped to repair the wall of Jerusalem (Neh. 3:29). [18] One who tried to intimidate Nehemiah (Neh. 6:10). [19] One who sealed the new covenant with God after the Exile (Neh. 10:8). [20] One who helped to purify the wall of Jerusalem (Neh. 12:36). [21] One at the dedication of the wall of Jerusalem (Neh. 12:42). [22] Father of the prophet Urijah (Jer. 26:20). [23] One who wanted the priests to reprimand Jeremiah (Jer. 29:24, 31). [24] Father of a prince of the Jews (Jer. 36:12). [25] *See* Shammua [3]. [26] A prince of Judah who took part in the dedication of the wall (Neh. 12:34). [27] A Levite of the line of Asaph (Neh. 12:35). [28] A chief of the priests who returned with Zerubbabel (Neh. 12:6–7).

Shemariah [Shamariah] (shem-a-rī′a [sham-a-rī′a]; *whom Jehovah guards*). [1] One who joined David at Ziklag (1 Chron. 12:5). [2] A son of King Rehoboam (2 Chron. 11:19). [3], [4] Two who married foreign wives during the Exile (Ezra 10:32, 41).

Shemeber (shem-ē′ber; *splendor of heroism*). The king of Zeboim in the days of Abraham (Gen. 14:2).

Shemed (shē′med). *See* Shamed.

Shemer [Shamer] (shē′mer [shā′mer]; *watch*). [1] Owner of the hill which Omri bought and on which he built Samaria (1 Kings 16:24). [2] A son of Heber, of the tribe of Asher (1 Chron. 7:34). Also called Shomer (1 Chron. 7:32).

Shemida [Shemidah] (she-mī′da; *fame of knowing*). A grandson of Manasseh (Num. 26:32; Josh. 17:2; 1 Chron. 7:19).

Shemidah (she-mī′da). *See* Shemida.

Shemiramoth (she-mīr′a-moth; *fame of the highest*). **[1]** A Levite in the choral service (1 Chron. 15:18, 20; 16:5). **[2]** One sent by Jehoshaphat to teach the Law (2 Chron. 17:8).

Shemuel (she-mū′el; *varient form of Samuel—name of God*). **[1]** One appointed to divide the land of Canaan (Num. 34:20). **[2]** Head of a family of Issachar (1 Chron. 7:2). **[3]** *See* Samuel.

Shen (shen; *tooth*). A place near which Samuel erected a stone memorial to the victory over the Philistines (1 Sam. 7:12).

Shenazar [Shenazzar] (she-naz′ar; *may [the god] Sin protect*). Son or grandson of Jeconiah (1 Chron. 3:18).

Shenir [Senir] (shē′ner [sē′nir]; *light that sleeps*). The Amorite name for Hermon (Deut. 3:9; Ezek. 27:5).

Shepham (she′fam; *wild*). A location on the northeastern boundary of the Promised Land near Riblah (Num. 34:10).

Shephathiah [Shephatiah] (shef-a-thī′a [shef-a-tī′a]; *Jehovah is judge*). **[1]** A son of David by Abital (2 Sam. 3:4; 1 Chron. 3:3). **[2]** Father of Meshullam who dwelled in Jerusalem (1 Chron. 9:8). **[3]** A valiant man who joined David at Ziklag (1 Chron. 12:5). **[4]** A prince of Simeon (1 Chron. 27:16). **[5]** A son of Jehoshaphat (2 Chron. 21:2). **[6]** An ancestor of returned captives (Ezra 2:4; Neh. 7:9). **[7]** One of Solomon's servants whose descendants returned from the Babylonian Captivity (Ezra 2:57; Neh. 7:59). **[8]** An ancestor of returned captives (Ezra 8:8). He is possibly identical with

[6]. **[9]** A descendant of Pharez whose descendants dwelled in Jerusalem (Neh. 11:4). **[10]** A prince of Judah in Zedekiah's time (Jer. 38:1).

Shepher (shē´fer). *See* Shapher.

Shephi [Shepho] (shē´fī [shē´fo]; *bare*). A descendant of Seir the Horite (1 Chron. 1:40). He is called Shepho in Genesis 36:23.

Shepho (shē´fo). *See* Shephi.

Shephupham (she-fū´fam). A form of Shephuphan.

Shephuphan (she-fū´fan). *See* Muppim.

Sherah (shē´ra). *See* Sheerah.

Sherebiah (sher-e-bī´a; *flame of Jehovah*). **[1]** A priest who returned from the Exile (Ezra 8:18, 24; Neh. 8:7; 9:4–5). **[2]** A Levite who sealed the new covenant with God after the Exile (Neh. 10:12; 12:8, 24).

Sheresh (shē´resh; *union*). A descendant of Manasseh (1 Chron. 7:16).

Sherezer (she-ē´zer). *See* Sharezer.

Sheshach (shē´shak; *humiliation*). A code word for Babel (Babylon) (Jer. 25:26). Some scholars view this as a part of Babylon or a Babylonian district.

Sheshai (shē´shī; *free; noble*). A son of Anak slain by Caleb (Num. 13:22; Josh. 15:14).

Sheshan (shē´shan; *free; noble*). A descendant of Judah through Jerahmeel (1 Chron. 2:31, 34–35).

Sheshbazzar (shesh-baz´er; *O [god] Shamash protect the father*). The prince of Judah into whose hands Cyrus placed the temple vessels. Many believe he is the same as Zerubbabel, but others deny this. They claim Sheshbazzar was governor under Cyrus and Zerubbabel under Darius (Ezra 1:8, 11; 5:14–16).

Sheth [Seth] (sheth [seth]; *compassion*). **[1]** A chief of the Moabites (Num. 24:17). **[2]** Third son of Adam and

Eve born after the murder of Abel (1 Chron. 1:1). Also
see Seth.

Sheth (sheth; *compassion*). A descriptive name given to a
Moabite chief (Num. 24:17). Possibly an ancient tribal
name of the Moabites.

Shethar (shē'thar; *commander*). One of the seven princes
of Persia and Media (Esther 1:14). Not to be confused
with Shetharboznai.

Shethar-boznai [Shethar-bozenai] (shē'thar-boz'nī
[shē'thar-boz'e-nī]; *starry splendor*). An official of the
king of Persia (Ezra 5:3, 6; 6:6, 13).

Sheva (shē'va; *self-satisfying*). **[1]** A son of Caleb (1 Chron.
2:49). **[2]** *See* Seraiah **[1]**.

Shibah (shī'ba). *See* Shebah.

Shibmah (shib'ma). *See* Sibmah.

Shicron [Shikkeron] (shik'ron [shik'e-ron]; *drunken-
ness*). A town on the northern boundary of Judah (Josh.
15:11).

Shihon [Shion] (shī'hon [shī'on]; *wall of strength*). A
town near Mount Tabor (Josh. 19:19). It is perhaps at
Modern 'Ayun esh-Sha'in.

Shihor [Sihor] (shī'hor [sī'hor]; *blackness*). The east
branch of the Nile River (1 Chron. 13:5; Jer. 2:18). Ide-
ally, this was to be Israel's southern boundary.

Shihor-libnath (shī'hor-lib'nath; *turbid stream of Lib-
nath*). A boundary stream of Asher (Josh. 19:26). It is
probably the Nahr ez-Zirka 9.7 km. (6 mi.) south of
Dor.

Shilhi (shil'hī; *dart-thrower*). Grandfather of King Jehoshaphat (1 Kings 22:42; 2 Chron. 20:31).

Shilhim (shil'him; *armed*). A city in southern Judah near
Lebaoth (Josh. 15:32). It is identified with Shaaraim
[2].

Shillem (shil′em; *retribution*). *See* Shallum [1].

Shillemites (shil′em-ītes). A tribal family descended from Shillem, the fourth son of Naphtali (Num. 26:49).

Shiloah [Siloah] (shi-lō′a [si′lōa]; *sent*). A waterway of Jerusalem (Isa. 8:6; Neh. 3:15). It carried water from the spring of Gihon to the Pool of Shelah to irrigate the Kidron Valley outside the city. It is identical with Siloam [1].

Shiloh (shī′lō; *peace*). A town in Ephraim (Josh. 18:1–10; Judg. 21:19). It is halfway between Shechem and Bethel.

Shiloni [Shilonite, Shelonite] (shī-lō′nī [shī′lo-nīte, she′lo-nīte]; *a Shilonite*). Father of Zechariah (Neh. 11:5).

Shilonite (shī-lōnīte). A name given to Ahijah the prophet, who was a native or resident of Shiloh (1 Kings 11:29).

Shilshah (shil′sha; *triad*). A son of Zophath (1 Chron. 7:37).

Shimea [Shimeah, Shimma] (shim′e-a [shim′e-a]; *God has heard* [*a prayer*]). [1] A descendant of Merari (1 Chron. 6:30). [2] Father of Berachiah (1 Chron. 6:39). [3] *See* Shammah [2]. [4] *See* Shammua [2]. [5] One of the family of King Saul whose descendants dwelled in Jerusalem (1 Chron. 8:32; 9:38). In the latter passage he is called Shimeam.

Shimeam (shim′e-am; *hearing*). *See* Shimeah [2].

Shimeath (shim′e-ath; *hearing*). Mother of one who aided in killing King Jehoash (2 Kings 12:21; 2 Chron. 24:26).

Shimeathites (shim′e-ath-ītes). A Kenite family of scribes who lived at Jabez in Judah (1 Chron. 2:55).

Shimei [Shimhi; Shimi] (shim′e-īt [shim′hī; shim′ī]; *Jehovah is fame*). **[1]** A son of Gershon and a grandson of Gershon (Exod. 6:17; Num. 3:18, 21; Zech. 12:13). **[2]** A descendant of Benjamin who cursed David when he was fleeing from Absalom (2 Sam. 16:5–13; 19:16–23). **[3]** A loyal officer of David (1 Kings 1:8). **[4]** An officer of Solomon (1 Kings 4:18). **[5]** Grandson of King Jeconiah (1 Chron. 3:19). **[6]** A man who had sixteen sons and six daughters (1 Chron. 4:26–27). **[7]** A descendant of Reuben (1 Chron. 5:4). **[8]** A son of Libni (1 Chron. 6:29). **[9]** Father of a chief of Judah (1 Chron. 8:21). **[10]** A Levite (1 Chron. 23:9). **[11]** A Levite in the temple song service in the days of David (1 Chron. 25:17). **[12]** One in charge of many vineyards (1 Chron. 27:27). **[13]** One who helped to cleanse the temple (2 Chron. 29:14). **[14]** A Levite in charge of the temple offerings under Hezekiah (2 Chron. 31:12–13). **[15], [16], [17]** Three men who took foreign wives during the Exile (Ezra 10:23, 33, 38). **[18]** Grandfather of Mordecai (Esther 2:5).

Shimeites (shim′ē-ītes). *See* Shimites.

Shimeon (shim′e-on; *hearing*). One who married a foreign wife (Ezra 10:31). Not to be confused with Simeon.

Shimhi (shim′hī). *See* Shimei, **[9].**

Shimi ((shim′ī). *See* Shimei **[1].**

Shimites (shim′ītes). A tribal family descended from Shimei, son of Gershon (Num. 3:21).

Shimma (shim′a). *See* Shammah **[2].**

Shimon (shī′mon; *trier; valuer*). A descendant of Caleb (1 Chron. 4:20).

Shimrath (shim′rath; *watch*). A descendant of Benjamin (1 Chron. 8:21).

Shimri [Simri] (shim′rī [sim′rī]; *Jehovah is watching*). **[1]** Head of a family of Simeon (1 Chron. 4:37). **[2]** Father of one of David's mighty men (1 Chron. 11:45). **[3]** Gatekeeper of the tabernacle in David's day (1 Chron. 26:10). **[4]** One who helped to cleanse the temple (2 Chron. 29:13).

Shimrith (shim′rith; *God preserves*). A woman of Moab, mother of Jehozabad who killed Joash (2 Chron. 24:26). She is called Shomer in Second Kings 12:21.

Shimrom [Shimron] (shim′rom [shim′ron]; *watch*). The fourth son of Issachar (Gen. 46:113; Num. 26:24; 1 Chron. 7:1). *See also* Shimron.

Shimron (shim′ron; *watch*). An ancient city belonging to Zebulun (Josh. 11:1; 19:15). It is possibly Semuniyeh 10.1 km. (6.3 mi.) west of Nazareth.

Shimron-meron (shim′ron-mē′ron). A royal city of the Canaanites, whose king was slain by Joshua (Josh. 12:20). Probably the full name of Shimron (q.v.).

Shimronites (shim′ron-ites). Descendants of Shimron, the fourth son of Issachar (Num. 26:24).

Shimshai (shim′shī; *shining one*). A scribe who, with Rehum, wrote to the king of Persia opposing the rebuilding of the wall of Jerusalem (Ezra 4:8–9, 17, 23).

Shinab (shī′ab; *Sin is my father*). The king of Admah attacked by Chedorlaomer and his allies (Gen. 14:2).

Shinar (shī′nar; *watch of him that sleeps*). The plains later known as Babylonia or Chaldea, through which the Tigris and Euphrates Rivers flow (Gen. 10:10; Isa. 11:11). *See* Sumer.

Shion (shī′on). *See* Shihon.

Shiphi (shī′fī; *Jehovah is fulness*). Father of a chief of Simeon (1 Chron. 4:37).

Shiphmite (shif′mīte). A native or inhabitant of

Shepham (Num. 34:10–11), a city in northeast Canaan, or perhaps of Siphmoth (1 Sam. 30:28), a city in southern Canaan.

Shiphrah (shif'ra; *beauty*). One of the Hebrew midwives at the time of the birth of Moses (Exod. 1:15).

Shiphtan (shif'tan; *judge*). Father of Kemuel, a chief of Ephraim (Num. 34:24).

Shisha (shī'sha; *distinction; nobility*). Father of two of Solomon's scribes (1 Kings 4:3). Possibly the same as Seraiah [1].

Shishak (shī'shak). Another name for Shishak I, king of Egypt. He sheltered Jeroboam against Solomon and in later years invaded Judah (1 Kings 11:40; 14:25; 2 Chron. 12).

Shitrai (shit'rī; *Jehovah is deciding*). A man in charge of David's herds in Sharon (1 Chron. 27:29).

Shittim (shit'im; *thorns*). [1] The final Israelite encampment before crossing the Jordan. Here Moses bade farewell and the Law was completed (Num. 25:1; Josh. 2:1). It was in Moab, east of Jordan, opposite Jericho. [2] A dry and unfruitful valley (Joel 3:18). The name may not denote any particular valley, but it may refer to the Kidron Wadi which starts northwest of Jerusalem, moves toward the east and runs toward the Dead Sea. It may also be a portion of the Arabah around the Dead Sea.

Shiza (shī'za; *splendor*). Father of one of David's valiant men (1 Chron. 11:42).

Shoa (shō'a; *kings*). A location mentioned along with Babylon, Chaldea, and Assyria (Ezek. 23:23); it probably refers to a settlement of the Sutu nomads of the Syrian Desert.

Shobab (shō'bab; *returning*). [1] A son of David (2 Sam.

5:14; 1 Chron. 3:5). [2] A son of Caleb (1 Chron. 2:18).

Shobach (shō′bak; *expansion*). Captain of the army of Hadarezer of Zobah (2 Sam. 10:16, 18); he is also called Shophach (1 Chron. 19:16).

Shobai (shō′bī; *Jehovah is glorious*). A tabernacle gate-keeper whose descendants returned from the Babylonian Captivity (Ezra 2:42; Neh. 7:45).

Shobal (shō′bal; *wandering*). [1] A son of Seir (Gen. 36:20, 23; 1 Chron. 1:38, 40). [2] A son of Caleb, son of Hur (1 Chron. 2:50, 52). [3] A son of Judah (1 Chron. 4:1–2).

Shobek (shō′bek; *free*). One who sealed the covenant with Nehemiah (Neh. 10:24).

Shobi (shō′bī; *Jehovah is glorious*). A man who helped David when he fled from Absalom (2 Sam. 17:27).

Shocho [Shochoh; Shoco; Socoh; Socho; Sochoh] (shō′ko [shō′ko; shō′ko; sō′ko; sō′ko; sō′ko]; *thorn–hedge*). [1] A town in lowland Judah or the hilly border of the Valley of Elah (Josh. 15:35; 2 Chron. 11:7; 28:18; 1 Sam. 17:1). [2] A town in Judah's hill country (Josh. 15:48). It is modern Khirbet Shuweikeh 16.1 km. (10 mi.) south-southwest of Hebron. [3] A place in one of Solomon's administrative districts (1 Kings 4:10). It is modern Tell-er-Ras about 16.1 km. (10 mi.) northwest of Samaria. [4] *See* Socho.

Shochoh (sho′ko). *See* Shocho.

Shoco (sho′ko). *See* Shocho.

Shoham (shō′ham; *a precious stone*). A descendant of Merari (1 Chron. 24:27).

Shomer (shō′mer; *keeper*). [1] *See* Shamer [2]. [2] *See* Shimrith.

Shophach (shō′fak). *See* Shobach.

S

Shophan (shō'fan; *burrow*). A fortress city east of the Jordan River that was captured and rebuilt by the tribe of Gad (Num. 32:35).

Shua [Shuah] (shoo'a [shoo'a]; *prosperity*). [1] A daughter of Heber (1 Chron. 7:32). [2] A Canaanite whose daughter Judah married (Gen. 38:2, 12; 1 Chron. 2:3).

Shuah [Shuhah] (shoo'a [shū'ha]; *bow down*). [1] A son of Abraham by Keturah (Gen. 25:2; 1 Chron. 1:32). [2] A brother of Chelub; descendant of Caleb (1 Chron. 4:11).

Shual (shoo'al; *fox*). The third son of Zophah (1 Chron. 7:36).

Shual (shoo'al; *fox*). A district north of Michmash (1 Sam. 13:17).

Shubael (shoo'ba-el; *God's captive*). [1] A son or descendant of Amram, a descendant of Levi (1 Chron. 24:20). [2] *See* Shebuel [2].

Shuhah *See* Shuah

Shuham (shoo'ham; *depression*). *See* Hushim [1].

Shuhamites (shū'hum-ites). The descendants of Shuham, of the tribe of Dan (Num. 26:42).

Shuhite (shū'hīte). A descendant of Shuah, son of Abraham and Keturah (Gen. 25:1–2; 1 Chron. 1:32).

Shulamite [Shulammite] (shū'lam-īte). A young woman mentioned in Song of Solomon 6:13). Many scholars interpret Shulamite as Shunammite—a woman from the city of Shunem (1 Sam. 28:4).

Shulammite (shū'lam-ite). *See* Shulamite.

Shumathites (shū'ma-thites). A family of Kirjath Jearim descended from Hur (1 Chron. 2:53).

Shunammite (Shū'na-mite). A native or inhabitant of Shunem. [1] Abishag, a young woman who ministered to David in his old age. [2] A woman who befriended the prophet Elijah (2 Kings 4:8–36).

Shunem (shoo'nem; *their sleep*). A town near Jezreel that was allotted to the tribe of Issachar (Josh. 19:18; 1 Sam. 28:4). It was opposite Mount Gilboa. The site is present-day Solem or Sulam.

Shuni (shoo'nī; *fortunate*). A son of Gad (Gen. 46:16; Num. 26:15).

Shupham (shoo'fam). See Muppim.

Shuppim (shup'im; *serpent*). [1] A gatekeeper in the days of David (1 Chron. 26:16). [2] See Muppim.

Shur (shoor; *wall*). A desert in the northwest part of the Sinai Peninsula (Gen. 16:7; 25:18). It was outside the eastern border of Egypt and was probably a caravan route between Egypt and Beer-sheba.

Shushan [Susa] (shoo'shan [soo'sa]; *a lily*). The capital of Elam inhabited by the Babylonians; later a royal residence and capital of the Persian Empire (Neh. 1:1; Dan. 8:2). The city was also known as Susa. The site is modern Shush on the Ulai River.

Shuthelah (shoo'the-la; *setting of Telah*). [1] A son of Ephraim (Num. 26:35–36; 1 Chron. 7:20). [2] Another descendant of Ephraim (1 Chron. 7:21).

Shuthalites ([**Shuthelathites**] (shū'thal-hītes [shuthel'a-thītes]). Descendants of Shuthelah, of the tribe of Ephraim (Num. 26:35–36; 1 Chron. 7:20).

Siaha [Sia] (sī'a-ha [sī'a]; *congregation*). Ancestor of returned captives (Ezra 2:44; Neh. 7:47).

Sibbechai [Sibbecai] (sib'e-kī [sib'e-kī]; *Jehovah is intervening*). A mighty man who killed a Philistine giant (2 Sam. 21:18; 1 Chron. 11:29; 20:4). He is called Mebunnai in Second Samuel 23:27.

Sibmah [Shibmah; Shebam] (sib'ma [shib'ma; shē'-bam] *to be cold*). A town of Reuben and Gad (Num. 32:38; Josh. 13:19). It is identical with Shebam (q.v.).

Sibraim (sib-rā'im; *twofold hope*). A northern boundary marker of Canaan (Ezek. 47:16). It is probably Sephar-vaim.

Sichem (sī'kem). *See* Shechem.

Siddim (sid'im; *tilled fields*). A valley near the Dead Sea (Gen. 14:3, 8, 10), full of bitumen pits.

Sidon [Zidon] (sī'don [zī'don]; *fortress*). Eldest son of Canaan, son of Ham (Gen. 10:15). He is called Zidon in First Chronicles 1:13. Possibly a reference to the in-habitants of the ancient city of Sidon.

Sidon [Zidon] (sī'don [zī'don]; *a fishery*). An ancient city of Canaan (Gen. 10:15, 19; Josh. 11:8; Luke 4:26).

Sidonians (sī'don-ē-ans). Natives or inhabitants of Sidon.

Sihon (sī'hon; *great; bold*). An Amorite king that was de-feated by Israel (Num. 21:21–31; Deut. 1:4; 2:24–32; Josh. 13:15–28).

Sihor (sī'hor). *See* Shihor.

Sikkuth [Sakkuth] (sik'kuth [sak'kuth]). A Babylonian god mentioned by the prophet Amos (Amos 5:26). Was the name Babylonians gave the planet Saturn.

Silas [Silvanus] (sī'las [sil-vā'nus]; *forest; woody*). An emi-nent member of the early church who traveled with Paul through Asia Minor and Greece and was imprisoned with him at Philippi (Acts 15:22, 32–34; 2 Cor. 1:19; 1 Thess. 1:1).

Silla (sil'a; *exalting*). A place near Millo where King Joash was murdered (2 Kings 12:20).

Siloah (sī-lō'a). *See* Shiloah.

Siloam [Shelah, Shiloah] (sī-lō´am [shē´la, shi-lo´a; *sent*). **[1]** A famous pool of Jerusalem at the south end of Hezekiah's tunnel (John 9:7). It is identical with Shiloah (q.v.). **[2]** A tower on the Ophel ridge near Siloam (Luke 13:4).

Silvanus (sil-vā´nus). *See* Silas.

Simeon [Simon] (sim´e-un [sī´mon]; *hearing*). **[1]** The second son of Jacob by Leah (Gen. 29:33; 34:25; 48:5; 49:5). His descendants became one of the twelve tribes of Israel. **[2]** A devout Jew who blessed the Christ child in the temple (Luke 2:25–34). **[3]** An ancestor of Jesus (Luke 3:30). **[4]** A disciple and prophet at Antioch (Acts 13:1); he was surnamed Niger ("black"). **[5]** Original name of Peter (q.v.). Simon is but another form of Simeon. Not to be confused with Shimeon.

Simeonites (sim´e-a-nites). Descendants of Simeon **[1]**.

Simon (sī´mon; *hearing*). **[1]** Original name of the apostle Peter (Matt. 4:18; 16:16–17; Luke 4:38; Acts 10:18). **[2]** Another of the twelve apostles, called Simon the Canaanite, indicating his fierce loyalty either to Israel or to his faith (Matt. 10:4; Mark 3:18; Luke 6:15; Acts 1:13). **[3]** One of Christ's brothers (Matt. 13:55; Mark 6:3). **[4]** A leper of Bethany in whose house Christ was anointed (Matt. 26:6; Mark 14:3). **[5]** A Cyrenian who was forced to bear the cross of Christ (Matt. 27:32; Mark 15:21). **[6]** A Pharisee in whose house the feet of Christ were anointed (Luke 7:40, 43–44). **[7]** The father of Judas Iscariot (John 6:71; 12:4; 13:2). **[8]** A sorcerer who tried to buy the gifts of the Holy Spirit (Acts 8:9, 13, 18, 24). **[9]** A tanner of Joppa with whom Peter lodged (Acts 9:43; 10:6, 17, 32).

Simon Peter. *See* Peter.

Simri (sim′rī). *See* Shimri.

Sin (sin; *the moon-god*). **[1]** A city on the eastern side of the Nile (Ezek. 30:15–16). It is possibly Pelusium; but is also identified with Syene, which is present-day Aswan at the first cataract of the Nile. **[2]** A wilderness area located between the Gulf of Suez and Sinai (Exod. 16:1; Num. 33:11–12).

Sinai [Sina] (sī′nī [sī′na]; *a bush*). **[1]** An area in the center of the peninsula that lies between the horns of the Red Sea, the Gulf of Suez, and the Gulf of Aqaba (Exod. 16:1; Acts 7:30–38). **[2]** A mountain, also called Horeb, where the Israelites received the Ten Commandments (Exod. 19:18). The location of the site is uncertain, although it is generally agreed to be in central Sinai. The traditional site is Jebel Musa, but other possibilities are Mount Serbal and Ras es-Safsafeh.

Sinim (si′nim; *south country*). A land from which the scattered Israelites were again to be gathered (Isa. 49:12). It probably refers to Syene on the southern Egyptian frontier where there was a Jewish garrison. Earlier scholars believed that China was indicated, but that view has been abandoned.

Sinite (sī′nīte). A tribe of Canaanites in northern Phoenicia (modern Lebanon, 1 Chron. 1:15).

Sion [Siyon] (sī′un [sī′yun]; *elevated*). **[1]** Another name for Mount Hermon (Deut. 4:48). **[2]** *See* Zion.

Siphmoth (sif′moth; *fruitful*). A place in southern Judah frequented by David (1 Sam. 30:28).

Sippai (sīp′ī). *See* Saph.

Sirah (sī′ra; *turning*). A well near Hebron where Abner was recalled by Joab (2 Sam. 3:26). It is probably modern 'Ain Sarah.

Sirion (sir´i-on; *breastplate*). The name given to Mount Hermon by the Sidonians (Deut. 3:9; Psa. 29:6).

Sisamai [Sismai] (sis´a-mī [sis´mai]; *Jehovah is distinguished*). A descendant of Jerahmeel, son of Pharez (1 Chron. 2:40).

Sisera (sis´er-a; *mediation; array*). [1] Captain of the army of Jabin who was murdered by Jael (Judg. 4:1–22; 5:26, 28). [2] One whose descendants returned (Ezra 2:53; Neh. 7:55).

Sithri (sith´ri). *See* Zithri.

Sitnah (sit´na; *hatred*). The second well dug by Isaac, located in the Valley of Gerar (Gen. 26:21).

Siyon (sī´yon). *See* Sion.

Smyrna (smur´na; *myrrh*). A city on the western coast of Asia Minor (Rev. 2:8–11). It is 64.4 km. (40 mi.) north of Ephesus.

So (sō; *vizier*). A king of Egypt, either Osorkon IV or Tefnakht. Others believe this name is a reference to a city (2 Kings 17:3–7).

Socho (sō´ko; *brambly*). A son of Heber (1 Chron. 4:18).

Socho (sō´ko). *See* Shocho.

Sochoh (so´ko). *See* Shocho.

Socoh (sō´ko). *See* Shocho.

Sodi (sō´dī; *God is my secret counsel*). Father of one of the spies sent into Canaan (Num. 13:10).

Sodom [Sodoma] (so´dom [sod´o-ma]; *their secret*). One of the five Cities of the Plain (Gen. 10:19; Rom. 9:29), destroyed because of its wickedness. The exact location of the site is unknown, but it is in the Dead Sea area.

Solomon (sol´o-mon; *his peace*). Son of David by Bathsheba and king of a united, strong Israel for forty years. His wisdom and sin stand out in his multi-faceted character (1 Kings 1:11; 2:11). He was an ancestor of Christ (Matt. 1:6–7).

Solomon's Pools. A repository of water built by Solomon near Bethlehem (Eccles. 2:6).

Solomon's Porch. A colonnade built by Solomon on the east side of the temple (John 10:23; Acts 3:11).

Sopater (sō′pa-ter; *savior of his father*). A man of Berea who accompanied Paul to Asia (Acts 20:4). Perhaps the same as Sosipater (q.v.).

Sophereth (so-fē′reth; *scribe*). Servant of Solomon whose ancestors returned from exile (Ezra 2:55; Neh. 7:57).

Sorek (sō′rek; *vine*). A valley in Gaza where Delilah lived (Judg. 16:4). It is modern Wadi es-Saran, which begins 20.9 km. (13 mi.) southwest of Jerusalem and twists northwest toward the Mediterranean.

Sosipater (so-sip′a-ter; *one who defends the father*). One who sent greetings to the Roman Christians (Rom. 16:21). He was Jewish (a "kinsman" of Paul) and is possibly the same as Sopater (q.v.).

Sosthenes (sos′the-nēz; *strong; powerful*). **[1]** Chief ruler of the synagogue at Corinth, beaten by the Greeks (Acts 18:17). **[2]** A believer who united with Paul in addressing the Corinthian church (1 Cor. 1:1). Some believe he was [1] after conversion.

Sotai (sō′tī). Head of a family of servants (Ezra 2:55; Neh. 7:57).

South Gate. A gate in the city wall of Jerusalem or the Temple area (1 Chron. 26:15).

South Ramoth. *See* Ramath.

South, The. *See* Negev.

Spain (spān; *rain*). A peninsula in southwestern Europe (Rom. 15:24). The nation was known as Hispania to the Romans.

Stachys (stā′kis; *ear of corn*). A believer of Rome to whom Paul sent greetings (Rom. 16:9).

Stephanas (stef′a-nas; *crown-bearer*). One of the first believers of Achaia (1 Cor. 1:16; 16:15–17).

Stephen (stē′fen; *crown-bearer*). One of the seven deacons. He became the first martyr of the church after Christ (Acts 6:5–9; 7:59; 8:2).

Suah (sū′a; *riches; distinction*). A son of Zophah, a descendant of Asher (1 Chron. 7:36).

Sucathites (sū′ka-thītes). *See* Suchathites.

Succoth (suk′oth; *tents*). **[1]** A town where Jacob built himself a house (Gen. 33:17; Josh. 13:27). It was east of the Jordan between Peniel and Shechem. Its probable location is Deir ʿAlla, about 1.6 km. (1 mi.) west of where the Jabbok bulges and turns south. **[2]** The first camping ground of the Israelites after leaving Egypt (Exod. 12:37; 13:20).

Succoth Benoth (suk′oth bin′nath). A Babylonian goddess, the mistress of Marduk (2 Kings 17:30).

Suchathites [Sucathites] (sū′ka-thites). A family of scribes who lived at Jabez in the territory allotted to Judah (1 Chron. 2:55).

Sukkiim [Sukkims, Sukkites] (suk′i-im [sūk′ims, sūk′ītes]; *booth-dweller*). A nation that assisted Shishak of Egypt when he invaded Judah (2 Chron. 12:3). Its population was probably of Libyan origin.

Sumer (sū′mer). The southern division of ancient Babylonia, consisting primarily of the fertile plain between the Tigris and Euphrates rivers. Referred to in the Old Testament as Shinar (Gen. 10:10; Isa. 11:11; Zech. 5:11) or Chaldea (Jer. 50:10; Ezek. 16:29).

Suph (sūff; *reeds*). An unknown place or region opposite the campsite in the Transjordan where Moses explained the Law to the Israelites (Deut. 1:1).

Supha (sū'fa). An unknown place associated with the border of Moab and the wilderness wandering early in Israelite history (Num. 21:14).

Sur (sur; *rebellion*). A gate in Jerusalem, possibly leading from the king's palace to the temple (2 Kings 11:6). The parallel passage calls it the Gate of the Foundation (2 Chron. 23:5).

Susa (soo'sa). *See* Shushan.

Susanchites (sū'san-kites). The inhabitants of Shushan, a nation of foreigners who repopulated Samaria after the city was captured by the Assyrians (Ezra 4:9).

Susanna (su-zan'na; *lily*). One of the women who ministered to Christ and was His follower (Luke 8:3).

Susi (sū'sī; *horselike*). Father of one of the spies (Num. 13:11).

Sychar (sī'kar; *end*). A town of Samaria near Jacob's well (John 4:5).

Sychem (sī-kem). *See* Shechem.

Syene (sī'ē'ne; *a bush*). A town on the southern frontier of Egypt (Ezek. 29:10; 30:6).

Syntyche (sin'ti-che; *fortunate*). A woman of the church at Philippi (Phil. 4:2).

Syracuse (sir'a-kūs; *that draws violently*). A city on the east coast of Sicily (Acts 28:12).

Syria (sir'i-a). The country lying north and east of Palestine (Judg. 10:6; 1 Kings 10:29; Acts 15:23). It stretched far inland from the Mediterranean and was bounded by the Taurus Mountains to the north.

Syrians (sir'i-ans). Inhabitants or citizens of Syria.

Syro-Phoenician (sī-rō-fe-ne'shun). A Gentile woman

from Phoenicia whose daughter was healed by Jesus (Mark 7:26).

Syrtis Quicksands (sur'tis; *shallows*). Two shoals off the coast of Africa between Carthage and Cyrene (Acts 27:17). The greater Syrtis is now called the Gulf of Sidra, the lesser Syrtis the Gulf of Gabes.

T

Taanach [Tanach] (tā'a-nak [tā'nak]; *who humbles thee*). An ancient city in Canaan whose king was conquered by Joshua (Josh. 12:21; 21:25; Judg. 1:27). Its ruins, Tell Ta'annak, are on the southern edge of the Valley of Jezreel about 8 km. (5 mi.) southeast of Megiddo.

Taanath-shiloh (tā'a-nath-shī'lo; *approach to Shiloh*). A border town between Manasseh and Ephraim (Josh. 16:6). It is now Khirbet Ta'na 11.3 km. (7 mi.) east-southeast of Shechem.

Tabbaoth (tab'a-oth; *spots; rings*). One whose descendants returned with Zerubbabel (Ezra 2:43; Neh. 7:46).

Tabbath (tab'ath; *celebrated*). A place where the Midianites stayed after Gideon's attack (Judg. 7:22). It is located in the Jordan Valley at Ras Abu Tabat.

Tabeal [Tabeel] (tā-bē-al [tā'be-el]; *God is good*). [1] Father of a man the kings of Israel and Damascus planned to make king of Judah (Isa. 7:6). [2] A Persian official who tried to hinder the rebuilding of the wall of Jerusalem (Ezra 4:7).

Tabeel (tā'be-el). *See* Tabeal.

Taberah (tab'e-ra; *burning*). A place three days north of Mount Sinai where Israel was punished for murmuring against God (Num. 11:3; Deut. 9:22).

Tabitha (tab'i-tha; *gazelle*). The Christian woman of Joppa whom Peter raised from the dead (Acts 9:36–42). Dorcas is the Greek form of the name.

Tabor (tā'ber; *height*). [1] A mountain located in the northern part of the Valley of Jezreel (Judg. 4:6, 12, 14; Psa. 89:12). It is now called Jebel el-Tur and is 8.8 km. (5.5 mi.) southeast of Nazareth. [2] A town of Zebulun given to the Levites (1 Chron. 6:77). Its location is uncertain. It may be the Chisloth-tabor of Joshua 19:12 or Khirbet Dabural, which is on a hill between Tabor and Nazareth. [3] An oak (not a plain as in KJV) in Benjamin (1 Sam. 10:3).

Tabrimon [Tabrimmon] (tab'rim-on; [*the god*] *Rimmon is good*). Father of Benhadad I, king of Syria (1 Kings 15:18).

Tachmonite [Tahchemonite, Tahkemonite] (tak' ma-nite; [tak'em-a-nīte]). The family name of Josheb-Basshebeth, chief captain in David's army (2 Sam. 23:8).

Tadmor (tad'mor; *palm tree*). A city known to the Greeks and Romans as Palmyra; it facilitated trade with the East (1 Kings 9:18; 2 Chron. 8:4). Its ruin is Tadmar in an oasis east-northeast of Damascus about midway between the city and the Euphrates. Some believe the reading in First Kings should be *Tamar;* the Masoretic Hebrew scholars read *Tadmor* in the margin but *Tamar* in the text. If we read Tamar then the reference is to a city probably in southern Judah.

Tahan (tā'han; *graciousness*). [1] A descendant of Ephraim

(Num. 26:35). [2] Another descendant of Ephraim (1 Chron. 7:25).

Tahanites (tā'han-ītes). Descendants of Tahan, son of Ephraim (Num. 26:35).

Tahapanes [Tahpanhes; Tehaphnehes] (ta-hap'a-nēz [ta'pan-hēz; tē-haf'ne-hēz]; *secret temptation*). An Egyptian city on the Pelusiac channel of the Nile (Jer. 2:16; 43:7–9; 44:1; Ezek. 30:18). It is identified with modern Tell Defneh.

Tahash (tā'hash). *See* Thahash.

Tahath (tā'hath; *humility*). [1] A descendant of Kohath (1 Chron. 6:24, 37). [2] A descendant of Ephraim (1 Chron. 7:20). [3] A grandson of the above (1 Chron. 7:20).

Tahath (tā'hath; *humility*). A desert encampment of the Israelites (Num. 33:26–27).

Tahpenes (ta'pan-hēz). An Egyptian queen, wife of the Pharaoh, who received the fleeing Hadad, an enemy of Solomon, (1 Kings 11:18–20).

Tahrea [Tarea] (ta'rē-a [tā'rē-a]; *flight*). Son of Micah, descendant of Saul (1 Chron. 8:35; 9:41).

Tahtim-hodshi (ta'tim-hod'shī; *lowlands of Hodshi*). A location between Gilead and Dan-jaan visited by Joab during the census of Israel (2 Sam. 24:6). The location of the site is unknown.

Talmai (tal-mi; *bold; spirited*). [1] A man or clan defeated by Caleb (Num. 13:22; Josh. 15:14; Judg. 1:10). [2] King of Geshur and father-in-law of David (2 Sam. 3:3; 13:27).

Talmon (tal'mon; *oppressor; violent*). A Levite in Ezra's day; a temple porter (1 Chron. 9:17; Ezra 2:42; Neh. 7:45).

Tamah [Thamah] (tā'ma [thā'ma]; *combat*). One whose descendants returned from the Babylonian Captivity (Ezra 2:53; Neh. 7:55).

Tamar [Thamar] (tā'mer [thā'mar]; *palm*). **[1]** The wife of Er, mother of Perez, and an ancestor of Christ (Gen. 38:6, 11, 13; Ruth 4:12; Matt. 1:3). **[2]** The daughter of David violated by Amnon (2 Sam. 13:1–32). **[3]** A daughter of Absalom (2 Sam. 14:27).

Tamar (tā'mer; *palm tree*). A place somewhere to the southwest of the Dead Sea; some identify the site with the village of Thamara, near Kurnub and Ain el-Arūs. Others deny this (Ezek. 47:18–19; 48:28).

Tanach (tā'nak). *See* Taanach.

Tanhumeth (tan-hū'meth; *comfort*). Father of one of Gedaliah's captains (2 Kings 25:23; Jer. 40:8).

Taphath (tā'fath; *a drop*). A daughter of Solomon (1 Kings 4:11).

Tappuah (tap-pū'a; *apple*). A descendant of Judah (1 Chron. 2:43).

Tappuah (tap-pū'a; *swelling*). **[1]** A city in the lowlands of Judah (Josh. 15:34). It is probably modern Beit Nettif 6.4 km. (4 mi.) north of Hebron. **[2]** A border town of Ephraim west of Shechem (Josh 16:8; 17:7–8). It is probably Sheikh Abu Zarad, about 12.9 km. (8 mi.) south of Shechem.

Tarah [Tara] (tā'ra; *wretch*). The twelfth Israelite encampment in the wilderness (Num. 33:27). It was between Tahath and Mithcah.

Taralah (tar'a-la; *strength*). A city allotted to the tribe of Benjamin (Josh. 18:27). It was near Irpeel.

Tarea [Tharshish] (tā're-a [thar'shish]). *See* Tahrea.

Tarpelites (tar'pa-lītes). Members of an Assyrian tribe

transported to Samaria by Shalmaneser of Assyria (Ezra 4:9).

Tarshish (tar′shish; *yellow jasper*). **[1]** A son of Javan and grandson of Noah (Gen. 10:4; 1 Chron. 1:7). Possibly a people who inhabited a region in Spain (Tartessus), near Gibraltar. **[2]** One of the seven princes of Persia (Esther 1:14). **[3]** A descendant of Benjamin (1 Chron. 7:10).

Tarshish [Tharshish] (tar′shish [thar′shish]; *yellow jasper*). A city in southern Spain with which the Phoenicians traded (Jer. 10:9; Ezek. 27:12; 1 Kings 10:22). It is believed to be modern Tartessus near Gibraltar.

Tarsus (tar′sus; *winged*). The most prominent city of Cilicia located on the river Cydnus in Asia Minor; it was the birthplace of Paul (Acts 9:11).

Tartan (tar′tan; meaning unknown). The title of a high Assyrian officer. There is evidence that the office was second only to the king. There are two tartans mentioned in Scripture (2 Kings 18:17; Isa. 20:1).

Tatnai [Tattenai] (tat′nī [tat-e-nī]; *gift*). A Persian governor of Samaria in the days of Zerubbabel (Ezra 5:3; 6:6, 13).

Tebah (tē′ba; *thick; strong*). A son of Nahor, the brother of Abraham (Gen. 22:24).

Tebaliah (teb-a-lī′a; *Jehovah has purified*). A Levite gatekeeper in the days of David (1 Chron. 26:11).

Tehaphnehes (te-haf′ne-hez). *See* Tahapanes.

Tehinnah (te-hin′na; *entreaty; supplication*). A descendant of Judah (1 Chron. 4:12).

Tekoa [Tekoah] (te-kō′a; *trumpet blast*). A town of Judah on the hills near Hebron (2 Sam. 14:2; Jer. 6:1). It is modern Taku ʽais, a ruined village 9.7 km. (6 mi.) south of Bethlehem.

Tekoite (te-kō'īte). A native or inhabitant of Tekoa (2 Sam. 23:26; Neh. 3:5).

Tel-abib [Tel Aviv] (tel-ā-bib' [tel a-vēv']; *heap of grain*). A town of Babylonia near the river Chebar where Jewish exiles were placed (Ezek. 3:15).

Telah (tē'la; *breach*). A descendant of Ephraim (1 Chron. 7:25).

Telaim (tē-lā'im; *lambs*). The place where Saul gathered and numbered his forces before the attack on Amalek (1 Sam. 15:4). It was probably in extreme southern Judah.

Telassar [Thelasar] (te-las'er [the-lā'ser]; *hill of Ashur*). A city near Harran and Orfa in western Mesopotamia (2 Kings 19:12; Isa. 37:12).

Telem (tē'lem; *a lamb*). A gatekeeper who divorced his foreign wife after the Exile (Ezra 10:24).

Telem (tē'lem; *a lamb*). A town in extreme southern Judah (Josh. 15:24).

Tel-harsa [Tel-haresha] (tel-har'sa [tel-har'e-sha]; *hill of workmanship*). A Babylonian village used as a grouping point for Jews returning to Palestine (Ezra 2:59; Neh. 7:61).

Tel-melah (tel-mē'la; *hill of salt*). A Babylonian town mentioned in Ezra 2:59; Nehemiah 7:61. It possibly was situated on the low salt tract near the Persian Gulf.

Tema (tē'ma; *south country*). A son of Ishmael (Gen. 25:15; 1 Chron. 1:30).

Tema (tē'ma; *south country*). A son of Ishmael (Gen. 25:15). The place his descendants dwelt was also called Tema (Job. 6:19). It was located in Arabia midway between Damascus and Mecca.

Teman (tē'man; *on the right hand*). [1] A grandson of

Esau (Gen. 36:11, 15; 1 Chron. 1:36). [2] A duke of Edom (Gen. 36:42; Chron. 1:53).

Temanite [Temani] (tē´man-īte [tē-man´ī]). A descendant of Teman or an inhabitant.

Temeni (tem´e-nī; *fortunate*). A son of Ashur (1 Chron. 4:5–6).

Temple. The structure in which the Israelites worshiped and offered sacrifices to God. There were three temples: Solomon's Zerubbabel's, and Herod's.

Terah [Thara] (tē´ra [thā´ra]; *turning; duration*). The father of Abraham and ancestor of Christ (Gen. 11:27–32; Luke 3:34).

Teresh (tē´resh; *solid*). A chamberlain of the Persian court that plotted against the crown (Esther 2:21; 6:2).

Tertius (tur´shi-us; *third*). The scribe to whom the Epistle to the Romans was dictated (Rom. 16:22). Some conjecture that he is Silas (q.v.).

Tertullus (ter-tul´us; *third*). An orator hired by the Jews to state skillfully their case against Paul before Felix (Acts 24:1–8).

Thaddeus (tha-dē´us; a name derived from an Aramaic word for the female *breast*). One of the twelve apostles (Matt. 10:3; Mark 3:18). He is the same as Judas, the brother of James (Luke 6:16; John 14:22; Acts 1:13). He was also named Lebbeus *(heart)*.

Thahash [Tahash] (thā´hash; *dolphin*). A son of Nahor, Abraham's brother (Gen. 22:24).

Thamah (thā´ma). *See* Tamah.

Thamar (thā´mar). Greek form of Tamar (q.v.).

Thara (thā´ra). Greek form of Terah (q.v.).

Tharshish (thar´shish). *See* Tarshish.

Thebes (thēbz; *city of the god* [Amon]). An ancient city in upper Egypt, 330 mi. (528 km.) south of Cairo, sacked by the Assyrians in 663 B.C. (Jer. 46:25; Ezek. 30:14–16; Neh. 3:8).

Thebez (thē´bez; *muddy*). A place in the district of Neapolis (Judg. 9:50). It was 20.9 km. (13 mi.) southwest of Scythopolis [Beth-shean].

Thelasar (the-lā´ser). *See* Telassar.

Theophilus (the-of´i-lus; *lover of God*). An unknown person, possibly a Roman official, to whom Luke addressed his Gospel and Acts (Luke 1:3; Acts 1:1).

Thessalonica (thes-a-lo-nī´ka; *victory at sea*). A city situated on the Macedonian coast at the head of the Thermaic Gulf (Acts 17:1, 11, 13; 27:2). It is known as Salonika today.

Theudas (thū´das; *gift of God*). Instigator of a rebellion against the Romans, which was crushed by them (Acts 5:36).

Thimnathah (thim´na-tha; *a portion*). A city in the allotment of Dan (Josh. 19:43). It was located between Elon and Ekron. Many identify it with Timnath [2]. *See also* Timnah.

Thomas (tom´as; *twin*). One of the twelve apostles of Jesus. When Christ rose from the dead, he was most skeptical (Matt. 10:3; Mark 3:18; John 20:24–29). His Aramaic name is Didymus in Greek.

Three Taverns[Three Inns]. A station on the Appian Way near the modern city of Cisterna (Acts 28:15).

Thyatira (thī-a-tī´ra; *sacrifice of labor*). A city between Pergamos and Sardis (Acts 16:14; Rev. 2:18–29). It was in Lydia in Asia Minor.

Tiberias (ti-bē´ri-as; *good vision*). [1] A city on the west coast of the Sea of Galilee (Josh. 6:1; 21:1). [2] A lake in northern Galilee (John 6:1; 21:1), the same as the Sea of Galilee.

Tiberias, Sea of. *See* Tiberias; Galilee, Sea of.

Tiberius (ti-bē′ri-us; *son of* [*the river*] *Tiber*). Third emperor of the Roman Empire (Luke 3:1).

Tibhath (tib′hath; *place of slaughter*). A city of Amam-Zobah (1 Chron. 18:8). It is identical with Betah (q.v.).

Tibni (tib′nī; *intelligent*). One who rivaled Omri for the throne of Israel (1 Kings 16:21–22).

Tidal (tī′dal; *splendor; renown*). King of Goyim [nations] who, with his allies, invaded the Cities of the Plain (Gen. 14:1, 9).

Tiglath-pileser (tig′lath-pi-lē′zer; Babylonian, *Tukulti-apil-Esharra—my trust is in the son of Asharra*). A king of Assyria who invaded Naphtali during the time of Pekah of Israel. He conquered northern Palestine and deported many from Naphtali (2 Kings 15:29; 16:7, 10; 1 Chron. 5:6, 26). His native name was Pul (2 Kings 15:19). Realizing he bore two names, we should translate First Chronicles 5:26, ". . . God . . . stirred . . . Pul king of Assyria *even* [not *and*] Tilgath-pileser king of Assyria."

Tikvah [**Tikvath**] [**Tokhath**] (tik′va [tik′vath, tōk′hath]; *expectation*). **[1]** The father-in-law of Huldah the prophetess (2 Kings 22:14; 2 Chron. 34:22). **[2]** The father of Jahaziah (Ezra 10:15).

Tilon (tī′lon; *mockery; scorn*). A descendant of Judah (1 Chron. 4:20).

Timeaus [**Timeus**] (ti-mē′us; *honorable*). Father of the blind Bartimaeus (Mark. 10:46).

Timeus (ti-mē′us). *See* Timaeus.

Timna [**Timnah**] (tim′na; *restraining*). **[1]** A concubine of a son of Esau (Gen. 36:12). **[2]** A daughter of Seir the Horite (Gen. 36:22; 1 Chron. 1:39). **[3]** A chief of

Edom (Gen. 36:40; 1 Chron. 1:51). **[4]** A son of Eliphaz (1 Chron. 1:36).

Timnah (tim'na; *allotted portion*). **[1]** A town on the northern border of Judah (Josh. 15:10). It was allotted to Dan and is called Thimnathah in Joshua 19:43. It was also known as Timnath (Gen. 38:12–14). Its site is Khirbet Tinah, 15 mi. from Jerusalem. **[2]** A town in the hill country of Judah (Josh. 15:57). Possibly identical with **[1]**. *See also* Timna.

Timnath (tim'nath; *allotted portion*). **[1]** A border town in Judah (Gen. 38:12–14). It is probably identical with Timnah. **[2]** A city in the territory of Dan near Philistia (Judg. 14:1–2, 5).

Timnath-heres (tim'nath-hē'rez; *portion of the sun*). A village in Ephraim (Judg. 2:9). It is identical with Timnath-serah.

Timnath-serah (tim'nath-sē'ra; *remaining portion*). The home and burial place of Joshua (Josh. 19:50; 24:30). It is probably modern Tibnah, 19.3 km. (12 mi.) northeast of Lydda. It is identical with Timnath-heres.

Timnite (tim'nīte). A native or inhabitant of Timnah (Judg. 15:6).

Timon (tī'mon; *honorable*). One of the seven deacons (Acts 6:1–6).

Timotheus [Timothy] (ti-mō'the-us [tim'o-thi]; *honored of God*). A young friend and convert of Paul; he traveled extensively with the apostle. He was from Lystra and was the son of Eunice, a Jewess, and a Greek father (Acts 16:1; 17:14–15; 1 Tim. 1:2, 18; 6:20).

Timothy (tim'o-thi). *See* Timotheus.

Tiphsah (tif'sa; *passage*). **[1]** A crossing located on the Euphrates River (1 Kings 4:24). It is probably modern Thapsacus. **[2]** A place mentioned in connection with

Tirzah (2 Kings 15:16). It may be the ruined village of Tafsah 10.5 km. (6.5 mi.) southwest of Shechem. Others identify it with Tappuah (q.v.).

Tiras (tī'ras; *longing*). Youngest son of Japheth (Gen. 10:2; 1 Chron. 1:5). Possibly the inhabitants of Thrace. Other scholars consider reference to be to the Tyrsenoi, a people who inhabited the islands and coastlands of the Aegean.

Tirathites (ti'ra-thites). A family of scribes who lived in Jabez, probably in Judah (1 Chron. 2:55).

Tirhakah (tir-hā'ka). A king of Ethiopia and Egypt who aided Hezekiah in his fight against Sennacherib (2 Kings 19:9; Isa. 37:9).

Tirhanah (tir-hā'na; *kindness*). A descendant of Hezron (1 Chron. 2:48).

Tiria (tir'i-a; *fear*). A descendant of Judah (1 Chron. 4:16).

Tirshatha (tur-shā'tha; *feared*). A title of the governor of Judea under Persian rule (Ezra 2:63; Neh. 7:65, 70; 8:9; 10:1).

Tirzah (tur'za; *delight*). Youngest daughter of Zelophehad (Num. 26:33; 27:1; Josh. 17:3).

Tirzah (tur'za; *delight*). A Canaanite city located north of Jerusalem (Josh. 12:24; 1 Kings 14:17). It was 48.3 km. (30 mi.) from Jerusalem.

Tishbe [Tishbeh] (tish'be [tish'be]; *the inhabitants*). A town in Gilead, the home of Elijah the prophet (1 Kings 17:1). Traditionally identified with el-Istib, about 7.5 mi. (12 km.) north of the Jabbok river.

Tishbite (tish'bīte). A name applied to Elijah the prophet (1 Kings 17:1; 21:17; 2 Kings 9:36); though some scholars believe he was from Thisbe, a town in Galilee.

Titius [Titius Justus] (tish′ē-us [tish′ē-us just′us]). A man of Corinth who worshipped God and whose house was next to the synagogue. Also *see* Justus.

Titus (tī′tus; *pleasant*). A converted Grecian entrusted with a mission to Crete (2 Cor. 2:13; Gal. 2:1; Titus 1:4).

Tizite (tī′zīte). A name of Joha, one of David's mighty men (1 Chron. 11:45).

Toah (tō′a; *humility*). An ancestor of Samuel the prophet (1 Chron. 6:34). He is called Nahath in verse 26 and Tohu in First Samuel 1:1.

Tob (tob; *good*). An area east of the Jordan between Gilead and the eastern deserts (Judg. 11:3, 5).

Tob-adonijah (tob-ad-o-nī′ja; *the Lord Jehovah is good*). One sent by Jehoshaphat to teach the Law (1 Chron. 17:8).

Tobiah [Tobijah] (to-bī′a [to-bī′ja]; *Jehovah is good*). **[1]** A Levite sent by Jehoshaphat to teach the Law (2 Chron. 17:8). **[2]** An ancestor of returning captives who had lost their genealogy (Ezra 2:60; Neh. 7:62). **[3]** An Ammonite servant of Sanballat who opposed Nehemiah (Neh. 2:10–20). **[4]** A leader who returned from the Babylonian Captivity (Zech. 6:10, 14).

Tobijah (to-bī′ja). *See* Tobiah.

Tochen (tō′ken; *measure*). A town of Simeon (1 Chron. 4:32), near Rimmon. It is identical with Ether [2].

Togarmah (to-gar′ma). A son of Gomer (Gen. 10:3; 1 Chron. 1:6). Possibly a people of the far north who inhabited the mountains northwest of Mesopotamia, between the Anti-Taurus and the Euphrates, or possibly the area on the upper Euphrates between Samosata and Melita.

Togarmah (to-gar′ma). A country that supplied horses and mules to the Tyrians and soldiers to the army of Gog (Ezek. 27:14; 38:6). Many identify this land with Armenia.

Tohu (tō′hu). *See* Toah.

Toi [Tou] (tō′e [tō′oo]; *error*). A king of Hamath who sent his son to congratulate David on his victory over Hadadezer (2 Sam. 8:9–10; 1 Chron. 18:9–10).

Tola (tō′la; *crimson worm*). **[1]** A son of Issachar (Gen. 46:13; 1 Chron. 7:1–2). **[2]** A judge of Israel (Judg. 10:1).

Tolad (tō′lad). *See* Eltolad.

Tolaites (to′lā-ites). The descendants of Tola (Num. 26:23).

Tophel (tō′fel; *ruin*). An area north of Bozra, toward the southeast corner of the Dead Sea (Deut. 1:1). It is perhaps Tafileh.

Tophet [Topheth] (tō′fet [tō′feth]; *a drum*). Once a part of a king's garden in Hinnom; it became a place where people in Jerusalem sacrificed their children (Isa. 30:33; Jer. 19:6, 11–14; 2 Kings 23:10).

Tou (tō′oo). *See* Toi.

Trachonitis [Traconitis] (trak-o-nī′tis; *hilly region*). A Roman province south of Damascus and north of Jordan (Luke 3:1). It is now called al-Seja.

Transjordan. A term for the large plateau east of the Jordan River, the Dead Sea, and the Arabah, often called "beyond the river" (Gen. 50:10–11; Deut. 3:20; Judg. 5:17; Isa. 9:1; Matt. 4:15; Mark 3:8).

Treasure Cities [Treasure House; Store Cities]. Designated cities at which the kings of the ancient world kept their treasures and tithes (Exod. 1:11; Ezra 5:17).

Troas (trō′az; *penetrated*). An important city on the coast of Mysia (Acts 16:8; 2 Tim. 4:13). It was in northern Asia Minor and is also called Alexandria.

Trogyllium (tro-jil´i-um; *fruit port*). A rocky projection of the ridge of Mycale and a town (Acts 20:5). They were both located on the western coast of Asia Minor opposite the island of Samos.

Trophimus (trof´i-mus; *nourishing*). A Christian convert and afterward a companion-in-travel with Paul (Acts 20:4; 21:29; 2 Tim. 4:20).

Tryphena [Tryphaena] (trī-fē´na; *dainty*). A Christian woman of Rome to whom Paul sent greetings (Rom. 16:12).

Tryphosa (trī´fō´sa; *delicate*). A Christian woman at Rome sent greetings by Paul (Rom. 16:12).

Tubal (tū´bal). [1] A son of Japheth (Gen. 10:2; 1 Chron. 1:5). [2] Possibly a reference to a people in eastern Asia Minor; they are called Tabal in Assyrian inscriptions. Tubal is mentioned by both Isaiah (Isa. 66:19) and Ezekiel (Ezek. 27:13) as a trader with Tyre.

Tubal-cain (tū´bal-kān; *the smith*). One of the sons of Lamech and an expert metal-smith (Gen. 4:22).

Twin Brothers, The. The figurehead of an Alexandrian ship which took the Apostle Paul from Malta to Puteoli (Acts 28:11).

Tychicus (tik´i-kus; *fortunate*). A disciple and messenger of Paul (Acts 20:4; Eph. 6:21; 2 Tim. 4:12).

Tyrannus (tī-ran´us; *tyrant*). A Greek rhetorician or Jewish rabbi in whose school Paul taught at Ephesus (Acts 19:9).

Tyre [Tyrus] (tīr [tīr´us]; *rock*). A city on the central coast of Phoenicia noted for its commercial activity (Josh.

19:29; 2 Sam. 5:11; Jer. 25:22). It is located halfway between Accho and Sidon.

Tyrus (tīr′us). *See* Tyre.

U

Ucal (ū′kal; *I can*; or a verb meaning *to be consumed*). *See* Ithiel.

Uel (ū′el; *will of God*). A son of Bani who had taken a foreign wife (Ezra 10:34).

Ugarit (yū′ga-rit). An ancient Canaanite city (modern Ras Shamra) in northern Syria where important archaeological discoveries were made which shed light on Ugarite (a Semitic language similar to Hebrew) and the religion of Baal. The Israelite prophets condemned the Israelite; and Judahites for their worship of Baal (2 Kings 17:1–20; 2 Chron. 36:9–12) but to little avail.

Ulai (ū′lī; *pure water*). A river surrounding Shushan in Persia (Dan. 8:2, 16). It is now called Kerah or Kerkhah.

Ulam (ū′lam; *leader*). [1] A descendant of Manasseh, the son of Peresh (1 Chron. 7:16–17). [2] A descendant of Benjamin whose sons were "mighty men of valor" (1 Chron. 8:39–40).

Ulla (ul′a; *burden*). A descendant of Asher (1 Chron. 7:39).

Ummah (ūm′a; *kindred*). A city of Asher on the Mediterranean coast (Josh. 19:30). It was near Aphek or Rehob; now it is called Alma.

Unni [Unno] (ū′nī [ū′no]; *answered*). [1] One of the Levites chosen as singers (1 Chron. 15:10, 18, 20). [2] A Levite that returned to the land with Zerubbabel (Neh. 12:9).

Unno (ū′no). *See* Unni.

Uphaz (ū′faz; *pure gold*). A city generally regarded as being identical with Ophir (Jer. 10:9; Dan. 10:5).

Upper Gate. A gate in the city wall or Temple area of Jerusalem (2 Kings 15:35; 2 Chron. 23:20; 27:3).

Ur (ur; *flame; light*). Father of one of David's mighty men (1 Chron. 11:35).

Ur (ur; *flame, light*). The city which Abram left to go to Haran (Gen. 11:28, 31). Ur is generally identified as ancient Ur (Uri), modern Tell el-Muqayyar located on the Euphrates in south Iraq.

Urbane [Urbanus] (ur′bān [ur-ba′nus]; *refined, polite*). A faithful Roman Christian whom Paul greeted (Rom. 16:9).

Uri (ū′rī; *my light*). A contracted form of Uriah. [1] The son of Hur, and father of Bezaleel (Exod. 31:1–2; 1 Chron. 2:20). [2] The father of Geber (1 Kings 4:19). [3] A porter of Levi who had married a foreign wife (Ezra 10:24).

Uriah [Urias; Urijah] (u-rī′a [u-rī′as; u-rī′ja]; *flame of Jehovah*). [1] A Hittite soldier in David's army. He was killed in a fierce battle, for David, desiring to marry his wife, Bath-sheba, had placed him on the front battle line (2 Sam. 11). [2] A priest under Ahaz who built a pagan altar on the king's command; then placed it in the temple (2 Kings 16:10–16). [3] A prophet whose message of judgment so offended Jehoiakim that he murdered him (Jer. 26:20–23). [4] A priest, the father of Meremoth (Ezra 8:33; Neh. 3:4, 21). [5] A man who stood by Ezra when he read the Law (Neh. 8:4). Possibly the same as [4]. [6] A priest whom Isaiah took as a witness (Isa. 8:2).

Urias (u-rī′as). Greek form of Uriah (q.v.).

Uriel (ū′ri-el; *flame of God*). [1] A chief of the sons of Kohath (1 Chron. 6:24; 15:5, 11). Possibly the same as Zephaniah [2]. **[2]** Father of Michaiah, one of Rehoboam's sons (2 Chron. 13:2).

Urijah (u-rī'ja). *See* Uriah.

Uthai (ū'thī; *Jehovah is help*). **[1]** A son of Bigvai who returned to the land of Israel with Ezra (Ezra 8:14). **[2]** A descendant of Judah (1 Chron. 9:4).

Uz [Huz] (uz [huz]; *counsel; firmness*). **[1]** Eldest son of Aram (Gen. 10:23). Possibly the name refers to an Aramean tribe or people. **[2]** A son of Shem (1 Chron. 1:17). The Septuagint makes this Uz identical with [1] naming Aram as his father. It is also possible the Hebrew text was abbreviated here. **[3]** A son of Dishan, son of Seir (Gen. 36:28). **[4]** The son of Nahor by Milcah (Gen. 22:21).

Uz (uz; *counsel; firmness*). **[1]** The country where Job lived (Job 1:1). The two most likely locations are Hauran, south of Damascus, and the area between Edom and north Arabia. **[2]** A kingdom not far from Edom (Jer. 25:20; Lam. 4:21). Perhaps identical with [1].

Uzai (ū'zī; *hoped for*). The father of Palal (Neh. 3:25).

Uzal (ū'zal; *wandering*). A son of Joktan (Gen. 10:27; 1 Chron. 1:21). Possibly the name refers to an Arabian tribe.

Uzza [Uzzah] (ūz'a [uz'a]; *strength*). **[1]** A man who was struck dead by God when he touched the ark of the covenant (2 Sam. 6:2–7; 1 Chron. 13:6–10). **[2]** A person in whose garden Manasseh, king of Judah, and Amon (Manasseh's son), also a king of Judah, were buried (2 Kings 21:18, 26). **[3]** A descendant of Merari (1 Chron. 6:29). **[4]** A descendant of Ehud (1 Chron. 8:7). **[5]** An ancestor of a Nethinim family that returned from Babylon (Ezra 2:49; Neh. 7:51).

Uzza, Garden of (ūz´a; *strength*). The place where Manasseh, king of Judah, and Amon, his son, were buried (2 Kings 21:18, 26).

Uzzah (ūz´a). *See* Uzza.

Uzzen-sherah [Uzzen Sheerah] (uz´en-shē´ra; *tip of Sherah*). A town established by Sherah, a daughter of Ephraim (1 Chron. 7:24). It was near the two Beth-horons and is now called Beit Sira.

Uzzi (uz´ī; *Jehovah is strong* or *my strength*). [1] A descendant of Issachar (1 Chron. 7:1–3). [2] Chief of a priestly family of Jedaiah (Neh. 12:19, 42). [3] Descendant of Benjamin (1 Chron. 7:7). [4] The overseer of the Levites at Jerusalem (Neh. 11:22). [5] The father of Elah, a descendant of Benjamin (1 Chron. 9:8). [6] A son of Bukki; even though in the line of high priests, he does not seem to have held this office (1 Chron. 6:5–6, 51; Ezra 7:4).

Uzzia (u-zī´a; *Jehovah is strong*). One of David's valiant men (1 Chron. 11:44).

Uzziah [Ozias] (u-zī´a [o-zī´as]; *Jehovah is strong* or *my strength is Jehovah*). [1] The eleventh king of Judah. When he attempted to offer incense unlawfully, God struck him with leprosy. He was also called Azariah (2 Kings 15:1–8; 2 Chron. 26). He was an ancestor of Christ (Matt. 1:8–9). [2] A Levite descended from Kohath and ancestor of Samuel (1 Chron. 6:24). [3] Father of Jehonathan (1 Chron. 27:25). [4] A priest who had married a foreign wife (Ezra 10:21). [5] A descendant of Judah (Neh. 11:4).

Uzziel (u-zī´el; *God is my strength* or *God is strong*). [1] The ancestor of the Uzzielites; the son of Kohath (Exod. 6:18). [2] Captain of the sons of Simeon (1 Chron. 4:42). [3] A son of Bela and grandson to Benjamin

(1 Chron. 7:7). **[4]** An assistant wall-builder (Neh. 3:8). **[5]** A Levite, son of Jeduthun, who helped to cleanse the temple (2 Chron. 29:14). **[6]** A musician set by David over the service of song in the temple (1 Chron. 25:4). Uzziel is the same as Azareel in verse 18.

Uzzielites (u-zī'el-ītes). Members of the tribal family of Uzziel (Num. 3:27; 1 Chron. 26:23).

V

Vajezatha (va-jez'a-tha; *born of Ized*). One of the sons of Haman slain by the Jews (Esther 9:9).

Valley Gate. A gate in the southwest wall of Jerusalem leading to the Hinnom Valley (Neh. 2:13).

Vaniah (va-nī'a; *praise, or nourishment, of Jehovah*). A son of Bani who divorced his foreign wife after the Exile (Ezra 10:36).

Vashni (vash'nī; *the second*). According to First Chronicles 6:28, the firstborn son of Samuel, but First Samuel 8:2 states Joel was his firstborn. Because of this, some scholars follow the Septuagint and Syriac versions, where verse 28 reads thus: "And the sons of Samuel: the firstborn, Joel, and *the second* Abiah."

Vashti (vash'tī; *beautiful woman; best*). The queen of Persia who was divorced by King Ahasuerus because she refused to come to his great feast (Esther 1:10–22).

Vineyards, Plain of the. A place east of the Jordan River, site of the battle in which Jephthah defeated the forces led by Ammon (Judg. 11:33). Many translations take this as a proper name and render it *Abel-cheramin*.

Vophsi (vof′sī; *fragrant; rich*). A descendant of Naphtali, the father of Nahbi the spy (Num. 13:14).

W

Water Gate. A gate on the east side of Jerusalem, above the spring of Gihon (Neh. 8:1, 3).

Waters of Merom. *See* Merom.

Wilderness. The area in which the Israelites wandered for 40 years before entering Canaan (Deut. 1:1; Josh. 5:6). Several places are encompassed in the designation Wilderness; these are listed under their individual names (e.g., Paran, Zin, etc.).

Willows, Brook of the. A small stream that marks the boundary between Moab and Edom (Isa. 15:7). It is possibly the lower course of Wadi el-Hesa where it meets the upper course of Seil el-Kerahi.

Wise Men. The men from the East led by a star to worship the infant Christ (Matt. 2:1, 7, 16). The Greek word for *wise* here *(magoi)* occurs as "astrologers" in the Greek Old Testament (the Septuagint; Dan. 1:20, 2:2) and as "sorcerers" in the New Testament (Acts 13:6, 8). Apparently the Magi were a caste of Medes who in the 5th century B.C. functioned as priests in the Persian Empire.

X

Xerxes (zurk′sēz) The Greek name of Ahasuerus, the Persian king who ruled from 486–465 B.C. (Esth. 1:1; 2:1; 3:1).

Y

Yaudi [Judah] (ya′ū-dē [jū′da]). A form of Judah used in 2 Kings 14:28. *See* Judah.

YHWH. The Hebrew name of the God of Israel, considered to be too sacred to pronounce. English versions of the Old Testament tend to translate this word as LORD or *Jehovah*. There is also a shorter form, *YAH,* which is used in several passages (Ps. 68:4; Isa. 12:2; 26:4, 38:11). In Exod. 3:14–16, the sacred name YHWH is given to Moses as a revelation of who God is. The word is a form of the verb *hayah, to be,* which is difficult to translate, though it may be rendered as, "I am who I am," or "I will be what I will be." *See* Jehovah.

Z

Zaanaim (za-a-nī′im). *See* Zaanannim.

Zaanan (zā′a-nan; *going out*). A town in Judah (Mic. 1:11). It is probably identical with Zenan (q.v.). The site is probably modern Arak el-Kharba.

Zaanannim [Zaanaim] (zā-a-nan′im [zā-a-nā-im]). A place on the southern border of Naphtali (Josh. 19:33; Judg. 4:11).

Zaavan [Zavan] (zā′van [zā′van]; *quake, terror*). A descendant of Seir (Gen. 36:27). Also called Zavan (1 Chron. 1:42).

Zabad (zā′bad; *endower*). **[1]** A descendant of Jerahmeel of Judah (1 Chron. 2:36–37). **[2]** A man of Ephraim and son of Tahath (1 Chron. 7:21). **[3]** Son of Alai and one of David's mighty men (1 Chron. 11:41). **[4]**, **[5]**, **[6]** Three who married foreign wives during the Exile (Ezra 10:27, 33, 43). **[7]** *See* Jozachar.

Zabbai (zab′a-ī; *roving about; pure*). **[1]** One who divorced his foreign wife after the Exile (Ezra 10:28). **[2]** Father of Baruch (Neh. 3:20).

Zabbud [Zaccur] (zab′ud; [za′kur]; *mindful, remembered*). One who returned from the Exile with Ezra (Ezra 8:14).

Zabdi (zab′dī; *Jehovah is endower*). **[1]** Father of Carmi (Josh. 7:1, 17–18); called Zimri in First Chronicles 2:6. **[2]** A descendant of Benjamin (1 Chron. 8:19). **[3]** One of David's storekeepers (1 Chron. 27:27). **[4]** An ancestor of Mattaniah (Neh. 11:17); also called Zichri (1 Chron. 9:15) and Zaccur (1 Chron. 25:2, 10; Neh. 12:35).

Zabdiel (zab′di-el; *my gift is God*). **[1]** Father of Jashobeam, David's captain (1 Chron. 27:2). **[2]** An overseer of the priests (Neh. 11:14).

Zabud (zā′bud; *bestowed*). Officer and friend of Solomon (1 Kings 4:5).

Zabulon (zab′u-lon). Greek form of Zebulun (q.v.).

Zaccai (zak′a-ī; *pure*). One whose descendants returned (Ezra 2:9; Neh. 7:14). Possibly the same as Zabbai [2].

Zaccheus (za-kē′us; *pure*). A publican with whom Jesus lodged during His stay at Jericho (Luke 19:1–10).

Zaccur [Zacchur] (zak′ur; *well remembered*). **[1]** A descendant of Simeon (1 Chron. 4:26). **[2]** Father of Shammua, one of the spies (Num. 13:4). **[3]** Descendant of Merari (1 Chron. 24:27). **[4]** *See* Zabdi [4]. **[5]** A Levite who sealed the covenant (Neh. 10:12). **[6]** Father of Hanan (Neh. 13:13); possibly the same as [5].

[7] One who rebuilt part of the wall of Jerusalem (Neh. 3:2). *See* Zabbud.

Zachariah [Zechariah] (zak-a-rī'a [zek-a-rī'a]; *Jehovah has remembered*). **[1]** Son and successor of Jeroboam II. He reigned only six months (2 Kings 14:29; 15:8–11). **[2]** Father of Abi or Abijah, mother of Hezekiah (2 Kings 18:2); written *Zechariah* in Second Chronicles 29:1.

Zacharias (zak-a-rī'as; Greek form of Zechariah—*Jehovah has remembered*). **[1]** The prophet whom the Jews stoned (Matt. 23:35; Luke 11:51). Some believe this prophet to be identical with Zechariah [11] or [16], though it is possible the reference is to an unknown prophet. **[2]** A priest, father of John the Baptist (Luke 1).

Zacher (zā'ker; *fame*). Son of Jeiel (1 Chron. 8:31); called Zechariah in First Chronicles 9:37.

Zadok (zā'dok; *righteous*). **[1]** A high priest in the time of David (2 Sam. 8:17; 15:24–36; 1 Kings 1:8–45). **[2]** Father of Jerusha, wife of Uzziah and mother of Jotham, both kings of Israel (2 Kings 15:33; 2 Chron. 27:1). **[3]** Son of Ahitub and father of Shallum or Meshullam (1 Chron. 6:12–13; Ezra 7:2). **[4]** A young man of valor (1 Chron. 12:28). **[5], [6]** Two who repaired the wall of Jerusalem (Neh. 3:4, 29). **[7]** One who sealed the covenant with Nehemiah (Neh. 10:21). **[8]** A scribe under Nehemiah (Neh. 13:13).

Zaham (zā'ham; *loathing*). A son of Rehoboam (2 Chron. 11:19).

Zahar (zā'har; *white*). A city that provided Damascus with wool (Ezek. 27:18).

Zair (zā-ir; *small*). The place in or near Edom where Joram defeated the Edomites (2 Kings 8:21). It is possibly Sa'ir, about 8 km. (5 mi.) north-northeast of Hebron. Some identify the city with Zior (q.v.).

Zalaph (zā'laf; *caper plant*). The father of one who repaired the wall of Jerusalem (Neh. 3:30).

Zalmon (zal'mon; *peaceable*). The Ahohite who was one of David's guards (2 Sam. 23:28). He is called Ilai ("exalted") in First Chronicles 11:29. Not to be confused with Salmon.

Zalmon [Salmon] (zal'mon [sal'mon]; *peaceable*). [1] A wooded area in Shechem (Judg. 9:48–49; Psa. 68:14). [2] The father of Boaz and an ancestor of Jesus (Ruth 4:20–21; Matt. 1:4–5). He is also called Salma (1 Chron. 2:11) and Sala (Luke 3:32, RSV).

Zalmonah (zal-mo'nah; *shade*). An Israelite encampment in the desert (Num. 33:41–42). It was probably east of Jebel Harien.

Zalmunna (zal-mun'a; *withdrawn from protection*). One of two Midianite kings slain by Gideon (Judg. 8:5–21). *See* Zebah.

Zamzummin (zam-zum'mem; *mumblers*). Ammonite name for the people called Rephaim (giants) by the Jews in their narrative of the conquest of Canaan (Deut. 2:20).

Zanoah (za-nō'a; *broken district*). One of the family of Caleb (1 Chron. 4:18).

Zanoah (za-nō'a; *broken district*). [1] A town in lowland Judah (Josh. 15:34; Neh. 3:13). It is Khirbet Zanu' or Zanuh about 4.8 km. (3 mi.) south-southeast of Bethshemesh. [2] A town in Judah's hill country about 2.1 km. (1.3 mi.) northwest of Yatta (Josh. 15:56; 1 Chron. 4:18).

Zaphnath-paaneah (zaf'e-nath-pa-nē'a; *savior of the*

world; revealer of secrets). Name given to Joseph by Pharaoh (Gen. 41:45).

Zaphon (zā'fon; *north*). A place allowed to the tribe of Gad in the Jordan Valley east of the river (Josh. 13:27).

Zara (zā'ra). Greek form of Zara or Zerah (q.v.).

Zarah (zā'ra). *See* Zerah.

Zareah (zā're-a; *wasp; hornet*). *See also* Zorah.

Zareathites (zār'e-a-thītes). *See* Zorathites.

Zared [Zered] (zā'red [zē'red]; *brook*). A brook and valley that marks the greatest limit of the Hebrews' wandering in the wilderness (Num. 21:12; Deut. 2:13–14). It was south of the Arnon, probably Wadi el-Hesa.

Zarephath (zar'e-fath; *dyeing place*). A town located near Zidon (Sidon) that was the residence of Elijah (2 Kings 17:9). It is probably modern Sarafand, 12.9 km. (8 mi.) south of Zidon.

Zaretan [Zarethan; Zartanah; Zarthan; Zeredathah] (zar'e-tan [zar'ta-na; zar'than; ze'red-a-tha]; *cooling*). A village near Beth-shean in the territory of Manasseh (Josh. 3:16; 1 Kings 4:12). It is probably Tell es-Sa'idiyeh. The city is probably identical with Zereda (q.v.).

Zareth-shahar [Zereth-shahar] (zā'reth-shā'har [ze'reth-shā'har]; *beauty of the dawn*). A town allotted to the tribe of Reuben (Josh. 13:19). It is probably at Zarat on the eastern shore of the Dead Sea.

Zarhites [Zerahites] (zar'hītes [zer'a-hites]). **[1]** A family of Simeonites (Num. 26:13). **[2]** A family of Judahites (Num. 26:20).

Zartanah (zar'ta-na). *See* Zaretan.

Zarthan (zar'than). *See* Zaretan.

Zattu [Zatthu] (zat'ū [zat-thu]; *lovely; pleasant*). **[1]** One whose descendants returned from the Exile (Ezra 2:8;

10:27; Neh. 7:13). **[2]** A cosealer of the new covenant (Neh. 10:14).

Zavan (zā'van). *See* Zaavan.

Zaza (zā'za; *projection*). A son of Jonathan (1 Chron. 2:33).

Zealotes (zē-lō'tēz). *See* Simon [2].

Zebadiah (zeb-a-dī'a; *Jehovah is endower*). **[1]** A descendant of Benjamin (1 Chron. 8:15). **[2]** A son of Elpaal (1 Chron. 8:17). **[3]** One who joined David (1 Chron. 12:7). **[4]** A descendant of Levi through Kohath (1 Chron. 26:2). **[5]** A son of Asahel (1 Chron. 27:7). **[6]** A Levite sent by Jehoshaphat to teach the Law (2 Chron. 17:8). **[7]** A son of Ishmael (2 Chron. 19:11). **[8]** Head of a famly who returned from exile (Ezra 8:8). **[9]** A priest who had taken a foreign wife (Ezra 10:20).

Zebah (zē'ba; *victim*). One of two Midianite kings slain by Gideon (Judg. 8:5–21). *See* Zalmunna.

Zebaim (ze-bā'im; *gazelles*). The home of one whose descendants returned from the Babylonian Captivity (Ezra 2:57; Neh. 7:59). It is perhaps identical with Zeboim (q.v.).

Zebedee (zeb'e-dē; *gift of Jehovah*). A fisherman of Galilee, husband of Salome, and father of the apostles James and John (Matt. 4:21; 27:56; Mark 1:19–20).

Zebina (ze-bī'na; *bought*). One who divorced his foreign wife after the Exile (Ezra 10:43).

Zeboim [Zeboiim] (ze-bo'im [ze-boi'im]; *gazelles*). **[1]** One of the five Cities of the Plain (Gen. 10:19; 14:2, 9). **[2]** A valley between Michmash and the wilderness to the east (1 Sam. 13:16–18). **[3]** A Benjamite town (Neh. 11:34). It is probably north of Lydda, perhaps at Khirbet Sabeyah.

Zebudah (ze-bū′da; *gift*). Wife of Josiah, king of Judah (2 Kings 23:36).

Zebul (zē′bul; *dwelling*). Ruler of Shechem (Judg. 9:28–41).

Zebulun [Zabulon] (zeb′u-lun [zab′u-lon]; *dwelling*). Tenth son of Jacob and ancestor of one of the twelve tribes (Gen. 30:20; 49:13; 1 Chron. 2:1).

Zebulun (zeb′u-lun; *dwelling*). The territory given to the tribe of Zebulun (Josh 19:27, 34). It was north of Issachar, east of Asher, and southwest of Naphtali.

Zebulunite (zeb′yū-la-nīte). A member of the tribe of Zebulun, or one who lived within its territory. In the second census of Israel in the wilderness, "the families of the Zebulunites" numbered 60,500 (Num. 26:27).

Zechariah (zek-a-rī′a; *Jehovah remembers*). [1] A chief of the tribe of Reuben (1 Chron. 5:7). [2] A Levite gatekeeper in the days of David (1 Chron. 9:21; 26:2, 14). [3] A Levite set over the service of song in the days of David (1 Chron. 15:18, 20; 16:5). [4] A priest in the days of David (1 Chron. 15:24). [5] A descendant of Levi through Kohath (1 Chron. 24:25). [6] A descendant of Levi through Merari (1 Chron. 26:11). [7] Father of Iddo (1 Chron. 27:21). [8] A prince of Jehoshaphat sent to teach the people (2 Chron. 17:7). [9] A Levite who encouraged Jehoshaphat against Moab (2 Chron. 20:14). [10] A son of Jehoshaphat (2 Chron. 21:2). [11] A son of Jehoiada who was stoned (2 Chron. 24:20). *See* Zacharias [1]. [12] Prophet in the days of Uzziah (2 Chron. 26:5). [13] A Levite who helped to cleanse the temple (2 Chron. 29:13). [14] A descendant of Levi (2 Chron. 34:12). [15] A prince of Judah in the days of Josiah (2 Chron. 35:8). [16] A prophet in the days of Ezra. His book still exists (Ezra 5:1; 6:14; Zech.

Z

1:1, 7; 7:1, 8). **[17]** A chief man of Israel (Ezra 8:3). **[18]** One who returned from the Exile (Ezra 8:11). The chief man in Ezra 8:16 was probably [17] or [18]. **[19]** One who took a foreign wife during the Exile (Ezra 10:26). **[20]** A prince with Ezra (Neh. 8:4). **[21]** A descendant of Perez (Neh. 11:4). **[22]** One whose descendants dwelled in Jerusalem (Neh. 11:5). **[23]** A priest (Neh. 11:12). **[24]** A Levite trumpeter (Neh. 12:35–36). **[25]** A priest who took part in the dedication ceremony (Neh. 12:41). **[26]** One whom Isaiah took as a witness (Isa. 8:2). **[27]** *See* Zachariah [2]. **[28]** *See* Zacher.

Zecher (zē′ker). A form of Zechariah.

Zedad (zē′dad; *mountainside*). A northern boundary mark of Canaan (Num. 34:8; Ezek. 47:15). It is probably a tower and has been identified with Sadad, southwest of Homs.

Zedekiah (zed-e-kī′a; *Jehovah my righteousness*). **[1]** A false prophet who encouraged Ahab to attack the Syrians at Ramoth-gilead (1 Kings 22:11, 24; 2 Chron. 18:10, 23). **[2]** A false prophet (Jer. 29:21–23). **[3]** A prince of Judah in the days of Jehoiakim (Jer. 36:12). **[4]** The last king of Judah; his rebellion spelled the doom of Judah (2 Kings 24:18—25:7; 2 Chron. 36:11–21). He is probably referred to in First Chronicles 3:16 as a "son" or successor of Jeconiah. *See* Mattaniah [1]. **[5]** *See* Zidkijah.

Zeeb (zē′eb; *wolf*). A prince of Midian slain by Gideon (Judg. 7:25; 8:3). Also *see* Oreb.

Zelah [Zela] (zē′la; *slope*). A town of Benjamin containing Kish's tomb (2 Sam. 21:14). It is probably Khirbet Salah northwest of Jerusalem.

Zelek (zē′lek; *split*). An Ammonite, a valiant man of David (2 Sam. 23:37; 1 Chron. 11:39).

Zelophehad (ze-lō′fe-had; *shadow of fear*). Grandson of Gilead (Num. 26:33; 27:1, 7; Josh. 17:3).

Zelotes (ze-lō′tēs; *full of zeal*). A nickname given to Simon, one of the twelve apostles of Jesus (Luke 6:15; Acts 1:13), to distinguish him from Simon Peter. Modern versions translate this as *the Zealot*.

Zelzah (zel′za; *noontide*). A town near Rachel's tomb (1 Sam. 10:2). It was 8 km. (5 mi.) southeast of Jerusalem.

Zemaraim (zem-a-rā′im; *double peak*). [1] A city north of Jericho (Josh. 18:22); we now know that it was 6.4 km. (4 mi.) away from Jericho. [2] A mountain in Ephraim's hill country (2 Chron. 13:4). Possible locations are Burkah and Kafr Nata.

Zemarites (zem′a-rītes). A Canaanite tribe (Gen. 10:18; 1 Chron. 1:16), probably living in northern Phoenicia in a town now called Sumra.

Zemer (zē′mer). A Phoenician city (Ezek. 27:8).

Zemira [Zemirah] (ze-mī′ra; *song*). A son of Becher, a descendant of Benjamin (1 Chron. 7:8).

Zenan (zē′nan; *place of flocks*). A village in the allotment of Judah (Josh. 15:37). It is probably identical with Zaanan (q.v.).

Zenas (zē′nas; *gift of Zeus*). A Christian who had been a teacher of the Law (Titus 3:13).

Zephaniah (zef-a-ni′a; *Jehovah has hidden*). [1] A prophet in the days of Josiah (Zeph. 1:1). [2] A Levite or priest, ancestor of Samuel (1 Chron. 6:36). Possibly the same as Uriel [1]. [3] Son of Josiah the priest (Zech. 6:10, 14). [4] A priest who opposed Babylonian rule (2 Kings 25:18; Jer. 21:1; 37:3).

Zephath (zē′fath; *watchtower*). A city of Canaan in the mountains of Kadesh near the Edomite border (Judg. 1:17). It was later called Hormah (q.v.).

Zephathah (zef′a-tha; *watchtower*). The valley in Judah's territory near Mareshah in which Asa and Zerah battled (2 Chron. 14:9–10). It is possibly modern Wadi Safiyeh.

Zephi [Zepho] (zē′fī [zē′fō]; *watchtower*). A son of Eliphaz (Gen. 36:11, 15; 1 Chron. 1:36).

Zepho (zē′fō). *See* Zephi.

Zephon (zē′fon; *expectation*). A son of Gad (Num. 26:15). Also called Ziphion in Genesis 46:16).

Zephonites (zef′ō-nītes). A Gadite family descended from Zephon (Num. 26:15).

Zer (zur; *flint, rock*). A fortress city of Naphtali (Josh. 19:35). It was located near the southwest bank of the Sea of Galilee. It may be Madon (q.v.).

Zerah [Zara; Zarah] (zē′ra [zā′ra; zā′ra]; *sprout*). [1] A son of Reuel (Gen. 36:13, 17; 1 Chron. 1:37). [2] Father of Jobab (Gen. 36:33; 1 Chron. 1:44). [3] A son of Judah (Gen. 38:30; 1 Chron. 2:4, 6). [4] A descendant of Gershon (1 Chron. 6:21). [5] A Levite (1 Chron. 6:41). [6] A king of Ethiopia who warred with Asa (2 Chron. 14:9). Also called a Cushite or Ethiopian. [7] *See* Zohar [2].

Zerahiah (zer-a-hī′a; *Jehovah has come forth*). [1] A priest of the line of Eleazar (1 Chron. 6:6, 51; Ezra 7:4). [2] Head of a family who returned from the Exile with Ezra (Ezra 8:4).

Zerahites (zer′a-hītes). *See* Zarhites.

Zered (zē′red). *See* Zared.

Zereda [Zeredah] (zer′e-da; *ambush*). A village in Manasseh (1 Kings 11:26). It was located to the north of Mount Ephraim about 24.1 km. (15 mi.) southwest of Shechem. It is identical with Zaretan (q.v.).

Zeredathah [Zeredah] (zer-e-dā′tha; *cool*). A village in the Jordan River Valley where Solomon erected foundaries which were used to forge the great bronze castings for the first Jerusalem Temple (1 Kings 7:13; 2 Chron. 4:17).

Zererah [Zererath] (zer′e-ra [zer′e-rath]). A town in the Jordan River Valley through which the Midianite army fled when defeated by Gideon's army (Judg. 7:22).

Zeresh (zē′resh; *gold*). Wife of Haman (Esther 5:10, 14; 6:13).

Zereth (zē′reth; *brightness*). A descendant of Judah (1 Chron. 4:7).

Zereth-shahar (zē′reth shā′har; *splendor of the dawn*). A town in Reubenite territory, possibly located about 20 mi. (32 km.) southwest of Medeba, on the shore of the Dead Sea.

Zeri (zē′rī; *balm*). A musician in the days of David (1 Chron. 25:3); perhaps the same as Izri (v. 11).

Zeror (zē′ror; *particle*). An ancestor of Kish (1 Sam. 9:1).

Zeruah (ze-roo′a; *smitten*). The mother of Jeroboam I (1 Kings 11:26).

Zerubbabel [Zorobabel] (ze-rub′a-bel [zo-rob′a-bel]; *seed of Babylon*). **[1]** The leader of a group who returned from exile; he began the rebuilding of the temple (Ezra 3—5; Neh. 7:7; 12:1, 47). He was an ancestor of Christ (Matt. 1:12–13). **[2]** An ancestor of Christ (Luke 3:27); perhaps the same as [1].

Zeruiah (zer-u-ī′a; *balm*). A daughter of Jesse and David's sister (1 Sam. 26:6; 2 Sam. 2:13, 18).

Zetham (zē′tham; *olive tree*). Son or grandson of Laadan (1 Chron. 23:8; 26:22).

Zethan (zē′than; *olive tree*). A descendant of Benjamin **Z** (1 Chron. 7:10).

Zethar (zē'thar; *conqueror*). A eunuch of Ahasuerus (Esther 1:10).

Zeus (zūs; *bright sky of day*). The principal god of the ancient Greeks, considered the ruler of the heavens and father of other gods. Barnabas was called Zeus (or Jupiter, the Roman equivalent) by the people after the apostle Paul performed a miracle at Lystra (Acts 14:12–13; 19:35).

Zia (zī'a; *terrified*). A descendant of Gad (1 Chron. 5:13).

Ziba (zī'ba; *post, statue*). A steward of Saul (2 Sam. 9:2–13; 16:1–4; 19:17–29).

Zibeon (zib'e-un; *hyena*). [1] A Hivite man (Gen. 36:2, 14). [2] A son of Seir (Gen. 36:20, 24; 1 Chron. 38:40).

Zibia (zib'i-a; *gazelle*). A descendant of Benjamin (1 Chron. 8:9).

Zibiah (zib'i-a; *gazelle*). Mother of King Joash of Judah (2 Kings 12:1; 2 Chron. 24:1).

Zichri (zik'rī; *renowned*). [1] A son of Izhar (Exod. 6:21). [2] A descendant of Benjamin (1 Chron. 8:19). [3] A descendant of Benjamin of Shishak (1 Chron. 8:23). [4] A descendant of Benjamin of Jeroham (1 Chron. 8:27). [5] A descendant of Eliezer in the days of Moses (1 Chron. 26:25). [6] Father of Eliezer, a descendant of Reuben (1 Chron. 27:16). [7] Father of Amaziah (2 Chron. 17:16). [8] Father of Elishaphat (2 Chron. 23:1). [9] A man of valor who slew the son of King Ahaz (2 Chron. 28:7). [10] Father of Joel (Neh. 11:9). [11] A priest of the sons of Abijah (Neh. 12:17). [12] *See* Zabdi [4].

Ziddim (zid'im; *flanks*). A fortress city of Naphtali (Josh. 19:35). It is possibly Hattim, 8.8 km. (5.5 mi.) northwest of Tiberias.

Zidkijah [Zedekiah] (zid-kī'ja [zed-e-kī-a]; *Jehovah my righteousness*). A chief prince of the Jews (Neh. 10:1).

Zidon (zī'don). *See* Sidon.

Ziha (zī'ha; *sunniness*). [1] One whose children returned from the Babylonian Captivity (Ezra 2:43; Neh. 7:46). [2] A ruler of the Nethinim (Ezra 2:43; Neh. 11:21).

Ziklag (zik'lag; *measure pressed down*). A city in the south of Judah (1 Sam. 30:1; 2 Sam. 1:1; 4:10). It is probably Tell el-Khut-weilfel about 16. 1 km. (10 mi.) north of Beer-sheba.

Zillah (zil'a; *shadow*). One of the wives of Lamech (Gen. 4:19, 22–23).

Zillethai (zil'e-thī). *See* Zilthai.

Zilpah (zil'pa; *myrrh dropping*). Mother of Gad and Asher (Gen. 29:24; 30:9–13; 35:26).

Zilthai [Zillethai] (zil'thī [zil'e-thī]; *God is a shadow*). [1] A descendant of Benjamin (1 Chron. 8:20). [2] A captain who joined David at Ziklag (1 Chron. 12:20).

Zimmah (zim'a; *counsel*). [1] A Levite of the family of Gershon (1 Chron. 6:20). [2] A Levite in the fourth or fifth degree of temple service (1 Chron. 6:42). [3] A Levite who assisted in cleansing the temple (2 Chron. 29:12).

Zimran (zim'ran; *celebrated*). A son of Abraham by Keturah (Gen. 25:2; 1 Chron. 1:32).

Zimri (zim'rī; *my protection*). [1] A disobedient Israelite slain by Phinehas (Num. 25:14). [2] A captain who slew Elah (1 Kings 16:9–20). [3] A son of Zerah of Judah (1 Chron. 2:6). [4] A descendant of Benjamin (1 Chron. 8:36; 9:42). [5] An unknown place or people (Jer. 25:25).

Zin (zin; *swelling*). A wilderness on the southern border of Canaan, not to be confused with the Wilderness of

Sin. It was either a part of the Wilderness of Paran or bordered on the wilderness which contained Kadesh-barnea (Num. 20:1; 27:14; Josh. 15:1–3).

Zina (zī'na; *fruitful*). Second son of Shimei (1 Chron. 23:10). He is called Zizah in verse 11.

Zion [Sion] (zī'on [sī'on]; *monument; fortress*). One of the hills on which Jerusalem stood. It came to be applied to the temple and the whole of Jerusalem and its people as a community whose destiny depends on God (2 Sam. 5:7; Psa. 48:11; Isa. 8:18; Joel 2:23). Zion also was a symbol of heaven (Rev. 14:1).

Zior (zī'or; *smallness*). A city in Judah near Hebron (Josh. 15:54). Some identify the city with Zair (q.v.).

Ziph (zif; *refining place*). [1] Grandson of Caleb (1 Chron. 2:42). [2] A son of Jehaleleel (1 Chron. 4:16).

Ziph (zif; *refining place*). [1] A city in southern Judah (Josh. 15:24). It was located between Ithnan and Telem and is probably modern ez-Teifah. [2] A town in Judah's hill country (Josh. 15:55; 2 Chron. 11:8). It is Tell Zif, 4 mi. southeast of Hebron.

Ziphah (zī'fa; *lent*). A son of Jehaleleel (1 Chron. 4:16).

Ziphim [Ziphites] (zīf'im [zif'ites]). The inhabitants of the city of Ziph [2] (Ps. 59, title; 1 Sam. 23:19; 26:1).

Ziphion (zif'i-on; *dark, wintry*). See Zephon.

Ziphites (zif'ites). See Ziphim.

Ziphron (zif'ron; *a stench* or *odor*). A place specified by Moses as the northern boundary of the Promised Land (Num. 34:9). It is probably Za'feranh southeast of Re-stan.

Zippor (zip'or; *bird*). Father of Balak, king of Moab (Num. 22:2, 4, 10, 16).

Zipporah (zi-pō'ra; *little bird*). The wife of Moses and daughter of Reuel (Exod. 2:21; 4:25; 18:2).

Zithri (zith-rī; *Jehovah conceals*). A descendant of Levi through Kohath (Exod. 6:22).

Ziz, Ascent of (ziz; *flower*). The pass that runs from the western shore of the Dead Sea north of En-gedi to the wilderness of Judah (2 Chron. 20:16). It is probably Wadi Hasasah.

Ziza [Zizah] (zī′za [zī′za]; *shining; brightness*). [1] A chief of Simeon (1 Chron. 4:37). [2] A son of King Rehoboam (2 Chron. 11:20). [3] *See* Zina.

Zoan (zō′an; *motion*). An ancient Egyptian city on the eastern bank of the Nile Delta on the Tanitic branch of the river (Ezek. 30:14). It was known to the Greeks as Tanis and is now San el-Hagar.

Zoar (zō′er; *small*). One of the five Cities of the Plain of the Jordan (Gen. 14:2; 19:22). It probably was located at the southeast end of the Dead Sea near es-Safi. The original site is believed to be under the Dead Sea's waters.

Zobah [Zoba] (zō′ba [zō′ba]; *bronze, copper*). A portion of Syria east of Coelesyria that was a separate empire during the days of Saul, David, and Solomon (1 Sam. 14:47; 2 Sam. 8:3; 10:6).

Zobebah (zō-bē′ba; *affable*). A descendant of Judah (1 Chron. 4:8).

Zohar [Jezoar; Izhar] (zō′har [jez′ō-ar; iz′har]; *nobility; distinction*). [1] Father of Ephron, from whom Abraham bought a field (Gen. 23:8; 25:9). [2] A son of Simeon of Judah (Gen. 46:10; Exod. 6:15). He is also called Zerah (1 Chron. 4:24). [3] A son of Helah, of the tribe of Judah (1 Chron. 4:7).

Zoheleth, Stone of (zō′he-leth; *creeping one*). A stone beside Enrogel near the Well of the Virgin. It was here that Adonijah sacrificed animals (1 Kings 1:9).

Zoheth (zō′heth; *strong*). A descendant of Judah (1 Chron. 4:20).

Zophah (zō′fa; *bellied jug*). A descendant of Asher (1 Chron. 7:35–36).

Zophai (zō′fī; *watcher*). A brother of Samuel (1 Chron. 6:26). He is called Zuph in verse 35.

Zophar (zō′fer; *twittering bird*). A Naamathite and "friend" of Job (Job 2:11; 11:1; 20:1).

Zophim (zō′fīm; *watchers*). A place on top of Pisgah where Balaam viewed the Israelite camp (Num. 23:14). It is possibly Tal′al es-Safa.

Zorah (zō′ra; *place of hornets*). A city in the lowlands of Judah allotted to the tribe of Dan (Josh. 19:41; 2 Chron. 11:10). The site is Sar′ah about 22.5 km. (14 mi.) west of Jerusalem. It is identical with Zorean (q.v.). It is called Zoreah [Zareah] in Joshua 15:33 and Nehemiah 11:29.

Zorathites [Zareathites, Zorites] (zō′ra-thītes [zar′e-a-thītes; zō′rites]). Descendants of Salma, of the tribe of Judah (1 Chron. 2:54).

Zoreah (zō′re-a; *place of hornets*). *See also* Zorah.

Zorobabel (zo-rob′a-bel). Greek form of Zerubbabel (q.v.).

Zuar (zū′er; *little*). Father of Nethaneel and a chief of Issachar (Num. 1:8; 2:5).

Zuph (zuf). An Ephraimite ancestor of the prophet Samuel (1 Sam. 1:1).

Zuph (zuf; *honeycomb*). A land or district where Saul searched for his father's donkeys (1 Sam. 9:5). The exact location of Zuph is not known but scholars believe that it was a district northwest of Jerusalem, in the land of Ephraim. Also *see* Zophai.

Zur (zur; *rock*). [1] A prince of Midian slain by Phinehas

(Num. 25:15; 31:8). **[2]** A son of Jehiel (1 Chron. 8:30; 9:36).

Zuriel (zū′ri-el; *God is my rock*). A chief of the Levites, descendant from Merari (Num. 3:35).

Zurishaddai (zū-ri-shad′ī; *the Almighty is a rock*). Father of Shelumiel (Num. 1:6; 2:12).

Zuzim, Zuzims (zū′zim; *powerfulness*). A primitive tribe that lived in Ham, a place east of the Jordan River between Bashan and Moab. The Zuzim were conquered by the Elamite King Chedorlaomer (Gen. 14:15).

Z

THE ANCIENT WORLD
GENESIS

MILES 0 25 50 100 200 300 400
KILOMETERS 0 50 100 200 300 400 500 600

JEROME S. KATES Cartographer
HERBERT G. MAY PH.D. Research Editor
COPYRIGHT 1948 THOMAS NELSON AND SONS

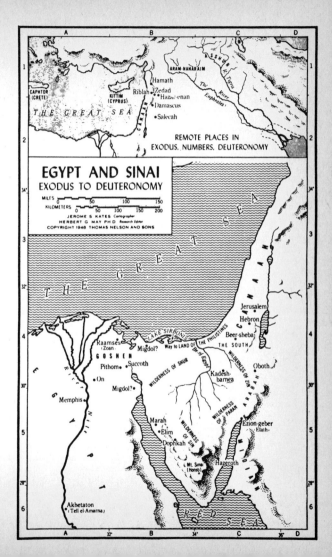

EGYPT AND SINAI
EXODUS TO DEUTERONOMY

MILES
0   50   100   150

KILOMETERS
0   50   100   150   200

JEROME S KATES Cartographer
HERBERT G MAY Ph D Research Editor
COPYRIGHT 1948 THOMAS NELSON AND SONS

REMOTE PLACES IN
EXODUS, NUMBERS, DEUTERONOMY

CAPHTOR
(CRETE)

KITTIM
(CYPRUS)

THE GREAT SEA

ARAM-NAHARAIM

ASSHUR

Hamath
Riblah Zedad
Hazar-enan
Damascus
Sakcah

The River Euphrates

CANAAN

THE GREAT SEA

CANAAN

Jerusalem
Hebron
Beer-sheba

Lake Sirbon

Way to LAND OF THE PHILISTINES

THE SOUTH

Raamses
(Zoan) Migdol?

GOSHEN

Pithom
Succoth

On

Migdol?

Memphis

THE RIVER NILE

WILDERNESS OF SHUR

WILDERNESS OF ETHAM

Kadesh-barnea

WILDERNESS OF ZIN

Oboth

WILDERNESS OF PARAN

WILDERNESS OF ARABAH

Marah
Elim
Dophkah

WILDERNESS OF SIN

Ezion-geber
Elath

Hazeroth

Mt. Sinai
(Horeb)

Akhetaton
(Tell el-Amarna)

RED SEA

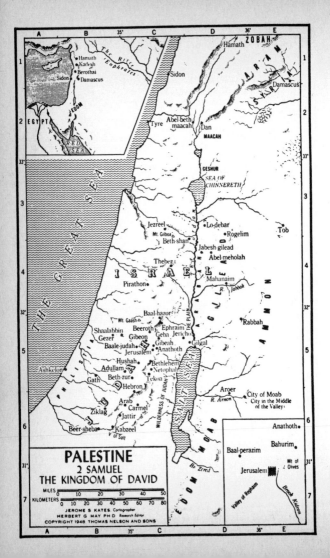

PALESTINE
2 SAMUEL
THE KINGDOM OF DAVID

MILES
0   10   20   30   40   50
KILOMETERS
0   10   20   30   40   50   60   70   80

JEROME S. KATES, Cartographer
HERBERT G. MAY PH.D. Research Editor
COPYRIGHT 1948 THOMAS NELSON AND SONS

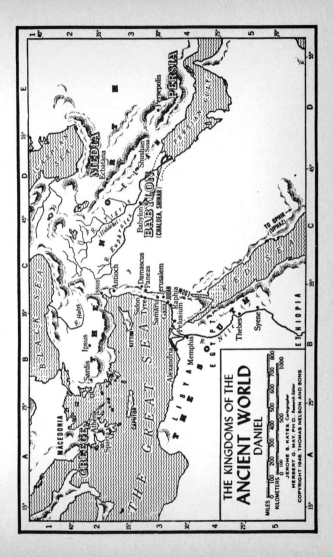

THE KINGDOMS OF THE
ANCIENT WORLD
DANIEL

MILES 0 100 200 300 400 500 600 700 800
KILOMETERS 0 100 500 1000

JEROME S. KATES, Cartographer
HERBERT G. MAY, PH. D., Research Editor
COPYRIGHT 1946, THOMAS NELSON AND SONS

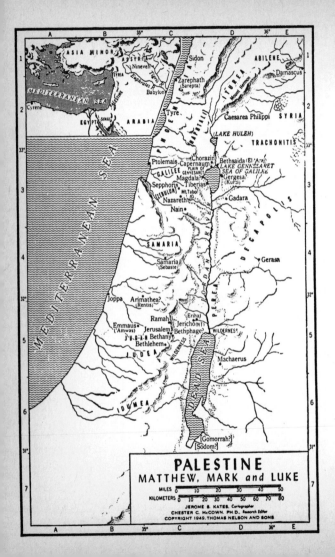

PALESTINE
MATTHEW, MARK and LUKE

MILES 0 10 20 30 40 50
KILOMETERS 0 10 20 30 40 50 60 70 80

JEROME B. KATES, Cartographer
CHESTER C. McCOWN, PH.D., Research Editor
COPYRIGHT 1949, THOMAS NELSON AND SONS

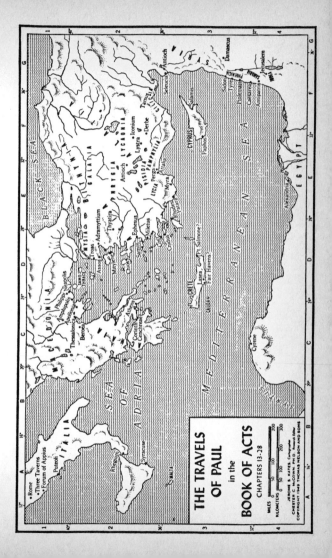

THE TRAVELS
OF PAUL
in the

BOOK OF ACTS

CHAPTERS 13-28

MILES
50   100   200   300
KILOMETERS
50 100 200 300

JEROME S. KATES, Cartographer
CHESTER C. McCOWN, Ph.D., Revising Editor
COPYRIGHT 1949 THOMAS NELSON AND SONS

Nelson's Quick-Reference™ Series

Nelson's Quick-Reference™ Bible Concordance
Gives you easy access to over 40,000 key Bible references that are most often sought. Save time and avoid the tedium that goes with wading through long lists of references less sought after. Keyed to the New King James Version, but useful with any.
400 pages / 0-8407-6907-5 / available now

Nelson's Quick-Reference™ Bible Dictionary
More like a "mini-encyclopedia" than a standard dictionary, this compact reference offers an A-Z way to discover fascinating details about the Bible—its characters, history, setting, and doctrines.
784 pages / 0-8407-6906-7 / available now

Nelson's Quick-Reference™ Bible Handbook
Helps you read each of the Bible's 66 books, plus those of the Apocrypha. Offers book introductions, brief summaries, historical and faith-and-life highlights, at-a-glance charts, and detailed teaching outlines. Suggests individual reading plans and schedules for group study.
416 pages / 0-8407-6904-0 / available now

Nelson's Quick-Reference™ Bible Questions and Answers
Learning is fun, lively, and exciting with the over 6,000 questions and answers covering the whole Bible. Variety keeps interest high—short answer, true/false, multiple choice, fill in the blank, and sentence completion.
384 pages / 0-8407-6905-9 / available now

Nelson's Quick-Reference™ Introduction to the Bible
Introduces the Bible as a whole and describes all its parts from an historical and evangelical theological perspective. Explore the fascinating variety in Scripture—story and song, poetry and prophecy, and more. Discover its divinely revealed answers to the most important questions of life.
approx 400 pages / 0-8407-3206-6 / available now

Nelson's Quick-Reference™ Bible Maps and Charts
Make any Bible a study Bible with this unique collection of maps, book charts, and other visuals that present clear information about Bible people, events, and teachings in ways that heighten your interest, retention, and understanding in Bible study. Seeing it helps you believe it!
approx 300 pages / 0-8407-6908-3 / April, 1994